THE MAKING OF
URBAN
AMERICA

THE MAKING OF
URBAN AMERICA

Raymond A. Mohl
Editor

A Scholarly Resources Imprint
Wilmington, Delaware

The paper used in this publication meets the minimum requirements of the American National Standard for permanence of paper for printed library materials, Z39.48, 1984.

Scholarly Resources Inc.
104 Greenhill Avenue
Wilmington, Delaware 19805-1897

Library of Congress Cataloging-in-Publication Data

The Making of urban America.

   Includes index.
   1. Cities and towns—United States—History.
2. Urbanization—United States—History.   I. Mohl,
Raymond A.
HT123.M286   1988   307.7'6'0973   87-23392
ISBN 0-8420-2270-8
ISBN 0-8420-2271-6 (pbk.)

Contents

Preface

Urban history is a relatively young subfield within the larger bailiwick of U.S. history. Only in the 1960s did scholars begin a systematic and wide-ranging examination of the historical dimensions of the American urban experience. Since that time the study of urban history has been marked by a vast investment of scholarly energy, as well as by a diversity of research strategies and interpretations. Some of this scholarly output has dealt with rather narrow facets of the subject, but many of the key works in the field address in imaginative and innovative ways some of the central interpretive questions of American history. Part of the large wave of social history that has flourished since the 1960s, careful and creative urban history research has probed deeply into the social and human experience of the American people.

Current syntheses of U.S. urban history are in short supply, however, and collections of material for teaching purposes are out of print or now outdated. This text is designed to fill a perceived need for a relatively short collection of essays that will introduce students of urban history to the recent interpretive literature in the field. The material presented in this book illustrates many of the important questions, issues, and ideas that American urban historians have been pursuing over the past decade. All but one of the essays have been written or published within the last ten years, most more recently. Taken as a group, they tend to emphasize the social and cultural aspects of urban history rather than the political or the economic. In that sense, these essays reflect the current research interests of urban history scholars.

The essays are presented within a three-part chronological context covering the preindustrial town and city, the industrial city, and the twentieth-century city. Each section begins with a narrative introduction laying out the pattern of urban development during that period, identifying the forces of change, and suggesting the interpretive questions that have intrigued urban historians. The essays within each section provide substantive illustration for the patterns of urban growth and social change. Part Four presents a detailed historiographical analysis of the subject. This bibliographical essay has been conceived as a guide for interested students through the thickets of published urban history.

Raymond A. Mohl
Boca Raton, Florida
March 1987

Part One

The Preindustrial Town and City

Introduction

Twentieth-century Americans live in an urban age. The process by which a group of small colonial settlements in an untamed wilderness grew into a highly industrialized and urbanized nation is one of the central stories of American history. Over a period of some 350 years, as the United States moved from colonial status to nationhood, Americans passed from a society characterized by small farms and villages to one dominated by huge central cities and massive sprawling suburbs. An understanding of the dynamic forces and values which nurtured, stimulated, and shaped American urban development is essential in comprehending the contours of contemporary America.

To a certain degree, urban life had been a regular feature of American society since the early colonial period. British and European settlers congregated in seaport towns and villages from the very beginning of the colonization effort. Many of the first colonists had been town or city dwellers in England or Europe, and they brought to the American wilderness urban values, attitudes, and aspirations. Although the populations of most colonial communities remained small through most of the prerevolutionary period, each colonial settlement, village, or town to some degree served traditional urban functions—that is, they became centers for the exchange of goods, services, and ideas. By the end of the seventeenth century, colonial Americans had created a fairly dynamic urban society. The larger seaport cities of Boston, Philadelphia, New York, Charleston, and Newport—which had populations ranging from about 2,000 to 7,000—exercised an influence throughout the colonies far out of proportion to their relatively small populations.

Several forces promoted colonial urban growth. In the early stages of settlement and on the colonial frontier, newcomers gathered together for security and mutual defense. These primitive colonial communities were often surrounded by a wall or wooden stockade, as in Plymouth, Jamestown, and Savannah, while others were clustered around a fortress, as in New York, Charleston, St. Augustine, and Mobile. Most of these early defensive communities rapidly became agrarian towns. This pattern prevailed especially in New England, where a community-centered society required towns to regulate effectively social and religious life. Town building also was promoted by English or European joint stock companies. Jamestown, Plymouth, New York, New Haven, and other colonial towns had such origins. English entrepreneurs and investors viewed towns as necessary for successfully tapping the raw materials and resources of the New World. Thus, they not only sponsored much of the early colonization effort, but they also provided the capital and manpower needs required to sustain the new overseas outposts during the early difficult years of community building.

Many of the largest colonial towns grew because of their political and administrative functions. British mercantilist policies required a close supervision and regulation of colonial trade. Moreover, each colony had its governing center: the residence of the colonial governor, the location of the administrative offices of government, and the meeting place of the colonial assembly. The imperatives of mercantilism and colonial government encouraged urban development, even in the southern colonies where geography and emerging agricultural and land distribution patterns militated against town life.

Above all, however, commercial activity in the colonies stimulated urbanization. By the end of the seventeenth century, colonial merchants and entrepreneurs had established a far-reaching and profitable trading network. Built primarily on the products of an extractive economy—fish and furs, tobacco and rice, wheat and indigo, lumber and livestock, naval stores and minerals— colonial trade with Britain, Europe, Africa, and the West Indies expanded and prospered. Returning ships carried new immigrants, slaves, sugar, manufactured goods, and products unobtainable in the New World. Intensive commerce of this kind promoted the growth of seaport towns and cities up and down the Atlantic coastline. These urban places became market cities where goods changed hands. As some urban geographers have noted, the colonial seaport cities served as an economic "hinge," central points for the collection of agricultural products for export and for the distribution of imported goods throughout the surrounding hinterland. In addition, the export-import function stimulated numerous supplementary industries in the towns. Most ports became centers for flour milling, shipbuilding, the processing of naval stores, and other simple manufacturing. Numbers of small shops produced rope, sails, barrels, and other products, while a growing class of urban craftsmen serviced expanding town and city populations. As a result of these advances in craft and commerce, the colonial economy prospered at times. The gradual expansion of the domestic market strengthened the cities' economic role, thus further intensifying the urbanizing trend.

The primacy of the colonial cities' economic functions contained the seeds of future social and political change. As historian Gary B. Nash has noted in *The Urban Crucible* (1979), the economically developing colonial seaport cities experienced social and class distinctions at a very early date. Although geographical mobility was always high, upward social and economic mobility was more limited in the cities than in other segments of colonial society. The continuous influx of new immigrants tended to keep wages down and economic opportunity circumscribed. More so than in agricultural and frontier regions, the colonial cities experienced a growing gap between the rich and the poor. In Boston, for instance, the class of propertyless laborers was increasing twice as rapidly as the population as a whole by the time of the American Revolution. In Philadelphia, the richest 5 percent of the population controlled equally as much wealth as the rest of the population combined. Thus, class lines were hardening by the mid-eighteenth century. At the same time, the colonial dependence on commerce meant that New World settlements had become part of an intricate web of world trade, subject to economic fluctuations due to war, depression, inflation, currency declines, and falling crop prices. As a result, most of the colonial urban economies suffered periodic economic stagnation and often severe problems of unemployment, poverty, and poor relief.

These social and economic conditions influenced the development of urban political thinking and political action. From the beginning, colonial society had been strongly deferential in nature—that is, it was a society in which men knew their place and accepted it, in which the middle and lower classes generally yielded decision-making authority to the local political and economic elites. However, people at every level of society shared certain basic assumptions about the mutual obligations of classes and the need for social harmony, good government, and personal liberty. When the urban elites challenged or undermined or violated these assumptions, the middle and lower classes often abandoned deferential attitudes and asserted their collective power in the streets in the form of a mob or riot to protect the old values and restore the old order. By the mid-eighteenth century, moreover, the growth of the market economy, with the new emphasis on individual profit and the new reality of periodic depression, led to lower class discontent, a decline of deference, and the rise of a popular and participatory politics in the seaport cities. As the artisans and the urban working classes developed an increasingly radical political consciousness, they began to take charge of their lives in new and dramatic ways. These changes, initiated in the colonial towns and cities, unleashed forces that hastened the coming of the American Revolution.

Indeed, the impact of the city on the coming of the Revolution cannot be overestimated. Historian Zane L. Miller has argued that "the Revolution had its roots in the cities," a judgment with which most historians would agree. During the revolutionary crisis, the colonial cities emerged as important centers of radical activity and propaganda. Based in the seaport cities, many colonial merchants saw urban prosperity and their own profits threatened by new British taxes and economic policies. The boycotts organized by the urban merchants and implemented in the port towns helped strike down the hated Stamp Act and the Townshend duties. The dissatisfaction and radicalism of urban workers, artisans, and sailors, stimulated by unemployment and the economic pressures of the 1760s, found expression in mobs and riots; the Sons of Liberty was primarily an urban group. Pivotal events such as the Boston Massacre originated in the conflict between colonial urbanites and British troops stationed in the cities, while the Boston Tea Party reflected urban concerns about Parliamentary control of the economy. Such urban radical organizations as the Boston Committee of Correspondence, along with widely read city newspapers, filled the countryside with revolutionary propaganda and justifications for independence. And, as historian Arthur M. Schlesinger suggested, the patterns of community life over the course of the colonial period provided a sort of "training in collective action" upon which patriot leaders drew during the intensifying revolutionary crisis.

The urban dimension of American life during the colonial period, then, was significant and influential in several respects. The colonial towns and cities became the economic, political, and cultural centers of a sparsely populated agricultural hinterland. They provided the arena for the emerging market-oriented commercial economy, which in turn pulled the American colonies into the wider, more interdependent, and more fragile network of world trade. Social and economic stratification intensified as the urban populations grew, stimulating discontent, some class conflict, and a new emphasis on democratic and participatory urban politics. As deference declined in the cities, simultaneous movements began seeking both independence from Great Britain and social and democratic change in America. By the end of the revolutionary era, about 5 percent of the American population—some 200,000 people—lived in twenty-four urban places of 2,500 or more residents. The proportion of urbanites was relatively small, but the growing cities dominated their surrounding regions and stimulated social, economic, and political change.

In the years between the American Revolution and the Civil War, the urban marketplace became indispensable to the national economy. The pace of urbanization speeded up considerably. New York emerged as a sort of "primate" city, a national metropolis dominating the economy of the entire country. A city of about 33,000 in 1790, New York increased in population by more than 50 percent each decade until 1860 (except the 1810–20 period). By 1860 more than 800,000 people crowded the island of Manhattan. The other eastern seaports also grew into large commercial metropolises. Philadelphia's 28,000 people of 1790 had multiplied to more than 565,000 by the time of the Civil War. Brooklyn, a small suburb of less than 5,000 in 1790, had become the nation's third largest city by 1860 with a population of over 265,000. Boston and Baltimore also had increased their populations at substantial rates during the early nineteenth century. The East Coast seaports comprised a regional system of cities. These marketplace cities each depended on commerce for growth and prosperity, while continuing to serve as regional marketing and distribution centers for expanding agricultural hinterlands.

Urbanization also spread into the interior of the continent during these preindustrial years. In the trans-Appalachian region, two new systems of cities spearheaded the westward movement and the settlement of the frontier. One group of cities sprouted along the Ohio and Mississippi rivers. Experiencing similar patterns of development, the cities of Pittsburgh, Louisville, Cincinnati, St. Louis, and New Orleans emerged as regional marketing and early manufacturing centers. Spurred by transportation innovations, notably steam navigation and canal building, a second system of cities grew up along the shores of the Great Lakes: Buffalo, Cleveland, Detroit, Chicago, and Milwaukee. Although Cincinnati was being promoted as the "Queen City" of the west and had become the nation's third largest manufacturing center by the Civil War, it was clear that Chicago was rising quickly as the western metropolis. These ten interior cities, which by 1860 ranged in population from about 45,000 to nearly 170,000, gave an urban aspect to the westward movement and to American society generally.

The catalyst for western urbanization was the transportation revolution of the early nineteenth century. New York merchants and promoters were especially active in supporting new transportation innovations, which in large measure accounted for the great success of the eastern metropolis. Perhaps more than any other single accomplishment, the opening of the Erie Canal in 1825 assured the commercial primacy of New York City. The completion of the Erie route set off a wave of canal building and then railroad construction, as other eastern cities sought to compete with New York for the trade and produce of the Ohio Valley. This so-called urban imperialism not only hastened the completion of new transportation arteries but also fostered urbanization in the western regions and along the routes of the new canals and railroads. A whole string of cities, for instance, grew up along the Erie Canal route between Albany and Buffalo.

Commerce and shipping, together with a host of supplementary trades and businesses, fueled the urban economy during most of this period. However, new technology as reflected in the steam engine and in textile machinery, the creation of the transportation network, and the growth of the domestic market in the mid-nineteenth century turned cities increasingly toward production for internal consumption. Factory production began in such industries as cotton textiles, woolen goods, finished clothing, boots and shoes, leather items, and iron products. Western cities, drawing on local resources and agricultural production, turned to flour milling, brewing, meat packing, mining, and lumbering. In New England, textiles and the footwear industry fostered the development of a number of smaller factory towns such as Lawrence, Lowell, Lynn, Haverhill, Fall River, New Bedford, and Manchester. A similar shift toward manufacturing was evident elsewhere, too, as cities ranging from Richmond and Lexington in the South to Newark, Paterson, Providence, Albany, and Troy in the North turned to factory production. By the 1850s the factory had become a recognizable feature of the urban landscape. Nevertheless, the commercial role of the cities remained predominant until the second half of the nineteenth century. By 1860, according to historian Eric Lampard, of the nation's fifteen largest cities, only five had more than 10 percent of their work force engaged in manufacturing. Thus, the industrial takeoff had not yet fully begun.

Like the growing factories, the social and political conditions of the preindustrial cities provided some hints about the shape of the urban future. European immigration, for instance, had begun to have a significant impact on the urban population. The immigrant tide began slowly at first in the early decades of the nineteenth century. During the 1830s, however, more than 490,000 newcomers arrived on American shores. During the 1840s, European immigration to the United States surged to more than 1.4 million, and during the 1850s the seaborne influx almost doubled to over 2.6 million. Mostly Irish, English, and German, these newcomers received their first introduction to American life in the immigrant arrival ports of New York, Boston, Philadelphia, Baltimore, San Francisco, and New Orleans. Large numbers of them moved on to interior towns or settled in the midwestern farm belt. But many remained in the cities, where their influence was increasingly felt in politics, culture, and the workplace. By 1860 immigrants made up more than 50 percent of the populations of St. Louis, Chicago, Milwaukee, and San Francisco. Close behind were New York, Buffalo, Cincinnati, Cleveland, and Detroit, where the proportion of foreign-born ranged from 45 to 48 percent of the total city population.

Internal migration and geographical mobility also affected the growing cities. While newcomers from abroad flooded into urban America in unprecedented numbers, native-born migrants from the farm and from rural towns boosted city populations as well, especially in the Northeast. This pattern continued into the late nineteenth century, as new agricultural technology displaced the rural peasantry of farm workers and hired hands. In addition, a substantial degree of population turnover within the cities contributed to the pace of urbanization and social change. Many early nineteenth-century observers noted the transiency and migratory habits of the lower stratum of urban society. The working classes and the poor were often described as a "floating" population or as being "constantly on the wing." Immigrants and natives alike passed in and out of the cities in search of jobs, better housing, or more opportunity. According to a study by Peter R. Knights, population turnover in Boston amounted to about 30 percent per year in the 1830s and 1840s and 40 percent per year in the 1850s. This sort of intensive internal migration and mobility reflected the dynamic character of the urbanization process in the United States, even in the preindustrial period.

While immigration and internal migration altered the composition and character of the American urban population, the preindustrial cities changed in other ways as well. The larger cities, for instance, had begun to experience, to a limited degree, some of the problems that later plagued city people and municipal governments. Pre-Civil War urban growth was disorderly and unplanned, as the older cities outgrew the more regular street plans of the colonial era. Heavy population increases imposed pressure on limited housing resources. Immigrants, workers, and the urban poor crowded into densely packed apartments, tenements, cellars, and shacks. Public health measures remained primitive, and most cities suffered periodic epidemics of typhoid, yellow fever, and cholera. Poverty, unemployment, crime, and violence became common. A rage of urban riots afflicted most large cities in the 1830s and 1840s, reflecting social, economic, religious, racial, and ethnic tensions. As these and other problems developed, city governments seemed weak and ineffective. Municipal governments were slow in providing services to the citizenry, and they were generally unable to regulate the bigger, more populous, more heterogeneous city of the mid-nineteenth century.

By the 1850s, therefore, the transition from the preindustrial to the modern industrial city was nearly complete. The process of modernization actually had been under way for some time. The colonial city was truly preindustrial in the sense described by sociologist Gidion Sjoberg in his book, *The Preindustrial City* (1960). For Sjoberg, the preindustrial city was characterized by the marketplace function and by patterns of handicraft and artisanal manufacturing. Animate sources of power—that is, human or animal power—were used in the system of production. Preindustrial urban workers labored in small shops with a few other craftsmen and apprentices. There was little specialization of work or division of labor. Using hand tools and individual skills, urban artisans created a finished product out of raw material. Skill was important and was transferred through the apprenticeship process.

The social organization of the preindustrial city was characterized by a high degree of order and stability, as well as by a shared sense of community.

Social segregation was rather limited and rich and poor lived close together, although they were not necessarily neighborly. Land uses were unspecialized, and very often living and working quarters were one and the same. Business and the household were intimately connected. Ethnic and religious homogeneity generally prevailed, although social diversity was on the rise by the revolutionary era. The social and political structure was dominated by a literate elite. In this hierarchical and deferential society, upward economic and social mobility was limited. Kinship ties were important, the extended family was more typical than not, and communication and personal contact was of the face-to-face variety. A sense of localism predominated, and change and innovation came slowly, if at all. All of these social and economic patterns prevailed in the American colonial town and city throughout most of the prerevolutionary period.

The first half of the nineteenth century, by contrast, was a period of substantial change, a period of transition and modernization. For example, the system of production began to undergo changes. The small shop pattern of the colonial years gave way to factories by the 1830s and 1840s. New technology brought new machinery, especially in textiles, supplanting the hand tools of the urban craftsman. The social organization of work was revolutionized in the factory setting. Skill became less important, since machines rather than men were doing the work. Division of labor and specialization of tasks rationalized the production process, but the constant repetition of a single task meant a lifetime of mindless monotony for the worker. New sources of inanimate power—first the harnessing of waterpower to drive gears, shifts, and pulleys and later the application of the steam engine to operate factory machinery—replaced the human and animal power of earlier years. Communication and transportation were hastened by the invention of the railroad and the telegraph, thus contributing to a breakdown of localism and personalized human contacts.

Similarly, the social order experienced changes during the early nineteenth century. By the 1830s increasingly heavy immigration and a substantial degree of rural-to-urban internal migration undermined social, ethnic, and religious homogeneity. The shared sense of community of the colonial town began to disappear, along with deferential attitudes and adherence to generally accepted behavioral norms. Mobility, at least of the geographical or residential sort, intensified, a development reflecting a loosening of the ties binding the individual to kin and community. Chances for upward economic mobility do not seem to have been improved by the breakdown of traditional society, for the loss of skill and the rise of the factory and commercial capitalism meant that the individual had less control over his economic destiny. In the modernizing city itself, various spatial changes were becoming recognizable. Land uses became more specialized and functional, as sections of the growing cities were given over to residential, retail, and productive purposes. Social segregation increased, as immigrants, workers, and the poor crowded older housing in city centers, while the urban political and economic elites moved from the center toward the periphery.

Above all, change and innovation were becoming commonplace. The fixed and timeless character of the preindustrial society was weakening before the forces of nineteenth-century change. The patterns of the transitional city also set the stage for the tremendous surge of urbanization and industrialization during the second half of the nineteenth century.

The essays that follow in Part One of this book demonstrate some of the interpretative concerns of recent historians about the early American town and city. DAVID R. GOLDFIELD illuminates the patterns of urbanization in the colonial South. Colonial America was overwhelmingly rural, and the South especially so. But Goldfield demonstrates that a town-centered civilization was struggling to be born during this early period. More important, the distinctive pattern of southern urban development was decipherable even at this early stage. Southern cities, the author contends, were shaped by a symbiotic link to the agricultural hinterland, by the ever-present reality of a biracial society, and by their economic subservience to a distant metropolis. These three characteristics continued to mold the southern city into the twentieth century. "The southern city is different," Goldfield has written, "because the South is different." Since so much has been written on community building in colonial New England, it is refreshing to get a slightly different perspective on colonial urbanization. It is also useful to begin thinking of the distinctive regional patterns that characterized American urban development from the very beginning of colonial settlement in the New World.

GARY B. NASH offers a new interpretative model for understanding the dynamics of urban social development in eighteenth-century America. The colonial cities, he notes, were located at the cutting edge of economic, social, and political change. His essay portrays urban change as an evolutionary process that reshaped community patterns, social networks, and group experience in the preindustrial city. Based on the exciting research of a new generation of urban and social historians, Nash's work reveals the growing ethnic, religious, and racial diversity of the early American city, a social pluralism that challenged and reshaped established ideas about community, conformity, and deference. New social realities were imposed on the cities by the growing numbers of free urban blacks and by a widening gap between rich and poor. The social geography of the urban areas also began to change, and physical growth was accompanied by spatial segregation of social and economic groups. Nash emphasizes the resilience of the human spirit—the ability of urban people to cope and adapt, individually and collectively, to the changing urban environment. In particular, the rise of a popular and participatory politics, along with the emergence of voluntary associations, reflected the active role of city people in adjusting and adapting to change. The social forces underlying the American Revolution carried into the early nineteenth century and formed the basis for new conceptions of community, social institutions, and political participation.

The final essay in this section illustrates the growing interest of scholars in the history of urban popular culture. In the first half of the nineteenth century, Philadelphia experienced a dramatic economic and social transformation. SUSAN G. DAVIS contends that the restructuring of the city's social and economic life was reflected in changing perceptions and uses of public space. The streets of Philadelphia became an arena for public expression, as various groups and classes celebrated, paraded, marched, demonstrated, rioted, and in other ways used public space for collective or group purposes. These new forms of public behavior, Davis argues, had important social meanings in the transitional city. From the festival and parade to the labor demonstration or nativist riot, city people used the streets and other public spaces to express political fervor, patriotism, joy, anger, resentment, and violence. The streets of the city, in short, came to be invested with symbolic importance in the display of collective behavior or in the quest for group power.

These three essays only begin to suggest the diversity and richness of recent historical interpretation on the preindustrial American city. They do, however, serve to introduce the reader to the historical imagination at work.

Pearls on the Coast and Lights in the Forest: The Colonial South

*David R. Goldfield**

L ike pearls on a string, the cities of colonial America lined the Atlantic coast from Boston to Savannah. We recall the maps in those otherwise forgettable textbooks of our childhood years: the cities in geographic single file, clinging to their watery niches. The distance between Boston and Savannah, though, was more than in miles. The New England settlers wrote to their British comrades across the sea of a wilderness that was abundant but very difficult, a challenge appropriate for testing the mettle of God's chosen. The letters from the southern latitudes likened the country to paradise—a lush, easy place where modest effort brought forth great rewards. It was not only a different way of looking at the world that separated northern and southern colonies; they were in fact different worlds.

Climate, geography, and geology facilitated life in the colonial South; they inhibited it in the colonial North. The rivers in the southern colonies ran deep into the interior, creating luxuriant bottomlands as they ran their courses. The mountain spine that divided eastern America from the Ohio country was conveniently deep into the southern interior. Even here, there lay a fertile valley—a highway for travel and a soil for cultivation. The climate, though a bit uncomfortable during the summer months, allowed a long growing season. The kaleidoscopic beauty of late October in the lower Shenandoah or the colorful floral array of Charleston in late March lifted southern hearts when New England was painted gray. Climate and geography made the South distinctive. The civilization, more particularly the urban civilization that grew from these natural conditions, would indelibly bear the character of land and weather.

Several decades ago, historians debated whether cities or farms were the first settlements on the American frontier. Richard C. Wade's book on the trans-Appalachian frontier of the late eighteenth and early nineteenth century was among the most influential statements on the subject. He contended that

*David R. Goldfield is Robert Lee Bailey Professor of History at the University of North Carolina, Charlotte. Reprinted by permission of Louisiana State University Press from Cotton Fields and Skyscrapers: Southern City and Region, 1607–1980 by David R. Goldfield. Copyright 1982 by Louisiana State University Press.

cities, not farms, were the spearheads of civilization on the frontier. Wade's "cities," however, were for the most part military outposts, artificially sustained by eastern supplies and capital. Were it not for the farmers who followed closely on the heels of the departing Indians, these settlements would have returned to forests. An agricultural surplus was necessary for the emergence of cities.

As British policymakers discovered ruefully, however, the existence of an agricultural surplus was a prerequisite but not a guarantee for urban development. Yet the British had several good reasons for wanting their colonists to "plant in towns." First, they could not conceive of civilization as they knew it to exist without towns. The colonies, in the midst of the wild frontier, could easily lose the trappings of Western culture and assume the manners and tastes of their surrounding environment. Second, the colonists as individual settlers were vulnerable against enemy attack—Indian, French, or Spanish. The English mind, only recently removed from the reality of walled cities and fortified towns, equated urban life with security. Anxious Carolina proprietors wrote to some prospective settlers in the 1660s: "We must assure you that it is your and our concern very much to have some good towns in your plantations for otherwise you will not long continue civilized or secure, there being no place in the world either of these without towns."

Finally, there were commercial-administrative reasons why the English government and its New World representatives urged the growth of towns. From their European experience, they saw towns, at the very least, serving as marketplaces—convenient gathering points—for agricultural and industrial production. The towns facilitated and financed production in a reciprocal arrangement: as the farms grew, so did the cities, encouraging expansion of cultivation, which in turn stimulated urban growth. In addition, the commercial legislation, weighted toward the mother country in a colonial economy, was most readily administered at urban focal points. The difficulties involved with overseeing the economic activities of a diffuse population were obvious.

Besides simple encouragement, there were periodic schemes designed to promote urban settlement in the face of an apparent southern colonial resistance to do so. In the 1660s, when the nonurban appearance of the Chesapeake colonies (Maryland and Virginia) was a source of both incredulity and concern in official circles, the Carolina proprietors published lengthy directives for the creation of agricultural villages that would also function as commercial centers. The combination of farming and urban activities was common throughout Europe and, as New England demonstrated, appeared in the New World as well, where such settlements solved the problems of food supply and commercial-administrative function. Later, in 1730, Governor Robert Johnson of South Carolina, looking more to security than to commercial-administrative problems, recommended the establishment of ten frontier towns to protect and thereby encourage interior settlement.

These plans, and the more general official encouragement, were unsuccessful. And here the influence of the distinctive geographic and climatic conditions of the colonial South is evident. The rivers that spread like fingers from the coastal plain to the interior discouraged concentrated settlement.

The fertile lands along the winding rivers proved ideal for agriculture, and their abundance from coast to fall line enticed thousands of settlers. For the traditionally land-starved Englishman, the plentiful supply of good land made huddling together in small villages unnecessary, unattractive, and unremunerative.

In addition, these rivers were navigable deep into the interior. This allowed the planters to market their own crops, removing one of the primary functions of towns. Ships, even oceangoing vessels in the Chesapeake colonies, sailed up to the docks of individual farmers, unloaded their goods from England, and took on tobacco or rice. The planter doubled as merchant, eliminating the middleman and therefore maximizing his profits (and risk as well).

This scenario was especially apt for the Chesapeake colonies, where the Chesapeake Bay and the rivers of the Virginia colony were like so many miniature seas. The respective colonial governments of Maryland and Virginia, in futile attempts to override nature, passed fourteen acts promoting town growth during the last half of the seventeenth century. By 1710, the failure of urban settlement was so complete that officials permanently abandoned legislative town-building efforts. As the Reverend Hugh Jones wrote in 1724, "neither the interest nor inclinations of the Virginians induce them to cohabit in towns."

The situation was much the same further south. The Carolina proprietors' agricultural village scheme failed. The abundance of good land, especially on the irregular coastal plain in North Carolina, resulted in scattered farms rather than the hoped-for villages. Governor Johnson's military villages fared little better in South Carolina sixty years later. Only one of Johnson's ten towns—Orangeburg—was permanently established. The nine others simply could not counteract the centrifugal tendencies of the population, even on the hazardous frontier.

If towns were to emerge in the colonial South—and they did—legislation and wishes were obviously poor incentives. The same geographic pattern that encouraged dispersed settlement would also dictate the nature and extent of the urban settlements that eventually emerged amidst the farms. As the Chesapeake and Carolina regions settled into staple production patterns, which abundant land and accommodating soil made possible by 1700, towns developed to service staple agriculture at various levels. The type of staple agriculture in turn determined the type of urban settlement.

The connection between staple production and urbanization was apparent with tobacco, the leafy monarch of the Chesapeake. The weed's popularity in Europe was such that as early as the 1620s tobacco grew in the streets of Jamestown, the forlorn first town of the Virginia colony. The marketing demands of the crop complemented the Chesapeake's geographic condition. Tobacco marketing in the colonial era did not require intermediaries. When the tobacco fleet arrived from England in October and November, the planter simply packed his crop into hogsheads (roughly four hundred pounds each) and rolled them to the nearest dock (frequently his own) where he bargained with the captain for the price.

By the early eighteenth century, however, Europeans had developed a discriminating taste for tobacco that required more quality control at the colonial end of the trade. Also, tobacco cultivation had become so extensive that the individual deals struck between captain and planter were becoming less feasible if the ships were not to remain in the colonies most of the fall and winter. Perhaps most important, the tobacco trade had become big business by the 1700s. London and Liverpool merchants were not content to entrust their profit margins to itinerant captains or refractory planters, so they sent agents to the Chesapeake to establish bases of operation to end the uncertainties of the traveling tobacco show.

The result in town building from these initiatives was quite small. Geography again limited what might have been an urban boom under the new arrangements, because the continued availability of good cropland, especially in Virginia, restricted population in the towns. Moreover, the numerous estuaries and rivers that dotted the Chesapeake made communication difficult if a traveler's or a cargo's destination was not along the same river. In order to negotiate the 120 miles between Williamsburg and Annapolis, for example, more than a dozen ferries and considerable hours were required. Hence the market area for the farms along these winding riverine highways was small, and as a consequence the towns that marketed the tobacco from these farms were also small. In fact, shipping tobacco was the only function performed by these communities. This activity did not serve as a base for developing other urban functions because such functions were unnecessary, given the geographic conditions of the Chesapeake colonies and the relatively uncomplicated marketing requirements of tobacco.

But urban Chesapeake was to get new life in the 1740s with the introduction of a new agriculture. The decline of tobacco prices and the increased food demands in Europe encouraged the cultivation of wheat in certain areas of the Chesapeake colonies. The marketing of wheat, unlike tobacco, required several procedures that could be conducted best in central locations, i.e., towns, and the processing and subsequent storage requirements of the crop facilitated the growth of larger urban settlements. Baltimore was a direct beneficiary of wheat cultivation, being able to tap the wheatfields of Pennsylvania and western Maryland. In the Piedmont and Valley regions of Virginia, where farmers began to shift to grains, Richmond, Fredericksburg, and Staunton grew as wheat markets to supplement an unstable tobacco trade. Whereas the tobacco trade had rarely sustained towns of more than three hundred residents, the wheat trade succeeded in building cities like Baltimore that exceeded six thousand people by the time of the Revolution. In the 1780s, tobacco regained profits and favor in southern and eastern Maryland and in Virginia, so these areas remained overwhelmingly rural.

The interaction between geography, staple cultivation, and urban development was equally apparent further south, where the string of pearls on the Atlantic thinned out considerably. There was Norfolk, a struggling little seaport of six hundred persons in 1775, existing as a rendezvous for the British navy and by the grace of royal commercial regulations. Williamsburg also appeared on the map, but despite its importance as a colonial capital, it could never generate more than two hundred permanent residents, and the only trading of importance conducted in Williamsburg was of a political nature. That Williamsburg achieved a reputation beyond its meager numbers is a tribute to the people who occasionally visited there to pass laws and swat mosquitoes and to its unique town plan, which introduced Baroque civic design to the New World.

The city, planned by Theodorick Bland, provided an excellent interplay between government buildings and street layout. The linear pattern featured one major thoroughfare—Duke of Gloucester Street—along which were located the major structures and activities of the community. At one end of the street, at the College of William and Mary, the linear pattern broke off into branches, a common Baroque device. However, Bland's interesting plan was insufficient to sustain a population, and only latter-day tourism has rescued the community from weeds.

Williamsburg was an interesting but insignificant (in terms of urban development) knot on the strand, and there was virtually nothing to fill the strand in the neighboring colony of North Carolina. The hazardous shoals of the Outer Banks precluded the emergence of an important seaport, and the small ports, more administrative than trading centers, like Edenton, New Bern (the colonial capital), and Wilmington served only their immediate hinterlands in the fertile coastal plain, much as the small Chesapeake tobacco ports did. Geography more than crop cultivation accounted for the colony's urban anemia. The navigable rivers flowing into backcountry North Carolina emptied into South Carolina, so the lumber and wheat cultivation that characterized interior North Carolina ultimately benefited the urban growth of Charleston.

Charleston was the major southern colonial urban center, with a population of ten thousand by the time of the Revolution. Its development reflected the history of crop cultivation and geography in the Carolina region. The city's early growth resulted from the deerskin trade, which demanded extensive storage facilities and produced sufficient capital to enable the city to become an important credit center as well, moving beyond the level of simple marketing functions. With this foundation, as well as an extensive commercial network in the backcountry, Charleston merchants helped to develop the rice, slave, and lumber trades that generated relatively rapid urban growth after 1730. When England allowed South Carolinians to export rice directly to southern Europe in that year, Charleston merchants reaped the benefits. Rice, like wheat, required extensive marketing, storage, and processing facilities. Finally, as the hub of rice cultivation, Charleston was also the leading slave market in the colonial South. The human cargo provided additional capital for its merchants, which in turn enhanced the city's influence as a credit center.

Rice cultivation spun a culture of its own in Charleston. City and country merged in the Carolina capital. The rice planters, some of whom had begun their careers in Charleston and all of whom had economic ties to the city, built comfortable townhouses of brick or cypress and yellow pine to complement their spacious country homes. Indeed, some interesting architectural forms appeared late in the colonial period as the planters attempted to duplicate the comfort and privacy of their plantation homes on a city lot. The result was a home with narrow street frontage and the ubiquitous porch or veranda extending back on the side of the long lot. These lots were sufficiently deep for servants' quarters, stables, a kitchen, and the usual garden. The symmetrical, well-proportioned exterior design of the houses and the hand-carved woodwork and paneled rooms in their interiors reflected the influence of the Georgian architecture then popular in England. As a combination urban plantation home and Georgian townhouse, the Charleston residence of the rice planter was a home away from home in more ways than one.

Charleston was a seasonal residence. Its life beat to an agricultural rhythm—vibrant in the winter months, languid during the rest of the year except for a few months in late summer when the "sickly season" in the low country brought planters and their families to the city. The activities during the winter season swirled about the planters in a perpetual round of balls, theater performances, dinner parties, and concerts. It was as if these sometime city residents were absorbing all of the social life they could to last them through the isolation of the growing season, when there would not be another white family for miles.

By the mid-1760s, the St. Cecilia Society had become a major focal point of Charleston social life. It was a men's club much after the London fashion. Initially, the society was a music appreciation association, but its concerts soon became secondary to the balls that followed them. These affairs were the highlights of the Charleston social season, a season that moved a dazzled St. Jean de Crèvecoeur to proclaim the Carolina port as "the most brilliant of American cities."

All was not dancing and frivolity in the rice capital, however. By the time the St. Cecilia Society had organized its first ball, the merchants of Charleston had been organizing a wide network of commercial partnerships that helped to link the backcountry with the coastal capital. Recalling the strand of pearls along the coast, it is perhaps easy to forget that urban civilization penetrated the interior forests of colonial America and in some instances would rival coastal counterparts in the nineteenth century.

Backcountry Carolina settlement began unpretentiously as military garrisons in the early eighteenth century. The forts soon expanded their security functions to supply soldiers and frontier traders. They were also convenient collection points for the important deerskin trade to Charleston. Here too, the nature of the deerskin trade—the need for storage and processing facilities—stimulated urban growth. After the 1730s when the deerskin trade declined in importance, these backcountry towns easily shifted to marketing wheat, hemp, and indigo to Charleston merchants.

Charleston entrepreneurs did not wait for backcountry resources to pour into their laps, however. After years of organizing the deerskin and later the rice commerce, they learned that organization meant efficiency. They nurtured the frontier outposts and lined their own pockets with the profits.

Camden, South Carolina, located 125 miles northwest of Charleston along a major trade road to the backcountry deerskin commerce, was one such Charleston protégé. Charleston merchants sent agents to the interior town, much as London merchants sent representatives to the Chesapeake tobacco towns, to serve as formal links between coast and backcountry and to ensure an orderly, steady flow of commerce in both directions. By the 1740s, Camden had transcended its initial function as a collecting point to engage in some minor industry. When the transformation of the backcountry from trapping to farming resulted in wheat cultivation in the Camden area, merchants in Camden erected mills to process wheat, which they then shipped to Charleston.

The growth of Camden reflected the growth of functions. No longer an appendage of Charleston, it was becoming an urban settlement in its own right with the development of backcountry agriculture. The town boasted a sawmill, a circuit court, a warehouse, two meetinghouses, a jail, and some fine residences. Commercial, industrial, and administrative functions had transformed the backwoods outpost into a full-fledged trading partner with Charleston.

The Camden experience was repeated throughout the colonial South wherever a primary coastal center, linked to the interior by roads or rivers, helped to build commercial bases in the backcountry. In Virginia, communities like Alexandria, Norfolk, Richmond, and Petersburg, located at the heads of river navigation, were no rivals to imperial Charleston, but they too stimulated interior development in such towns as Dumfries and Colchester, downriver from Alexandria, and Leedstown and Hobbes Hole, down the Rappahannock from Fredericksburg.

Here, in outposts of fifty to one hundred citizens, the line between rural and urban was surely blurred—a characteristic of a frontier society. Frequently, these types of communities began as mere extensions of a plantation where an enterprising planter had established a gristmill, some warehouses, and a country store for the benefit of neighbors and the profit of himself. In fact, descriptions of larger plantations, especially those in the Carolina low country, read much like accounts of small towns. One such plantation, not atypical, included a dairy, a large gristmill, a sawmill, and a store stocked with the latest inventory from Charleston. The clearing in the forest, the farm with a gristmill and a store shared characteristics of both urban and rural environments, but were neither.

By the 1750s, however, a remarkable wave of immigration to the Carolina backcountry established and expanded previously marginal settlements into full-fledged urban places with their economic livelihood firmly grounded with the farmers in the surrounding countryside. During the 1750s, settlers from western Pennsylvania and Virginia streamed into backcountry Carolina attracted by land and the security against Indian attack. Immigration increased during the 1760s to include an ethnic mix that still characterizes these backcountry areas today. The German and Swiss settled in already existing outposts such as New Windsor and Saxa Gotha; the Scotch-Irish in Ninety-Six and the Waxhaws; and the Welsh Baptists, Irish Quakers, and French Huguenots in similar interior settlements, giving the backcountry a unique international flavor.

The development of Saxa Gotha indicated the vagaries of backcountry urbanization. The town was one of Governor Johnson's frontier settlements of the 1730s, but it languished until some seventy Swiss families moved there in the 1740s, and soon a church and school appeared as landmarks of civilization. The town's location on a river that penetrated further into the backcountry led to the establishment of a gristmill once farmers began cultivating the surrounding region. Charleston merchants also established their interests in the town by the 1760s, and inns, warehouses, and homes soon filled out the growing community. By that time, the story of Saxa Gotha was similar to the evolution of Camden, though on a much smaller scale.

By the time of the Revolution, similar urban settlements had evolved as far as three hundred miles from Charleston. Considering the distances and the primitive transportation available, the ties with the coast were quite tenuous. The very distance from the coastal capital forced, in effect, the creation of central locations in the interior to supply the frontier population, serve as temporary security, and eventually serve as a marketplace for surplus agricultural production. Nevertheless, when the British attempted to force the backcountry to capitulate by blockading Charleston, they understood that however independent these backcountry communities seemed, their lifeline to Charleston—for capital and goods—was unmistakable. For Charleston, the Camdens and the Saxa Gothas enabled that pearl of the Atlantic to maintain and increase its luminescence.

The diligence of Charleston merchants in establishing commercial links to the interior received additional inspiration when a rival city appeared on the strand to the south of the Carolina port. Savannah was indeed a gem of the ocean. At least, that is what its imaginative mentor, James Oglethorpe, had in mind when he planned the city in 1733. The outlines of his good sense can still be seen in the tree-lined streets and periodic interruptions of parks and rest places. Well into the nineteenth century, Savannah was one of the few cities in the country that provided sufficient open spaces for its citizens.

The same ideas that influenced the Carolina proprietors and South Carolina's Robert Johnson affected Oglethorpe: the belief in the importance of urban settlement, yet the recognition that rural features were necessary to temper the urban landscape. In Oglethorpe's view, the city and the country could be mutually reinforcing environments. The result—a middle landscape—would integrate the best from both worlds. Oglethorpe grew up with a generation that was beginning to see the problems of concentrated urban settlement. Indeed, a half century before Savannah appeared on the Georgia coast, William Penn had designed Philadelphia as a "green garden town" with spacious lots, an orderly gridiron street pattern, and five squares that served as America's first public parks.

Oglethorpe was aware of Penn's plan—Savannah copied the Philadelphia gridiron street pattern—and sought to improve upon it. The city was constructed of building-block units, or wards, each of which contained ten or a dozen house lots with an open square at the center. Since the city controlled surrounding lands, the expansion of Savannah could be easily regulated with the simple addition of wards as the need arose. This allowed for considerable expansion without the formless sprawl that was already evident in Philadelphia. In order to provide food for the community and to inject pastoral activities and values in the urban milieu, Oglethorpe surrounded the city with garden plots and larger farms. As one contemporary observer described it, "each Freeholder . . . has a Lott . . . beyond the Common of 5 Acres for a Garden. . . . Each Freeholder of the Tything [ten houses equaled one tything] has a Lott or Farm of 45 Acres. . . . Beyond . . . commerce Lotts of 500 Acres; these are granted upon Terms of keeping 10 servants."

As both city and countryside developed, the idea of the urban farmer became less plausible. The collection of plots and farms into larger units and the permanent residence of citizens either on the farm or in the city were becoming more common by the time of the Revolution. The city itself, however, with its relatively slow growth, was able to preserve the basic features of the "green garden town" plan, the disappearance of which had so frustrated William Penn.

English settlers were not the only southern colonists who appreciated the middle landscape ideal. The French in their European communities had compromised urban and rural life-styles. The wide avenues and formal gardens that were characteristic of urban planning during the reign of Louis XIV, as well as the smaller, less formal squares, were simultaneous attempts at the elegant and the pastoral. The French influence in the colonial South was confined to the Gulf Coast, an area that remained of only peripheral concern to the empire. After the establishment of Mobile in 1710, the French embarked on their most ambitious scheme in the area with the founding of New Orleans in 1722 by Jean Baptiste Le Moyne, sieur de Bienville. He held lofty aspirations for the city at the Mississippi delta. He intended a great capital, and his plan reflected these intentions. The focal point of Bienville's city was the *place d'armes*, a formal open ground now called Jackson Square. The formal *place*, a common French planning device at the time, was centered perfectly on the river and dominated by St. Louis Cathedral. Later, government buildings and apartments of wealthy and prominent citizens joined the church on the *place*. Architecture historian Christopher Tunnard has called this grouping "the most important architectural plaza in the United States."

New Orleans did not achieve the hoped-for grandeur. The siting of the town may have been militarily efficacious, but for almost every other purpose it was unfortunate. Settlers constantly battled floods, tropical diseases, and virtual isolation from other settlements. The potentially rich farmlands in the area were hardly worked, so the city's economic potential went largely unfulfilled during the colonial period. Still, as early as 1727, there were nearly one thousand people in this mainly administrative and military outpost. By the late eighteenth century, Americans were arriving in significant numbers, bringing with them more aggressive business methods and staple-crop cultivation.

The isolation of New Orleans, though extreme, was not unique to that city. By the time of the American Revolution, urban civilization existed in the colonial South, but certainly not in an integrated urban network or a well-defined urban system with a distinctive hierarchy of urban places. Transportation, whether by roads or rivers, was problematic and seasonal. The type of steady reciprocal commercial flow characteristic of an urban network was missing in certain areas. Indeed, in some regions, towns of any size were missing. All settlements were small, with the exceptions of Charleston and New Orleans, and limitations on size implied limitations of functions that would preclude the evolution of an urban hierarchy. The frontier environment, in addition, was too unstable to support an urban network. Settlements were founded and frequently disappeared. Finally, the metropolis or primary city so necessary for the development of any system was absent.

Despite London's general failure to encourage urban settlement during the seventeenth century, the commercial policies of the eighteenth century had some impact on the growth and decline of towns. In 1691, when monarchs William and Mary designated certain ports of entry in Virginia, urban growth suddenly blossomed in that once-barren environment for towns. When royal officials attempted to pump some life into the sagging tobacco trade during the 1740s by consolidating tobacco shipments in certain Maryland towns, those communities not favored by the legislation literally disappeared.

The pattern of urbanization in the colonial South was similar to urban development in feudal Europe, which is not surprising considering the primitive surroundings and the lower-order economic activities. That pattern was decentralized, revolving around relatively parochial economies. The pattern reached an extreme in the Chesapeake, where geographic configurations produced a new economic region every ten miles or so. The towns of Virginia and Maryland, though in the same geographic area, probably had more communication with London than they had with each other.

It appeared that a network of some sort was in the process of creation by the 1770s. The river towns in the Chesapeake had established ties with smaller places along the river system. In the Valley of Virginia, a series of towns evolved by the 1760s with ties both to the coastal communities and to the towns in the western backcountry. The functional and size distinctions between these places were not sufficiently great to warrant the term *hierarchy*, however. These links, moreover, were irregular, and there was rarely contact with towns in other colonies.

In the Carolinas, the connections between low country and up-country, especially in the case of Charleston and its partners, were more developed, but they had little communication beyond the Carolina region. As with the Virginia towns, the distinctions between the dozens of settlements on the Carolina frontier were so minor that a hierarchical structure did not exist. The basic materials were there, however: coastal cities and backcountry towns that would later evolve into a system with connections beyond the region.

This development seemed evident, given the evolution of the urban South during the colonial period. Urbanization went through three general periods. During the seventeenth century, urban development was slight. The abundance of fertile land, the limited nature of staple-crop cultivation, and geographic patterns counteracted the directives and intentions of royal officials. The first half of the eighteenth century was the seedbed for sustained urban development in the colonial South. Staple cultivation burgeoned—wheat and rice production in particular—and increased manipulations by England's merchants and legislators stimulated urban growth. Finally, beginning in the 1740s, the establishment of Charleston as the colonial South's most important city, the growth of backcountry towns and cultivation, and the links between coast and frontier marked the third stage of urban development.

Urbanization throughout much of the period, though, was insignificant—indeed all of colonial America remained overwhelmingly rural up to and considerably beyond the Revolution. Even the appearance of urban settlements during the late colonial era was quite modest, certainly when compared with the more precocious northern towns, which benefited from a more diverse agricultural hinterland and, especially in New England, the relative scarcity of good climate, geography, and soil. Yet the colonial period is a crucial era for southern urbanization because the themes that characterized the distinctive development of the South's cities up to the present first appeared at that time.

To begin with, whatever direction southern urbanization would take in the post-Revolutionary era, it seemed evident that the peculiar characteristics of the region—its geography, climate, and crop cultivation, for some major examples—would mold the character of its cities. If the region were distinctive, so would its cities be distinctive. The colonial era had demonstrated that within the same colonial empire, very different patterns could emerge.

Second, a biracial society was emerging. Certainly, blacks, both free and slave, resided in areas outside the colonial South. The black population was greater in the South, however, and here staple-crop agriculture, particularly such labor-intensive crops as tobacco and rice, encouraged the use of black labor. The abundance of land—and large tracts of it—made the use of gang labor feasible and efficient. In a colonial society where labor was scarce, the African provided an excellent adaptation to soil, climate, and geography. Such a fixed capital investment ensured adherence to staple agriculture.

Slavery, however, was an urban institution as well. In the colonial era, when the line between slavery and freedom was unclear, the urban slave probably enjoyed more freedom than he would at any future time. Southern urban residents were just beginning to cope with the implications—legal and philosophical—of a biracial society by the time of the Revolution.

A practical and more immediate consequence of a biracial society was the creation of a class of low consumers. What towns existed maintained low functional levels in part because the demands and the capital of the surrounding population—in some areas over three-quarters slave—were limited. The relative absence of towns, especially of major ports of entry other than Charleston, discouraged the immigration of a free population. The growth of Boston and Philadelphia in the eighteenth century resulted in great part from the demand generated by the free white families who required provisions, implements, and livestock during their first years in the New World. This is not to say that slavery discouraged or retarded urbanization; slavery, after all, existed throughout colonial America. But it is evident that the large slave population and the relative absence of free migration reinforced the shallow urban development already evident in the colonial South.

The importance of the metropolis in determining the urban and economic future of a region was a third theme that first emerged in the colonial era. By the eighteenth century, the colonial administration in London had sufficient influence to enhance or inhibit urban growth in the American colonies. The power of legislation, especially commercial legislation, was understood in the colonies. Where possible, detrimental laws were avoided, but where this was not possible, oblivion and economic ruin were realistic concerns. This point was evident with all colonists, regardless of region, and more so in the cities where the economic stakes were highest. When avoidance was impossible, or when threatening measures seemed imminent, revolution was the alternative. Of course, the origin of the American Revolution was not as simple as that. But the colonists' long experience with the real and potential power of the metropolis was a crucial factor in fomenting revolutionary sentiment once that power was used in an adverse way.

The metropolis could affect urbanization in more subtle ways as well. Capital accumulation and consequently credit were constant problems in colonial economic life, and some colonies resorted to inflationary paper money to "solve" the difficulties of inadequate capital. The absence of banks in the colonial economy threw the responsibility of capital accumulation and credit upon urban merchants and planter-merchants. The system worked adequately in Charleston, for example, but ultimately the reins of capital were held in London. The coastal financiers were typically middlemen in the credit network. In fact, some planters dealt directly with London capitalists, bypassing local lenders. London had the banks, controlled the specie circulation (chronically short in the colonies), and therefore had as much influence on economic growth as the colonial financiers. This situation merely describes a typical colonial condition. It was, nevertheless, a well-remembered legacy of the colonial era. Banking, in fact, was a dominant issue during the first half century of national existence.

These, then, were to become the persistent themes of southern urbanization: the influence of the rural landscape and especially of staple agriculture, the presence of a biracial society, and the impact of the metropolis. The same forces, of course, affected the entire region. And that is the point. In the next period of southern history, the antebellum era, southerners would capitalize on the first, accommodate themselves to the second, and fight the third. In the process, they would become increasingly set apart from the rest of the nation, and so would their cities.

The Social Evolution of
Preindustrial American Cities,
1700–1820

*Gary B. Nash**

As the eighteenth century began, the population of Boston, the largest city in the English overseas world, stood at 7,000. New York City bustled with 5,000 inhabitants, while the villages of Philadelphia and Charleston, with only a few score buildings that had progressed beyond framed to brick structures, had about 2,000 people each. Four generations later, as the century ended, Boston had grown to 25,000, New York to 60,000, Philadelphia to 62,000, Charleston to 13,000, and Baltimore, a newcomer on the urban scene, to 27,000. Twenty-eight other towns exceeded 2,500 inhabitants and just over 6 percent of the American population lived in urban centers of more than 2,500. Much greater growth lay just ahead, with Philadelphia and New York burgeoning to 118,000 and 131,000, respectively, by 1820. But even as Thomas Jefferson assumed the presidency, population increase and commercial development had reconfigured what had been an almost cityless landscape at the beginning of the century into one studded with urban places. Relative to England, probably the most urbanized country in the world in 1800, the United States lagged behind by half a century. Occupied after the Revolution in the business of expanding across the continent, land-hungry Americans remained largely a rural people for more than a century. Hence, not until 1840 would the United States be able to match the 15 cities over 20,000 in population that England boasted in 1800, and not until the 1880s would 30 percent of the population live in towns of 2,500 or more, as did this percentage of the English population in 1800.[1] Nor would the kind of industrial cities that grew so rapidly in the second half of the eighteenth century in England—cities such as Manchester, Liverpool, and Birmingham—be found in America at this time (Table 1). Yet like all modern nations, the United States was

*Gary B. Nash is professor of history at the University of California, Los Angeles. Reprinted from Gary B. Nash, "The Social Evolution of Preindustrial American Cities, 1700–1820: Reflections and New Directions," Journal of Urban History 13 (February 1987): 115–45. Copyright 1987 by Sage Publications. Reprinted by permission of Sage Publications.

Table 1
Population of English and American Cities, 1700–1800

1700	1750	1800
Norwich (30,000)	Norwich (36,000)	Manchester (90,000)
Bristol (20,000)	Bristol (25,000)	Liverpool (88,000)
Manchester (10,000)	Birmingham (24,000)	Birmingham (74,000)
BOSTON (7,000)	Liverpool (22,000)	Bristol (64,000)
Leeds (6,000)	Manchester (19,000)	PHILADELPHIA (62,000)
Birmingham (6,000)	BOSTON (16,000)	NEW YORK (61,000)
NEW YORK (5,000)	NEW YORK (13,000)	Leeds (53,000)
Liverpool (5,000)	PHILADELPHIA (13,000)	Norwich (37,000)
Portsmouth (5,000)	Sheffield (11,000)	Bath (34,000)
	Portsmouth (10,000)	Portsmouth (33,000)
	Leeds (10,000)	Sheffield (31,000)
		BALTIMORE (27,000)
		BOSTON (25,000)

Sources: C. W. Chalkin, *The Provincial Towns of Georgian England* (London, 1974); B. R. Mitchell, *European Historical Statistics, 1750–1820,* 2d ed. (New York, 1980); Gary B. Nash, *The Urban Crucible: Social Change, Political Consciousness, and the Origins of the American Revolution* (Cambridge, MA, 1979); U.S. Bureau of the Census, *Return of the Whole Number of Persons within the Several Districts of the United States [1800]* (Washington City, 1802).

launched on the historic course that would make it a nation of urban rather than rural people.

What did it mean for an urban center to increase from 5,000 to 60,000 over four generations? How did social relations, political life, and patterns of association change in the course of such development? Elsewhere I have argued that the seaboard cities were the cutting edge of change in early America. It was here that almost all the alterations associated with the advent of modern capitalist society first occurred, and then slowly radiated outward to the small farming communities of the hinterland. In the colonial cities, people first made the transition from an oral to a literate culture, from a moral to a market economy, from an ascriptive to a competitive social order, from a communal to an individualistic orientation, from a hierarchical and deferential polity to a participatory and contentious civic life. In the cities factory production first began to replace small-scale artisanal production and the first steps were taken to organize work by clock time rather than by sidereal cycles. These were, in fact, among the critical changes that Ferdinand Tonnies identified as constituting the transition from *gemeinschaft* to *gesellschaft*— a historic process that he identified as quintessentially an urban phenomenon.[2]

How, amid such changes, did urban people experience life differently and, most important, how did they confront these changes? Following Thomas Bender's seminal suggestion, I propose that we reconsider the *gemeinschaft* to *gesellschaft* formulation of change in which the vocabulary of analysis is composed of words like decay, decline, dissolution, and disintegration of community. This analytic model is not without its uses for urban historians.

However, enough has been discovered about the dynamics of urban social development in eighteenth-century towns to keep us mindful that communities change at different rates of speed, sometimes in different directions, not always in unilinear fashion, and rarely with all members of the community cleaving to the same values and responding identically to the same stimuli. Moreover, the organizing notion of decline and decay implicitly, if unintentionally, consigns to a passive role the city dwellers themselves, and especially those who were most adversely affected by change.[3]

The tendency has been almost irresistible to interpret the rise of materialistic, self-interested, contentious, class-oriented urban polity as a sign of social declension and shattered harmony. As in most things, we look backward to what we imagine were better days—a simpler time when mutuality, order, and a universal regard for the commonweal prevailed. Social cohesion and harmony, alas, were never so prevalent in the prerevolutionary cities as sometimes imagined, even if the richest and poorest inhabitants lived next door to each other, even if the poor were succored with familial forms of relief, even if journeymen lived with masters and worked with them under one roof. Moreover, the emerging urban social order of the late eighteenth century, while at many times difficult and hardly bearable, brought compensating advantages that offset some of the strains. Free black Americans, for example, were usually denied respect and equal access to jobs, education, and political rights when they migrated into these cities; but none of them would have traded their lot for their prior status as slaves, for freedom in the postrevolutionary cities, with all its disadvantages, was preferable to slavery, even in its mildest forms. Struggling shoemakers in the age of Jefferson no longer lived across the street from the mayor or worshiped in the same church as lofty merchants; but such socially integrating mechanisms had never guaranteed them employment in "the old days." Moreover, in their emerging working-class neighborhoods, where they frequented their own taverns, churches, and craft organizations, they found the opportunity to create a stronger culture of their own than had proven possible in the more class-mixed and socially mobile cities of the eighteenth century. Journeymen no longer lived with the master and ate at his table, but when it came time to vote, they were more likely to be found at the polls and went there more autonomously than before. *Gesellschaft*, in some of its forms, was in fact more likely to occur in cities where growing social stratification and social zoning occurred than in the less stratified and more socially integrated cities of the past.

Bender aptly asks: "Why cannot *gemeinschaft* and *gesellschaft* simultaneously shape social life," for both are "forms of human interaction that can act reciprocally on each other?"[4] Extending this, it may be asked whether homogeneity and smallness are the indispensable elements of community and viable social relations. In seeking to substitute new paradigms of social change for the overused *gemeinschaft* to *gesellschaft* model, it may be best to begin by observing life as close to the street level and the kitchen hearth as possible, searching for signs of how urban people struggled to create, adapt to, oppose, defend, or legitimize new circumstances. Rather than nostalgically tracing the *eclipse* of community, we need to trace the continuously evolving *process* of community. We need to look for the *different* meanings (rather than the *less satisfactory* ones) that urban life took and the various strategies of living that people devised as their cities grew in size and complexity. In important ways, this article argues, the kinds of structural changes occurring in the cities created conditions that encouraged—even necessitated—the fabrication of communities within communities by energized and mobilized groups that had previously often been politically and socially quiescent and detached from group activity, except in churches.

E ven in their earliest years, the capitals of Massachusetts, Pennsylvania, New York, and South Carolina were not so ethnically and religiously homogeneous as is sometimes supposed. But they were relatively unified by their settlers' common religious orientations and social backgrounds, with East Anglican Puritans, Dutch Calvinists, English Quakers, and West Indian Anglicans shaping the early social contours of the four provincial capitals respectively. This religious homogeneity broke down rapidly in Manhattan in the late seventeenth century and in Philadelphia and Boston in the eighteenth, despite efforts to maintain it in Boston and because no one attempted to maintain it in Philadelphia. After the Peace of Utrecht in 1713, Philadelphia became the port of entry for thousands of immigrants from Ulster, the Rhine, the West Indies, and other points of the compass. In Boston, although as late as 1718 five boatloads of Ulster immigrants would be hustled out of town and directed to the New Hampshire frontier, the process eventually was much the same. Street signs would never be rendered both in German and English in John Winthrop's Boston, as in William Penn's Philadelphia, but the immigrants came, particularly after the Revolution, when the volume of immigration was heavier than previously believed according to recent estimates, to complete the process that the early town fathers had so much feared—the diversifying of a community formerly composed of supposedly like-minded souls.[5]

Urban historians still know very little about the exact patterns of migration—from the rural hinterland, from other mainland colonies, and from overseas—that spurred growth and turned American towns into ethnic and religious bouillabaisses that in England had a counterpart perhaps only in Liverpool and London. But while the timing and dynamics of this rapid diversifying of the urban populaces is murky, the overall effects would have been obvious to any visitor strolling the streets of the major seaport cities on a Sunday morning in 1800. In Philadelphia, for example, such a visitor would have witnessed people crowding into thirty-five churches representing fourteen denominations and eight ethnic groups, whereas a century before worshipers had attended only the churches of four English denominations and one Swedish chapel. Even in Boston, less than half the size of Philadelphia, nineteen churches of eight denominations existed at the end of the eighteenth century.[6]

Amid this growing cosmopolitanism, religious persecution, if not religious prejudice, faded. In the process, the early Boston meaning of "community"—a collection of like-minded believers who extended to "strangers" only the freedom "to be gone as fast as they can, the sooner the better"—was eclipsed by the Philadelphia meaning of "community"—a collection of believers, disbelievers, mystics, agnostics, and nihilists who learned to see themselves linked to those around them by material rewards and social necessities rather than by heavenly quests. In this growing acceptance of the idea that diversity could be the cement rather than the dissolvant of unity lay the roots of the pluralism that was to become a mainstay of American society. That it set American cities off from their English counterparts, London excepted, seems apparent from the comments of English visitors, who often remarked on the multichromatic and multilingual melanges in the American cities.

One immigrant group of a special character, largely absent in every English town except London, figured importantly in the urban landscape. At the beginning of the century the cities contained only small numbers of America's involuntary immigrants—the sons and daughters of Africa. But their proportion of the population grew rapidly between 1720 and 1760, spurred by the demand for labor in the growing towns and, during the Seven Years' War, by the nearly complete stoppage of the indentured servant trade. Boston's slave population grew from about 300 to 1,544 between 1710 and 1752; slaves in New York City increased so rapidly in the same era that by 1746 half the white households held slaves. In Philadelphia, where those investing in bound labor had chosen Irish and German indentured servants more often than African slaves in the first half of the century, merchants and artisans alike purchased record numbers of Africans during the Seven Years' War, multiplying the black population to above 1,400 by war's end. In Charleston, capital of the colony with the highest proportion of slaves in British North America, 54 percent of the city's 11,000 residents were slaves in 1770.[7]

In the last third of the century, however, this rapid growth of black laborers underwent two enormous changes. First, slave imports to the growing cities came to an abrupt halt except in Charleston. The depression that followed the Seven Years' War convinced many urban capitalists of the advantages of free laborers, whom they could hire and fire as economic cycles dictated. The growth of abolitionism in the cities and their occupation by the British during the Revolution put the finishing touches on slave imports. All over the northeastern seaboard the black slave populations in the cities plummeted in the revolutionary era, as dying slaves went unreplaced by new recruits from Africa and as younger slaves fled to the British when they occupied the towns.

The second change was the dramatic rise of the free black populations in the postrevolutionary cities, including those in the South such as Norfolk, Baltimore, Savannah, and Charleston. In the northern cities, just as quickly as the black slave population had diminished between 1765 and 1780, the free black population rose from 1780 to 1800. Philadelphia, the southernmost of the northern cities, was especially notable. Its free black population of perhaps 250 on the eve of independence approached 10,000 by 1810. Almost every northern seaport exerted a powerful magnetic force upon freed blacks, for the city represented a place to make a living (which was very difficult in the countryside for those lacking capital to invest in land and equipment), a place to find marriage partners and compatriots, a place, in short, to start a community within a community.[8] In the southern cities, the free black population also grew rapidly, far outstripping increases in the white and slave populations. In Baltimore, where only a handful of free blacks resided at the end of the Revolution, nearly 6,000 free blacks congregated by 1810. Richmond and Petersburg, Virginia, and Charleston, South Carolina, all had free black communities exceeding 1,000 by 1810 (Table 2).[9]

America's northern city dwellers, in an average person's lifetime, witnessed the rapid growth of slavery, a sudden black depopulation during the war, the dismantling of urban slavery, and then a swift repopulation of the cities by free blacks, many of them streaming in from the hinterland and the upper South. New York lingered half a generation behind in this manumission process, and the southern cities represented a different case altogether, but in all the cities the urban character of modern Afro-American life was taking shape. When Cato, Cudgo, and Betty, who had formerly lived *in* the houses of merchants and artisans as lifelong servants, became Cato Freeman, William Thomas, and Elizabeth Anderson, who lived *down the street* as free persons who controlled their own destinies, white and black urbanites both had to make psychological adjustments. Some could not, and consequently the black emancipation process was fraught with difficulties. Nonetheless, growing black populations smithied out the elements of modern Afro-American life and culture on the anvil of urban coexistence with those who had formerly been their masters. In the southern cities (and in New York City until about 1820), free blacks lived precariously among blacks still enslaved. They too, albeit under more difficult circumstances, formed neighborhoods, established families, and organized churches, schools, and benevolent societies.[10] One important urban group had made the transition from individuals whose collective action was strictly prohibited to persons who eagerly formed religious and social groups and acted collectively in a number of other ways.

Table 2
Urban Free Black Population, 1790–1810

	Free Black Popul.		Percent Change, 1790–1810		
	1790	1810	Free Blacks	Whites	Slaves
Boston	761	1,484	+ 95	+ 90	NA
Providence	427	865	+ 103	+ 56	− 88
New York	1,101	8,137	+ 639	+ 192	− 29
Philadelphia	2,078	9,653	+ 365	+ 17	− 99
Baltimore	323	5,671	+ 1,656	+ 204	+ 272
Richmond	265	1,189	+ 349	+ 138	+ 153
Petersburg	310	1,089	+ 251	+ 92	+ 72
Charleston	951	1,472	+ 55	+ 31	+ 29

Sources: U.S. Bureau of the Census, *Heads of Families at the First Census of the United States Taken in the Year 1790: Pennsylvania* (Washington, DC, 1908); *Aggregate Number of Persons within the United States in the Year 1810* (Washington, DC, 1811).

Blacks emerging from the house of bondage in the late eighteenth-century cities sought opportunity as other poor immigrants had done for decades. The parallel was closest with those who had arrived as indentured servants and worked off their labor contract. However, manumitted blacks at the end of the eighteenth century (along with newly arriving immigrants) were entering an economy that differed markedly from that which humble aspirants had found before the Revolution. The early eighteenth-century towns were filled with men who had risen to modest wealth from artisan backgrounds, mostly through the mechanism of urban land speculation or military subcontracting in time of war. Still young and fluid, the cities were arenas of opportunity for the industrious and bold. Benjamin Franklin was everyone's model of the plucky, shrewd, and frugal leather-apron man who might advance rapidly from apprentice to journeyman to master. Many, like Franklin, watched their wives replace the pewter spoon and earthern porringer at the breakfast table with a silver spoon and china bowl, symbolizing the ascent beyond a "decent competency" that was the artisan's self-proclaimed goal in the preindustrial city. Of course, only a handful rose so rapidly and stylishly as Poor Richard in the early years; yet few ever imagined that their families would go hungry or that they might awaken one morning inside an almshouse. More and more that fate awaited those who entered urban life at the bottom of the social ladder in the last third of the century.

Even those who faithfully followed Poor Richard's precepts of industry and frugality sometimes fell into poverty in the prerevolutionary generation. Boston suffered earlier and more intensively than other towns, its economy wracked after the 1720s by war-induced inflation and heavy taxes and its coffers strained from supporting hundreds of war widows and their fatherless children. By midcentury, New England's commercial center was the widow capital of the Western world with one of every three married women heading a husbandless household. By the early 1750s Boston officialdom was describing the abodes of the poor where "scenes of Distress we do often behold! Numbers of Wretches hungry and naked shivering with Cold, and, perhaps, languishing with Disease."[11] Although it has been axiomatic among historians that poverty corroded the lives of ordinary people to a far greater extent in English than in American towns, the selectmen, in this same year, ventured to claim that poverty was so widespread that they were obliged to expend relief monies double those of any town of equal size "upon the face of the whole Earth."[12]

In all the cities poverty spread during the deep recession following the Seven Years' War. Nobody in the cities of Cotton Mather, Robert Hunter, and James Logan could have imagined a report such as came from the Philadelphia almshouse managers, who wrote, as the Continental Congress was conducting its epic debate over independence a few blocks away, that "of the 147 Men, 178 Women, and 85 Children [admitted to the almshouse during the previous year] most of them [are] naked, helpless and emaciated with Poverty and Disease to such a Degree, that some have died in a few Days after their Admission."[13] To control the strolling poor, whose support drove up poor taxes and whose very appearance threatened social disorder, town leaders tightened residency requirements, systematically examined and expelled nonresidents, and built workhouses and almshouses with harsh daily regimens to control those who qualified for relief.[14]

Research conducted by a second wave of those who have followed in the wake of the pioneering work done on tax lists a generation ago by Robert E. Brown and Jackson T. Main has led to the discovery that urban poverty on the eve of the Revolution was far more extensive than ever imagined. We now know that the tax lists that once were regarded as snapshots of the entire community do not include a very large group of urban adult males. In Providence and Newport, Rhode Island, for example, about 30 and 45 percent of all adult males were too poor to be included on the assessors' lists on the eve of the Revolution.[15] In Philadelphia, at least a fifth of the population, mostly people who lived as roomers in boarding houses or rented back buildings, sheds, and crude apartments in alleys, courtyards, and side streets, are missing from the assessors' rolls.[16] This large floating population, associated conceptually with a society in which opportunities are restricted and in which geographical rather than social mobility gives rise to the term "strolling poor," lends an entirely new look to the contours of urban society on the eve of the Revolution. It was into this altered urban scene that newly emancipated blacks would stride during and after the war.

The postwar reconstruction of the American cities, most of which were physically ravished during the British occupation, by no means eliminated urban poverty. In fact, it grew as the cities suffered through several severe trade depressions in the decade after the Peace of Paris. Struggling to absorb new waves of immigrants, particularly poor Irish sojourners who often could not find work, urban people were also scourged repeatedly by yellow fever at the end of the century. In the worst microbic attack ever to afflict American cities, the fever struck unremittingly from New York to New Orleans in the 1790s, especially striking down laboring families who could not afford to flee to the countryside, as did their social superiors. In several cities yellow fever claimed nearly 10 percent of the population in a single year (which amounts to something like 15 percent of the working classes), and strained poor relief resources in every municipality.[17]

The urban centers of the new American republic, while busy centers of growing overseas trade and early manufacturing, also became the centers of the highest mortality, criminality, and poverty rates ever known on the eastern seaboard. What a visiting committee of the Methodist Hospitable Society found in Philadelphia in 1803 was by no means unusual. Prowling the back alleys and the laboring-class neighborhoods on the edge of the city, the Methodists described scores of families living "in rooms with shattered furniture, in tenements almost in ruins, [some] laying on straw with a few rags to cover them."[18] This kind of urban immiseration, primarily associated by historians with European cities or with the industrializing, immigrant-filled American cities of the mid-nineteenth century, was, in fact, much in evidence by the time of Jefferson's presidency.

Alongside urban poverty rose urban elegance, architecturally visible in the handsome Georgian mansions that rose in the cities in the last third of the century; and evident in the cobbled streets—twisted in Boston, curved in New York, and straight in Philadelphia—as a growing battalion of four-wheeled carriages rolled by. One of the by-products of this new urban wealth, which also produced a broader middle class than existed earlier, was the growth of a consumer ethos. The sheer range of articles available for purchase in the cities grew enormously in the eighteenth century, as can be traced in newspaper advertisements, in urban occupational specialization, and in inventories of wealth in the probate records.[19]

A revolution fought for liberty and equality, but also for property and the right to acquire it as plentifully and competitively as people knew how, did nothing to retard the polarization of wealth and the growing material appetites of middle- and upper-class urbanites. The Revolution, in fact, removed several obstacles to the quest for wealth. Among the casualties of the victory over England was the concept of the commonweal and of a corporate economy in which the guarantee of the right to eat outweighed private pursuit of gain. Such a traditional ideology, with roots deep in the medieval past, had been losing ground steadily in the eighteenth century, even among master craftsmen. However, it had a revival amid the millennial fervor of the early years of revolution when many men hoped the conflict would achieve a double victory: independence from corrupt and oppressive England and self-purification through a restoration of civic virtue, spartan living, and disdain for worldly things. The yearning of an urbanite like Samuel Adams for a return to ancestral virtue and communal attachment quickly dissipated, however, even before the war's end. The *novus ordo seclorum* that large numbers of city dwellers sought was not Adams's "Christian Sparta" but an unfettered stage on which a drama composed by Adam Smith could be played out by actors who spoke not of the fair wage and the just price but of the laws of supply and demand and the greater benefits to the community of unbridled competition and consumer choice freed from the restraining hand of government.

The changes wrought in the second half of the eighteenth century, during a protracted period of war, economic volatility, and commercial expansion, were systematically recorded in the tax lists and the probate records of the period. These records, although understating the case because they do not include large numbers of the poorest city dwellers, confirm what was evident architecturally in the cities—that a substantial redistribution of wealth occurred, particularly, it appears, in the period from 1740 to 1765 when a number of large fortunes, based on overseas trade and urban land speculation, created America's first truly wealthy urban elite (Table 3). More important than the shifting proportion of wealth held by each stratum of urban society was the fact that the concentration of the community's resources in the hands of the elite was accompanied by a hefty increase in the proportion of propertyless and indigent urban dwellers. This growing economic inequality might have continued for some time without objections if middle- and lower-class city dwellers had not seen the amassing of great fortunes as one of the main causes of the growing poverty and indigency that afflicted every city in the second half of the eighteenth century.[20] From the revolutionary era to the

Table 3
Wealth Held by Richest Ten Percent of Urban Population

	Late 17th Century	Mid-18th Century	Late 18th Century
Boston (t)	46	64	65
Boston (i)	41	60	56
New York (t)	45	46	61
Philádelphia (t)	45	66	61
Philadelphia (i)	36	60	72

Sources: Nash, *Urban Crucible*, 395–98, Tables 3, 5; Allen Kulikoff, "The Growth of Inequality in Postrevolutionary Boston," *William and Mary Quarterly*, 28 (1971), 381; Billy G. Smith, "Inequality in Late Colonial Philadelphia: A Note on Its Nature and Growth," Ibid., 41 (1984), 629–45; Gloria Main, "Inequality in Early America: The Evidence from Probate Records of Massachusetts and Maryland," *Journal of Interdisciplinary History*, 7 (1977), 559–81; Bruce Martin Wilkenfeld, *The Social and Economic Structure of New York City, 1695–1796* (New York, 1978), pp. 161–62.

Note: t = based on tax assessment; i = based on probated inventories of wealth.

early nineteenth century, the distribution of urban wealth seems to have changed less rapidly. Then, during a period of early industrialization from about 1820 to 1850, a second major period of wealth redistribution further widened the gap between the top and bottom of urban society and left in the purses of the bottom half of society little more than 10 percent of the community's assets—about half as much as they had possessed a century before.[21]

It has been suggested that these changes in the division of economic resources stemmed primarily from the increasing youthfulness of eighteenth-century American society and that propertylessness was primarily a function of "social age." The propertyless, according to this argument, were mostly younger sons waiting for their landed inheritance. Because they were increasing as a proportion of the population, it appears that wealth became less equally divided when, in reality, it was age inequality that had spread.[22] This argument may hold for rural communities where ownership of land was the rule and sons waited far beyond the taxable age of eighteen to acquire their fathers' estates. However, in the cities, where propertylessness was becoming the rule at the lower ranks of society, changes in the age structure of the population, according to the one empirical study available, do not account for the widening disparity between rich and poor.[23]

In urban centers, enhanced opportunities for amassing great wealth among those positioned advantageously increased the relative wealth of those at the top of the social pyramid. Meanwhile, depressed real wages (partly caused after the Revolution by the increase in immigrant labor available in the cities), cyclical economic buffetings that struck hardest at those with the thinnest margin of security, and the vengeful yellow fever of the 1790s, which was America's first class disease, appear to have been the main factors bearing on the deepening social inequalities. Benjamin Franklin Bache, a Philadelphia newspaper editor, understood the growing disparity of wealth in much this way. "Is it not heart rending," he wrote in 1797 "that the laboring poor should almost exclusively be the victims of the disease introduced by that commerce, which, in prosperous times, is a source of misery to them, by the inequality of wealth which it produces?"[24]

Although comparable data for provincial towns in England are not available, it seems possible, because the old English provincial towns were exporting their dispossessed while American seaboard towns were absorbing them, that by the end of the eighteenth century the American cities harbored as many or possibly more transient poor than their English counterparts. By 1790, if one can generalize from one case study of Philadelphia, more than a third of the population was too poor to pay even the most modest tax— and this ratio would increase to more than half by 1830.[25] The smokestack towns that were already growing rapidly in Manchester, Liverpool, and Birmingham were still a generation away in America as the eighteenth century closed, so the proper comparison is between the American cities and the older provincial towns such as Norwich, Bath, and Bristol. The unflattering comments of almost all Americans who traveled in England notwithstanding, these towns may have differed in their social structure from their English counterparts primarily in that the English urban poor were indigenous and white (and therefore noticed) whereas in America the poor were immigrant and black (and therefore overlooked).

While a century of urban growth increased the gap between gentry and common folk, it also transformed the spatial patterns of working and living, and, perforce, social relations. Much of the changing social geography stemmed from the rapid rise of urban land values in the old cores of the seaport towns. Before the Revolution, except in the stagnant town of Boston, land values multiplied many times, making real estate investment a greater source of wealth than trade. After the Revolution, land values again soared. In Manhattan, they climbed 750 percent between 1785 and 1815 alone, and a similar trend prevailed in other cities.[26] In Philadelphia, "A Friend to Equal Justice" complained bitterly in 1793 that rents (which reflected the market value of land) had doubled, trebled, and even quadrupled after Congress moved to Philadelphia from New York in 1789.[27]

The century-long rise of land values and rents, because it far outstripped advances in the wages of artisans and laborers, led to two historic changes in the social geography of the cities. First, property ownership became more concentrated in the hands of merchants, professionals, shopkeepers, and speculative builders. As the price of urban land spiraled upward, leather-apron men found that a building lot cost four or five years' wages, rather than the four or five months' pay it had cost their grandfathers earlier in the century. Hence, tenancy rates climbed from about 30 percent of all heads of household at the beginning of the eighteenth century to about 80 percent one hundred years later.[28] In Baltimore, a young town where the entire process of social formation lagged several generations behind that of the older cities, the proportion of lower artisans without real property increased from about 48 percent to 69 percent in a single decade after 1804.[29]

Second, facing the urban real estate market with wages that increased only slowly in the second half of the eighteenth century, working people were obliged to seek cheaper land and rental housing on the periphery of the city. This, in turn, led to another change—the separation of the place of residence from the place of production. Thus emerged the pattern of concentric residential zones that became common to all growing urban centers of the Atlantic basin. Towns whose neighborhoods had previously been integrated by occupation and class now began to develop a core dominated by the wealthy, a surrounding belt containing primarily the middle class, and a periphery populated by the laboring poor. This "social zoning," as Peter Clark has termed it, has been traced in several cities where inspection of the tax lists had revealed median assessments in the core from four to ten times as great as on the outlying edges.[30]

Overlapping this increasing class segregation, which was still in the early stages at the beginning of the nineteenth century, was a growing racial clustering that occurred when free blacks establishing their own residences replaced slaves living with masters throughout the cities. The modern term "segregation," connoting a racial separation imposed by the dominant group, is not entirely appropriate in the early nineteenth-century American context because the concentration of black families in certain neighborhoods, as they worked their way free of the residual effects of bondage after the Revolution in the northern cities, or made their way thence from the upper South, was partly the result of their own desire to live near the independent black churches they built, near the schools associated with these churches, and near relatives, friends, and associates.[31] Nonetheless, the physical separation of blacks and whites, if we can generalize from the Philadelphia example, increased rapidly, with the index of dissimilarity growing from .149 in 1790 to .514 in 1820.[32]

As well as reflecting rising land values and rents, the social geography of the cities changed with the reorganization of work. Early in the century, apprentices and journeymen, working within a household mode of production, had usually lived with the master artisan in a familial setting in which residence and work location were merged. By the end of the century, a larger scale production led many masters to relocate their shops away from their place of residence, journeymen usually lived independently of the master, typically in rented rooms or in that new urban phenomenon of the late eighteenth century—the boardinghouse. Moreover, journeymen increasingly found themselves in an antagonistic relationship with their masters, for by the early nineteenth century the traditional pathway that led from apprentice to master craftsman was becoming severely clogged.[33] In Boston, for example, where as late as 1790 a majority of journeyman carpenters could expect to become masters, only one in five achieved that goal in the decades after 1810.[34] By the early nineteenth century, artisans who formerly would have expected to achieve the status of master were increasingly obliged to depend on others for wage work. "The time before long will come," decried one craftsman, "when we shall tread in the steps of Old England."[35] The term "walking cities" still applies at the end of the eighteenth century because urban geographical spread was still not very great, and people of many stations lived within hailing distance of each other. But while the geographical proximity of urban social classes remained relatively close, the social distance grew between employers and employees, rich and poor, black and white.

For urban women somewhat different changes in the social environment of work were taking place, particularly in the late eighteenth and early nineteenth centuries. First, the gradual transfer of male productive labor from the household to a commercial place of business "reduced the transmission of business and craft knowledge within the family" and thus decreased the likelihood that widows would continue their husbands' enterprises after their death.[36] A trend away from female proprietorships, noted in the case of Boston many years ago by Elisabeth Dexter on the basis of newspaper advertisements, has been statistically demonstrated for Philadelphia in a study of women's occupations listed in city directories. As late as the 1790s the probability remained high that widows would manage their deceased husbands' businesses—including the widows of ironmongers, pewterers, printers, coopers, turners, and tallow chandlers. However, by the antebellum era, the likelihood of this had been much reduced, and midwivery, although for different reasons, was also being taken out of women's hands.[37] In these areas of work, women of middling rank were pushed out of the public realm and into the private sphere.

At the same time the middle-class female proprietorships were decreasing, lower-class female household production in one important area—textiles— grew rapidly after the middle of the eighteenth century. The first attempts to utilize the labor of poor urban women—and increasingly their children— came in Boston, the capital of impoverished widowhood in America. But women balked at the separation of domestic responsibilities and income-producing work, and this resistance played a large part in the failure of the linen manufactory that merchants opened in 1750. However, women adapted readily to the putting-out system under which they spun thread in their homes, while simultaneously discharging familial responsibilities.[38] In most of the cities after the Revolution, merchant-entrepreneurs established large putting-out networks for the domestic spinning of cotton yarn. Where immigrant labor was available, as in Philadelphia, the system soaked up the labor of poor urban women until as late as the 1830s, thus maintaining the home as a workplace.[39] In other cities, such as Boston and Pawtucket, the mechanization of cotton spinning drew large numbers of women and children out of their homes and into textile factories as early as the 1790s, in imitation of the much more developed practice in English industrial towns.[40] Thus began a long history of urban women and children of the lower orders in textile work—a chapter of urban history that would take another turn in the antebellum years with the movement of poor women and their children into the needle trades.[41]

In the last generation, historians have discovered much more about structural changes in eighteenth-century urban society than they have about how people responded to these alterations. The utilization of quantifiable sources, such as deeds, tax and probate documents, and poor relief records, has advanced our knowledge of what Tonnies called "gemeinschaft of locality"—the physical life of the community—more than our comprehension of what he termed "gemeinschaft of mind"—the mental life of the community. Hence, any agenda of research in eighteenth- and early nineteenth-century urban history ought to be headed by topics relating to the individual and collective strategies of urban people as they sought to cope with their changing environment.

Insofar as they have inquired into the mental and behavioral responses of urban people to the passage of their locales from seaport villages to commercial and protoindustrial cities between 1690 and 1820, historians have looked primarily to the realm of politics. Some of them have argued that while the chasm between rich and poor grew and movement between the tiers of society decreased, conditions associated with the transition from *gemeinschaft* to *gesellschaft*, the reverse was happening in the political arena. The urban upper class in the American cities, as in England, had long believed in a system of political relations defined by gentle domination from above and willing subordination from below—a contractual arrangement that historians call deference politics. However, deference eroded markedly in the eighteenth-century cities, especially during critical periods when unemployment and declining real wages impoverished many working people and threatened the security of many more, thus sharpening their consciousness of inequalities of wealth and status. When artisans (and even laborers and mariners) mobilized politically, no longer believing that the elite managed affairs in the interest of the whole community, then the traditional rules of genteel politics began to change.

Long before the Revolution the instrumentalities of popular politics appeared in the cities—outdoor political rallies, vitriolic campaign literature, petition drives, club and caucus activity, and attacks on the wealthy as subverters rather than protectors of the community's welfare. During the Revolution this transformation of mechanic consciousness ushered in a new era of politics in which laboring people began to think of themselves as a distinct political entity. This led in turn to campaigns for transforming the political process through annual elections, secret balloting, universal male suffrage, rotation of office holding, inclusion of artisans as candidates for municipal offices, formation of extralegal committees for enforcing trade restrictions, self-convened outdoor political assemblages, and the opening of legislative debates to the public.[42] In the drawing rooms of polite society, men sputtered that "the Mechanics have no Right to *Speak* or *Think* for themselves," and should not presume to "intermeddle in state affairs."[43] The genie was out of the bottle, however, and would never be imprisoned again.

The political self-empowerment that was occurring in the revolutionary cities is often seen as a breakdown of an older social system in which interclass relations were marked by harmony, trust, mutual respect, and a sense of partnership within hierarchy. To some extent this notion of a prior social equilibrium is a convenient fiction created by historians who wish to chart change from a golden age. But the *relative* social equilibrium that had prevailed in the cities before the 1760s *was* in disarray because the conditions necessary for its survival were crumbling—an economy in which laboring people could fulfill their goals of earning a "decent competency," achieving an independent status, and obtaining respect in their communities.

Yet the overturning of the old system of political management partially mitigated the social disequilibrium because it offered the possibility that through a democratic political system each interest group in the urban polity could contend equally for its particular advantages. In time, the new system would be celebrated as uniquely American, although many urban nabobs could never accept the active participation in the political process of the "mere mechanics," the "rabble," the "unthinking multitude." This popularization of politics continued after the Revolution, despite a conservative reaction in the last decade of the century. While economic development, population growth, and the differential effects of war on urban society had led to a widening chasm between the top and bottom of urban society, in politics the increasingly distinct social ranks were forced into a common political process in which it was entirely legitimate for the lower orders to raise their voices, take to the streets, and formulate demands arising from their understanding of how the social system was changing. For those panjandrums who sat at the pinnacle of the more sharply defined social pyramid, popular politics carried the horrifying ring of anarchy, especially after the outbreak of the French Revolution. Beneficiaries of the advancing social exclusiveness, they were obliged to tolerate a growing political inclusiveness. Their discomfort was made all the more acute by the popular attacks mounted against them in the postrevolutionary era—fusillades that increased in intensity by the end of the century and escalated further as merchant capitalists organized banks, built factories, and penetrated such crafts as shoemaking and house building.[44]

Eventually finding a home in the Democratic-Republican party that formed in the 1790s, urban working men, often led by small merchants, professionals, and master artisans turned manufacturers, pressed hard for a more democratic system of politics and for specific changes in the way power was distributed in such varied aspects of urban life as the availability of credit, schooling, taxation, militia duty, and indebtedness laws. Strains of the old corporatist ethic remained alive in artisan republicanism, although the upward movement of many master craftsmen into the ranks of manufacturers carried them into a realm where Madisonian political economy was particularly congenial.[45]

Meanwhile, within the lower orders the egalitarian ideology enunciated during the Revolution was refurbished from about 1790 to 1830 and adapted to the new conditions of labor taking hold in the first third of the nineteenth century. Running deeply through this thought of the radical urban democracy was a deep suspicion of wealth and of the concentrated power that lower-class and many middle-class city residents believed was its handmaiden. The belief grew that republican "simplicity and equality of manners essential to equal rights" was being undermined by a parasitic class of merchant capitalists—nonproducers whose unrestrained acquisitiveness and lack of concern for the community led, eventually, to the degradation of productive labor. As William Duane, the fiery immigrant editor of the Philadelphia *Aurora* expressed it in 1806 (in the context of the conviction of striking journeymen shoemakers for conspiring to restrain trade), "the doors of industry are to be closed so that a breed of *white slaves* may be nursed up in poverty to take the place of the *blacks* upon their emancipation."[46]

This is not to argue that the lower orders were able to use their newly gained political voice to transform the conditions under which they lived and worked in urban society. Far from it. There emerged in the postrevolutionary era no crystallization of artisan consciousness or all-craft solidarity, and short-term working-class victories were outweighed by long-range defeats. Despite structural changes in shoemaking, tailoring, printing, and other trades that were separating journeymen from masters, it proved difficult for working people to unite in a society in which the ideology of laissez-faire had penetrated deeply. In New York, it took until 1804 for those who did not own property—a growing proportion of the laboring population—even to obtain the vote in municipal elections, and thereafter they were able to accomplish much less than they hoped for at the ballot box. In Philadelphia, prosperous mechanics, allied with professionals and some merchants, even formed their own wing of the Jeffersonian party in the early nineteenth century, adopting positions on economic and fiscal issues that made them hardly distinguishable from the Federalists. Such men did not share the radical social perspective that inspired the periodic insurgency of the lower artisans, mariners, and laborers, who imbibed a small producers' ideology stressing egalitarianism and communitarianism—and who were less than a generation away from embracing socialism and from founding workingmen's parties in all the major cities.[47]

In spite of the effects of westward movement and political cooptation in dissipating political radicalism in the seaboard cities, the revolutionary and postrevolutionary experience heightened artisan consciousness and brought working people into the political arena as never before. Once in that arena, they did not unify completely or act collectively at all moments. But the realization spread that the changes overcoming urban society could not be addressed by autonomous individuals who singly exercised their political rights but only by collective actions and intertrade alliances. The advent of a "gemeinschaft of mind" was hastened, moreover, by the residential class clustering that was emerging. For the first time in the history of American cities political alignments became closely connected with neighborhoods and wards and were reflected not simply in national and state political parties but also in the subcommunities that gathered themselves in trade associations, militia companies, and mutual aid societies.[48]

Much remains to be done on urban politics, especially in the neglected period between the end of the Revolution and the beginning of the Jacksonian era. Preoccupation with the emerging national party system has obscured the dynamics of local politics, which seem, to judge by a few recent studies, to have been far more clamorous and less cleansed of mob activity than is usually supposed (although there is no gainsaying the fact that public authorities became less tolerant of mob activity and moved ruthlessly to suppress it after the Revolution). There may be much more continuity between the revolutionary period and the 1820s than meets the eye. By the latter decade, the democratic strivings inherited from the revolutionary era were bursting through the boundaries of conventional Jacksonian party politics in most of the cities, and an extraordinary set of characters—Paineite free thinkers, Jacobin feminists, Owenite visionaries, radical political economists, and early socialists—were mobilizing the lower orders and sometimes middle-class people with their various formulas for reforming a republic that they believed had turned its back on the revolutionary promise of freedom, equality, and the elimination of corruption and exploitation. The work of Sean Wilentz and Paul Gilje on New York's plebian politics after the 1780s and Susan Davis's fruitful explorations of the rise of the folk street drama "as a mode of political communication" in early nineteenth-century Philadelphia are just three of the new

pioneering works that are illuminating the neglected period in the history of
the early republic in ways that suggest the responses outside the formal realm
of politics devised by urban people who saw themselves contending with
threatening new situations.[49]

A brief look at voluntary organizations in the postrevolutionary cities provides evidence of one important way in which urban people knit themselves together in subcommunities in order to cope with the forces of social
change that were rending the larger community. Three decades into the
nineteenth century Alexis de Tocqueville would marvel at the fervor of Americans to join local voluntary groups. "Americans of all ages, all conditions,
and all dispositions," he wrote, "constantly form associations. They have not
only commercial and manufacturing companies . . . but associations of a
thousand other kinds, religious, moral, serious, futile, general or restricted,
enormous or diminutive."[50] What the French observer described had its roots,
in fact, in the postrevolutionary seaboard cities where a phenomenal growth
of voluntary associations occurred.

For Tonnies, voluntary associations were a characteristic of a system of
gesellschaft because they were special interest groups directed at particular,
not universal, ends and were based on contractual agreements among their
members, whose principal aim was to advance their own wealth. In a *gesells-
chaftlich* society, "which presupposes every individual person with separate
spheres of rational will," Tonnies argued, these associations provided "the
only possible type of interrelationship." Yet after witnessing the rise of producer and consumer cooperatives among the laboring poor of Germany in
the early twentieth century, Tonnies discerned in these associations the revival
of "a principle of gemeinschaft economy" that might lead to the resuscitation
of "other forms of gemeinschaft."[51]

The potential of voluntary associations in the postrevolutionary era to
act as antipodal centers of urban group activity deserves much more attention
from historians. Voluntary societies were not new to the postrevolutionary
cities, of course. Charitable societies and fire companies had existed since the
early eighteenth century, and journeymen's societies were not far behind. The
latter, established to buffer aspiring craftsmen against the economic cycles
that could undermine the security of those living close to the margin, served
first as mutual aid associations but almost as importantly as nodal points of
social and political organization.

After 1760, urban voluntary associations multiplied rapidly, if we are to
judge by the cases of New York and Boston, the two cities that have been
most closely examined in this regard.[52] Volunteer fire companies, reform-
minded benevolent organizations, volunteer militia companies, and literary,
artistic, and scientific groups mushroomed, attracting thousands of city dwellers to endeavors that provided them with the satisfactions of sociability as
well as service. Composed only of men before the Revolution, such associations
began forming among urban women as well by the late 1780s, bringing into
collective activity the social group that had been traditionally most restricted
to functioning within the family and whose options in the economic sphere

were beginning to narrow at this time. By 1800, at least seventy-eight voluntary organizations were meeting in Boston, whereas only fifteen had existed in 1760.[53] Parallel growth, as yet charted only imperfectly, seems to have occurred in other cities as well. Among urban women, the 1790s and the first decade of the nineteenth century witnessed a spectacular growth of such groups, which far more than their male counterparts were devoted to religion, reform, and supporting the marginal people of the growing cities—the poor and sick, the orphaned and insane, and criminals and prostitutes.[54]

Why did this movement that made America a nation of joiners blossom in the late eighteenth-century cities? To some extent the new concept of citizenship ushered in by the Revolution, which enjoined the active involvement of citizens, nourished the desire to enlist in order to improve and perfect the new republic. Apathy, the revolutionary generation learned, was the enemy of a virtuous, improving people. A number of voluntary associations in the cities, founded out of educational, artistic, and reformist motives, fit this explanation. But a larger number of voluntary groups seem to have originated as mechanisms for buffering people against the forces of change or as a means of promoting or resisting change. Some organizations were explicitly meant to advance or defend the interest of a group, such as the journeymen's societies that grew rapidly between 1780 and 1820. Others were purposefully exclusionary, offering members a "surrogate community of harmony" in a world that had thrown off the patriarchal ideal and, in its political ideology, had abandoned hierarchy.[55] The best example here is the Masonic lodges, which grew at a dizzy pace in the late eighteenth-century cities. Modeling their organization to recapture the world as they thought it used to be, the Masons instituted an elaborate hierarchy, maintained strict deference between ranks, and prized harmony and stability.[56] Their fraternity was, in fact, a surrogate family, although by drawing heavily on the leisure time and emotional resources of their male members, they may have simultaneously weakened traditional family life.

More research is needed on urban voluntary associations to determine the composition and motives of their members and their meaning to those who joined. Tentatively, it appears that they were of many kinds and purposes; but all of them served particular segments of much enlarged and diversified urban populations by creating communities within communities. Facilitating interpersonal contact, providing small-scale arenas for self-improvement and mutual reinforcement, and training ordinary people in organizational skills, they helped to stitch together urban centers that sometimes seem, in historical perspective, to have been coming apart at the seams. Often engaging in highly ritualized public display, such associations sharpened their members' group consciousness and impressed upon their fellow urbanites the extent to which various groups regarded themselves as distinct. Yet the marching of Masons through the streets, or the procession of artisans under emblems of their trade, also made visible how extensively urban life involved group as against individual activity.[57]

The eighteenth-century cities, in sum, while places of rapid change, were also places of continuous readjustment. Urban people had to be resilient, for they were regularly buffeted by serious blows from economic and natural sources. Bostonians, for example, suffered major fires on ten occasions between 1653 and 1760 that wiped out as much as a tenth of the town's buildings with each conflagration. They withstood eight raging smallpox epidemics between 1640 and 1730, sustained military casualties proportionate to World War II death tolls four times from 1690 to 1780, and twice between 1740 and 1780 experienced hyperinflation that nearly wiped out the value of currency. Yet Boston, like other cities, survived, recovered, and grew. To a considerable extent this was possible because city people became adept at creating viable subcommunities, ranging from neighborhoods to voluntary associations, and they learned to use them to defend their interests, perpetuate sociability, and cope with (and sometimes counteract) structural changes affecting urban life.

NOTES

[1]P. J. Corfield, *The Impact of English Towns, 1700–1800* (Oxford, 1982), 7–8; the population data for American towns are drawn from the published decade censuses.

[2]Gary B. Nash, *The Urban Crucible: Social Change, Political Consciousness, and the Origins of the American Revolution* (Cambridge, 1979), passim; Ferdinand Tonnies, *Community and Society*, translated and ed. by Charles P. Loomis (East Lansing, MI, 1957).

[3]Thomas Bender, *Community and Social Change in America* (New Brunswick, NJ, 1978), ch. 1–2.

[4]Ibid., 31, 33. In attenuated form this had been Tonnies's original formulation. See *Community and Society*, 227.

[5]Henry A. Gemery, "European Emigration to North America, 1700–1820: Numbers and Quasi-Numbers," *Perspectives in American History*, New Series, 1 (1984), 283–342.

[6]The churches are listed in the Boston and Philadelphia city directories for 1800.

[7]Statistics on urban slave populations are taken from Nash, *Urban Crucible*, passim, and, for Charleston, from Evarts B. Greene and Virginia S. Harrington, *American Population Before the Census of 1790* (New York, 1932), 178. On the absence of blacks in all English towns except London, see James Walvin, *Black and White: The Negro and English Society, 1555–1945* (London, 1973), ch. 4.

[8]Gary B. Nash, "Forging Freedom: The Emancipation Experience in the Northern Seaport Towns, 1775–1820," in Ira Berlin and Ronald Hoffman, eds., *Slavery and Freedom in the Age of the American Revolution* (Charlottesville, VA, 1983), 3–48.

[9]Ira Berlin, *Slaves Without Masters: The Free Negro in the Antebellum South* (New York, 1974), ch. 2.

[10]Among the new community studies of free blacks are Jay Coughtry, *Creative Survival: The Providence Black Community in the 19th Century* (Providence, RI, 1982); Robert J. Cottrol, *The Afro-Yankees: Providence's Black Community in the Antebellum Era* (Westport, CT, 1982); Leroy Graham, *Baltimore: The Nineteenth Century Black Capital* (Washington, DC, 1982); Susanne Lebsock, *The Free Women of Petersburg: Status and Culture in a Southern Town, 1784–1860* (New York, 1984).

[11]*Industry and Frugality Proposed as the Surest Means to Make Us a Rich and Flourishing People. . .* (Boston, 1753), 8–10.

[12]*Reports of the Record Commissioners of the City of Boston* (39 vols., Boston, 1876–1908), XIV, 222, 240.

[13]"Report of the Contributors to the Relief and Employment of the Poor," in *Pennsylvania Gazette*, May 29, 1776.

[14]John Alexander, *Render Them Submissive: Responses to Poverty in Philadelphia, 1760–1800* (Amherst, MA, 1980); Raymond A. Mohl, *Poverty in New York, 1783–1825* (New York, 1971); Douglas Jones, "The Transformation of the Law of Poverty in Eighteenth-Century Massachusetts," *Publications of the Colonial Society of Massachusetts*, 62 (1984), 153–190; Lynn Withey, *Urban Growth in Colonial Rhode Island: Newport and Providence in the Eighteenth Century* (Albany, 1984), ch. 4.

[15]Withey, *Urban Growth in Colonial Rhode Island*, 123.

[16]Sharon V. Salinger and Charles Wetherell, "A Note on the Population of Prerevolutionary Philadelphia," *Pennsylvania Magazine of History and Biography*, 109 (1985), 369–386.

[17]J. H. Powell, *Bring Out Your Dead: The Great Plague of Yellow Fever in Philadelphia in 1793* (Philadelphia, 1949); John Duffy, *A History of Public Health in New York City, 1625–1866* (New York, 1968).

[18]*The Nature and Design of the Hospitable Society* (Philadelphia, 1803), quoted in Ronald Douglas Schultz, "Thoughts Among the People: Popular Thought, Radical Politics, and the Making of Philadelphia's Working Class" (Ph.D. dissertation, University of California, Los Angeles, 1985), 322.

[19]Among the occupations listed on the 1789 Philadelphia tax assessor's list that indicate the specialization occurring within the luxury trades were bucklemaker, combmaker, muffmaker, looking glass maker, fan maker, and piano maker. On the rise of a consumer ethos see the forthcoming book by Carole Shammas.

[20]The causal connection that many urban commentators perceived between the simultaneous rise of great wealth and dire poverty was expressed repeatedly from the 1760s onward. See Nash, *The Urban Crucible*, passim.

[21]Peter H. Lindert and Jeffrey Williamson, *Inequality in America: A Macroeconomic History* (New York, 1980); James A. Henretta, "Wealth and Social Structure," in Jack P. Greene, and J. R. Pole, eds., *Colonial British America: Essays in the New History of the Early Modern Era* (Baltimore, 1984), 276.

[22]John J. Waters, "Patrimony, Succession, and Social Stability: Guilford, Connecticut in the Eighteenth Century," *Perspectives in American History*, 10 (1976), 156; Jackson Turner Main, "The Distribution of Property in Colonial Connecticut," in James Kirby Martin, ed., *The Human Dimensions of Nation Making: Essays on Colonial and Revolutionary America* (Madison, WI, 1976); and James A. Henretta, "Families and Farms: *Mentalité* in Pre-Industrial America," *William and Mary Quarterly*, 35 (1978), 6–8.

[23]Billy G. Smith, "Inequality in Late Eighteenth-Century Philadelphia: A Note on Its Nature and Growth," *William and Mary Quarterly*, 41 (1984), 629–645.

[24]Quoted in James Douglas Tagg, "Benjamin Franklin Bache and the Philadelphia 'Aurora'," (Ph.D. dissertation, Wayne State University, 1973), 155.

[25]Tom W. Smith, "The Dawn of the Urban-Industrial Age: The Social Structure of Philadelphia, 1790–1830" (Ph.D. dissertation, University of Chicago, 1980), 151. The exclusion of a large percentage of free black householders from the assessment lists is not usually noted by historians; when this omission is corrected, the percentage of unassessed in the urban population by the early nineteenth century grows to about 50–60 percent.

[26]Betsy Blackmar, "Rewalking the 'Walking City': Housing and Property Relations in New York City, 1780–1840," *Radical History Review*, no. 21 (1980), 131–148; Arthur L. Jensen, *The Maritime Commerce of Colonial Philadelphia* (Madison, WI, 1963), 126–27.

[27]*Federal Gazette*, April 27, 1793.

[28]Blackmar, "Walking City," 132–139; Smith, "Dawn of the Urban-Industrial Age," 151, Table 60; Sharon V. Salinger and Charles Wetherell, "Wealth and Renting in Prerevolutionary Philadelphia," *Journal of American History*, 71 (1985), 829.

[29]Charles G. Steffen, *The Mechanics of Baltimore: Workers and Politics in the Age of Revolution, 1763–1812* (Urbana, IL, 1984), 40; Smith, "Inequality in Late Colonial Philadelphia," 633, Table 1.

[30]Peter Clark, ed., *The Transformation of English Provincial Towns, 1600–1800* (London, 1984); Allan Kulikoff, "The Progress of Inequality in Revolutionary Boston," *William and Mary Quarterly*, 28 (1971), 375–412; Smith, "Dawn of the Urban-Industrial Age," 278–279; Carl Abbott, "The Neighborhoods of New York, 1760–1775," *New York History*, 55 (1974), 35–54.

[31]Nash, "Forging Freedom," 40–43; Leonard P. Curry, *The Free Black in Urban America, 1800–1850: The Shadow of the Dream* (Chicago, 1981), ch. 4.

[32]Smith, "Dawn of the Urban-Industrial Age," 278, Table 89.

[33]Steffen, *Mechanics of Baltimore*, ch. 2, 5; Sean Wilentz, *Chants Democratic: New York City and the Rise of the American Working Class, 1788–1850* (New York, 1984), ch. 1–2, passim; Bruce Laurie, *Working People of Philadelphia, 1800–1850* (Philadelphia, 1980), ch. 1–2, passim.

[34]Lisa Lubow, "Journeymen and Masters: The Changing Relations of Artisan Labor [in Boston]," (dissertation in progress, University of California, Los Angeles).

[35]*1820 Census of Manufactures*, National Archives, Return of Robert Wellford [Philadelphia], quoted in Schultz, "Thoughts Among the People," 320.

[36]Claudia Golden, "The Changing Status of Women in the Economy of the Early Republic: Quantitative Evidence" (paper delivered at the Social Science History Association Conference on Quantitative Methods in History, California Institute of Technology, March, 1983), 13.

[37]Ibid., 13–18. Golden's findings largely confirm what Mary Beard argued four decades ago in *Women as Force in History: A Study in Traditions and Realities* (New York, 1946).

[38]Gary B. Nash, "The Failure of Female Factory Labor in Colonial Boston," *Labor History*, 20 (1979), 165–188.

[39]Cynthia Shelton, "The Role of Labor in Early Industrialization: Philadelphia, 1787–1837," *Journal of the Early Republic*, 4 (1984), 365–394.

[40]Kulikoff, "Progress of Inequality," 379; Gary Kulik, "Pawtucket Village and the Strike of 1824: The Origins of Class Conflict in Rhode Island," *Radical History Review*, no. 17 (1978), 5–37; Barbara M. Tucker, *Samuel Slater and the Origins of the American Textile Industry, 1790–1860* (Ithaca, NY, 1984).

[41]Christine Stansell, "The Origins of the Sweatshop: Women and Early Industrialization in New York City," in Michael H. Frisch and Daniel J. Walkowitz, eds., *Working-Class America: Essays on Labor, Community, and American Society* (Urbana, IL, 1983), 78–103.

[42]Edward Countryman, *A People in Revolution: The American Revolution and Political Society in New York, 1760–1790* (Baltimore, 1981); Gary B. Nash, "Artisans and Politics in Eighteenth-Century Philadelphia,"

in Margaret Jacob and James Jacob, eds., *The Origins of Anglo-American Radicalism* (London, 1984), 162–182; Steven Rosswurm, "'As a Lyen out of His Den': Philadelphia's Popular Movement, 1776–1780," in ibid., 300–323; Richard Walsh, *Charleston's Sons of Liberty: A Study of the Artisans, 1763–1789* (Columbia, SC, 1959). For a contrasting view of prerevolutionary urban politics and the tension between capitalist development and the structure of urban values see Christine Leigh Heyrman, *Commerce and Culture: The Maritime Communities of Colonial Massachusetts, 1690–1750* (New York, 1984). Heyrman's study stops on the eve of the Seven Years' War and therefore is not altogether comparable to the studies cited above.

[43]*Pennsylvania Gazette* September 27, 1770.

[44]Alfred F. Young, *The Democratic-Republicans of New York: The Origins, 1763–1797* (Chapel Hill, NC, 1967), passim; William Bruce Wheeler, "Politics in Nature's Republic: The Development of Political Parties in the Seaport Cities in the Federalist Era" (Ph.D. dissertation, University of Virginia, 1967); Schultz, "Thoughts Among the People," ch. 4–5; Steffen, *Mechanics of Baltimore*; Howard B. Rock, *Artisans of the New Republic: The Tradesmen of New York City in the Age of Jefferson* (New York, 1979).

[45]Drew R. McCoy, *The Elusive Republic: Political Economy in Jeffersonian America* (Chapel Hill, NC, 1980); Schultz, "Thoughts Among the People"; Wilentz, *Chants Democratic*; Rock, *Artisans of the New Republic*; Steffen, *Mechanics of Baltimore*.

[46]Philadelphia *Aurora*, January 14, 1807; November 28, 1805, quoted in Schultz, "Thoughts Among the People," 296, 303.

[47]Schultz, "Thoughts Among the People," and Wheeler, "Politics in Nature's Republic" are the two best studies to consult.

[48]Rock, *Artisans of the New Republic*; Steffen, *Mechanics of Baltimore*; Schultz, "Thoughts Among the People."

[49]Wilentz, *Chants Democratic*; Thomas Slaughter, "Mobs and Crowds, Riots and Brawls: The History of Early American Political Violence" (unpublished), 18–22, 47; Paul A. Gilje, "Mobocracy: Popular Disturbances in Post-Revolutionary New York City, 1783–1829" (Ph.D. dissertation, Brown University, 1980); Susan G. Davis, *Parades and Power: Street Theatre in Nineteenth-Century Philadelphia* (Philadelphia, 1986); Amy Bridges, *A City in the Republic: Antebellum New York and the Origin of Machine Politics* (Cambridge, 1984).

[50]Alexis de Tocqueville, *Democracy in America*, quoted in Richard D. Brown, "The Emergence of Voluntary Associations in Massachusetts, 1760–1830," *Journal of Voluntary Action Research*, 2 (1973), 64.

[51]Tonnies, *Community and Society*.

[52]Brown, "Voluntary Associations in Massachusetts," 64–73; Jacquetta Mae Haely, "Voluntary Organizations in Pre-Revolutionary New York City, 1750–1776," (Ph.D. dissertation, SUNY, Binghamton, 1976); Anne M. Boylan, "Women in Groups: An Analysis of Women's Benevolent Organizations in New York and Boston, 1797–1840," *Journal of American History*, 71 (1984), 497–523.

[53]Brown, "Voluntary Associations in Massachusetts."

[54]Boylan, "Women in Groups," passim.

[55]Brown, "Voluntary Associations in Massachusetts," 71.

[56]Dorothy Ann Lipson, *Freemasonry in Federalist Connecticut* (Princeton, NJ, 1977), ch. 2.

[57]Davis, *Parades and Power*, passim.

Street Theatre in Nineteenth-Century Philadelphia

*Susan G. Davis**

Philadelphia's parade traditions were formed during a radical restructuring of urban economic and social life. What could, could not, and did take place in the city streets resulted from the interactions of a changing physical world, an explosive social environment, and shifting definitions of appropriate public behavior. More particularly, the city's festive calendar formally and informally codified the reasons people found to make street theatre. At the same time, changes in and conflicts over the calendar, festivals, and the popular uses of public space reveal how powerfully the city's transformation molded its parade traditions. This complicated context framed the gatherings, parades, and ceremonies of the populace and infused public performances with particular and general social meanings.

Economic Change and Social Structure

Between 1790 and 1860, Philadelphia shed its character as a center for the exchange of goods and money and became a powerful manufacturing metropolis. The rise of manufactures broke down and restructured older ways of life, affecting all levels of social life and culture. Spurred by the construction of canals and railways, the opening of new markets for urban manufactures drove the transition to industrial capitalism. The city began to produce light consumer goods for its own population, the region, and the rural hinterland.[1] Between 1800 and 1850, migrants in search of new kinds of work followed transport networks to Philadelphia, increasing the population at an unprecedented rate. The urban area quintupled its population—from 81,000 to 408,000—in five decades. Especially after 1820, the city absorbed many newcomers from the British Isles and still more from the Pennsylvania countryside.[2] As the city's industrial system changed unevenly but decisively, migrants

*Susan G. Davis is associate professor of communication at the University of California, San Diego. Reprinted from Parades and Power: Street Theatre in Nineteenth-Century Philadelphia by Susan G. Davis. Copyright 1986 by Susan G. Davis. Reprinted by permission of Temple University Press and Susan G. Davis.

45

sought work in a growing number of factories, manufactories, and workshops. Textile factories, introduced first as an experiment in "bettering" local paupers, soon became the centers of Manayunk, Spring Garden, and Kensington, tightly clustered working-class neighborhoods.[3] Other innovations in making glass, iron, furniture, shoes, and clothes brought large numbers of workers under one roof and one master, beginning the destruction of domestic industries and the restructuring of work patterns.

The transition to industrial capitalism widened older social and economic inequalities. Despite recurrent and devastating depressions, Philadelphia's rate of economic growth rose steadily between 1800 and 1850, and per capita wealth increased strikingly; but beyond the rosy measures of expansion lay desperation. The city housed more poor and working people than ever before, and growing numbers of workers depended solely on wage labor for their livelihood.

Wealth burgeoned, but its distribution grew more lopsided as a shrinking number of people controlled a swelling share of invested capital, property, and goods for export, in addition to personal income.[4] Although a stratum of merchants and professionals was emerging to ally with the wealthy and propertied, few rose from small beginnings to great wealth. The myth of the self-made man notwithstanding, most of Philadelphia's wealthy and powerful citizens had inherited their riches and social status from their fathers. Members of Philadelphia's patriciate kept their hands in the world of commerce and finance as they speculated in manufactures, transport, and private corporations.[5]

Although eighteenth-century Philadelphia had a large stratum of propertyless poor people, in the early nineteenth century differences between rich and poor sharpened. The worker's living standard did not rise with the merchant's swelling wealth, and industrial labor and overcrowding fostered impoverishment and health problems. A new kind of social relationship was being created, defining the amount and kinds of control people had over their lives. As more workers were less likely to own their own tools and dwellings, and as skills were devalued and reorganized in new modes of production, fewer people found the independent means of subsistence so valued by eighteenth-century workers. To live, most had to work for someone else, and for many, powerlessness to change their material situations defined their lives. Neither could the wealthy fully control the changes wrought by industrial capitalism: during economic crises, urban leaders were unable to alleviate widespread destitution and unrest.[6]

Political Development and Social Conflict

Differences in wealth and power were countered by a hopeful sign, the extension of political rights. Whereas in the eighteenth century political activity had been the domain of men of wealthy families and well-to-do artisans, nineteenth-century political participation took novel, extended forms. In Pennsylvania, white males enjoyed manhood suffrage, and by the 1830s they participated enthusiastically in political parties. Political participation, although broadened, may have masked widening class differences. In the first decades of the century, political leaders were still drawn from the city's wealthy and respectable families; by the 1830s merchants, businessmen, master artisans, and lawyers and other professionals dominated elective offices and political parties as they would for the rest of the antebellum period.[7]

In this period of fluidity and uncertainty, new forces and ideas entered the political arena. Men organized not only to influence the machinery of government, but also to challenge and control the pace and direction of social and economic change. Workers' associations, labor organizations, and a short-lived but important workingmen's movement injected urban, working-class concerns into politics, analyzing and attacking the forces reshaping workers' lives. Mechanics and artisans argued that the growing inequalities of wealth and power could not be ignored; they addressed the morality of accumulation, monopoly, and speculation, and they questioned the place of private economic power in a democracy.[8]

Philadelphians participated enthusiastically in another kind of nongovernmental political activity, the voluntary association built upon neighborhood life and concerns. Ethnic benefit societies, temperance and reform groups, churches, and clubs bound men and women in networks of sociability and special interest. However, Tocqueville's hope that voluntary associations would mediate tensions and rival the power of the "mercantile aristocracy" was unfulfilled. Associations and clubs were more than means for advancing ideas and platforms: the most elite of them provided the means by which Philadelphia gentlemen maintained control over important issues and institutions. At lower levels, neighborhood reform societies and clubs were structures through which merchants, businessmen, and professionals became respected authorities and local leaders. So, the purposes and activities of voluntary organizations that bound men across class lines tended to be defined by men allied with business.[9]

Economic and social changes provoked bitter, almost constant social conflict, and Philadelphia's associations expressed and engaged in more conflicts than they mediated. Hibernians and Orangemen, abolitionists and slavery's advocates, Whigs and Democrats, nativists and Catholics, teetotalers and tipplers, workers and factory masters all used associations to propagandize their positions and attack each other. The city's streets were the prime location for public expression of conflict, in both symbolic and physical modes. If most clubs and societies attacked their opponents only in the symbolic realm, many Philadelphians communicated social antagonism with bricks, laths, cobblestones, and bullets in the city's riots. Philadelphia was wracked by mob violence in the 1840s and 1850s; its notorious street upheavals frightened the gentle, antagonized the propertied, and contradicted Thackeray's praise for its "grave, calm, kind" atmosphere.[10]

Spatial Change and the Uses of the Street

Before the Civil War, the city underwent dramatic physical and social-geographic changes. In a sense, the city's parade traditions were themselves ways people found to make the altered street and the expanding city understandable and knowable. Like other settlements, Philadelphia was initially conceived as a combined garrison and commercial venture, and its form reveals these mixed purposes. The shapes of medieval European cities and their early modern rebuildings recognized the performances central to church and state power. North American commercial cities, in contrast, were designed to move traffic and develop land, not house spectacles.[11]

Spaces formally designed for public activities were part of Philadelphia's seventeenth-century heritage, although they were not used as planned. William Penn's draftsman laid out a grid of streets, with two avenues intersecting at a midpoint forming Center Square, and four smaller squares defining the town's quadrants. Penn reserved Center Square for governmental buildings and activities; the other four were declared public domain, reserved for future recreation and gatherings of all the people.[12] As it worked out, Center Square was far removed from the hub of everyday life, the Delaware docks, and a half-timbered courthouse met government's needs in the city's markets at Second and High (now Market) streets. In the 1730s the city corporation moved the business of government out of the disorderly docks into orderly Georgian offices on a square surrounded by Fifth, Sixth, Walnut, and Chestnut streets. The yard around these buildings opened a sixth formal public space inside Philadelphia's boundaries, and the new State House became the site of corporate ceremony.[13]

In the eighteenth century, the squares served as commons with recreational and symbolic uses. Center Square boasted a tavern, a race course, and a militia parade ground. The city corporation used the large open field to stage public hangings, its infrequent but most popular spectacles, and twice-yearly fairs. The southeastern square found use as a potter's field, a burial ground for black and white paupers, and as a spot for slaves' festive dances.[14] The northeastern, northwestern, and southwestern squares served informally as drill, play, and burial grounds and offal dumps, uses which city leaders later rejected and reformed.

Throughout the eighteenth century and well into the next, privately owned, multifunctional open space lay at the city's edge. The city was surrounded by the outlying villages and a rural landscape of marshes and farmland, which Philadelphians used for fishing, swimming, hunting, and skating. Within walking distance of a city dwelling, open ground sheltered customary illegal sports such as bearbaiting, cockfighting, horseracing, and pugilism, and forage in the countryside buffered the poor in hard times. Semirural areas existed within the city in open yards and lots used as cow pastures, gardens and orchards, playgrounds, and work areas.[15]

Economic growth altered Philadelphia's colonial appearance and older spatial patterns. Open space was increasingly exploited for commercial use, and private property rights took precedence over older, informal uses. Open lots were filled with new buildings and the city moved outward, replacing farms and fields. The downtown surrounded the old city on the Delaware River, but private builders and speculators erected fine buildings on the westward streets, concentrating, investing, and displaying wealth in handsome domestic structures.[16] A great deal of money could be made by housing workers and the poor; thus black and Irish immigrants were crowded into suburbs and into the city's newly opened alleys and courts. Whole working-class districts sprang up around factories on the fringe of the urban grid. As the compact and walkable city, once an incomplete plan, became a large, densely populated terrain, neighborhoods acquired separate identities based on industry or ethnicity. Territorialities or specific conflicts were expressed in the streets, in fights, brawls, and riots.[17]

In the nineteenth century, the streets were the most accessible open space in the city; their layout and size testified to the city's preoccupation with the manufacture and movement of goods. Conduits for commodities and information, Philadelphia's streets extended in a grid of right angles north and south (between Vine and Cedar streets) and east and west (from the Delaware River to Center Square, and later to the Schuylkill). Some visitors found this rectangular plan monotonous. Frances Trollope, for example, declared her short downtown walk boring, and Rebecca Harding Davis felt oppressed and confined by her downtown neighborhood. But regular streets aided traffic flow, and the easy movement of goods to shipping points was important as Philadelphia became a major manufacturing center.[18] The regularity and spacing of the streets made them easy, walkable transit ways. Houses faced the street, and doors fronted on the traffic, with only a few steps between interior and exterior. To step out one's door was to step into an intensely social milieu. Information, goods, experience, neighborliness (and perhaps anonymity) could be had for the walking.[19] To enter the street was to join and help create social communication.

Social life in neighborhoods and downtown streets took shape around a variety of commercial establishments, from grand to modest, and these multiplied along the transit ways and in side streets. Corner taverns flourished, and new institutions—oyster cellars, pleasure gardens, dance halls—hedged the street with sociability. Bow windows advertised goods of all kinds, and commercial theatres, forbidden in the eighteenth century, flowered first at the city's southern boundary and later in the district around the State House. By 1830 the theatre district featured the work of the most popular playwright of the period, Shakespeare, on the same stage with pantomimes and fairy shows, with blackface minstrelsy, circuses, panoramas, and automata.[20]

Street Life and Class Perception

The density of buildings and people and cultural, human, and commercial variety swelled and pressed on the street, amplifying its possibilities as a milieu for communication. Yet this variety and openness were problematic. Affluent and respectable Philadelphians were discomfitted by the disgusting scenes of vernacular culture unfolding in theatre and pub, street and square. The commercial theatre now played to a strongly working-class audience; refined theatre-goers, horrified by conduct in the galleries, sought refined theatrical spheres for themselves. At the same time, they decried the moral effects of stage spectacles on the excitable plebs.[21]

Moral reformers noted that working and poor people conducted much of their social, domestic, and working lives outdoors. As Christine Stansell has argued, the uses of nondomestic space for activities seen as properly familial and private became evidence of working-class ignorance and degeneracy.[22]

People whose occupations depended on the street came under attack. Rag-pickers, food vendors, hawkers, beggars, scavengers, and petty criminals used the street's rich resources but were increasingly harassed by the city watch and laws.[23]

Degeneracy was perceived everywhere in the public sphere, but especially in working-class social life and petty economic activities. Reformers made piecemeal efforts to banish unseemly customs and trades. For example, City Councils attempted to suppress street vendors' cries, bells, and horns as early as the 1830s. Others, often radical artisans, defended the rights of peram-bulating sellers, asserting that tradesmen's noise was a kind of public infor-mation.[24] There was also local defense of neighborhood street use: vendors fought for the right to keep carts and stalls, and residents resisted the intro-duction of railroad and streetcar tracks that ruptured familiar residential patterns and fractured street life. People from the same districts banded together and sometimes fought to keep their streets free of watchmen, fine collectors, and strikebreakers, even as they defended their territories against foreigners, blacks, and outsiders.[25]

With more leisure and domestic space at its command, the business class responded to the street's culture by creating distance. Men moved their occu-pations out of the house, and family life and domestic labors withdrew from public view, to be defended by new standards of domestic manners, privacy, and gentility.[26] Try as they might, genteel citizens could not fully escape. Residential space was increasingly stratified by class and ethnicity, but the city was densely populated and poor neighborhoods persisted in alleys, courts, and the back streets of fashionable blocks. While separation was incomplete, an irritating physical proximity influenced perceptions and prompted more differentiation of behaviors and manners. Back alleys and working-class blocks were seen as "regions" populated by "demons" who menaced peace and morality.[27]

Reorganization and Reinterpretation of Space

Lacking the ability to "renew" whole neighborhoods, affluent Philadelphians concentrated on accessible and symbolic spaces, notably the squares and, later, through the establishment of the police, the central streets. The potter's field, for example, was a miasma of collapsed graves and polluted water by the 1820s. In 1832 the Washington Centennial gave City Council members and militia volunteers the impetus to complete a proposed redesign of the square. William Strickland was commissioned to design a monument and commemorative square that would serve as a patriotic shrine and a fashion-able resort for the neighborhood. Although the monument was never erected, the cornerstone was laid with military fanfare, and the square refurbished. Franklin, Logan, and Rittenhouse squares, in poor condition by the 1830s, were similarly reinvented in the nineteenth century. Logan and Rittenhouse had been used for decades as offal dumps, and Franklin had been illegally annexed for a churchyard. Poor neighbors around Rittenhouse Square com-plained of its condition as a threat to their health and safety, but it was the desire of affluent new residents for parks that finally spurred improvements.[28]

Throughout the nineteenth century, Philadelphians treated State House Square as the city's symbolic heart and most sacred site. The place was laden with local memories of the Revolution. On the day the Declaration of Independence was read, the crowd dragged the king's arms out of the hall and publicly burned them, making the square thoroughly revolutionary and North American.[29] During the war, the meetings of Congress, the speeches, and frequent military drills there had firmly attached the city's "affections" to the State House. Before the Civil War, the Democratic Party favored State House Square as a ceremonial spot and the city corporation used it as a reception hall for dignitaries and honored patriots. Philadelphians voted there and gathered there in civil emergencies; during strikes workingmen and unionists used Independence Hall's steps as a stage from which to read declarations of independence from their masters.[30] The Square served as the starting and ending point for many of the city's parades.

Paradoxically, while the social life of the city became more complicated and varied, some of the uses of open space were more contested, as the propertied worried about how public spaces should be used and what public events communicated. The squares were a case in point. State House Square had recreational as well as ceremonial uses. As the five squares became parks, however, problems arose over recreation in these public places. In the 1830s, John Watson recalled a history of complaints about the uses of State House Square dating back to "the year of the war's conclusion [1783]," when the yard became "a place of general resort," "the haunt of many idle and profligate people."[31] In nineteenth-century City Council meetings, Philadelphia's leaders continually debated monitoring the behavior of the idle and profligate as well as protecting public spaces from indecorous users.

Collective uses of open space prompted more anxiety and were less susceptible to constraint than individual cases of inappropriate behavior. Center Square always drew working-class crowds on holidays, especially the Fourth of July. Officials repeatedly tried to restrain festivities, and finally banned booths and tents there in 1823. Expressing concern over crowds at spectacles, the state legislature removed hangings from public view. After the last open-air public execution in 1837, hangings were conducted inside Cherry Hill Prison.[32]

Space for Working-Class Political Activities

From the working-class point of view, access to space for political activities was constrained in the antebellum period. Any trade union gathering could be labeled conspiratorial in the early nineteenth century; although workingmen relied on taverns and hotel dining rooms for regular meetings, their leaders had trouble finding halls for larger ceremonies and speeches. As Robert Dale Owen pointed out, workers needed their own spaces if they were to construct a fully autonomous political movement:

> You will be told there are public buildings enough in your city already. There are buildings enough, but whose are they? . . . [Churches] offer teaching without challenge or reply . . . and are not churches closed six days a week? . . .

Neither the churches nor the State House are under the control of the people, the strange unrepublican fact is that while each of your hundred ministers of religion has a public building at his command, the people have not one at theirs.[33]

As the general strike of 1835 taught workers, the clergy often sided with employers. In that year, tens of thousands of men massed regularly in State House Square to hear speeches, but demonstrators ordinarily had to ask city officials for permission to use the yard and building.[34] Workingmen and the unemployed customarily held large meetings on street corners and in lots, where the back of a wagon served as a podium. On one hand, open-air gatherings could reach the city at large; on the other, weather could thwart such efforts, and it was difficult to conduct business with regularity.

As Owen emphasized, obtaining a building for collective use required money, resourcefulness, and a cause that those in power considered legitimate. Ironically, this limitation contrasted with an increase in the construction of "public" buildings—lycea, lecture halls, theatres, and museums—by businessmen, merchants, and private associations.[35] Black congregations, for example, struggled for decades to erect churches in which to center their communities.[36] Once constructed, black churches were given no guarantee that the city would protect them from racist mobs. Opponents of slavery— black and white, male and female—were always in danger when they held meetings, as the burning of the abolitionists' Pennsylvania Hall in 1838 demonstrated.[37]

The Popular Uses of the Street

The streets enabled workers, poor people, and racial minorities to broadcast messages to large numbers of people, which partly explains the vibrant popularity of parades of all kinds and the variety of autonomously produced mobile performances. The street was shared more equally than any other space. A decision to strike, a meeting's outcome, or a festive gathering could move quickly from an assembly into a marching line that conveyed a message to coworkers, neighbors, and the city at large.

The grid of streets built for commerce suited the circulation of important messages, and parades fit the informal milieu of the street. Parades and processions occupied a crucial terrain of behavior between personal interactions at corners or dooryards and more formal ritual behavior, such as commemorations, oratory, or reenactments. Especially in the dense downtown area where work and domestic life were adjacent, parades took place within sight of home and neighbors, and within view of wide varieties of people. Characteristically, the early nineteenth-century line of march repeatedly doubled back on itself as it wound around familiar residential blocks.

Some of the deep, entwined roots of hostility to popular gatherings can be traced to colonial times. European historians have shown that Puritan antagonism to early modern vernacular culture led to recurrent attempts at suppression and reform.[38] In North America, the battle between the older superstitious plebeian culture and Protestant rationality, between Carnival and Lent, was often drawn around the issues of dramatic enactment and popular festivity. Because Pennsylvania's Quakers, like other Puritans, opposed marking any day as more sacred than another, they viewed the "irrational" behavior and revelries of traditional holidays and rituals as obnoxious and morally corrupting. Seventeenth- and eighteenth-century Quaker authorities had tried to eliminate festive Christmas customs, such as disguise, drum-beating, firing guns, noisemaking, drinking, and feasting.[39] Distrust of enactments and entertainments lay behind a long tradition of restricting theatre within Philadelphia.

Dramas and gatherings were neither easily contained nor easily abolished. The "great gatherings of people," the twice-yearly fairs in Center Square, were sources of complaint as early as the 1690s, and were called disruptions of the peace and corrupting influences on apprentices, servants, and youth. At such festive times, slaves, too, had permission to hold dances. But the fairs' economic functions made them difficult to abolish until the 1770s; like fairs, Afro-American revels were outlawed on the eve of the Revolution and never revived.[40]

Uneasiness over the regular gatherings of poor people stemmed as much from the social organization of labor in the city, and the social makeup of crowds, as from religious or cultural hostility to "irrational" behavior. The city depended heavily on unfree labor in the eighteenth century, that is, the labor of slaves, indentured servants, and apprentices. From the 1740s, petitioners urged City Councils to suppress "tumultuous meetings and disorderly doings of Negroes, Mullatoes, Indians, Servants and Slaves" who met in the marketplace after dark to talk and play music. Such demands for legal controls on the uses of the marketplace were repeated throughout the eighteenth century.[41] Antagonism to gatherings, fairs, and dances expressed owners' and masters' understanding that autonomous and unsupervised uses of free time by the unfree might endanger the social order. If uprisings of slaves and servants were unlikely in Philadelphia, autonomous recreation provided opportunities for these workers to build networks of communication and culture that might support insubordinate attitudes and shield runaways.

By the early nineteenth century, hostility to large gatherings of working people was still strong, perhaps having roots in memories of the Revolution. The city's working class pushed for radically democratic social change; several times the "lower orders" came close to seizing the Revolution from its elite leaders.[42] But new class relations, as much as memory, made crowds threatening. Ignoring the democratic heritage preserved in the people's right to assemble, some fearful commentators suggested that public gatherings be banned altogether.[43] They supported the position of employers and political leaders who opposed any manifestation of working-class radicalism, whether in the Revolutionary War's crowd violence and direct action, or in the new trade union meetings. More generally, opposition to public gatherings grew out of an awareness that workers' relationships to their superiors had changed. If employers owed workers nothing more than wages, and laborers owed masters little loyalty, where might a mass meeting lead in hard times? Under conditions of widespread poverty, growing population, and cyclical, recurring depressions, large gatherings of people were dangerous. As the riots of the 1830s, 1840s, and 1850s showed, Philadelphians could express or be manipulated to express violent hatreds. But riots were the most extreme example of problematic crowd behavior, and most Philadelphia riots were aimed at outsiders, social inferiors, and proponents of unpopular causes like abolition, rather than at factory owners.[44]

Even during peaceful times, the level of business-class suspicion remained high. Gathered in large groups, workers might recognize and examine their common interests, spread word of their discovery, and learn ways to act collectively. Fear of class recognition, more than dread of riots, prompted attacks on the working-class public presence and fed hostility toward seemingly innocent gatherings at theatres and parades.

These strains of antagonism surfaced in criticism of working-class festivity, which was becoming more explosively jubilant as the city's population boomed. Festivals were free time that the populace could structure alternatively and use collectively. As industrial capitalism transformed the uses of time in the workplace and home, festivals held appealing possibilities for autonomous recreation, something hard-pressed workers desperately needed. Autonomous uses of collective time also suggested the development of an oppositional working-class culture, a possibility that disturbed the business class. When employers and respectable citizens complained about Christmas revelry and Fourth of July street battles, they acknowledged a reordered relationship between labor and sociability, workday and holiday. The opponents of festivity, seeing older ways of life disappear before their eyes, recognized their inability to control the present and the future.

Time and Public Culture

Time and the social structuring of time codified in the calendar constituted another dimension of context for parades and ceremonies. From the city's cycle of festivals, people developed major reasons for gatherings, street dramas, and processions. Like space, festival and the uses of free or nonlaboring time had a history, particular to Philadelphia, which included conflict.

The city's growing strength in manufactures restructured collective and individual clocks and calendars. On one hand, industrial progress did not immediately destroy older urban and agrarian work rhythms. As in an agrarian culture, patterns of labor and leisure were still influenced by climate. Many industries were hand or water powered, and much work took place outdoors. New textile factories could halt for weeks at a time because of frozen or overflowing streams. The major avenues of commerce were rivers, which, when free of ice, supported longshore and shipbuilding trades, fishing, and oyster dredging; thus, in the coldest days of winter, whole industries dragged to a halt. Conversely, for many workers summer was a period of intense activity. For instance, construction workers often called strikes in July to put extra pressure on employers who expected high productivity in good weather. Many occupations fluctuated with the seasons, affecting everyday life and public culture as long as hand power and water power dominated work processes.[45]

New forms of industrial organization began to revolutionize the way individuals and groups sensed and used time. As Bruce Laurie has shown, a range of work processes and environments—from factories to sweatshops to handcrafts and casual labor—could be found in the antebellum city. Each productive process placed different demands on the worker, and Laurie argues that the work experience helped shape styles of social life and ideologies. Philadelphians who worked in mechanized mills were forced to learn punctual habits and pay constant attention to a rapid and repetitive machine-driven task. This intense discipline left little room for older patterns of drinking and socializing on the job. Douglas Reid has shown that employers in nineteenth-century Sheffield stepped up this discipline and restructured the work week when they introduced expensive steam power, which they were unwilling to waste on dilatory "hands." Hard-pressed and poor, the new factory workers were especially vulnerable to the demands of evangelical piety and temperance, which stressed a guilty self-discipline and a harsh rejection of irrational habits.[46]

The majority of city workers, however, had some control over work and more relaxed attitudes toward free time. Many men toiled in small manufactories, in workshops, or at home; another large proportion were day laborers in the streets or docks, while working women plied trades at home or hired out as domestic servants. This pattern of productive organization, combining small-scale production with increasing division of labor processes, relied on the semiskilled and unskilled and was bolstered by waves of immigrant labor.

At the top of labor's hierarchy, skilled artisans and masters of small workshops had some control over their work pace and its influence on their lives. Those with greater autonomy read, argued and socialized at work, and chose their days off. Some skilled workers transmitted the radical artisanal heritage of natural rights philosophy, based on the writings of Thomas Paine, self-education, and mutual aid. These rationalists tended to oppose the rowdy, free-and-easy ways of the unskilled and uneducated, while they attacked the revivalists as irrational ranters.[47]

In the city's seasonal festivals, urban workers found a terrain in which to preserve the relaxed, if sometimes boozy, life of the workshop and tavern. As traditional liberties were assaulted in workplaces, churches, and lecture halls, time and room were found for them on days and in places freed from the dictates of time clocks and ministers. Philadelphia's festivals became the apotheosis of workers' autonomy, as men and women whose lives were constrained by harsh labor abandoned themselves to the temporary liberties of festive recreations. Those on the fringe of the work world—the unemployed, the casual laborer, the young, and the poor—joined artisans and mechanics in extending flexible labor patterns into license and revelry.[48]

Festivity and Public Order

Some Philadelphians who criticized local festivities complained of streets being overrun by an ethnically and racially mixed rabble who lacked decorum, deference, or restraint. Especially after 1830, three major breaks in the working year—Christmas, Muster Day, and the Fourth of July—drew complaints of outrageous, disgusting behavior.

Christmas was a time for relaxation and the reaffirmation of social bonds, but it was also an interval when urban moral order threatened to come undone. As occupations came to a halt, work made way for a week of customary recreations: drinking and dancing, sacred and secular rituals, skating parties, ox roasts, pigeon shoots, pig chases, and lotteries. Commercial theatres counted heavily on holiday audiences for special harlequinades, pantomimes, circuses, and minstrel shows during Christmas week. Militia troops, firemen, and other associations held balls and promenade concerts; ladies gave church fairs; Methodists "watched in" the New Year; and cookshops sold seasonal specialties. Hundreds of pubs, groggeries, and taverns treated their customers "with extra liberality."[49]

For working people there was a fine line between seasonal relaxation and distress. Unemployment rose sharply in the winter city. The sense of a special, heightened time persisted from rural life, but many working people, cut off from older means of subsistence and self-sufficiency by the rise of wage labor, found the slowed pace of winter a threat to health and livelihood. To the growing alarm of observers and reformers, drink, relaxation, and despair combined with rollicking recreations to transform the Christmas streets into scenes of fighting. In the 1840s, authorities claimed that Christmas and New Year's night celebrations disgraced the city; they annually declared working-class districts out of control during the holidays.[50]

On Christmas Eve, 1833, for instance, "riot, noise and uproar prevailed uncontrolled and uninterrupted in many of our central and most orderly streets. Gangs of men and boys howled as if possessed by the demon of disorder."[51] Christmas was also marked by mob attacks on blacks, fighting among black and white gangs, firemen's riots, arson, and great throngs in the central streets and squares. City officials and middle-class observers viewed Christmas revelry as public disorder and attempted to contain it. Compared with solemn ceremonies and decorous balls, Christmas masking, noisemaking, and street performances seemed to challenge dominant ideals.

Battalion or Muster Day revelry in spring also prompted criticism. The legally required mustering and drilling of the men enrolled in public companies (theoretically, all those between eighteen and forty-five years of age) took up several days in May, during which time parades took over the city. Alongside the public companies marched the city's elite private militia, until thousands of uniformed and nonuniformed men jammed the streets and parade grounds. To city authorities Muster Day was a cumbersome, unruly holiday. Because Muster Day was required by law, it warranted a day off from work for enrollees, many of whom were mechanics, artisans, journeymen, and laborers; thus underage employees and apprentices were set free for the day. These young men swelled the crowds of ineligible blacks, children, the curious, and "criminals" who flocked to the parade grounds. In rural Pennsylvania farmers used Muster Day as a time for visiting and business, as well as drilling, celebrating it with drinking, dancing, and the selling of food and trinkets;[52] in the city, Muster Day had all these features on a grand scale.[53]

Complaints about Muster Day point to its festive tone, the suspension of

work, and the extralegal activities that often accompanied it. "The jubillee
of general idleness," it was despised for the "din and turmoil of reviews."[54]
In 1828 a grand jury sitting at Philadelphia presented the parade ground at
Bush Hill as "an ill governed and disorderly place, where all sorts of vices
are practiced day and night, particularly on parade days."[55]

A welter of reasons existed for the dislike of Muster Day. Those compelled to drill resented the loss of their working time, but took the opportunity
to enjoy the day—or lessen its burdens—with drink and recreation. Disorderly
parade days also undermined the work discipline demanded by employers
because musters encouraged absenteeism on the part of both the enrolled
and nonenrolled. Employers who struggled to get men to relinquish "Saint
Monday" had little enthusiasm for a legally mandated day—which could
stretch into a week—of work's suspension. Reformers and Sabbatarians, who
hoped to teach workers to use free time piously and rationally, viewed the
informal pleasure fair as a nest of vices.

Reform of the militia system, a thorny issue through the years before
1860, turned in large part on the issue of public parade days. Raucous parade-
ground activities cast doubt on the muster's value to the nation's military
strength. But proposals for reform echoed manufacturers' objections as much
as workingmen's dissatisfactions. In 1837, one Adjutant Small, running for
the post of major in the city's Ninth Regiment, assured citizens that he
"opposed all kinds of militia parades except at such times as will be least
inconvenient to men of business and citizens generally."[56] Since few businessmen would have belonged to the public militia companies because of the
system of exemptions, Small addressed them as concerned employers of
enrollees.

Philadelphians celebrated competing versions of Independence Day. For
the well-to-do and politically powerful, the Fourth of July was a temporal
arena for political rhetoric and displays of partisan and civic values. Despite
differences in political opinions, leaders of opposed factions shared common
notions about the proper way to celebrate the anniversary—with elegance,
decorum, and respectability. From the gentlemanly, enlightened culture of
those who led the Revolution, along with customs of the earlier Georgian
men's clubs, Freemasonry, and eighteenth-century corporate ceremony, grew
an annual pattern of elite events, a mix of open and private ceremonies.
Cannon and bells announced the day to everyone, and militia troops circulated
through the central streets and squares. The day's political meanings found
formal reconstruction and interpretation in church sermons, orations, and
long, sumptuous dinners. Planned by committee and held in hotels, subscription dinners were designed for and attended by like-minded men—the Society
of the Cincinnati, the Sons of Saint Tammany, Federalists, Jeffersonians,
Democratic Republicans, and later Whigs and Democrats of various stripes.[57]
Though these men reveled separately, they shared the same festive forms. In
the vigorous political life of Philadelphia's upper reaches, men who ate and
drank together on this day shared more than opinion or patriotic sentiment,
for dinners were only one event in a year-round cycle of male mutuality and
commensalism connecting family, business, and politics.[58]

The city's small reading public learned about these gentlemanly ceremonies through party press reports. The committee of arrangements always furnished newspaper editors with the texts of toasts and speeches.[59] Onlookers were aware of the presence of eminent diners from painted window illuminations, flags, and buntings. Most important among the techniques of self-advertisement was the dining company's parade from meeting place to hotel, announcing to spectators that the day was being commemorated with appropriate pomp by those most fit to celebrate. Processions such as those of the Society of the Cincinnati always filed from the sacred spot—the State House— to church and then to private dining rooms. Likewise, volunteer militia troops dramatically bridged the worlds of street and private club with fancy dress parades.[60] The Fourth of July created by affluent men joined together in voluntary associations presented an elegant, dignified, and patriotic face— an image projected through the combination of orderly private ceremonies and public street dramas. Dinners and orations framed the ideas about nationhood, progress, and patriotism held by all-white, all-male organizations and parties. Not surprisingly, these expressions furthered particular interests while remaining embedded in universal-sounding values.[61]

The obverse of the decorous Fourth unfolded in the streets, squares, and fields, where semicommercial popular recreations were the heart of working-class celebrations. Tavern frolics and informal excursions were popular from early in the century.[62]

With breaks in the working year crowded increasingly into the few new national holidays and the solstices as old craft holidays disappeared, the Fourth of July became less an anniversary and more a jubilantly popular festival.[63] Yet the Fourth was not observed everywhere with work's suspension. Independent artisans probably took the day off, but whether large employers granted a holiday or workers took it for themselves is unclear. One Manayunk textile operative writing in the 1830s described the Fourth as a customary day off. A study of small textile mills on Brandywine Creek, however, reports that employers tried to force workers to labor on the Fourth, and that workers took the day off by striking.[64] Customary prerogatives must have varied with the type of industry, the size of the workplace, and the needs and predilections of both employer and employee.

Complaints about working-class behavior focused on Center Square, the end point of militia company parades, where hucksters and gamblers assembled around the company tents and tavern. As with Muster Day, municipal authorities and the press found vice and corruption. A tirade published in 1822 cited the great degree of drunkenness and "bare-faced violations of the liquor laws."[65] In 1823 Mayor Robert Wharton banned stalls and booths from the site on that day.[66] Undaunted, petty entrepreneurs shifted their operations to "the hill opposite Fairmont" at the city's edge, where unlicensed liquor sales, betting, fighting, and the enticements of prostitutes persisted. In 1839 the *Public Ledger* complained that "the licentious portion of the community have made preparations to . . . desecrate the day" and deplored "the crowds of our youth of all ages . . . reeling and staggering . . . troops of abandoned females . . . gambling, both dice and cards."[67] In 1844 the *Ledger* again called on respectable citizens to set an example and reform the Fourth of July by replacing "the saturnalia of passion" with a "jubilee of reason."[68]

Class recognition continually informed criticism of Independence Day: in the 1850s, editorials denounced riots and gunfights in working-class districts.[69]

Criticism forced some changes in festive behavior, but reform from within the working class was limited to small circles. For instance, when working people tried to shape festivity for their own political causes, they often felt compelled to adopt their critics' forms and styles. Some artisans, for example, tried to mold the Fourth's popular nationalism into a temperate republicanism. Leaders of the General Trades' Union and the Workingmen's Party defended workers' rights to festivity, but they urged their brothers to mark the day with restraint and propriety. A manifesto issued in 1829 claimed the Fourth for workingmen, but urged them to accept the gentlemen's way of celebrating:

> No class of the community has so generally and constantly manifested a sense of hilarity on the Fourth of July as the Working People. While the more wealthy classes have gradually withdrawn themselves from all public display on this national holiday as *ungenteel*, the toil worn artisan has continued to set it apart with mirth and jollity, in so much as to incur sometimes the charge of exuberant levity and small discretion from those who never knew a working day. The Fourth will soon be upon us with happy auspices; for the overworked and undignified mechanic is about to take his station with the magnates of the land and boldly enter on the race for equal rights and equal intelligence. We venture therefore to suggest our friends and fellow workmen . . . adopt the most dignified and established mode of conducting *The Day*.[70]

This mode, the *Mechanics' Free Press* argued, was exemplified by the all-male subscription dinner with patriotic oratory, rather than street socializing, dancing, and gambling. Decorous toasts would dramatize the convergence of previously separate interests and establish an "interchange of sentiment and community feeling, . . . adding to our union, respectability and intelligence."[71] Respectability was the watchword: forced to defend their right to exist at all, workers' associations framed social criticism with genteel devices. Mechanics and artisans thought that respectability would foster political development, but the gentlemanly forms of their gatherings foreclosed the possibility of a broader, more angry and moral appeal to the whole city and, thus, the creation of a larger audience. The techniques of citywide appeals to popular nationalism would be taken to their limits by more reactionary political movements, especially the nativists of the American Republican Party.[72]

The business class reacted to the explosion of rowdy and disreputable festive behavior by withdrawing from general participation and elaborating their own modes of celebration. Beginning in the 1820s, affluent Philadelphians made a custom of leaving town on the Fourth of July.[73] As for the street, proclamations attempted to contain crowds and collective recreations. Sheriffs and watchmen kept an eye on dance halls, oyster cellars, and "disorderly houses" (brothels); aldermen heard complaints against street vendors, musicians, July Fourth revelers, Muster Day brawlers, and Christmas mummers. Even before the establishment of a professional police force in 1854, ordinances attempted to limit street vendors' occupations and popular recreations. With the introduction of the police, street life and festivity could, theoretically, be brought under more uniform surveillance. It took most of the century, and concerted reform efforts begun after the Civil War, to make urban festivals safe for the city.[74]

Respectable Philadelphians countered disreputable festivity with another response: they expanded the familiar calendar to create a public ceremonial presence for themselves, and they elaborated their own styles for performance. Like ordinary citizens, well-to-do white men inherited a range of traditions for ritualizing social relations. But because these men tended (or tried) to control public spaces and techniques for making performances legitimate, they could invent their own version of the calendar and its dramas, thus fathering the city's official tradition. To state that the business class shaped festivity through processes of definition and legitimation is not to claim that they conspiratorially commandeered public culture. As previously argued, the invention of traditions took place gradually, informally, and unofficially. It was, however, predictable that men or associations who presented themselves as leaders should try to gain the foremost ceremonial place for themselves. By the late 1820s, merchants, businessmen, and governmental leaders were intent on producing edifying spectacles that highlighted their social and personal roles as leaders. Dramas sponsored by merchants and businessmen tended to represent social relations from the point of view of the business class. Whether affluent men planned street ceremonies to counter the carryings-on of their employees, servants, and other inferiors is unknown. But solemn Fourth of July parades by the Cincinnati and precise, elegant military parades on Muster Day took part of their meaning from their glaring contrast with the surrounding crowds. The tension between respectable and rowdy street theatre followed, and was understood to follow, class lines. In turn, these tensions flooded the whole of public culture with class significance.

Within the context of conflict over the uses of space, time, and dramas, parades and ceremonies flourished as important modes of communication for different classes and groups. For working people under pressure to differentiate themselves from their rowdy neighbors, street dramas could articulate claims to respectable status. During desperate times, street marches could raise angry defiance of the social order. For the poor, immigrants, and marginal workers, street performances were rites of local solidarity; they could also be used to construct images of alternative social orderings. The business class used street dramas in a variety of ways, all of which helped construct images of the rightness of its own power.

Despite all this variety and possibility, the rights to street performance were as significantly patterned by social difference as space and time. By the early decades of the century, rights to ritual self-presentation roughly traced the definition of citizenship: white manhood. This is not to say that only white males performed in the streets; rather, for all others, attempts at street performance could be physically or symbolically dangerous.

Blacks' and abolitionists' attempts at collective public display met with mockery, scorn, and violence. Abolitionists had long used their own versions of the Fourth of July for political purposes: they devoted the day to fund-raising, sermons, and oratory that used the Declaration to explore the dichotomies between American principle and practice. As the sectional crisis gathered force, this oratory became a volatile countertheatre.[75] Black abolitionists moved from the pulpit to the street, inventing counter-Independence parades out of the familiar July Fourth militia march and the fife-and-drum band of black popular culture. At first, blacks marched on the fifth of July to avoid the wrath of white crowds, as well as to make a temporal and kinesic distinction underscoring their separate but unequal status. After Parliament freed the slaves of the British West Indies in 1834, an event of enormous importance to Afro-Americans, blacks had a true Independence Day to celebrate on the first of August.[76]

Parades of all kinds demonstrated blacks' unwillingness to acquiesce in their inferior status. At the same time, limitations on their street presence grew more severe as racism intensified in the 1830s and 1840s. In August 1842, for example, a black Temperance Society's Independence procession was attacked by a white mob and the melee set off days of destruction in black neighborhoods. Rumors forced the mayor to display the Society's offending banner, which depicted, not bloodthirsty slaves burning San Domingo as rioters had claimed, but a freed man with his chains at his feet. Nevertheless, city officials lost no time in claiming that the Temperance Society caused the riots by parading.[77] Other black uses of the street met with white retaliation. An early account of Christmas masking in the city describes an attack on a black fife-and-drum troop by a white gang.[78]

Whites found blacks barely acceptable when they stayed inside the circle of their own private, domestic activities, and when their social life took place in cellars, alleys, and back streets. But when the image of a unified black community with moral and political claims on the rest of society was projected into the streets, whites felt their prerogatives threatened. John Watson reflected on this challenge from a widely shared point of view: "In the olden time, dressy blacks and dandy coloured beaux and belles as we now see them issuing from their proper churches were quite unknown. . . . Now they are vainglorious and overweaning . . . and want to be called coloured people." Watson added that he found blacks' "fondness for imitating whites in processions and banners" particularly irritating.[79]

Different limits constrained the public activities of white women. In contemporary opinion, women made themselves "public women" or "women of the streets" when they assumed performative roles outside the home. Women who mounted the speaker's platform in the cause of abolitionism or feminism were not only vilified for their ideas, but also attacked for daring to manifest them in public, a move critics interpreted as a betrayal of their gender's nature.[80] Working women, who had little choice but to participate in the life of the street, who held traditional roles as market hucksters, and who joined corner sociability with enthusiasm, thereby lost any claim to respectability. Working women became prostitutes, if only metaphorically, by their economic activity. This logic extended to female participation in street parades, so that when respectable women made their rare appearances in processions, they were either escorted protectively by men or dressed as caricatures of purity. Nevertheless, not all women accepted this exclusion. In letters to newspapers, commenting on plans for great processions, women complained that they held political and patriotic concerns as deeply as men, and resented being excluded from public ceremonies.[81]

Philadelphia's large Irish Catholic immigrant population used the streets to display ethnic unity on Saint Patrick's Day, although city fathers tried to discourage parades, especially during times of intense anti-immigrant sentiment. While municipal officials were sometimes uneasy about Saint Patrick's Day, they found no reason to ban inflammatory anti-Catholic spectacles, such as the mass processions by native Americans, which called for the restriction of Irish-American civil rights. On Saint Patrick's eve, the burning of "stuffed Paddy" effigies was a venerable nativist tradition.[82]

Labor associations and striking workers often used processions, sometimes legitimating their cause—which was considered illegal and illegitimate for most of the nineteenth century—with elaborate fraternal costumes, banners, and bands of music. Less respectably, strikers marched to call other men away from work, announce their grievance, and muster community solidarity behind their cause. The representation of conflict between masters and employees antagonized city officials. Militant strike parades and demonstrations were contained physically, decried by mayors and municipal authorities, and discouraged by some labor leaders.

In a variety of ways, conflict between classes and groups gave meaning to competing definitions of public culture and the popular uses of public space in the city. At the same time, access to spaces and to roles for performance was limited by race, ethnicity, gender, and class. Although city officials and propertied citizens could not achieve full control over the uses of open spaces and free time, or which versions of social relations might be enacted in city streets, they tried to reshape urban culture. Slowly, they succeeded. Through initial suppressions of street life and attacks on festivity, through the construction of a repertoire of respectable public performances, the city's image and imageries were recast.

The history of the patterning of public culture needs to be drawn in more detail; it had multiple dimensions and was shaped by several forces. Concerns over property and ideas, customary privileges and legal prerogatives, and the tensions between material and symbolic quests for power all interacted. As a stage for culture, the city offered a field of places and practices useful for framing and disseminating ideas, shaping powers and opinions, but as a human construction, this stage did not yield all residents equal time, space, and power to perform.

NOTES

[1]Diane Lindstrom, *Economic Development in the Philadelphia Region, 1810–1850* (New York: Columbia University Press, 1978), pp. 1–54; Bruce Laurie, *Working People of Philadelphia, 1800–1850* (Philadelphia: Temple University Press, 1980), pp. 3–30.

[2]Lindstrom, *Philadelphia Region*, pp. 24–25; Laurie, *Working People*, pp. 8–10; James T. Lemon, *The Best Poor Man's Country: A Geographical Study of Early Southeastern Pennsylvania* (Baltimore: Johns Hopkins University Press, 1976), pp. 73–92; Sam Bass Warner, *The Private City: Philadelphia in Three Periods of Its Growth* (Philadelphia: University of Pennsylvania Press, 1968), pp. 56–57.

[3]Cynthia Jane Shelton, "The Mills of Manayunk: Early Industrialization and Social Conflict in the Philadelphia Region, 1787–1837," doctoral dissertation, University of California, Los Angeles, 1982, pp. 110–69.

[4]Lindstrom, *Philadelphia Region*, pp. 1–24; and Jeffrey Williamson and Peter Lindert, "Long Term Trends in American Wealth Inequality," in James D. Smith, ed., *Modelling the Distribution and Intergenerational Transmission of Wealth* (Chicago: University of Chicago Press, 1980), pp. 9–93.

[5]Edward Pessen, *Riches, Class, and Power Before the Civil War* (Lexington, Mass.: D. C. Heath, 1973), pp. 73–163.

[6]For information on the eighteenth century, see Gary B. Nash, "Up from the Bottom in Franklin's Philadelphia," *Past and Present* 77 (1977): 58–83; for the rise of economic inequality, see Laurie, *Working People*, pp. 3–104. Historians disagree about how to name early nineteenth-century American class structure; nevertheless, the rise of systematic, structural inequalities of wealth and power has been amply demonstrated. The distinction between two classes, the working class and the propertied or business class, follows Michael B. Katz, Mark J. Stern, and Michael Doucet, *The Social Organization of Early Industrial Capitalism* (Cambridge: Harvard University Press, 1982). The term *middle class* has been avoided because of its theoretical vagueness. Despite evidence of some social mobility and the fact that some workers and artisans straddled the boundaries between the working class and the business class, it is not clear that a "middle class" existed in early nineteenth-century America as a discrete entity, separate in interests and sources of power from both labor and capital; see ibid., and Anthony Giddens, *The Class Structure of Advanced Societies* (New York: Harper & Row, 1975). As Chapter Five will show, new values that mediated between the working class and the propertied were emerging—and very important—in the antebellum era.

[7]Pessen, *Riches, Class, and Power*, pp. 281–301.

[8]Louis H. Arky, "The Mechanic's Union of Trade Associations and the Formation of the Working-men's Movement," *Pennsylvania Magazine of History and Biography* 76 (1952): 142–76; William A. Sullivan, "A Decade of Labor Strife," *Pennsylvania History* 17 (1950): 23–38; William A. Sullivan, *The Industrial Worker in Pennsylvania, 1800–1840* (Harrisburg: Pennsylvania Historic and Museum Commission, 1955); Laurie, *Working People*, pp. 67–83, 161–87; and Sean Wilentz, *Chants Democratic: New York City and the Rise of the American Working Class, 1788–1850* (New York: Oxford University Press, 1984).

[9]Lindstrom, *Philadelphia Region*, pp. 24–54; Walter S. Glazer, "Participation and Power: Voluntary Associations and the Functional Organization of Cincinnati in 1840," *Historical Methods Newsletter* 5 (1972): 151–68; Mary P. Ryan traces the formation of male and female networks of interest and sociability in *Cradle of the Middle Class: The Family in Oneida County, New York, 1790–1865* (Cambridge: Cambridge University Press, 1981), pp. 105–44; Katz, Stern, and Doucet, *Early Industrial Capitalism*, pp. 50–53, 64–107, 356–62; and Pessen, *Riches, Class, and Power*, pp. 251–80.

[10]Michael Feldberg, "The Crowd in Philadelphia History," *Labor History* 15 (1974): 323–36; Elizabeth Geffen, "Violence in Philadelphia in the 1840s and 1850s," *Pennsylvania History* 36 (1969): 381–410; and W. M. Thackeray, quoted in Joseph Jackson, *Literary Landmarks of Philadelphia* (Philadelphia: David McKay, 1939), frontis.

[11]For the history of European cities as stages for culture, see Anthony Vidler, "The Scenes of the Street: Transformations in Idea and Reality, 1750–1871," in Stanford Anderson, ed., *On Streets* (Cambridge: M.I.T. Press, 1978), pp. 29–111. For medieval cities, see Lewis Mumford, *The City in History: Its Origins, Its Transformations, and Its Prospects* (New York: Harcourt, Brace and World, 1961), pp. 163, 167, 277–80. For the North American commercial city forms, see Ian Davey and Michael Doucet, "Appendix One: The Social Geography of a Commercial City, ca. 1853," in Michael B. Katz, *The People of Hamilton, Canada West: Family and Class in a Mid-Nineteenth-Century City* (Cambridge: Harvard University Press, 1975), pp. 319–42.

[12]Sylvia Doughty Fries, *The Urban Idea in Colonial America* (Philadelphia: Temple University Press, 1977), pp. 97–101.

[13]Harold Donaldson Eberlein and Courtlandt Van Dyke Hubbard, *The Diary of Independence Hall* (Philadelphia: J. B. Lippincott, 1948), pp. 13–14, 23, 59, 92.

[14]J. Thomas Scharf and Thompson Westcott, *The History of Philadelphia, 1609–1884*, 3 vols. (Philadelphia: L. H. Everts, 1884) 1:649 and 2:857; and John F. Watson, *The Annals of Philadelphia and Pennsylvania* (Philadelphia: Carey & Hart, 1830), and rev. ed. in 3 vols., ed. Willis P. Hazard (Philadelphia: Edwin S. Stuart, 1900) 1:350–51.

[15]Watson, *Annals* 1:276–81, 436–41, 477–83, 485–98.

[16]In the eighteenth century, the city was tightly clustered along the north-south streets close to the Delaware; after 1800 it spread west, north, and south. For the social geography of late-eighteenth-century Philadelphia, see Mary Schweitzer's unpublished paper, "Occupation, Residence and Real Estate Values in Philadelphia, 1790" (Philadelphia Center for Early American Studies Seminar, October 26, 1984). See also, Fries, *Urban Idea in Colonial America*, pp. 89–96; Gwendolyn Wright, *Building the Dream: A Social History of Housing in America* (Cambridge: M.I.T. Press, 1981), pp. 24–40; and Pessen, *Riches, Class, and Power*, pp. 183–89.

[17]Class and occupational neighborhoods were recognized by Philadelphians at least as early as 1790; see Schweitzer, "Occupation, Residence and Real Estate Values." For speculation in housing and real estate, see Sam Bass Warner, *The Private City*, pp. 49–62, 126–40; for territoriality, see Bruce Laurie, "Fire Companies and Gangs in Southwark," in Allen F. Davis and Mark Haller, eds., *The Peoples of Philadelphia: A History of Ethnic Groups and Lower Class Life, 1790–1940* (Philadelphia: Temple University Press, 1973), pp. 71–87; for Philadelphia's wealthy neighborhoods, see Pessen, *Riches, Class, and Power*, pp. 183–89.

[18]Fries, *Urban Idea in Colonial America*, pp. 89–96; Frances Trollope, *Domestic Manners of the Americans* (London, 1832), p. 210; for Rebecca Davis, see Tillie Olsen, "Rebecca Harding Davis," in *Silences* (New York: Dell, Laurel Ed., 1978), p. 116.

[19]Thomas Czarnowski, "The Street As Communications Artifact," in Anderson, ed., *On Streets*, pp. 207–12; and François Bedarida and Anthony Sutcliffe, "The Street and The Structure of Life in the City," *Journal of Urban History* 6 (1980): 379–96.

[20]For prohibition of theatre and entertainments in the city, see William S. Dye, "Pennsylvania Against the Theatre," *Pennsylvania Magazine of History and Biography* 55 (1931): 333–71. For the history of theatricals in the early nineteenth century, see Arthur H. Wilson, *A History of the Philadelphia Theatre, 1835–1855* (Philadelphia: University of Pennsylvania Press, 1935); and Lawrence W. Levine, "William Shakespeare and the American People: A Study in Cultural Transformation," *American Historical Review* 89 (February 1984): 34–66.

[21]For class relations in the theatre, see Alexander Saxton, "Blackface Minstrelsy and Jacksonian Ideology," *American Quarterly* 27 (1975): 3–28; and Peter Buckley, "'A Privileged Place': New York Theatre Riots, 1817–1849" (paper presented at the annual meeting of the Organization of American Historians, Philadelphia, April 1, 1982). For criticism of the moral effects of theatres and plays, see A Friend to the Theatre, *An Enquiry into the Conditions and Influence of the Brothels in Connection with the Theatres at Philadelphia* (Philadelphia, pamphlet, 1834). Peter Buckley and Michael Meranze generously shared their research on reformers' opposition to the theatre.

[22]Christine Stansell, "Women, Children and the Uses of the Street: Class and Gender Conflict in New York City, 1850–1860," *Feminist Studies* 8 (1982): 308–35.

[23]Sean Wilentz, "Crime, Poverty and the Streets of New York: The Diary of William H. Bell, 1850–51," *History Workshop* 7 (1979): 126–55; and "Disgusting Exhibitions," *Public Ledger* (Philadelphia), June 26, 1844. Philadelphia instituted a Department of Beggar Detectives during the Panic of 1857; City of Philadelphia, Department of the Beggar Detectives, *Report*, 1857–58, Philadelphia City Archives.

[24]See, for example, a letter from "Veron," *Mechanics' Free Press* (Philadelphia), April 26, 1828. Objections to the suppression of charcoal vendors and scavengers claimed vendors' customary right to use a cry or bell and commented on the unquestioned use of rattles by the night watch; ibid., October 23, 1830.

[25]For resistance to fines collectors, see *Niles' Weekly Register* (Baltimore), April 4, 1835, p. 76; July 20, 1833, p. 344; and September 14, 1833, p. 47. For resistance to the destruction of markets to make way for railroads, see *United States Gazette* (Philadelphia) June 5, 1835. For opposition to the corporate use of streets to build rail lines, phrased in terms of the streets' public nature, see *Public Ledger*, June 22, 1842. For resistance to strikebreakers, see *Public Ledger*, August 19, 1842.

[26]Stansell, "Class and Gender Conflict"; and Nancy F. Cott, *The Bonds of Womanhood: 'Woman's Sphere' in New England, 1780–1835* (New Haven: Yale University Press, 1977).

[27]Warner, *Private City*, pp. 49–62, 126–40; Stuart Blumin, "Residential Mobility in Nineteenth-Century Philadelphia," in Davis and Haller, eds., *Peoples of Philadelphia*, pp. 37–51. The Schuylkill side of the city, for example, had a neighborhood named "Rotten Row," and the Schuylkill docks were thought of as an underworld; see Howard O. Sprogel, *The Philadelphia Police, Past and Present* (Philadelphia, privately published, 1887), pp. 622–30. For a description of Southwark as a demonic region, see *Public Ledger*, January 3, 1854.

[28]Fries, *Urban Idea in Colonial America*, pp. 97–101; Scharf and Westcott, *History of Philadelphia* 3:1845; Watson, *Annals* 2:397; and Samuel Hazard, ed., *Register of Pennsylvania* (Philadelphia) 12 (July 1833): 8.

[29]Watson, *Annals* 2:265; and Eberlein and Hubbard, *Independence Hall*, pp. 175–80.

[30]Ibid., pp. 219, 286, 312, 358. For the importance of public reading aloud, proclamation, and ritual in the Revolution, cf. Rhys Issac, "Dramatizing the Ideology of Revolution: Popular Mobilization in Virginia, 1774–1776," *William and Mary Quarterly*, 3rd ser., 37 (1980): 29–52.

[31]Watson, *Annals* 1:397.

[32]*United States Gazette*, July 1, 1823; Scharf and Westcott, *History of Philadelphia:* 1:649 and 2:857. For the history of the movement to abolish spectacular public punishment in Pennsylvania, see Michael Meranze, "The Penitential Ideal in Late Eighteenth-Century Philadelphia," *Pennsylvania Magazine of History and Biography* 108, no. 4 (October 1984): 419–40.

[33]*Mechanics' Free Press*, October 3, 1829.

[34]*Pennsylvanian* (Philadelphia), June 3–7, 9, 10, 12, 1835. The *North American* (Philadelphia), November 12, 1857, provides an example of the need to obtain a permit to use the Square.

[35]See, for example, Donald M. Scott, "The Popular Lecture and the Creation of the Public in Mid-Nineteenth Century America," *Journal of American History* 66 (1980): 791–809.

[36]Gary B. Nash, "'To Arise Out of the Dust': Absalom Jones and the African Church of Philadelphia, 1785–1795" (paper presented to the Philadelphia Center for Early American Studies Seminar, September 24, 1982).

[37]Geffen, "Violence in Philadelphia"; *History of Pennsylvania Hall, Which Was Destroyed by a Mob on the 17th of May, 1838* (Philadelphia, 1838; repr. ed., New York: Negro Universities Press, 1969).

[38]Christopher Hill, "The Uses of Sabbatarianism," in *Society and Puritanism in Pre-Revolutionary England*, 2nd ed. (New York: Schocken, 1967), pp. 145–218; Peter Burke, *Popular Culture in Early Modern Europe*

(London: Temple Smith, 1978); and R. W. Malcolmson, *Popular Recreations in English Society, 1700–1850* (Cambridge: Cambridge University Press, 1973).

[39]Dye, "Pennsylvania Against the Theatre."

[40]Eric Foner, *Tom Paine and Revolutionary America* (New York: Oxford University Press, 1976), pp. 50–51.

[41]Hazard, *Register* 1 (April 1828): 154 (a complaint from 1732), 255 (from 1738), 271 (from 1741).

[42]The most dramatic eruption of popular radicalism in the city was the Fort Wilson riot, which is analyzed by Steven J. Rosswurm in "Arms, Culture and Class: The Philadelphia Militias and the 'Lower Orders' in the American Revolution," doctoral dissertation, Northern Illinois University, DeKalb, 1977, pp. 430–61.

[43]*Democratic Press* (Philadelphia), May 12, 1825. Crowds also got out of control at pleasure gardens; see *Niles' Weekly Register*, October 31, 1819, pp. 143–44; and Geffen, "Violence in Philadelphia."

[44]Geffen, "Violence in Philadelphia"; David Grimstead, "Rioting in Its Jacksonian Setting," *American Historical Review* 77 (1972): 361–97.

[45]Laurie, *Working People*, pp. 3–30; and Shelton, "Mills of Manayunk," pp. 192–94.

[46]Laurie, *Working People*, pp. 33–52; Douglas Reid, "The Decline of Saint Monday, 1766–1876," *Past and Present* 71 (1976): 76–101; E. P. Thompson, "Time, Work-Discipline, and Industrial Capitalism," *Past and Present* 38 (1967): 56–97; and Sidney Pollard, "Factory Discipline in the Industrial Revolution," *Economic History Review*, 2nd ser., 16 (1963): 254–71.

[47]Laurie, *Working People*, pp. 53–104.

[48]The history of how festivity, industrial work, and poverty are related remains to be written. For some contributions, see J. H. Plumb, "The Commercialization of Leisure in Eighteenth-Century England," in J. H. Plumb, Neil McKendrick, and John Brewer, eds., *The Birth of a Consumer Society: The Commercialization of Eighteenth-Century England* (Bloomington: Indiana University Press, 1982); Roy Rosenzweig, *Eight Hours for What We Will: Workers and Leisure in an Industrial City, 1870–1920* (Cambridge: Cambridge University Press, 1983); James Walvin, *Leisure and Society, 1830–1950* (New York and London: Longmans, 1978); Peter Bailey, *Leisure and Class in Victorian England: Rational Recreation and the Quest for Control, 1830–1885* (London: Routledge, Kegan Paul, 1978); Reid, "Decline of Saint Monday"; and Herbert H. Gutman, *Work, Culture and Society in Industrializing America* (New York: Vintage, 1977), pp. 3–78.

[49]Susan G. Davis, "'Making Night Hideous': Christmas Revelry and Public Order in Nineteenth-Century Philadelphia," *American Quarterly* 34 (1982): 185–99; and Alfred Shoemaker, *Christmas in Pennsylvania: A Folk-Cultural Study* (Kutztown: Pennsylvania Folklife Society, 1959).

[50]Davis, "'Making Night Hideous.'"

[51]*Daily Chronicle* (Philadelphia), December 26, 1833.

[52]J. Ritchie Garrison, "Battalion Day: Militia Muster and Frolic in Pennsylvania Before the Civil War," *Pennsylvania Folklife* 26 (1976–77): 2–12.

[53]See, for example, *Democratic Press*, April 30, 1808.

[54]*Public Ledger*, May 10, 1836.

[55]*Saturday Evening Post* (Philadelphia), June 4, 1828.

[56]*Public Ledger*, July 12, 1837.

[57]Dinners organized by political clubs are described in papers sponsored by parties and factions. The party press was the predominant newspaper form in the United States until the rise of the labor press and the cheap or "penny" press in the 1830s. Some examples of these accounts appear in *Poulson's American Daily Advertiser* (Philadelphia), July 3, 1801; *True American* (Philadelphia), July 4, 1805; and *Democratic Press*, July 6, 1810. The dinner as a forum for oratory is discussed in Howard H. Martin, "Orations on the Anniversary of American Independence, 1776–1876," doctoral dissertation, Evanston, Northwestern University, 1955, pp. 11–94. Fletcher M. Green details the context of southern toasting traditions in "Listen to the Eagle Scream: One Hundred Years of the Fourth of July in North Carolina, (1776–1876)," *North Carolina Historical Review* 31 (1954): 295–320, 529–49.

[58]See, for example, "Extracts from the Diary of Thomas Franklin Pleasants, 1814," *Pennsylvania Magazine of History and Biography* 39 (1915): 322–31.

[59]For size of the party presses' readership, see Frank Luther Mott, *American Journalism—A History, 1690–1960*, 3rd ed., (New York: Macmillan, 1962), pp. 202–3, 303; and Dan Schiller, *Objectivity and the News: The Public and the Rise of Commercial Journalism* (Philadelphia: University of Pennsylvania Press, 1981), pp. 12–13.

[60]For numerous examples, see W. A. Newman Dorland, "The Second Troop Philadelphia City Cavalry," *Pennsylvania Magazine of History and Biography* 47 (1923): 264, 269, 362–63; see also *United States Gazette*, July 5, 1821, and July 5, 1834.

[61]Martin, "Orations," pp. 11–94.

[62]*Record of Burials, 1730–1831*, Old Swedes' Church (Gloria Dei), Philadelphia, contains notes on informal July Fourth frolics, or dances, in the Southwark district; for an example from 1801, see p. 176. This source was brought to my attention by Susan Klepp.

[63]Some Philadelphia crafts and trades celebrated traditional occupational holidays, such as the shoemakers' holiday, St. Crispin's Day. Early in the nineteenth century Philadelphia printers celebrated

Benjamin Franklin's birthday. These practices seem to have been more vigorous and popular in New York City than in Philadelphia. See Sean Wilentz, "Artisan Republican Festivals and the Rise of Class Conflict in New York City, 1788–1837," in Michael H. Frisch and Daniel J. Walkowitz, eds., *Working-Class America: Essays on Labor, Community and American Society* (Urbana: University of Illinois Press, 1983), pp. 37–77.

[64]Shelton, "Mills of Manayunk," pp. 199–200; and William Sisson, "From Farm to Factory: Work Values and Disciplines in Two Early Textile Mills," *Working Papers from the Regional Economic History Research Center* 4 (1981): 15.

[65]*Poulson's Daily Advertiser*, July 6, 1822.

[66]*United States Gazette*, July 1, 1823.

[67]*Public Ledger*, July 4, 1839.

[68]Ibid., July 4, 1844.

[69]*Pennsylvanian*, July 6, 1850.

[70]*Mechanics' Free Press*, June 6, 1829.

[71]Ibid., June 20, 1829.

[72]Nativists' uses of the Fourth of July have never been studied in their own right, but see David Montgomery, "The Shuttle and the Cross: Weavers and Artisans in the Kensington Riots of 1844," *Journal of Social History* 5 (1972): 411–46.

[73]Sidney Fisher, for example, loathed the day; see Nicholas B. Wainwright, ed., *A Philadelphia Perspective: The Diary of Sidney George Fisher* (Philadelphia: Historical Society of Philadelphia, 1967), pp. 224, 258, 476, 518; and *North American*, September 4, 1839.

[74]This story is still untold, but see Davis, "'Making Night Hideous'"; and Rosenzweig, *Eight Hours for What We Will*, pp. 153–68.

[75]Frederick Douglass, "What to the Slave is the Fourth of July?" *Black Scholar* 7 (1976): 32–37; Philip S. Foner, "Black Participation in the Centennial of 1876," *Phylon* 39 (1974): 283–86; Leonard I. Sweet, "The Fourth of July and Black Americans in the Nineteenth Century: Northern Leadership Opinion Within the Context of Black Experience," *Journal of Negro History* 61 (1976): 256–75; and Benjamin Quarles, "Antebellum Free Blacks and the 'Spirit of '76,'" *Journal of Negro History* 61 (1976): 229–42.

Philadelphia had a long-standing free black community clustered at the southeastern edge of the old city center and along Cedar (South) Street. From the early nineteenth century on, blacks competed with white neighbors for jobs and resources, achieving relative strength in unskilled trades, in a few guilds, and in the exclusivity of black-defined occupations before the Civil War. Social and political conditions worsened for Philadelphia blacks after the 1830s, when Pennsylvania rescinded their right to vote and interracial attempts at labor organization collapsed. See Emma J. Lapsansky, "A Haven for Those Low in the World: South Street Philadelphia, 1762–1854," doctoral dissertation, University of Pennsylvania, 1975; and W. E. B. DuBois, *The Philadelphia Negro* (repr. ed.; New York: Schocken, 1970).

[76]Sweet, "Fourth of July and Black Americans."

[77]*Public Ledger*, August 2 and 3, 1842. In contrast, late-eighteenth-century black and white Philadelphians working together in the antislavery cause appeared together in ceremonial, public roles. See Nash, "'To Arise Out of the Dust.'"

[78]*Public Ledger*, December 28, 1840.

[79]Watson, *Annals* 2:261.

[80]Doris Yoakum, "Women's Introduction to the American Platform," in William N. Brigance, ed., *A History and Criticism of American Public Address*, vol. 1 (New York and London: McGraw-Hill, 1943), pp. 153–89; Gerda Lerner, *Black Women in White America: A Documentary History* (New York: Pantheon, 1972), p. 83; Gerda Lerner, *The Grimké Sisters of North Carolina: Pioneers for Women's Rights and Abolition* (New York: Schocken, 1971), pp. 187–89; Eleanor Flexner, *Century of Struggle: The Women's Rights Movement in the United States* (New York: Athenaeum, 1973), pp. 21–28, 51; and Angela Y. Davis, *Women, Race and Class* (New York: Random House, 1981), pp. 30–69. Delores Hayden has expanded our understanding of women's relation to public spaces in *Redesigning the American Dream: The Future of Housing, Work and Family Life* (New York: Norton, 1984), pp. 24–28, 209–24.

Historians who argue that nineteenth-century American women had no public role overstate the case and underestimate women's social and political activism: Antebellum women in the eastern part of the country had invented a variety of influential public roles and stances. Public roles and public *ceremonial* presence, however, are not the same thing. The limitations on female self-representation in the streets and on hustings, despite women's political energies, underscore the special, highly charged nature of public terrains; see Nancy A. Hewitt, *Women's Activism and Social Change: Rochester, New York, 1822–1872* (Ithaca: Cornell University Press, 1984).

[81]*Poulson's American Daily Advertiser*, February 17, 1832. Women dressed as figures of purity appeared in temperance processions; see *Public Ledger*, July 2–4, 6, 1840.

[82]Dennis Clark, *The Irish Relations: Trials of an Immigrant Tradition* (Rutherford, N.J.: Fairleigh Dickinson University Press, 1982), pp. 193–203; and *Niles' Weekly Register*, April 3, 1819, pp. 71–72, and April 5, 1823, pp. 105–7.

Philadelphia was home to many Protestant (Ulster) Irish and Catholic Irish. Thus, July 12 (the anniversary of defeat of the Catholic Republican forces by William of Orange at the Battle of the Boyne) and Saint Patrick's Day became traditional days for parades and factional brawling between Orangemen and the Sons of Erin (Hibernians).

Part Two

The Industrial City

Introduction

By the time of the Civil War, the United States was poised on the threshold of the industrial era. In the years between 1860 and 1920, the face of urban America was reshaped and restructured by technology, transportation, economic development, demographic shifts, and the rise of corporations and other large bureaucratic organizations. Powerful and dynamic forces such as capitalism, competition, individualism, and consumerism triggered economic and social changes. Driven by the profit motive, the process of modernizing change did not always have pleasant results. The large American industrial city—for the most part ugly, congested, noisy, smelly, smoky, unhealthy, and ill governed—emerged during this period. At the same time, city people sought to understand, manage, and overcome the new forces and conditions reshaping the cities. Heterogeneous groups of immigrants and rural migrants, unaccustomed to urban life and work, struggled to adjust to new conditions. As the cities grew to enormous size, they also became more socially divided, segmented, and disorderly.

One of the most noticeable differences between the industrial city of the late nineteenth century and the commercial metropolis of the pre-Civil War period was population size. New York, with less than 1 million people in 1860, exceeded 5.5 million by 1920. Chicago, which had little over 100,000 in 1860, neared the 3-million mark in 1920. Most of the older eastern and midwestern cities grew at a startling pace. In addition, explosive urban growth occurred in a number of smaller cities in the South, the trans-Mississippi, West, and the Pacific Coast, as evidenced by Omaha, Kansas City, Minneapolis, Denver, Seattle, Portland, San Francisco, Oakland, Los Angeles, Atlanta, and Birmingham. By 1920 the U.S. census revealed that more than 50 percent of all Americans lived in urban places, a vast jump from the less than 20 percent who lived in cities in 1860. "We cannot all live in cities," New York editor Horace Greeley wrote in 1867, "yet nearly all seem determined to do so." Greeley's analysis was not far off the mark, for the nation had become truly "citified" by the early twentieth century.

The rapid urban population growth of the period was the consequence of a great release of rural population, both in the United States and in Europe. A rising birthrate, a falling death rate, and annexation by cities of surrounding areas accounted for some of the increase, but most of the new urbanites came from rural America and peasant villages in Europe. Agricultural depressions and the hardships of farm life forced American farmers and their families off

71

the land and into the cities in search of economic opportunity. Many young people from the farms also were lured to the city by its active social, cultural, and recreational life.

Simultaneously, millions of European peasant farmers and villagers cast their lot with the cities in migrating to the "land of opportunity." During the century after 1820, about 34 million immigrants arrived in the United States. The first wave consisted primarily of Irish, German, British, and Scandinavian newcomers. By the 1880s southern and eastern Europeans began arriving at the immigrant ports, as well. In the twentieth century, the European influx to the cities was swelled by the migration of rural southern blacks to cities in the North, West, and South. And by the 1920s migrants from rural Mexico had joined the movement to the American city, not just in California and the Southwest, but as far away as Chicago, Minneapolis, and Detroit.

These demographic shifts contributed to the reshaping of the modern American city. The presence of such large numbers of rural newcomers, unaccustomed to city ways and industrial labor, drastically altered the fabric of urban life. Ethnic, religious, and racial diversity became common in almost every city. The foreign-born presence was especially pervasive. By 1910 more than 70 percent of the populations of New York, Chicago, Boston, Cleveland, Detroit, Buffalo, and Milwaukee was composed of immigrants or their American-born children. The percentage of foreign stock ranged between 50 and 70 percent in such other major cities as St. Louis, Philadelphia, Cincinnati, Pittsburgh, Newark, and San Francisco. Swelling the inner districts of the cities where housing was cheap and jobs were available, the immigrants made the city look, sound, and feel different.

Strangers in new surroundings, the immigrants sought identity in common with their fellows. They could not recreate the village society of peasant Europe, but old institutions such as family and church remained strong; they established new community agencies such as newspapers, benevolent societies, and unions that helped maintain their group identities. At the same time, through the public school, the political system, and the workplace, the assimilation process began. Industrial cities of the late nineteenth century, then, served as huge centers for social interaction and cultural change. In the process of community building, farmers and peasant folk became city people, shepherds and fruit growers became factory workers, Sicilians and Calabrians became Italians, and foreigners became Americans. These changes were occurring simultaneously at different levels and at different rates. Moreover, change of this kind was a constant feature of life in the city because new immigrants continued to arrive until the restrictive legislation of the 1920s. If anything, the industrial city was a place of continual social and cultural change.

If population changes dramatically affected urban life during this period, so also did new transportation technology that did away with the "walking city." Beginning with the horse-drawn omnibus in the 1830s, a series of transportation innovations revolutionized life in the city by the late nineteenth century. These innovations—the commuter railroad, the horsecar, the electric trolley, the cable car, and finally the subway and the elevated railroad—

brought structural and spatial change to the city. In the first place, new transportation opened up distant peripheral areas to development and permitted the physical expansion of the city. New housing sprouted along streetcar, trolley, and subway lines. Wealthy and middle-class residents moved from the central districts to the outer fringes and suburbs, as city workers and immigrants began occupying older housing vacated in the center.

The transportation lines focused on the city center, driving up land prices, creating downtown shopping districts, and bringing workers to centrally located businesses and factories. Land uses became differentiated and specialized. Functionally, urban regions split between the center (comprising older, low-income housing and industrial, commercial, and business establishments) and the outlying ring of suburbs; often separating the two was a "zone of emergence," or working-class districts on the urban periphery. By the end of this period the motor truck and the automobile had begun to have an impact, intensifying some of the earlier patterns of physical development but creating new ones as well.

New methods of urban transit had other long-range results. Physical growth of the city promoted social fragmentation, as community life tended to segregate by class, ethnicity, and race. The personal and face-to-face contacts that had characterized the walking city were replaced by looser and more impersonal human relationships. The sense of community that had prevailed in earlier years eroded in the industrial city; the common value structure of a prior era had little impact on a heterogeneous population composed of numerous ethnic, religious, and racial subcultures. Similar patterns prevailed in the streetcar suburbs, which most new residents conceived of only as an escape from the city and where, according to some interpretations, community life seemed to be less centered than in the older urban neighborhoods.

Transportation innovations between cities also had a powerful effect on urban life and economic development. Railroad mileage increased from 30,000 miles in 1860 to 190,000 miles in 1900, reflecting the completion of an integrated national railroad network by the end of the nineteenth century. During these years, smaller rail lines were consolidated into large railroad empires, and the transcontinental railroads pushed out across the Great Plains and the Rocky Mountains to Pacific Coast cities. These developments, linking far-flung cities and fostering the growth of new ones, brought a national market within reach of manufacturers and businessmen and helped make an industrial revolution possible after the Civil War.

By the late nineteenth century the stage was set for the rise of the large, sprawling industrial city. Population growth had created a huge internal market, and transportation innovations offered a means of gathering raw materials and distributing finished products and consumer goods. The rural migrants and new immigrants pouring into the cities provided a ready pool of cheap labor. Technology supplied the skills and machinery needed for industrial output and mass production, and new sources of energy such as steam, oil, and electricity provided the necessary power. The emergence of finance capitalism, as opposed to the older and more localized merchant capitalism, made investment funds readily available for new industrial endeavors. New and consolidated forms of business organization, especially the corporation, tended to cut competition, facilitate economies in production, and spur large-scale economic activity. And, finally, in a variety of ways government promoted economic growth as a desirable end. The unregulated, laissez-faire atmosphere of the era enabled the new corporations to flourish without much governmental intervention. The concatenation of these developments brought an industrial revolution to the American city.

As a result of this revolution, American cities had become massive centers for manufacturing and related economic enterprise. The cities of the period differed markedly from the mercantile and commercial cities of the pre-Civil War years. The largest urban centers in the Northeast and the Midwest all developed highly diversified economies, while smaller cities often gained reputations for specialized manufacturing. Most big cities also served regional financial and marketing functions, as subsidiary industries and businesses emerged.

In addition, the growth of the urban market encouraged a consumer revolution. The new downtown shopping districts boasted popular department stores and chain stores, all stocking standardized products, while promotional advertising helped to create a mass consumer market. The new mail-order houses of Sears, Roebuck and Montgomery and Ward, centered in Chicago and relying on widely distributed catalogs, typified the businessman's new approach to capturing the consumer dollar. Even in the midst of the industrial era, the growth of a mass consumer society was causing a shift of the work force toward a variety of service occupations. The giant corporations, for example, developed huge bureaucracies of managers and office workers, and mass marketing required tens of thousands of service workers to move the product to the consumer.

Technology, capitalism, and the widespread American faith in competition, consumerism, and economic growth propelled the United States into the industrial era. By the end of the nineteenth century, the value of American industrial output surpassed the combined totals for Britain, France, and Germany, the world's industrial leaders in 1860. Emerging in the late nineteenth century, the American industrial city became an economic center with wide-reaching functions. It was a center for manufacturing, wholesaling, and retailing; it was the point of concentration for financial and corporate decision making; and it was the place of work for millions of new urbanites. Clearly, the changes introduced by transportation, economic growth, and industrialization had important and longlasting impacts on life in the American city.

Changes of this kind can be perceived in urban political developments during the industrial era. City politics provided an arena for conflicting interest groups. Not surprisingly, municipal politics reflected the emerging residential pattern that encouraged the creation of urban neighborhoods and communities according to class, ethnicity, and race. These groups vied for city council positions, school board seats, municipal patronage, and a share of power in the allocation of funds for urban physical development. As individuals sought economic gains in the competitive society, so also did special interest groups compete for city jobs for relatives and friends, better parks and streets in their neighborhoods, or governmental favoritism of one kind or another.

Holding these fragmented political communities together was the political machine and the city boss. Numerous recent studies have demonstrated that the urban bosses did more than simply rob the public treasuries. As sociologist Robert K. Merton has noted, the machine had a number of "latent functions"— services beyond those provided by the official government. Such services could take the form of a municipal job, a Christmas turkey, winter fuel for the poor, a utility or transit franchise for the businessman, or a free hand to gamblers, saloon-keepers, and prostitutes. The machine, however, exacted something in return such as votes, graft, kickbacks, or protection money. The link between machine politicians and such popular sports as baseball, boxing, and horse racing, as sports historian Steven A. Riess has noted, also suggests the complex ways in which the bosses played to a varied urban constituency.

It also appears now that most of the classic urban bosses—Tweed in New York, Shepherd in Washington, DC, Cox in Cincinnati, the Pendergasts in Kansas City—supported and promoted urban physical development. They lavishly spent municipal funds for new streets and docks, public buildings, schools, parks, transit facilities, public utilities, and other services. Important sectors of the business community, such as real estate interests, banking, building and construction concerns, and transit and power companies, often found an ally in the boss, who provided cheap municipal land, bank deposits of municipal funds, construction contracts, tax exemptions, franchises, and other payoffs. The costs were high and the political corruption reprehensible, but, according to recent interpretations, the bosses mastered the fragmented metropolises, brought order out of chaos, and provided a kind of positive government. At the same time, the boss was something of a philanthropist and social reformer, promoting the interests and serving the needs of a large immigrant and working-class constituency.

The strong prodevelopment position of most urban bosses stands in marked contrast to the policies advocated by the so-called municipal reformers. As recent historians have suggested, these middle-class, good-government advocates were often "structural" reformers who promoted changes in the constitutional structure of city government. They sought city charter changes granting home rule, creating stronger mayors and smaller councils, consolidating school boards, and in general centralizing authority. They advocated a streamlined government administered by experts, an objective thought achievable through the city manager or commission form of municipal government. Their goals included greater efficiency, more honest government, less extravagance, and lower taxes. Thus, these structural reformers usually took an antidevelopment stance, and they opposed huge expenditures for urban physical development.

Drawn from the professions and the bureaucracy of the new corporate structure and often residents of the periphery and the suburbs, the middle-class reformers fought the bosses and the machines for control of urban government. In one sense, as historian Bruce M. Stave has suggested, it was a struggle "between the center-as-residence (for the bosses and their immigrant following) and the center-as-place-of-business (for the reformers)." The reformers represented the forces of centralization, while the machines sought to preserve the decentralized structure held together by the ward heeler, the precinct captain, and the boss. When elected, the reformers found it difficult to retain the support of the voters who wanted services and patronages and the business groups that thrived on urban development. Thus, although reformers were periodically swept into office on a wave of revulsion against corruption and the machine, the bosses were just as regularly put back into power by a constituency fed up with efficiency experts, moral preaching, the merit system, reduced social programs, and rigorous law enforcement in the immigrant neighborhoods. In short, over the long span of American urban history, machine politics has demonstrated a surprising strength and resiliency. It was a political system that fit remarkably well with the business values of the industrial era.

Machine politics is not the only legacy of the industrial city. The competitive spirit carried over into other areas of urban life, as well. For example, the physical and spatial configurations of American cities have been determined largely by entrepreneurial values. Urban land in the United States has been conceived of as a private resource; city landowners sought to use their land in the most profitable ways, without much regard for public convenience or human welfare or physical consequences. The resulting mixed patterns of land use left much to be desired. Valuable business property in downtown areas was gobbled up for factories, railroad yards, and office and storage buildings. Entire neighborhoods were uprooted in the interests of business and industrial groups, and the impact upon the urban environment was ignored. When zoning ordinances and city planning commissions were introduced in the early twentieth century, these tools generally served the interests of the business leaders and affluent property owners who controlled the urban economy.

The city planning profession which emerged in the industrial era reinforced such patterns. The planners usually worked for the real estate developers or for municipal governments dominated by business interests. The widespread adoption of the rectangular, gridiron street pattern typified the orientation of the planners; the gridiron brought a monotonous sameness to American cities, but it was the most efficient and profitable method of dividing urban land for business purposes and for speculation. There were some creative planners, of course, such as Daniel Burnham in Chicago, Horace Cleveland in Minneapolis and St. Paul, and Frederick Law Olmsted in New York. But those with wealth and power and political influence generally determined the planning and physical development of the city. Predominant entrepreneurial values and business purposes prevailed in the planning and building of American cities.

These values also affected many other aspects of American urban life in the industrial era. In the competitive society, the business ethic prevailed; economic success and individual achievement were valued over human welfare and the idea of community. In a large range of areas—housing, sanitation, public health, education, working conditions, wages—the bulk of urban residents and workers suffered abominably. The overcrowded tenement house came to typify living conditions in large metropolises like New York City, while unsightly two- and three-family structures characterized Boston, Chicago, and St. Louis, and dingy bungalows prevailed in working-class districts in smaller industrial cities like Detroit, Buffalo, and Milwaukee. By the twentieth century, new technology had only begun to bring improvements in municipal sewage systems, sanitation, and public health. Public schooling for most city children encompassed only the elementary years, and thousands of children were annually thrown onto the labor market and forced into "dead-end" jobs. Factory, mine, and mill jobs were dangerous and industrial accidents common. Social services for sick, injured, unemployed, or otherwise dependent persons were inadequate. Incredibly, during the long depressions from the 1870s to the 1880s, public relief was abolished in many big cities.

For those who could not compete there were few rewards, but, even for many who did compete by selling their labor for wages, the rewards were differential—that is, they were distributed in inequitable ways. Industrial laborers were buffeted by the periodic depressions of the industrial era; unprotected by unions, they worked long hours at subsistence or even below subsistence wages. Women and children slaved away in garment "sweatshops" or in the factories, mines, and mills.

Conditions were even worse for black Americans in the city. Rural southern blacks envisioned northern cities as a kind of "promised land" in the post-Civil War years. Over the entire period from 1870 to 1920, about 1,100,000 southern blacks became northern urban dwellers. The movement was especially strong after 1900 because of the promise of economic opportunity. The jobs were there, but white workers, faced with competition for work and housing, responded with discrimination, racism, and violence. Tension often resulted in bitter racial conflicts by the end of the period. Race riots in East St. Louis in 1917 and in Chicago in 1919 exemplified these patterns of response and reaction. The racial ghettos so common in mid-twentieth-century America were first created during the industrial era.

The urban society which emerged during the industrial era, then, contained the seeds of the contemporary American city. Population changes, transportation and other technological innovations, and economic advances all combined to thrust the city into the industrial revolution. The competitive drive for entrepreneurial success, a phenomenon most apparent in the cities, moved the United States into the front ranks of the modern industrial nations. But the same kinds of values—individualism, consumerism, competition, and economic achievement—made acceptable the appalling kinds of social and working conditions that prevailed in the city. Neighborhoods and communities often were divided by class, race, and ethnicity. Cities were fragmented functionally and politically. Bosses and businessmen, both driven by the dollar, controlled urban destinies. Economic growth and urban expansion were unplanned and unregulated. Most Americans conceived of such growth in positive ways, but social and environmental costs were ignored in the process. In many of its physical aspects, the city represented the triumph of expedience and profits over aesthetic and environmental considerations.

The city had its problems, but there was a positive side to the urban pattern, especially as reflected in the ways in which the human spirit not only survived but also thrived in the urban centers. Indeed, it has been argued that man's best achievements have been encouraged by urban life, particularly in the cultural, artistic, and intellectual sense. Recent historians, moreover, have emphasized the persistence of old communal and cultural values in the modern industrial city. Despite the pressures for adaptation and conformity to American and urban ways, newcomers from the farm and from across the

seas maintained their old life ways to a remarkable degree. The family structure, religious patterns, and group life remained strong, and the sense of
community among the new urbanites could not be extinguished.

The essays that follow illustrate some of the recent interpretive ideas of
American historians about the industrial city, particularly in its political
and social context. STANLEY K. SCHULTZ and CLAY McSHANE push beyond the
traditional account of urban political and administrative history, with its
focus on the struggle between machine politicians and political reformers.
Instead, the authors emphasize the complexity of the late nineteenth-century
urban environment, especially the hazardous pollution and public health
problems created by rapid industrial growth in the city. Nineteenth-century
municipal government evolved slowly in response to the emerging problems
of urban America. The provision of professional municipal services, such as
police and fire protection, only gradually came to be the norm by midcentury.
Advances in medical knowledge by the 1880s, especially the germ theory of
disease, led city governments to apply new technological innovations to human
and social problems. Improved water supply, city planning techniques, and
sewage and other sanitation systems resulted. The hiring of city engineers,
city planners, and eventually city managers came to typify the changing
administrative pattern of municipal government. The application of technological solutions to urban problems, the authors contend, contributed significantly to the professionalization and bureaucratization of city government.
Indeed, some historians have suggested, the city engineer may have been
more important than the urban boss in shaping the development of the
modern industrial city.

STEVEN A. RIESS offers a different perspective on urban politics, focusing
on sports and machine politicians in New York City. Organized sport grew
up in the industrializing city of the late nineteenth century, taking on such
modern characteristics as bureaucratic organization and specialization of
function. Mass spectator sports such as boxing, baseball, and horse racing
attracted large popular audiences. But these sports provided more than just
commercialized entertainment for the urban masses. As Riess demonstrates,
sport became intricately linked with machine politics and various facets of
urban crime, particularly gambling. The politicians not only profited financially from their sporting and gambling connections but also broadened their
political appeal as purveyors of Sunday baseball, offtrack betting, and the
manly bachelor subculture of boxing. All three sports remained highly politicized throughout the industrial era, which detracted not in the least from
their widespread popular appeal to city people.

The ubiquitous urban saloon reflected another facet of culture during the
industrial era. JON M. KINGSDALE contends that the working-class saloon served
important social and cultural functions in urban and ethnic neighborhoods.
These male-dominated institutions became neighborhood gathering places,
centers for recreation and amusement, and essential cogs in the local political
machine. Many saloon patrons were attracted by free lunches, by the sociability of the male drinking subculture, or perhaps by the unsavory and illegal
offerings of gambling and prostitution. Whatever the reason, the saloon was

an enormously popular institution until the beginning of prohibition in 1919. Kingsdale suggests that prohibition came as the culmination of a long reform agitation against the saloon by middle-class women. The antisaloon crusade also reflected reformist and nativist concerns that democracy was being corrupted by barkeep politicians, and that the saloon promoted ethnic culture and retarded assimilation. Few social institutions in the industrializing city played such an important role in working-class culture as the saloon, and few stirred such angry passions among nativists, temperance advocates, and opponents of the political machine.

The corner saloon rarely opened its doors to women, but working-class girls and women were developing their own leisure-time culture in the city. KATHY PEISS illustrates the social impact of changing work patterns in the industrializing city. As late as 1880 most working women in the city labored in domestic service or other home-based occupations. A dramatic transformation in the social organization of work by 1900 created new opportunities for working-class women. Increasingly, by the twentieth century, women worked in factory settings, especially in the garment trades. The centralization of retailing and corporate activities in the city also opened up jobs for women as sales clerks in department stores and as secretaries, typists, and telephone operators in business offices. For a variety of reasons, the workday was shortened as well, leaving more time for female recreation and leisure. Peiss contends that a distinctive women's work culture developed during this era, one through which women collectively gained some degree of control over the workplace and over their pleasure-oriented, leisure-time activities. Peiss's essay represents a blending of new approaches to labor history, women's history, and cultural history.

Recent historians also have offered new interpretations of immigration and ethnic group life in urban America. Earlier views portrayed the immigrants as uprooted peasants whose traditional cultures were undermined and extinguished during the assimilation process in the United States. RUDOLPH J. VECOLI presents a quite different analysis. In examining some sixteen separate Italian immigrant communities in industrial era Chicago, Vecoli demonstrates the distinctive old-country village and regional basis for Italian group life in America. Through chain migration and cultural affinity, Italian immigrants tended to cluster together, reconstituting community along the lines of old-world origins. These cohesive communities, persisting in many cases beyond the immigrant generation, facilitated ethnic cultural maintenance. Rather than assimilating rapidly, the newcomers retained their ethnic culture, which became a powerful determinant of social experience in the industrial city. While the specific details often differed, most other immigrant groups in the industrial city shared the settlement and adjustment patterns that Vecoli described for Italians.

The final essay in Part Two provides a comparative perspective on the urban adjustment of two groups of newcomers—southern blacks and immigrant Poles—in early twentieth-century Pittsburgh. Historians JOHN BODNAR, MICHAEL WEBER, and ROGER SIMON analyze the differential patterns of urban adaptation, particularly in the occupational arena, demonstrated by the two groups in the Steel City. Blacks, like the Poles, came to Pittsburgh in search of economic opportunity, and both groups had some industrial labor experience prior to migration. Similarities ended on that point, however. Poles established elaborate kinship networks in obtaining jobs for newcomers, resulting in ethnic clustering in a few major industries. By contrast, because of racist hiring practices, blacks were unable to rely on kinship networks in the job market, which resulted in the widespread distribution of black workers throughout the city's economy. In Polish households, younger workers lived with parents longer and contributed earnings to family needs, while young black workers left home earlier and had little tradition of contributing to household support. The two groups also differed on such measures as household structure and occupational mobility. Using a unique blend of oral history, family history, and quantitative analysis, the authors demonstrate conclusively the dissimilar models of urban accommodation followed by blacks and Poles. They suggest the importance of premigration traditions in the modernizing city, but they also posit the patterns of change created by interaction with the urban environment.

These six essays suggest some of the exciting and innovative research currently being pursued by urban and social historians. Each offers important interpretive perspectives on several significant facets of the human experience during the industrial era.

To Engineer the Metropolis: Sewers, Sanitation, and City Planning in Late Nineteenth-Century America

Stanley K. Schultz and Clay McShane*

A Baltimore engineer who sought public construction and ownership of a city-wide sewer system drew a parallel in 1905 between the efficiency of sewers and the quality of a civilization. Referring to Europe, he stated that "completely sewered, with a low death rate," Paris is "the center of all that is best in art, literature, science and architecture and is both clean and beautiful. In the evolution of this ideal attainment," he continued, "its sewers took at least a leading part, for we have only to look at conditions existing prior to their construction to see that such a realization would have been impossible before their existence." Although his sentiments were overblown, his statement conveyed some truth. A growing number of urbanites in early twentieth-century America recognized an intimate relationship between technology and the social, economic, and governmental structure of cities. To harness new technologies to social needs was the aspiration of many so-called "progressives." As landscape architect John Nolen put it in 1909: "Intelligent city planning is one of the means toward a better utilization of our resources, toward an application of the methods of private business to public affairs, toward efficiency, toward a higher individual and higher collective life."[1]

The central watchwords of many political reformers during the late nineteenth and early twentieth centuries, as Nolen suggested, were conservation, corporate-like government, efficiency, and social engineering. Each goal required the application of technology to the solution of human problems. Each demanded innovative methods of administration to serve best the public interest. The Baltimore engineer added his voice to a swelling chorus of city leaders and political pundits who urged stronger public control of such services as water and sewer systems, transportation facilities, electric lighting—indeed, all those services that improved the quality of the urban physical

*Stanley K. Schultz is professor of history at the University of Wisconsin at Madison. Clay McShane is associate professor of history at Northeastern University. Reprinted from Journal of American History *65 (September 1978): 389–411. Reprinted by permission of the Organization of American Historians.*

environment. To achieve these aims, numerous reformers called for municipal ownership of utilities and for new governmental institutions to administer the services.[2]

As the French philosopher Jacques Ellul observed, modern administrative organization in both the economic and political spheres matured with the application of formerly private techniques to questions of public concern. The moment that new techniques "proved themselves able to operate efficiently on the masses, they ceased to be purely private. The state could no longer remain disinterested." Twentieth-century economic and political administration emphasized several characteristics, including a centralized, permanent bureaucracy staffed by skilled experts, and a commitment to long-range, comprehensive planning. These served as goals for many political reformers during the late nineteenth and early twentieth centuries. Thus, if seeking the origins of modern municipal administration, especially if searching for the beginnings of so-called "comprehensive" city planning, scholars can do no better than to explore competing technological systems and ideas in cities over the last half of the nineteenth century. Sewers become important after all.[3]

Of the many crises confronting nineteenth-century urbanites, none loomed more obvious or important than environmental pollution. Unpaved or poorly paved streets, inefficient or nonexistent collection of garbage, excrement from thousands of horses, the sooty dust from small manufacturing establishments—these and other problems threatened the physical comfort and safety of most urban Americans by midcentury. Successive cholera, typhoid, and diphtheria epidemics claimed the lives of thousands. With each epidemic city fathers established and then folded public boards of health, but made no permanent effort to enforce standards of hygiene until after 1866, when New York's newly formed Metropolitan Board of Health served as a model. As late as 1850, only New York City, Boston, Chicago, and Philadelphia had even semiadequate public water supplies. Integrated sewer systems were unknown; at best, cities depended upon a few private sewers or a few large storm sewers built only in part by tax monies. Add to those conditions the increasing density of urban populations and the pressures on the existent stock of housing, and who could have quibbled with the Massachusetts sanitary surveyors in 1850: "It has been ascertained that the inhabitants of densely populated places generally deteriorate in vitality. . . . This is a significant fact, which should be generally known. Cities are not necessarily unhealthy, but circumstances are permitted to exist, which make them so."[4]

To understand why citizens permitted such circumstances to exist, the structure of antebellum municipal government must be explored. During the late eighteenth and early nineteenth centuries the tasks of municipal administration began to shift from the exclusive promotion and regulation of trade to a more general concern for residents' well-being. By the eve of the Civil War, most city governments still more closely resembled their medieval predecessors than today's city administrations. State legislators saw cities principally as sources of patronage. Mayors were figureheads. Common councils exercised quasi-executive, quasi-judicial authority. Individual aldermen often retained control over most expenditures in their own wards. City employees such as policemen came into and left office in the revolving door of each election. Real estate speculators generally controlled land-use decisions and almost alone anticipated future growth; their major goal was to subdivide land to maximize short-run profits. Because of their traditional mistrust of centralized government, Americans usually turned to the local ward politicians or even to private groups or individuals for such vital urban services as water supply, street sanitation, and even fire protection. With the power to govern scattered in bits and pieces among a bewildering variety of offices, boards, and commissions, in effect no one governed.[5]

Changes in scientific knowledge and popular ideas about illness and death around the middle of the century fostered new perceptions of the urban environmental crisis. Many citizens, of course, still wanted to blame human frailty for the unhealthy conditions of the cities, and found convenient scapegoats in the growing numbers of native poor and foreign immigrants in their midst. But careful investigators of the cities' plight—such as physicians, sanitary surveyors, landscape architects, and civil engineers—began to identify other sources of urban ills. However much human attitudes and habits appeared at fault, the problems of environmental pollution were physical. Their solution would be physical and technological as well—or so an increasing number of urban Americans came to believe over the last half of the century.[6]

City officials had long appreciated the importance of adequate water supplies. Fear of epidemics and fires, coupled with the pollution of wells by seepage from graves and privies, forced city fathers to tap new sources and often to bring in water from outside municipal boundaries. Philadelphia built a public waterworks system in the 1790s. New York, Boston, and a few other large cities followed suit some forty years later. Various physicians and public health reformers advertised the sanitary reasons to provide not only water, but pure water. But who should construct and administer the new systems, the private sector or government? Until the 1850s most cities relied upon private firms, but in most cases the private efforts failed technically and economically, especially in the largest cities. Few private entrepreneurs or corporations had the capital, the condemnation power, the concern for public health, or the economic will to build and maintain water supply systems that would serve the entire public. Concerned about profits, few private companies proved to be willing to serve poorer people from whom they could expect meager revenues. Thus, municipal ownership and administration gained slowly between the 1860s and the 1890s. By the turn of the century, however, only nine of the fifty largest cities still had privately owned water supplies. By 1910, more than 70 percent of cities over 30,000 population owned their waterworks. Over the last half of the century, city officials discerned sanitary, technological, and political reasons to provide this service at municipal expense and under municipal control.[7]

The addition of adequate water did not end environmental pollution. To some extent, it increased it, for now cities had to dispose of vast quantities of water brought in by the new aqueducts. Existent surface drainage was inadequate. The new water closets of the 1860s and 1870s overflowed the old privy waste disposal systems, soaked the urban water tables, and converted large portions of city land and streets into a stinking morass. Once again the solution was physical and technical. During the 1870s and 1880s, city leaders undertook expensive programs of sewer building. They also began massive paving programs to improve drainage and to cover the wastewater-saturated soil of urban streets. The engineers who shepherded these projects emphasized their sanitary functions nearly as much as their traffic-bearing functions.[8]

There was little doubt in the minds of many sanitarians, physicians, and engineers that a good sewer system meant investment in the present and future health of the citizenry. In Chicago during the mid-1850s, for example, Ellis S. Chesbrough, chief engineer of the first sewerage commission, was so persuasive that the city expended in excess of $10,000,000 to construct nearly fifty-four miles of sewers and to raise the grade of the street for drainage purposes by as much as twelve feet in the emerging central business district. John Bell, a Philadelphia physician reporting in 1859 for a committee on the internal hygiene of cities, argued that "paving ought to precede the erection of houses, and drainage follow habitation at a very early period. A neglect of these two preliminary conditions for public health has been productive, in all ages, of a fearful waste of life." By the late 1870s, George E. Waring, Jr., perhaps the most influential sanitary engineer of the late nineteenth century, vividly stated the relationship between sewers and health. Speaking of the old sewers of New York and Boston, Waring charged that they were "highest at the lower end, lowest in the middle, biggest at the little end, receiving branch sewers from below, and discharging at their tops; elongated cesspools, half-filled with reeking filth, peopled [sic] with rats, and invaded by every tide." He labeled such sewers "huge gasometers, manufacturing day and night a deadly aeriform poison, ever seeking to invade the houses along their course; reservoirs of liquid filth, ever oozing through the defective joints, and polluting the very earth upon which the city stands."[9]

Waring was a leading proponent of the sewer gas theory of disease, the notion that decaying organic matter, such as human and other animal wastes, exuded an odorless gas that caused innumerable infectious and noninfectious illnesses. Although widely debated, the idea was accepted by many involved in the public health movement. Engineering periodicals often supported the theory and offered technical schemes for preventing the escape of the gas. Not until the triumph of the germ theory of disease during the 1890s and early 1900s did the sewer gas theory completely evaporate.[10]

The discovery during the 1880s that many diseases, especially the killer typhoid, were waterborne accelerated campaigns for pure water, for sewer construction, and for the filtration of both water and sewage. In 1890 only twenty-six cities among those of 10,000 population or more had no sewers at all. By 1907, nearly every city in the nation had sewers. The filtration of water and sewage brought a dramatic drop in typhoid mortality rates, a drop that averaged 65 percent in selected major cities. The sewer gas theory, then, together with other theories and medical discoveries, lent weight to the arguments favoring technological solutions to public health problems.[11]

The lessons were clear. Water and sewer systems were a city's lifelines. As such, they were too vital to be left to either the good intentions or the caprices of private enterprises alone. On this point the opinion of the Massachusetts Drainage Commission of 1884–85 was firm and typical of attitudes developing in a number of cities and states. The commission recommended that "the supervision of matters pertaining to water supply, sewerage, and the pollution of waters generally, be assigned to some board . . . to enable it to introduce system and method in these important departments of the common welfare." Municipal construction and control of water and wastewater systems grew so in public acceptance over the last three decades of the century that by 1910 the standard text on urban public health, *Municipal Sanitation in the United States* by Charles V. Chapin, could state succinctly: "Even the need for sewers has scarcely to be urged by health officers. The public so well appreciates their advantages that they are usually demanded when needed, even if they must be entirely paid for by the abutters." Chapin also pointed out that cities rarely called upon health officers to advise about sewer construction. "In recent times," he noted, "since sewers have been constructed by the municipality and with engineering advice, details have been wisely left to the engineers.[12]

By "wisely" leaving the matter to engineers, city administrators accomplished at least three results. First, they recognized and supported the growth of a new profession in the United States—municipal engineering. Second, they set in motion processes that ultimately would help restructure the organization of urban governments. Third, local administrations and the public at large implicitly came to accept the concept of comprehensive city planning, if not always the actual practice. From city-wide water and sewer systems to plans for every feature of the urban physical environment was but a short step of the imagination. A major engineering journal developed this logic in 1877:

> If the grading, drainage, paving, cleansing, and policing of towns are worthy of careful and systematic control, so are also the general shaping of the towns, the preservation or destruction of the natural features of their sites, and the distribution of their population and residence. Just what are the proper limits of public interference in such matters is a political question upon which we cannot venture; but public neglect has shown itself to be both costly and pernicious.

An examination of their part in reshaping the urban physical environment will underscore the importance of engineers to governmental reorganization and to city planning.[13]

Engineers did not raise solitary voices in calling for physical solutions to environmental problems. Sanitarians, landscape architects, and engineers formed a troika that tried to pull citizens and officials alike from the mire of governmental inaction to the higher ground of municipal planning and administration. Over the last half of the nineteenth century, urban public health officers assessed the spatial distribution of diseases, using the survey techniques of the engineers. Sanitarians supported municipal regulation of food, of air pollution, and of housing. They urged the rapid construction of water and sewer systems, rapid transit systems, and parks. But rarely, except in times of epidemics, did public health officers exert influence over most matters of municipal policy and administration. Landscape architects such as Frederick Law Olmsted, George Kessler, and Horace Shaler Cleveland—each of whom had some engineering training—propagandized planning concepts. Usually their physical solutions to health problems rested upon the construction of large urban parks as "lungs" for the city or upon the creation of upper-class suburbs as escape valves for the fortunate few. Occasionally their ideas roamed farther afield. Olmsted proposed parkways (even coining the term) as not only transportation arteries, recreational areas, and pollution shields for urban watercourses, but also as hubs of comprehensively planned communities. He was an early advocate of restrictive covenants to regulate housing developments. Still, with few exceptions, the landscape architects contributed little to the reformulation of public policy or to changes in the administrative reach and authority of municipal governments. Although the troika often worked together, exchanged ideas, and supported similar goals, the municipal engineers were the most influential group.[14]

The functions of modern municipal administration were inherent in water and wastewater technology. Sewer and water supplies required permanent construction; hence they necessitated long-range planning. If engineers did not plan systems to accommodate future growth, the city would have to lay new aqueducts and trunk sewers each time the population increased even slightly. City officials learned that acquiring new sources of water or reconstructing sewer systems considerably increased costs over the long run. They also learned that if they ignored the use of experts in the construction and administration of sewer systems, disastrous health and financial consequences resulted. In the early 1870s, for example, Alexander Shepherd, boss of the District of Columbia, wasted a $5,000,000 bond issue when contractors hired for political rather than engineering reasons built lateral sewers that ran uphill into the main sewers. Partly because of this fiasco, the District lost home rule to a federally appointed commission which had to include at least one officer of the Army Corps of Engineers. St. Louis had to reconstruct its water supply and Cincinnati its sewer system within ten years after completion; both city administrations had rejected engineers' proposals in favor of politically popular decisions to cut costs. Hazen Pingree, Detroit's reform mayor during the 1890s, complained bitterly about politics having been more important than engineering in the construction of the sewer system when its concrete pipes began to crumble into dust during his regime. Of all major cities, Baltimore delayed longest in building a sewer system. The city paid for that folly with one of the two highest typhoid death rates in the nation. Not until 1905–06 did the city fathers begin to modernize and centralize the sewers under public control.[15]

Sewer and water systems required centralized administration. There were economies of scale in building only one reservoir and one main aqueduct. An integrated sewer system with a trunk sewer at the lowest grade level and an outfall at a site that minimized pollution problems also considerably reduced costs. Thus, the new technology necessitated a permanent bureaucracy to acquire land, oversee construction, administer on a day-by-day basis, and to plan for long-term needs. The public works could be built most efficiently by technological and managerial experts who could survey the topography, choose appropriate construction materials, and draw readily upon the experiences of their counterparts in other cities.

Engineers and their projects served to centralize metropolitan administration of problems common to areas larger than the central core city. Topography ignored municipal boundaries. An efficient sewer system that followed natural gradients to achieve a gravity flow usually violated a city's political limits. The dumping of one community's sewage might and often did pollute the system of a neighboring community. Newark, for instance, drew its water supply from the Passaic River at a point below the sewer outflows of Paterson and Passaic. Mill towns in the Merrimac Valley were notorious for fouling one another's water supplies. To combat pollution in such locales the engineering press began urging regional cooperation in water and sewer services during the early 1870s. Although there were earlier isolated examples of such metropolitan "authorities," usually public health boards and park planning commissions, permanent administrative bodies seem to have arisen in the late 1880s and early 1890s in response to pollution problems. City officials gained state legislative approval to create metropolitan water and sewer districts such as Boston's Metropolitan Sewage Commission (1889), and similar districts in Chicago, the Passaic Valley, and elsewhere. Municipal governments vested authority for such extramunicipal projects in their city engineer's office. By the early 1890s, also, engineers in a few cities had obtained the power to approve plats in areas beyond city limits to ensure that subdividers used street plans that would facilitate travel and accommodate the installation of subsurface utilities. In some cities engineers could abate nuisances beyond city limits, thus gaining authority to protect watersheds and to engage in an early form of housing regulation as well.[16]

Engineers also contributed to the rationalization of fiscal techniques. Recurrently throughout the 1880s and 1890s articles in the engineering press outlined the organization and division of responsibility within engineering offices, provided model forms for paperwork, and suggested standardized systems for monitoring costs. Before organizations like the National Conference for Good City Government and the National Municipal League published data on tax and budgetary policies, the engineering press identified most of the major issues and shaped the framework for discussion.[17]

Labeling themselves neutral experts, engineers professed to work above the din of local politics. Usually they tried to isolate themselves from partisan wrangles, and often succeeded. In the creation of administrative bureaucracies, engineers apparently were the earliest municipal officials to achieve anything like job security. Chesbrough, chief engineer of the Chicago Board of Sewerage, 1855–61, served as that community's first city engineer from 1861–79, an extraordinary career at a time when most municipal jobs changed hands with every election. Others had equally long terms. E. P. North, director of the Croton Water Works for New York City; Robert Moore, municipal engineer of St. Louis; and, George Benzenberg, city engineer of Milwaukee, all had twenty years of continuous service before 1900. Cost savings, of course, resulted from retention of an engineer familiar with the local system. In some jurisdictions, courts reinforced this tendency by declaring that engineers held title to whatever plans they made. A city that fired its engineer might lose the blueprint to its sewer system with his departure.[18] Still, longevity in office for engineers stemmed from more than simple cost considerations. Their

political caution, growing stature as problem solvers, and their professionalization all worked to the engineers' advantage.

Civil service reformers repeatedly praised engineers as models of efficient
bureaucrats. Reform literature often cited the District of Columbia, largely
administered by the Army Corps of Engineers, as an excellent example of
good government. European cities with autonomous engineer-administrators,
usually military officers like Baron Georges E. Haussmann in Paris, also
garnered plaudits from the reformers. Thus, engineers were among the earliest
municipal employees to receive civil service protection, in most cases a *de jure*
recognition of a *de facto* situation.[19]

Operating in a cosmopolitan, not a local, context, engineers were as much
responsive to their professional peers as to local pressures. They institutionalized the role of the consultant. Some, like Waring or Rudolph Hering, the
two most prominent sanitary engineers of the period, worked only as consultants, moving from one city to another. Others, like Chesbrough, Benzenberg, Moses Lane of Milwaukee, Joseph P. Davis of Boston, and Colonel
Julius W. Adams of Brooklyn were home based but traveled widely to consult
on major projects in other cities. The consultant role was a measure of the
status of engineers and of their independence from partisan politics. Nineteenth-
century city leaders viewed their communities in keen competition with others
for economic growth and population. A reputation for excellence in public
works and health served local boosters well in the wars of urban imperialism.
Yet, various city engineers were so important as in-house experts that local
politicians could not deny them the opportunity of advising hated rival cities.

As an emerging "strategic elite," in sociologist Suzanne Keller's telling
phrase, engineers secured job tenure through professionalization.[20] At a time
when few if any clearinghouses for the exchange of ideas and practices benefited cities nationwide, the engineers built up a remarkable communications
network among themselves. Their common training, whether in the relatively
few engineering schools of the period or in shared apprenticeships, usually
on the major railroads, bound them together. The practice of review by outside
consultants reinforced these connections. Engineers belonged to the same
national organizations. The majority held membership in the American Society of Civil Engineers that frequently published papers on municipal engineering with appended comments from experts throughout the nation. They
also belonged to local professional clubs that corresponded with one another,
publishing and exchanging reports about conditions in their individual cities.
Numerous professional journals provided forums for discussion and debate.
During the late 1870s and again in the late 1880s the most prestigious of
these journals, the *Engineering News*, printed lengthy series comparing cities
around the country. Reports described water supply, sewerage, streets, parks,
housing design, transportation terminals, and other elements of municipal
planning. They dealt also with administrative and legal questions, subjects
on which some engineers had special competence. Of active civil engineers
born before 1820, almost 28 percent underwent legal training in addition to
their technological training. The engineering press also published reports on
European developments, paying particular attention to the important research
trips abroad of Chesbrough and Hering. Finally, in 1894, the professionals

involved principally with urban problems formed their own national organization, the American Society for Municipal Improvements.[21]

The engineers, then, were well aware of each other's activities, in contact with innovation in their profession, alert to employment opportunities throughout the nation, and not bound to the petty squabbles of local politics. Decades before early twentieth-century political reformers depicted their ideal administrator, municipal engineers embodied all the administrator's attractive characteristics—efficiency, expertise, and an allegedly disinterested, incorruptible professionalism.

Over the last half of the nineteenth century, engineers often demonstrated the value of long-range planning to municipal administration. Not only did the profession offer solutions to physical problems such as water and sewer supply, but it also contributed comprehensive planning schemes that repeatedly illustrated the interaction of technology with the social, economic, and political structure of cities. Planning ideas that evolved from the construction of water supply and sewer systems between the 1850s and the 1890s presaged the later city plans of men such as Nolen, Daniel Burnham, George B. Ford, and others. In many respects the engineers' proposals surveyed the physical city more thoroughly than did the plans of the early twentieth century. Certainly the engineers, and their colleagues the landscape architects and the sanitarians, generally showed a deeper understanding of the health needs of the populace than did many planners after the turn of the century.

The engineering press propagated the ideas of the sanitarians. *Van Nostrand's Engineering Magazine*, for instance, reprinted in 1876 a utopian scheme of the British sanitarian B. W. Richardson. "Hygeia—A City of Health" outlined the elements of climate, site selection, water supply, sewerage, street layout, park system, and housing design that together could reduce mortality figures and transform the city into an ideal environment. The Chicago sanitarian J. M. Gregory told the Chicago Medical Society, in a speech promptly reprinted by *Engineering News*, that "a great city is a vast laboratory, in which the energies imported in the food supplies and stored in the atmosphere are transmitted into human life, or rather, into thousands of human lives, but which are momentarily and perpetually exposed to that further transmutation which crumbles organized being back to its chemical elements." Waring presented his utopian view of "New York, A.D., 1997—A Prophecy," predicting the city of the future built upon the solid foundations of well-designed transportation, adequate water and sewer systems, the use of electrical power, streets rid of the filth of horses and other domestic animals, universal public education, and efficient government freed of bossism and political corruption. Engineers, accustomed to thinking about unified systems, joined with sanitarians in viewing the city as an ecosystem, a vast, integrated unit with the efficient functioning of one part dependent upon the efficient functioning of all the parts.[22]

Comprehensive planning meant nothing more nor less than focusing attention on all the interconnected parts of the urban system. A good example of this vision was the work prepared by the Engineer's Club of Philadelphia during the early 1880s. Lewis Haupt, an influential engineering professor at the University of Pennsylvania, presented a number of papers on street layout and the need for rapid transit. In form and recommendations, these proposals resembled but antedated the Progressive era transit and traffic surveys by engineer Bion Arnold and the consultant firm of Kelker, De Leuw. Haupt even tried to devise a method to forecast future population growth. Hering, then resident in Philadelphia, gave a paper on "The Future Sewerage Requirements of Philadelphia" that saw the city as a sprawling but integrated unit. Other papers dealt with housing regulation, water supply, and bridge and harbor improvement. All the papers emphasized the necessity of comprehensive physical planning. Throughout the 1880s and the following decade, other local engineering clubs in St. Louis, Chicago, Cleveland, Kansas City, and elsewhere, prepared similar reports. Most reports stressed the engineers' role as planners and managers in sentiments like these expressed in 1894:

> The city engineer is to the city very much what the family physician is to the family. He is constantly called upon to advise and direct in all matters pertaining to his profession. . . . He does know the character, constitution, particular needs and idiosyncrasies of the city, as the family physician knows the constitutions of the family. . . . The city engineer is becoming the most important director of the material development of cities, and his office is becoming more and more a permanent one. He is thus to a certain extent responsible for holding the successive political officials to a consistent, progressive policy in all the branches of work under his charge. To him, even more than to the successive mayors, falls the duty of serving as the intelligence and brains of the municipal government in all physical matters.[23]

Engineers began promoting their "physician" role as early as the 1850s. During the immediate post-Civil War years a number of broad-ranging plans embodying the comprehensive viewpoint appeared. City fathers implemented some, others remained part of a paper brigade. Two examples—the development of Boston's Back Bay and a partially aborted plan for the Bronx—illustrated the scope of the planners' vision.

For two decades following the late 1850s, Boston undertook a massive landfill operation and development project for its Back Bay area. Other historians have recounted the full story, but for present purposes several elements should be highlighted.[24] The city used restrictive covenants in deeds for lots on the newly filled land to establish common house setbacks, to impose height restrictions, and to limit nonresidential use of land—in other words, an early effort at zoning.[25] The entire area pivoted around a principal traffic artery, Commonwealth Avenue. On the model of European boulevards, the artery included a strip of park down the middle. Land-use restrictions and the boulevard served both to enhance the attractiveness of the area and to diminish the quantities of sewer gas and other miasmic materials in the air and thus, by contemporary standards, to ensure physical health. Boston also undertook a major reconstruction of its sewer system so that wastes drained into the South Bay rather than filling the more stagnant waters of the Back Bay. The city forced railroad lines to relocate from the Back Bay to a freight yard on newly filled land in the South Bay, thereby turning that district into an attractive site for industrial activities.

While the Back Bay project continued, an enterprising landscape architect, Robert Morris Copeland, seized the opportunity to advance a comprehensive plan for redoing all of Boston. "We have supposed that, for some unnamed reason," Copeland observed, "planning for a city's growth and progress could only be done as it grows; . . . this is a fallacious belief." Directly confronting the tradition of unfettered individualism in American cities, he argued that the best way to protect private property rights was to plan carefully for the future. Boston's physical, economic, and social wants could be "digested for its future progress" by dividing the city into parts and by measuring the relationship of each of the parts to the whole. "The city whose area is carefully studied, which shows by plans where wharves may be built, where new avenues are to be laid out, and where factories may congregate; where parks, gardens, and palaces, if desired, may be made, will grow," Copeland predicted, "in a sure, orderly, and progressive way." He was certain that thoughtful engineering would satisfy all the city's needs: "merchandise can be easily transported, business done, water and gas supplied, amusements furnished, fires limited, and sewage provided for." Although the primary emphasis of his plan was to assure the rational conduct of business as vital to the strength of the community, Copeland demonstrated an understanding of the city as organism—a concept similar to that held by engineers. "A city or town," he affirmed, "is to be considered as a whole, and in relation to all of its wants, as well as its necessities." Boston did not adopt Copeland's plan. Still, he contributed significantly to the continuing public discussion over comprehensive planning for the urban future. Certainly his plan, in connection with the Back Bay project, taught Bostonians the importance of conceiving the city as a whole greater than the sum of its parts.[26]

Later, in the 1880s, when engineers and builders had finished most of the Back Bay development, the city sought to complete the project with yet another engineering scheme. To reduce further pollution of the bay and to provide additional recreational and health amenities, the city hired Olmsted to lay out a park system (the Back Bay Fens) along the Muddy River that drained into the bay. This carefully engineered project was an example of intelligent planning that sparked enthusiasm for similar actions in other cities.[27]

Between 1865 and 1877, John J. R. Croes, a civil engineer, and Olmsted surveyed and prepared a thorough plan for a portion of territory in the Bronx recently annexed to New York City. Charged with the responsibility of planning a street system and a rapid transit steam railroad to connect the annexed wards to the city, Croes and Olmsted instead proposed comprehensive development of the area as a suburb before any property could be sold to residents. Implicitly, their design argued for thorough planning of all the undeveloped areas that one day would comprise Greater New York City.

The Croes-Olmsted plans, presented in three reports, called for the development of a central business district bordered by a residential section on the high ground around the center of the area, with suburban homes on the northern and western edges. They offered street patterns that would provide drainage by gravity, thereby lessening the costs of subsurface water and sewer facilities. They urged construction of wide north-south avenues along valley bottoms and the tops of the ridges that dominated the topography of the Bronx. These avenues would cover water and sewer lines and also accommodate elevated railroads built up the middle, with consequent minimum disturbance to the surrounding environment. Parkways through proposed linear parks that would protect creeks and the Bronx River from pollution also would facilitate travel to the downtown. The most scenic lands in the area would be preserved for recreational and health purposes. Croes and Olmsted suggested granting of extramunicipal powers to city engineers to abate nuisances in the Westchester County headwaters of Bronx streams. Thus, the city could prevent industrial location along the small, slowly flowing waterways and ensure the area's healthfulness.

Throughout their reports the two planners minimized private development decisions and elevated the role of the public agency, in this case the Board of Commissioners of Public Parks, in comprehensive planning. But the desires of the board and of real estate speculators to populate the area quickly by the traditional means of private development won the day. Nuisance abatements, restrictive covenants as a land-use and housing control, and thorough planning before settlement were too radical to please the special interest groups involved. Croes and Olmsted lost their battle.[28]

While nothing as comprehensive as the Back Bay development or the Bronx plan appeared again in the United States until after the turn of the new century, bits and pieces of these plans did recur elsewhere. By 1900, Chicago, Kansas City, and Buffalo, among others, had built or at least had begun multipurpose park systems that went far beyond the mere provision of recreational land usage. All of these plans protected streams and rivers from inordinate industrial pollution; all provided new transportation systems that improved travel conditions in and about the city; all promised solutions to the public health problems of the cities; and all projected the improvement of housing facilities for large numbers of the urban population.[29]

The last half of the nineteenth century thus saw remarkable innovations in technology, municipal administration, and city planning. Virtually the only problems successfully attacked by nineteenth-century urban leaders were those susceptible to engineering expertise. Cities dramatically lowered their disease and mortality rates with the construction of efficient water supply and sewage systems. The administrative techniques of engineers, and their reputations as problem solvers, carried great prestige into the early years of the twentieth century. Within their specialized functions, engineers had developed centralized agencies capable of long-range, comprehensive planning and staffed by cosmopolitan experts. They also had advocated, with some success, the extension of their brand of organization to municipal administration as a whole. Albert F. Noyes, one of the leading city engineers of the period, echoed conventional wisdom among his colleagues in 1894 when he noted that "the office of the municipal engineer is of the greatest importance to the community. . . . In fact, the city government of today is in a large measure a matter of municipal engineering, and the character of the city engineer's department is a safe index to the intelligence shown in the development of a municipality."[30]

That city engineers trumpeted their own importance was not surprising. The core of professionalism is the assertion of knowledge and skills available only to in-group members. Although little contradictory evidence exists (and a great amount in support), the engineers' claims of political neutrality may be suspect. Surely their growing importance as managers of the physical city involved them intimately with elected officials and posed potential abuses of power similar to those associated with Robert Moses in twentieth-century

New York City.[31] But, one fact is certain. Many political reformers of the early twentieth century found themselves in agreement with the opinions of Noyes and other engineers. In both process and personnel, various changes in the structure of municipal government during the Progressive era drew heavily on the technological and administrative skills exhibited by engineers over the last half of the nineteenth century. The cumulative impact of the engineers' contributions helped to create two new professions in early twentieth-century America—city planners and city managers. Both substantially altered the administrative functions and reach of municipal government.[32]

The role of engineers in the emerging profession of city planning was considerable. Nelson P. Lewis, author of one of the earliest city planning texts, dedicated his 1916 volume "To the Municipal Engineers of the United States, the first men on the ground in City Planning as in City Building." Of the fifty-two charter members of the American Institute of Planning (AIP) in 1917 (then the American City Planning Institute), thirteen were engineers. Only the landscape architecture profession provided more members, and several of them had some engineering training. In that same year the American Institute of Architects published a nationwide survey, *City Planning Progress*, in which the editors noted that "the Committee has laid particular stress on the economic and engineering side of city planning, because it believes that that is fundamental to progress." The newly formed AIP included the individuals, principally the engineers and the landscape architects, who had prepared most of the city plans advanced since 1905. Mel Scott, the plutarch of the planning profession, observed that during the 1920s most smaller cities still delegated responsibility for planning to their city engineer's office. With the solitary exception of Delos Wilcox, a political reformer, engineers dominated the most important of the new planning specialties, transportation planning.[33]

While engineers played a central part in the growth of the city planning profession, their direct contributions to the restructuring of municipal governments during the early years of the twentieth century were even more impressive. However much reformers disagreed about specifics of structural change, they agreed that the proper direction lay in the professionalization and bureaucratization of government. No political change better reflected the emphasis on efficiency and the demands for accountability so characteristic of progressive structural reform than the managerial revolution in urban governments.

The new city manager form of government, as attested by the National Municipal League in 1913, promised administrative unity, clear lines of responsibility, expertise in the head of the administration, and discipline and harmony among the ranks of government servants. By 1919, the league incorporated the position of city manager into its model charter for urban governmental reform. The new professionals brought administrative expertise, a taste for bureaucracy, and the battle cry of "efficiency" to the management of scores of small and middle-sized cities over the first few decades of the twentieth century.[34]

A profile of members of the new profession revealed commonality of backgrounds. The first city managers of Staunton, Virginia, and Dayton, Ohio, the initial laboratories of the experiment, were both practicing civil engineers. H. M. Waite, who took up his Dayton post in 1914, came directly from a highly successful career as city engineer of Cincinnati. The 1919 *Yearbook* of the City Managers' Association showed that 48 percent of the total membership were engineers. In 1920, a survey of California city managers stated that of the twenty-one listing their backgrounds, thirteen were engineers. Surveys taken during the 1920s and 1930s demonstrated that less than 3 percent of all managers who graduated from college had majored in public administration or political science, the disciplines one might expect to have provided the best education for an administrator. Of those with B.A. degrees, 75 percent had trained as engineers. By the time the "typical" manager assumed his job, he had engaged in some engineering work and had held one or more posts in government, usually as a department head. As late as 1940, a major survey related that more than 63 percent of city managers over the previous twenty-five years had trained as engineers.[35]

Historians interested in tracing the strands of continuity in municipal government should find fascinating the engineering backgrounds of city managers. This new profession, which many contemporaries considered the high-water mark of progressive reforms in municipal administration, recruited primarily from another profession that long since had proved its central importance to the orderly functioning of cities. During the half century preceding the Progressive era, the job of municipal engineer developed into a profession that reshaped the physical landscape of urban America. But, of equal significance, it provided a corps of experienced experts and a model of administrative skill that latter-day progressives would use as a basis for the structural reform of urban government.

Behind the political reforms of the progressive years lay decades of technological changes in the physical growth patterns of American cities. The increasingly complex metropolitan environment of the last half of the nineteenth century had deepened the awareness of urbanites about the role of technology in the comfort, health, and order of their daily lives. That awareness in turn helped foster new conceptions of the role of government in serving the expectations of the citizenry. Just as the physical problems of the expanding cities had called forth a new profession of experts to provide solutions, so did the political administrative problems require a new profession of skilled managers.

In both the technological and the political arenas, municipal engineers played an increasingly important part. They stamped their long-range visions of metropolitan planning on the public consciousness over the last half of the nineteenth century. Their successful demands for political autonomy in solving the physical problems of the cities contributed to the ultimate insistence for efficient government run by skilled professionals. At the heart of physical and political changes in the administration of American cities, indeed at the very core of city planning, stood the work of the municipal engineers.

NOTES

[1]Baltimore *Sun*, April 24, 1905; John Nolen, "City Making," *The American City*, I (Sept. 1909), 19.
[2]The best summary of reformers' demands was by Frederic C. Howe, *The City: The Hope of Democracy* (New York, 1906).

[3]Jacques Ellul, *The Technological Society* (New York, 1964), 234, 3–13, 171–83, 229–39. See also R. J. Forbes, *The Conquest of Nature: Technology and Its Consequences* (New York, 1968) and Herbert J. Muller, "The Social Environment: The City," *The Children of Frankenstein: A Primer on Modern Technology and Human Values* (Bloomington, Ind., 1970), 258–77.

[4]*Report of a General Plan for the Promotion of Public and Personal Health, Devised, Prepared and Recommended by the Commissioners Appointed Under a Resolve of the Legislature of Massachusetts, Relating to a Sanitary Survey of the State* (Boston, 1850), 153–54. On pollution and attempts to deal with it, see Lawrence H. Larsen, "Nineteenth-Century Street Sanitation: A Study of Filth and Frustration," *Wisconsin Magazine of History*, 52 (Spring 1969), 239–47; Martin V. Melosi, "'Out of Sight, Out of Mind': The Environment and Disposal of Municipal Refuse, 1860–1920," *The Historian*, XXXV (Aug. 1973), 621–40; Joel A. Tarr, "Urban Pollution—Many Long Years Ago," *American Heritage*, XXII (Oct. 1971), 65–69, 106; Nelson Manfred Blake, *Water for the Cities* (Syracuse, 1956). On public health boards see, among others, Barbara Gutman Rosenkrantz, *Public Health and the State: Changing Views in Massachusetts, 1842–1936* (Cambridge, 1972) and John Duffy, *A History of Public Health in New York City, 1625–1866* (New York, 1968).

[5]Jon C. Teaford, *The Municipal Revolution in America: Origins of Modern Urban Government, 1650–1825* (Chicago, 1975), 47–110; Sam Bass Warner, Jr., *The Private City: Philadelphia in Three Periods of Its Growth* (Philadelphia, 1968), 49–157; Seymour J. Mandelbaum, *Boss Tweed's New York* (New York, 1965); Ernest S. Griffith, *A History of American City Government: The Conspicuous Failure, 1870–1900* (New York, 1974), 52–62.

[6]See, for example, Charles E. Rosenberg, *The Cholera Years: The United States in 1832, 1849 and 1866* (Chicago, 1962); George Rosen, *A History of Public Health* (New York, 1958), 237–46; Stanley K. Schultz, *The Culture Factory: Boston Public Schools, 1789–1860* (New York, 1973), 92–100, 209–51; and, for an apology about immigrants' part in fostering disease, absolving them and blaming instead the physical environment, see J. G. Pinkham, *The Sanitary Condition of Lynn, Including a Special Report on Diphtheria* (Boston, 1877), 58.

[7]Blake, *Water for the Cities*; M. N. Baker, ed., *The Manual of American Water Works* (New York, 1897); Samuel W. Abbott, *Past and Present Condition of Public Hygiene and State Medicine in the United States* (Boston, 1900); C.-E. A. Winslow, *The Evolution and Significance of the Modern Public Health Campaign* (New Haven, 1923), 38; J. J. Cosgrove, *History of Sanitation* (Pittsburgh, 1909), 87–88.

[8]Henry I. Bowditch, *Public Hygiene in America* (Boston, 1877), 103–04; "Early Sanitary History of Chicago, 1832–1874 and Sketch of the Early Drainage and Sewerage of Chicago 1847–1879," City of Chicago Municipal Reference Library, Frederick Rex, Librarian (n.p., n.d.); R. Isham Randolph, "A History of Sanitation in Chicago," *Journal of the Western Society of Engineers*, XLIV (Oct. 1939), 227–40; Samuel C. Busey, "History and Progress of Sanitation of the City of Washington and the Efforts of the Medical Profession in Relation Thereto," *The Sanitarian*, XLII (March, 1899), 205–16; Geo. W. Rafter and M. N. Baker, *Sewage Disposal in the United States* (New York, 1894), 169–86; Leonard Metcalf and Harrison P. Eddy, *American Sewerage Practice* (3 vols., New York, 1914), Vol. I: *Design of Sewers*; Richard Shelton Kirby and Philip Gustave Laurson, *The Early Years of Modern Civil Engineering* (New Haven, 1932), 185–239; Charles V. Chapin, *Municipal Sanitation in the United States* (Providence, 1901), 172–92; Henry B. Wood, "Street Work in Boston, As Applied to Brick Pavements, Filling Joints of Granite Pavements, Street Watering and Street Cleaning," *Association of Engineering Societies Journal*, XI (Aug. 1892), 427–38; and George W. Tillson, *Street Pavements and Paving Materials* (New York, 1901), 167. Joel Tarr and David Wojick of Carnegie-Mellon University made suggestions about the evolution and interdependence of water and wastewater systems.

[9]E. S. Chesbrough, *Report and Plan of Sewerage for the City of Chicago, Illinois* (Chicago, 1855); "Up from the Mud: An Account of how Chicago's Streets and Buildings were Raised," Workers of the Writer's Program, WPA in Illinois for Board of Education (Chicago, 1941); Louis P. Cain, "Raising and Watering a City: Ellis Sylvester Chesbrough and Chicago's First Sanitation System," *Technology and Culture*, 13 (July 1972), 353–72; and James C. O'Connell, "Chicago's Quest for Pure Water" (Washington, 1976). John Bell, *Report on the Importance and Economy of Sanitary Measures to Cities* (New York, 1859), 35; and George E. Waring, Jr., *House-Drainage and Sewerage* (Philadelphia, 1878), 11.

[10]James H. Cassedy, "The Flamboyant Colonel Waring: An Anti-Contagionist Holds the American Stage in the Age of Pasteur and Koch," *Bulletin of the History of Medicine*, XXXVI (March-April 1962), 163–76. Among numerous contemporary comments about the sewer gas theory, see G. E. Waring, Jr., *Earth Closets and Earth Sewage* (New York, 1870); C. W. Chamberlain, "Erysipelas and Sewer Gas," *Public Health*, I (Aug. 9, 1879), 81–82; John Lambert, "Sanitary Reform and Preventive Medicine," *ibid.*, I (Aug. 16, 1879), 97–101; Victor C. Vaughan, "Healthy Homes and Foods for the Working Classes," *American Public Health Association* (Concord, N.H., 1886), 15–18; and the graphic depiction, "Sewer Gas Poisoning," *Scientific American*, LXIII (Nov. 29, 1890), 344. On the triumph of the germ theory see Charles V. Chapin, "The End of the Filth Theory of Disease," *Popular Science Monthly*, LX (Jan. 1902), 234–39; Rosen, *History of Public Health*, 285–335; and Richard Shryock, "The Medical History of the American People," Richard Shryock, *Medicine in America* (Baltimore, 1966), 22–30.

[11]George C. Whipple, *Typhoid Fever, Its Causation, Transmission and Prevention* (New York, 1908); Frederic L. Hoffman, "American Mortality Progress," Mazÿck P. Ravenal, ed., *A Half Century of Public Health* (New York, 1921), 102; U.S. Bureau of the Census, *Financial Statistics of Cities Having a Population of Over 30,000: 1910* (Washington, 1913), 134–43; Cosgrove, *History of Sanitation*, 87–88; and Edward Meeker, "The Improving

Health of the United States, 1850–1915," *Explorations in Economic History*, 9 (Summer 1972), 366–73 and Table 6; Edward Meeker, "The Social Rate of Return on Investment in Public Health, 1880–1910," *Journal of Economic History*, XXXIV (June 1974), 392–421.

[12]"Report of the Massachusetts Drainage Commission, 1884–85," portion reproduced in Rafter and Baker, *Sewage Disposal*, 115; Chapin, *Municipal Sanitation*, 296–97.

[13]Raymond H. Merritt, *Engineering in American Society, 1850–1875* (Lexington, Ky., 1969), 136–76; and, for the pre-Civil War experience, Daniel Calhoun, *The American Civil Engineer: Origins and Conflict* (Cambridge, 1960). The quotation appeared in *Engineering News*, IV (July 7, 1877), 173.

[14]For discussion of the sanitarians, in addition to those works on public health cited above, see James H. Cassedy, *Charles V. Chapin and the Public Health Movement* (Cambridge, 1962); Wilson G. Smillie, *Public Health, Its Promise for the Future: A Chronicle of the Development of Public Health in the United States, 1607–1914* (New York, 1955); Duncan R. Jamieson, "Towards a Cleaner New York: John H. Griscom and New York's Public Health, 1830–1870" (doctoral dissertation, Michigan State University, 1971); and Jon A. Peterson, "The Impact of Sanitary Reform upon American Urban Planning, 1840–1890" (paper delivered at the Organization of American Historians meeting, St. Louis, April 9, 1976).

[15]Busey, "History and Progress of Sanitation of the City of Washington," 210–12; Constance McLaughlin Green, *Washington, Village, and Capital, 1800–1878* (Princeton, 1962), 241–60; M. L. Holman, "Historical Aspects of the St. Louis Water Works," *Journal of the American Engineering Society*, XIV (Jan. 1895), 1–9; A. L. Anderson, "The Sanitary Conditions of the Cincinnati Sewer," *Engineering News*, V (Nov. 14, 21, 1878), 324, 372; Arthur S. Hobby, "The Sewerage of Cincinnati," *ibid.*, V (Nov. 18, 1878), 377–78; Melvin G. Holli, *Reform in Detroit: Hazen S. Pingree and Urban Politics* (New York, 1969), 26–27; William Travis Howard, Jr., *Public Health Administration and the Natural History of Disease in Baltimore, Maryland, 1797–1920* (Washington, 1924); and James B. Crooks, *Politics & Progress: The Rise of Urban Progressivism in Baltimore, 1895 to 1911* (Baton Rouge, 1968), 132–36.

[16]Rafter and Baker, *Sewage Disposal*, 579–85; Commonwealth of Massachusetts, *Acts of 1889* (Boston, 1890), Chap. 439, and *First Annual Report of the Board of Metropolitan Sewerage Commissioners* (Boston, 1890); "Troy, N.Y.," *Engineering News*, IV (Nov. 3, 1877), 359–69. "The Better Water Supply of Northeastern New Jersey," *Engineering News and American Railway Journal*, XIX (March 24, 1888), 230–31. See also "Municipal Co-operation a Possible Substitute for Consolidation," *Engineering News*, XLI (Feb. 16, 1899), 104–06; Paul Studenski, *The Government of Municipal Areas in the United States* (New York, 1930), 33–34, 49–59, 105–13. On extra-municipal powers, see Nelson Tibbs, "The Sanitary Protection of the Watershed Supplying Water to Rochester, N.Y.," *Engineering News and American Railway Journal*, XIX (April 28, 1888), 531; Olmsted, Vaux & Co., *Report on the Parkway Proposed for the City of Brooklyn* (n.p., 1868); "How to Subdivide Land in Illinois," *The Engineer and Surveyor*, I (April 1874), 4; and Mel Scott, *American City Planning Since 1890* (Berkeley, 1969), 110–269.

[17]On the organization of offices in numerous cities, see, for example, *Journal of the Association of Engineering Societies* (March 1893) and the series that ran in *Engineering News* from Jan. 6, 1886, through Dec. 25, 1886.

[18]American Society of Civil Engineers, *A Biographical Dictionary of American Civil Engineers* (New York, 1972), 23–24; Calhoun, *American Civil Engineer*, 68–78.

[19]Charles W. Eliot, "One Remedy for Municipal Misgovernment," *Forum*, XII (Oct. 1891), 153–68; "Engineers as Commissioners of Public Works," *Engineering News and American Railway Journal*, XXXI (Feb. 1, 1894), 82. References to Washington include: John Ficklen, "The Municipal Condition of New Orleans," *Proceedings of the Second National Conference on Good City Government* (Dec. 8–10, 1894), and "Municipal Reports," *Municipal Engineering*, XVII (Jan. 1900), 56–58. On civil service protection see A. Marston and G. W. Miller, "The Methods of Choosing City Engineers," *Engineering Record*, XLVII (Dec. 21, 1903), 198–99.

[20]Elites "refers first of all to a minority of individuals designated to serve a collectivity in a socially valued way. . . . Socially significant elites are ultimately responsible for the realization of major social goals and for the continuity of the social order." Furthermore, "only certain leadership groups have a general and sustained social impact. . . . We refer to these groups as *strategic elites* . . . [who] comprise not only political, economic, and military leaders, but also moral, cultural, and scientific ones. Whether or not an elite is counted as strategic does not depend on its specific activities but on the scope of its activities, that is, on how many members of society it directly impinges upon and in what respects." Suzanne Keller, *Beyond the Ruling Class: Strategic Elites in Modern Society* (New York, 1963), 4, 20.

[21]For example, see "European Systems of Sewerage," *Engineering News*, IX (Jan. 28, 1882), 33–35; "Municipal and Sanitary Engineering in the City of London," *Engineering News and American Contract Journal*, XVI (Aug. 21, 28, 1886), 122–23, 134–35. Information on the legal training of engineers may be found in American Society of Civil Engineers. *Biographical Dictionary of American Civil Engineers*. For the E. S. Chesbrough and Rudolph Hering reports see E. S. Chesbrough, *Report of the Results of Examinations Made in Relation to Sewerage in Several European Cities, in the Winter of 1856–7* (Chicago, 1858) and Rudolph Hering, "Reports of an Examination Made in 1880 of Several Sewerage Works in Europe," *Annual Report of the National Board of Health, 1881* (Washington, 1882), 200–12.

[22]B. W. Richardson, "Modern Sanitary Science—A City of Health," *Van Nostrand's Eclectic Engineering Magazine*, XIV (Jan. 1876), 31–44. For a discussion of the issue, see James H. Cassedy, "Hygeia: A Mid-Victorian Dream of a City of Health," *Journal of the History of Medicine and Allied Sciences*, XVII (April 1962), 217–29. J. M. Gregory, "The Hygiene of Great Cities," *Engineering News*, VII (Jan. 10, 1880), 17; metaphors comparing the city to organisms or machines were frequent in the engineering press. George Waring's piece was published together with a biography in Albert Shaw, *Life of Col. Geo. E. Waring, Jr.: The Great Apostle of Cleanliness* (New York, 1899).

[23]L. M. Haupt, "Rapid Transit," *Proceedings of the Engineering Club of Philadelphia*, IV (Aug. 1884), 135–38, which appeared to be modeled on an 1875 survey of rapid transit undertaken by the American Society of Civil Engineers for New York City, published as "Rapid Transit and Terminal Freight Facilities," *ASCE Transactions*, IV (1875), 1–80. Lewis Haupt, "The Growth of Cities as Exemplified in Philadelphia," *Proceedings of the Engineering Club of Philadelphia*, IV (Aug. 1884), 148–75. Rudolph Hering, "Future Sewerage Requirements," *ibid.*, II (1880), 36–50. Similar reports from other cities included "St. Louis Boulevards in the Business District," *Journal of the Association of Engineering Societies*, XII (March 1894), 190; "Civil Engineering," *Engineering Magazine*, III (June 1892), 418–20; Robert Gilliam, "Work for Our Engineers' Club," *Journal of the Association of Engineering Societies*, XII (June 1893), 305–13. The quotation appeared in John C. Olmsted, "Relation of the City Engineer to Public Parks," *Journal of the Association of Engineering Societies*, XIII (Oct. 1894), 594–95.

[24]Walter Muir Whitehill, *Boston, A Topographical History* (Cambridge, 1968), 141–73; Norman T. Newton, *Design on the Land: The Development of Landscape Architecture* (Cambridge, 1971), 290–306; Lawrence J. Friedman, *A History of American Law* (New York, 1973), 397.

[25]For an excellent discussion of this process in another city, see Andrew J. King, "Law and Land Use in Chicago: A Prehistory of Modern Zoning" (doctoral dissertation, University of Wisconsin, 1976).

[26]Robert Morris Copeland, *The Most Beautiful City in America. Essay and Plan for the Improvement of the City of Boston* (Boston, 1872), 10–12. In some specifics, tone, and in comprehensive sweep, Robert M. Copeland's plan resembled the much earlier work of Robert Fleming Gourlay, *Plans for Beautifying New York, and for Enlarging and Improving the City of Boston. Being, Studies to Illustrate the Science of City Building* (Boston, 1844). Today, Robert Gourlay is nearly forgotten as a pioneering city planner. Walter Muir Whitehill mentions him, but the only "modern" studies that exist are Janet Carnochan, "Robert Gourlay," *Publications of the Niagara Historical Society*, No. 18 (1909), 35–47 and Fletcher Steele, "Robert Fleming Gourlay, City Planner," *Landscape Architecture*, VI (Oct. 1915), 1–14.

[27]Laura Wood Roper, *FLO: A Biography of Frederick Law Olmsted* (Baltimore, 1973), 385–88; Newton, *Design on the Land*, 290–94.

[28]The series of reports included *Preliminary Report of the Landscape Architect and the Civil and Topographical Engineer, upon the Laying Out of the Twenty-third and Twenty-fourth Wards*, and *Report of the Landscape Architect and the Civil Topographical Engineer, Accompanying a Plan for Laying out That Part of the Twenty-fourth Ward, Lying West of Riverdale Road* (New York, 1876); *Report of the Civil and Topographical Engineer and the Landscape Architect, Accompanying a Plan for Local Steam Transit Routes in the Twenty-third and Twenty-fourth Wards* (New York, 1877); and *Communication for the Landscape Architect and the Civil and Topographical Engineer, in Relation to the Proposed Plan for Laying out the Central District of the Twenty-third and Twenty-fourth Wards, Lying East of Jerome Avenue and West of Third Avenue and the Harlem Railroad* (New York, 1877). See also E. B. Van Winkle, "Drainage of the Twenty-third and Twenty-fourth Wards, This City," reprinted in *Engineering News*, VIII (Aug. 18, 20, 1881), 321–27, 337–49; S. S. Haight, "Surveying, Laying out and Monumenting the New Wards of New York," *Engineering News*, VIII (March 5, 1881), 96; Roper, *FLO*, 354–56; and Albert Fein, *Frederick Law Olmsted and the American Environmental Tradition* (New York, 1972), 50, 159, and fig. 78.

[29]Newton, *Design on the Land*, 307–36; and the voluminous collection of park planning reports in the Francis Loeb Library, Harvard School of Design (Cambridge).

[30]Albert F. Noyes, "Organization and Management of a City Engineer's Office," *Journal of the Association of Engineering Societies*, XIII (Oct. 1894), 541, 544.

[31]Robert A. Caro, *The Power Broker: Robert Moses and the Fall of New York* (New York, 1974).

[32]On the planning profession see Scott, *American City Planning*; Roy Lubove, *The Progressives and the Slums: Tenement House Reform in New York City, 1890–1917* (Pittsburgh, 1962), 217–45; Roy Lubove, *The Urban Community: Housing and Planning in the Progressive Era* (Englewood Cliffs, 1967), 1–22; John L. Hancock, "Planners in the Changing American City, 1900–1940," *Journal of the American Institute of Planners*, XXXIII (Sept. 1967), 290–304; John W. Reps, *The Making of Urban America: A History of City Planning in the United States* (Princeton, 1965), 497–525; and Thomas S. Hines, *Burnham of Chicago: Architect and Planner* (New York, 1974). On the city manager profession, see John Porter East, *Council-Manager Government: The Political Thought of Its Founder, Richard S. Childs* (Chapel Hill, 1965); Clarence E. Ridley and Orin F. Nolting, *The City-Manager Profession* (Chicago, 1934); Richard J. Stillman II, *The Rise of the City Manager: A Public Professional in Local Government* (Albuquerque, 1974); and Harry Aubrey Toulmin, Jr., *The City Manager: A New Profession* (New York, 1915).

[33]Nelson P. Lewis, *The Planning of the Modern City: A Review of the Principles Governing City Planning*

(New York, 1916); Scott, *American City Planning*, 163–64, 228; George B. Ford and Ralph F. Warner, *City Planning Progress* (Washington, 1917), iii.

[34]Griffith, *A History of American City Government*, 167–68.

[35]Lewis, *Planning of the Modern City*, 415; Toulmin, *The City Manager*, 78–81; "City Manager Plan Widely Endorsed," *Engineering News-Record*, LXXXV (Oct. 7, 1920), 703; Stillman, *Rise of the City Manager*, 38–39; Harold Stone, Don K. Price, and Kathryn H. Stone, *City Manager Government in the United States: A Review After Twenty-five Years* (Chicago, 1940), 57.

Sports and Machine Politics
in New York City, 1870–1920

*Steven A. Riess**

American historians since Frederic Paxson and Arthur M. Schlesinger, Sr., have portrayed that city as the primary site for the rise of organized sport in the post-Civil War era. As the urban setting became increasingly complex and organized, sport developed modern characteristics, including specialization of roles, bureaucratic organization, and a degree of equality of opportunity. At the same time, sport became a popular form of commercialized entertainment. The modernization and maturation of sport was largely the product of urbanization. The city also served as the locus of the dynamic social development of sport as that institution became linked with the processes that constituted urbanization—namely, the interaction of physical setting, social organization, and collective behavior. This essay examines the relationship between the development of sport and the evolution of modern political institutions and political behavior. Professional politicians, particularly machine politicians, played an important role in the development of urban recreation. They were among the major promoters and facilitators of commercialized urban spectator sports from 1870 until about 1920, when they began to be supplanted by urban elites and syndicate criminals.[1]

This study focuses on the three major professional sports in New York City at the turn of the century: baseball, boxing, and horse racing. By far the largest city in the United States, New York had a population in 1910 of 4,766,883, greater than the combined total of the next three biggest cities (Chicago, Philadelphia, and St. Louis). More importantly, as the sporting capital of America, New York was emulated by other urban areas. The city was the center of thoroughbred racing supervised by the prestigious Jockey Club, the preeminent racing association in America. It also served as the principal site for boxing, the second city after New Orleans to have legalized prizefights. Finally, in 1903, New York became the only city with three major league baseball teams. Tammany politicians and their cronies played a crucial role in promoting and facilitating professionalized spectator sports. In turn, organized sports had important ramifications for the city's political culture

*Steven A. Riess is professor of history at Northeastern Illinois University. Original essay printed by permission of Steven A. Riess.

and became central to the nexus existing between urban politics and organized crime.

I

Machine politicians generally held a prominent place in New York's largely Irish, male, bachelor subculture. Participants engaged in a wide variety of "manly" recreations such as gambling, drinking, wenching, and athletics, frequently at a saloon where they gathered to gossip, gamble, or attend to business. At a time when an exclusively male culture dominated sport, politicos held a leading place in the sporting fraternity. As youths, Tammany Bosses Richard Croker and Charles F. Murphy gained local reputations as boxer and baseball player, respectively. As adults, they frequented billiard-saloons, ballparks, racetracks, and boxing clubs. They were heroes and role models to newspaper boys and other working-class youths. Machine politicians, gangsters, entertainers, and other members of the sporting fraternity attended sporting events together, bet with each other, and socialized late into the evening after sporting contests. These political figures achieved a celebrity status, and the press always noted their presence at opening-day ball games, major stakes races, and championship fights.[2]

Not just famous sports fans, professional politicians also facilitated the expansion of mass participatory sport, which undoubtedly improved their standing among constituents. On a modest level, political organizations sponsored athletic clubs, baseball teams, and outings that attracted young men to their colors. Tammany-sponsored picnics usually drew from 200 to 800 boys and men for such sports as baseball, football, track and field, even Gaelic football. The grandest and most famous picnics were sponsored by the Timothy D. Sullivan Society of the Lower East Side. Sullivan was the local district leader and the number two man in Tammany Hall. On September 10, 1900, the society sponsored its greatest outing as a memorial to the end of prizefighting, banned just ten days before. Transported by boats to a Long Island resort, some 6,000 people enjoyed a day of sports, drinking, and revelry. They marked their return to Manhattan that evening with a parade through the Bowery. The five-dollar tickets for the outing were paid for by saloon-keepers and other Bowery businessmen trying to stay on good terms with Boss Sullivan.[3]

Urban politicians also encouraged participatory sport by nonenforcement or selective enforcement of penal codes impinging on sport. The most important legal restrictions on sports were Sunday blue laws supported by pietistic, native-born Protestants who believed in preservation of the Sabbath. Advocates of the American Sabbath sought to regulate the moral conduct of the entire community, particularly urban immigrants who needed indoctrination in the traditional American value system. Nearly every state had Sunday blue laws, although enforcement varied from region to region. The Midwest and far West were rather lenient, and cities like Chicago and Denver had professional Sunday baseball in the late nineteenth century. In the South, blue laws were strictly enforced by common consent. In the Northeast, rural-dominated, state legislatures ardently supported the American Sabbath as a real and symbolic means of insulating against immigrant-congested cities regarded as centers of vice, crime, and corruption. In New York City, Tammany's working-class, immigrant constituents preferred a Continental Sabbath on their only day off and vigorously opposed the Sunday blue laws. Resentment built up against elite New Yorkers who played golf and tennis on Sundays at their resorts, while urban youth were being arrested for playing ball. Tammany strongly supported reform of the blue laws. The organization had little success in Albany in repealing the detested penal codes, but Tammany judges usually discharged those arrested for Sabbath-breaking sport. Some Tammany politicians had ulterior motives: they owned semiprofessional teams that regularly played on Sundays and sought protection against police harassment.[4]

The most important contribution by politicians and city government to the rise of mass sport participation was the development of municipal parks. By the mid-nineteenth century, New York was already terribly overcrowded, with limited available open space for sports or healthful outdoor recreation. Even in the era of the walking city, most New Yorkers found sports fields increasingly inaccessible. In 1855 city and state governments, with backing from Mayor Fernando Wood, approved the construction of the 840-acre Central Park in Manhattan. It was expected to be a panacea providing harmony, social uplift, improved health, and an escape valve for hardworking people living in New York's unhealthy environment. However, park planners Frederick Law Olmsted and Calvert Vaux opposed sport activities that injured the natural environment. They advocated a philosophy of receptive recreation, by which parkgoers would receive pleasure without conscious exertion as they enjoyed the beauty of nature. In time, parkgoers began to use the grounds actively for sports. Ponds were being used for ice-skating by the winter of 1859–60, but no ballplaying was allowed until the 1880s.[5]

Central Park and, in the 1890s, Pelham Bay and Van Cortlandt parks were supported by Tammany because their development provided sources of patronage jobs and graft. Indeed, the Republican state government was so worried about Democratic use of Central Park for graft and patronage that it took over the park site in 1857, about the same time the state took control of the city's police department. Construction supervisor Olmsted was under enormous pressure to provide jobs to party workers. During the depression, his house was broken into by job seekers, and a few days later his office was besieged by over 5,000 laborers, led by politicians trying to impress their constituents. When the Democrats captured the state legislature in 1870, a new city charter was quickly approved, thereby returning the park to city control. Olmsted was fired by Boss William M. Tweed's lieutenant, Peter "Brains" Sweeney, but left office proud that he had held out against political pressure. Tammany thereafter milked the park for make-work projects for thousands of laborers at a cost of $8 million. The carefully landscaped beauty of the park was destroyed in the process. The abuse of the park ended in 1871 with the collapse of the Tweed Ring.[6]

Despite the needs of constituents for accessible breathing spaces, Tammany did not have much interest in the small parks movement of the 1890s and early 1900s. Small, inner-city parks offered limited opportunities for graft and patronage, and construction costs were high at a time when New York was in financial distress. One historian has noted, moreover, the considerable community opposition to the neighborhood park concept amongst Lower East Side Jews. Residents of the Lower East Side feared that knocking down buildings for parks would destroy needed housing in the neighborhood.[7]

This pattern of neglect was not unique to New York, for Chicago's local ward machines also ignored the small park movement. In Boston, however, Democratic machine politicians representing poor Irish districts worked vigorously to secure small parks for their constituents. They opposed distant and inaccessible park sites until city leaders supported small, inner-city parks and playgrounds as well. In the mid-1890s, under the direction of Boss John F. Fitzgerald, pressure from poor sections of Boston succeeded in getting a park built in the North End at Charlestown, as well as improvements for the Charlesbank Gymnasium in the West End. These community breathing spaces came under local control and were used for the active recreation prohibited in the beautiful suburban parks.[8]

II

The close connection between commercialized sport and urban politics was probably first evident in prizefighting. As early as the 1830s and 1840s, gangs of New York youths worked actively with Tammany Hall in seeking the immigrant vote for the Democratic party. Gangs helped bring out the vote, and "shoulder hitters" made sure the electorate voted correctly. The first politician to organize the gang leaders was Captain Isaiah Rynders. Tammany boss of the Sixth Ward, Rynders established the Empire Club in 1843, which served as the focal point of ward political activity and as "the clearing house of all gangster activities which had to do with politics." Other Democratic factions had their own shoulder hitters, as did the Whigs and Nativists. In the antebellum era, all leading New York boxers were aligned with politicized gangs. Perhaps the most famous was Irish-born John Morrissey, the American boxing champion from 1853 to 1858. Later a big New York gambler, Morrissey utilized his fame in getting elected to the U.S. Congress after the Civil War. Ward leaders and public officials in this era often became boxing patrons, arranging bouts for side bets at hangouts like Harry Hill's Dance Hall, a favorite meeting place for the sporting crowd. Politicians often rewarded favored fighters with such jobs as emigrant runners, bouncers, tavern keepers, and policemen.[9]

The need of politicians for shoulder hitters declined after the Civil War. Political parties marshaled their use of supporters by more rational means, including patronage and payoffs. By 1893, Tammany had become virtually omnipotent in New York City, although it suffered some defeats following episodes of outrageous corruption revealed by public investigations. Tammanyites remained interested in boxing, but formal matches were difficult to pull off because the violent and bloody sport was illegal. Contests had to be fought in out-of-the-way sites such as barns, barges, or saloon backrooms. Some of the important exhibitions in the early 1880s were held at Madison

Square Garden, a refurbished railroad station. The big attraction was usually John L. Sullivan, the heavyweight champion of the world after 1882, who fought a number of four-round fights there until 1885, when the promoters gave up after repeated police interference.[10]

In the 1880s the center of boxing shifted to New Orleans, where local promoters and politicians used various techniques to circumvent proscriptive laws. In 1890 the city and the state passed laws permitting "glove contests" sponsored by regularly chartered athletic clubs. Athletic clubs began promoting organized boxing matches in indoor arenas, selling tickets for admission. Boxers fought for a specified purse rather than side bets, although betting continued to be important. Contests were increasingly fought under the new Marquis of Queensberry rules, requiring gloves and rounds with time limits. In New Orleans on September 7, 1892, James Corbett defeated Sullivan for the championship in the first heavyweight championship fight under the new rules. Corbett won the $25,000 purse and a $10,000 side bet.[11]

Prizefighting staged a revival in the New York metropolitan area in the early 1890s, and New York regained its preeminence in the sport. The main site of bouts was Coney Island, a wide-open resort that was becoming a major sporting center. Known as "Sodom by the Sea," Coney Island was infamous as an area of low-life amusements. The local political boss was John T. McKane, a former Democratic president of Kings County, who after 1884 served concurrently as president of the local town board, chief of police, and head of the water and health boards. The principal boxing club there was the Coney Island Athletic Club (CIAC), organized in May 1892 by McKane and various machine politicians. McKane owned the arena, provided political protection, and prevented any big bouts at Coney Island unless he had a share of the action. Police Justice Dick Newton was the matchmaker, and Magistrate James T. Tighe handled financial affairs. The club staged a number of important bouts, reputedly earning $150,000 in under five months. But the CIAC was not omnipotent and in 1893 was forced to cancel the Jim Corbett-Charley Mitchell championship bout because of public pressure.[12]

The CIAC was only one of several boxing clubs in the metropolitan area sponsored and protected by local politicians. These clubs operated even though professional boxing was illegal. For example, in 1895 the New Puritan Boxing Club of Long Island City held its matches at a site owned by the town's former mayor, James Gleason. His partners included Big Tim Sullivan and former Justice Dick Newton, recently released from a jail sentence for corrupt electioneering.[13]

Tim Sullivan was first elected to the state assembly in 1886 at the age of twenty-three and moved on to the Senate in 1893. He served in the U.S. Congress from 1902 to 1906, but in 1908 he returned to his power base in the state senate. Sullivan's last victory came in 1912, when he was again elected to Congress, but he was never sworn in because of failing health; he died one year later. Sullivan was associated early in his career with such gangsters as Monk Eastman, Kid Twist, and Paul Kelly, who provided him with intimidators and repeaters at election time. In return, organized crime was allowed to flourish. Big Tim was idolized by his constituents as a friend of the poor. He provided them with patronage, relief, outings, and any other assistance. Sullivan was a great sportsman. He raced horses, gambled heavily, and, after 1895, dominated the New York poolroom business. Furthermore, by 1898 he also monopolized boxing in New York State, except in Brooklyn, where the new CIAC was protected by Democratic Boss Hugh McLaughlin.[14]

In 1896, under Sullivan's guidance, a bill passed the legislature and was approved by the governor legalizing "sparring" matches of up to ten rounds at licensed athletic clubs. New York became the only state with legalized boxing because Louisiana had banned the sport after the death of a New Orleans fighter in 1894. New York's 1896 Horton Act seemed, on the surface, to outlaw prizefights (boxing for a purse), contests regarded as brutal and unscientific and where the object was to pummel an opponent into unconsciousness. But in reality the new law legitimized prizefighting. Police thereafter rarely interfered with bouts, especially after New York Police Commissioner Theodore Roosevelt attended a rough contest at Sullivan's Broadway Athletic Club and told the press that the match had complied with the law.[15]

Tammany control of the police department further obviated any fears of harassment at the politically connected athletic clubs. Police Chief Bill Devery rarely interfered with boxing bouts, even well-advertised matches like the heavyweight championship match in 1899 between titleholder Bob Fitzsimmons and challenger James J. Jeffries at the new CIAC, a club politically allied with Hugh McLaughlin. Devery had joined the police department in 1878 and owed his rise to the sponsorship of Boss Croker and Tim Sullivan. His career was marked by several episodes of incompetence and corruption. In 1894, Devery was fired from his captaincy because of criminal charges resulting from the Lexow Investigation, but he was acquitted on a technicality and regained his post. Five years later the Mazet Investigation documented his corrupt activities as chief. His work was so scandalous that the state legislature abolished his position in 1901 in favor of a commissioner. But the new head of the police simply appointed Devery his deputy and left the department in his care. When Seth Low was elected mayor on a Fusion ticket that year, he fired Devery immediately.[16]

Legalized boxing lasted only until 1900, when the state legislature repealed the Horton Act because of the sport's brutality, the gambling menace, and the Tammany influence in boxing. Approximately 3,500 contests had been staged over five years, mainly in New York City. The cheapest tickets were fifty cents for club fights (equal to the cost of general admission at baseball parks), while tickets to top-flight matches ranged between one and three dollars. Admission to championship bouts went for five to twenty-five dollars. Most of the profits came from box office receipts, but additional revenue came from the sale of movie rights to championship bouts. The single largest gate of the Horton era was Jeffries's title defense in 1900 against former champion Jim Corbett, which brought in $60,000.[17]

The repeal of the Horton Act did not completely stop boxing, since it survived surreptitiously in saloon backrooms and at club smokers. Private clubs circumvented the law by holding three-round exhibitions for the entertainment of "members," who paid a one-dollar "fee" to join the club. The most prestigious of the membership clubs was Tim Sullivan's National Athletic Club, which reputedly had 3,000 members. By 1908 fifteen clubs in New York held weekly bouts. The police generally did not interfere and seldom made arrests. However, if promoters became too audacious, or drew too much public attention by scheduling big-name fighters, the police were pressured to stop the bouts.[18]

Tammany politicians tried in vain for several years to legalize boxing again. Prospects brightened in 1911 when the Democrats gained control of both the state legislature and the governor's mansion for the first time in years. This enabled Senator James J. Frawley, a former president of the Knickerbocker Athletic Club, to pass a bill legalizing ten-round, no-decision boxing contests. The sport was placed under the supervision of an unpaid three-man State Athletic Commission responsible for licensing athletic clubs and fighters. A 5 percent tax was levied on the box office take, which came to nearly $50,000 in 1912. The Frawley Act resulted in a renewed interest in boxing, and by the end of 1912 there were eighty-nine licensed boxing clubs in the state, forty-nine in New York City. The bouts were held in small neighborhood boxing clubs and large downtown arenas like Madison Square Garden.[19]

Prizefighting operated under the Frawley Act until 1917, when the law was repealed by a Republican administration. The prestige of the sport remained low. Its brutality, the low-life types associated with it, and incessant gambling and rumors of fixes did little to improve the standing of boxing as a sport. The Athletic Commission never fully enforced its guidelines. Its public image further suffered once it had become overtly politicized by the Republicans, who regained control of the state legislature and the governorship in 1915. Governor Charles Whitman's new athletic commissioners were patronage appointees with substantial salaries. That was not enough, apparently, because the commission chariman was fired by the governor in 1917 after an investigation revealed that he extorted money from promoters and fight managers. Shortly thereafter a fatality occurred in the ring at a match attended by two commissioners. This episode convinced Whitman that he had to abolish the sport. Yet despite its many problems, boxing had its friends in the state legislature, and the governor's first efforts at repeal were badly defeated. Whitman called for repeal late in the session as a party measure, getting his bill approved on a strict party vote. Not one Democratic senator voted to abolish boxing. Whitman's battle against boxing was a politically astute move signifying to upstate voters that the Republican party stood for tradition and high moral values, unlike the Democrats who had supported an immoral blood sport with dubious connections to urban political machines and gangsters.[20]

The repeal of the Frawley Act was a major blow to American prizefighting. The sport was legal in twenty-three states in 1917, but it was severely restricted, if not completely outlawed, in the major markets of New York and Chicago. Even in San Francisco, which had temporarily supplanted New York as the boxing capital after the repeal of the Horton Act, the sport was greatly curtailed by a 1914 state law limiting matches to four rounds. The outlook for boxing improved markedly during World War I, however, because the sport was used to help train soldiers for combat. Consequently, boxing's image became much better. Even the reform-minded *New York Times* became an advocate of pugilism. Nevertheless, boxing supporters failed to get a bill through the legislature in 1918 restoring the sport. One year later a measure favoring pugilism passed the Senate but was defeated in the lower chamber by conservative Republicans. Legislators had just approved the legalization of Sunday movies and baseball, and, as one ranking Republican suggested, "We can't afford to be too liberal." Then, in 1920, under the direction of Senate Minority Leader Jimmy Walker, a loyal son of Tammany, the legislature enacted a law permitting twelve-round matches, with judges empowered to choose a victor if the contests went the distance. An unpaid athletic commission was established to supervise the sport and license boxing clubs, trainers, and fighters.[21]

The passage of the Walker Act enabled New York City to regain its position as the national center of boxing. In the 1920s local fight clubs became important sources of top-flight fighters. Most major American bouts were held at Madison Square Garden. The promoter there was Tex Rickard, probably best known for his successful work in pulling off the Jeffries-Johnson championship fight of 1910 in Reno, Nevada. Rickard's first promotion in New York was the Willard-Moran heavyweight championship fight in 1916. An out-of-towner, Rickard generated a lot of jealousy among local promoters and politicians, compelling him to provide passes, favors, and bribes to bring off the match. By 1920, Rickard had learned his lesson and developed important connections in Tammany Hall. His backers included Governor Al Smith, who interceded on Rickard's behalf with owners of Madison Square Garden, helping the promoter get a ten-year lease for $400,000. Smith believed that Rickard was the only man with the imagination and promotional flair to operate the huge arena successfully. Rickard succeeded in making boxing a respectable and profitable sport. Boxing was soon legalized in other important states like Illinois, and the sport's heroes, particularly Jack Dempsey, were among the most admired Americans in the 1920s.[22]

III

Politics ominated not only the "sport of pugs" but also the "sport of kings." Despite the aristocratic image of the sport, horse racing often came under severe moral scrutiny from church leaders and moral reformers because of the gambling, crooked races, and animal abuses associated with the turf. More than any other sport, racing depended upon betting for its appeal and survival. Consequently, thoroughbred racing at the turn of the century was widely forbidden. Where the sport did operate, as in New York, it was heavily influenced by machine politicians and politically active elites, such as William C. Whitney, Thomas Fortune Ryan, and August Belmont II. These men used sport to facilitate cross-class coalitions in the Democratic party to help protect their transit franchises. Streetcar executives out of necessity became intimately involved in urban politics; they needed inside information, long-term leases, and rights of way. Elite sportsmen like Ryan and Belmont owned and operated racetracks. Along with machine politicos like Croker and Tim Sullivan, they owned, bred, and raced thoroughbreds, and they wagered heavily at the track. Sullivan and other professional politicians were also prominent in the business of gambling, usually as organizers and protectors of bookmaking and offtrack poolroom, or betting parlor, syndicates. The elite and plebeian members of the sporting fraternity worked together on issues of mutual concern, such as the facilitation of racetrack operations and the legalization of ontrack betting. They were bitter enemies, however, when it came to offtrack betting.[23]

Thoroughbred racing was a popular elite diversion in the Colonial era. The sport subsequently enjoyed a boom in the 1820s and 1830s but faltered in the North after the depression of 1837. The center of racing then shifted to New Orleans, where it remained a vital institution until the Civil War. The turf did not revive in the North until 1863, when John Morrissey staged races at the resort town of Saratoga Springs to attract elite vacationers. He was supported by wealthy sportsmen Leonard Jerome, William R. Travers, and John Hunter, who apparently were not adverse to working with a former Tammany shoulder hitter.[24]

The Saratoga experiment was such a resounding success that Jerome, Chairman August Belmont of the national Democratic party, and other elite sportsmen organized the American Jockey Club (AJC) in 1866 to sponsor races in the vicinity of New York City. Jerome played a leading role in securing 230 acres in Westchester, where a racetrack was built and named Jerome Park in his honor. The goals of the AJC were to improve the breed and maintain racing as an elite sport. The jockey club introduced several important innovations, such as holding three meets each year and replacing the traditional long distance heat with the shorter English dash system. This resulted in more races on each card, which meant more betting to attract turf fans. Larger purses, averaging about $13,000 per meet, attracted better horses, particularly annual stakes races like the Belmont, initiated in 1867 in honor of the AJC's first president. Expenses were met by gate receipts, at least $3,000 per day, along with daily fees paid by auction pool-sellers and concessionnaires and the entrance fees paid by horsemen for the right to race thoroughbreds.[25]

Not all of the 862 original members of the AJC between 1866 and 1867 were socially elite. Some were horse fanciers of more modest origins. The membership included such politicians as the notorious Tammany Boss William M. Tweed. Boss Tweed was also interested in Monmouth Park, established in 1870 at Long Branch, New Jersey, by gambler Joseph Chamberlain who hoped to turn Monmouth Park into another Saratoga. Chamberlain's other associates included robber barons Jay Gould and Jim Fisk, Jr., who "practically owned the Legislature."[26]

New York horsemen needed considerable political savvy to circumvent the legal barriers to gambling, the backbone of the sport. An antipool law was passed by the state legislature in 1877 in response to the widespread wagering on the Tilden-Hayes election. Despite fears that this law would hurt track attendance, the turf continued to flourish, largely because the auction pool system of betting was replaced by bookmaking. The locus of racing moved to the Coney Island area, a forty-cent, one-hour train ride from midtown Manhattan. Local politicians were expected to protect the tracks from rigorous enforcement of the penal codes. In June 1879, William A. Engeman, builder of the Brighton Beach Hotel and politically well connected, established a proprietary racetrack at Brighton Beach. The track was quite successful, and, by 1882, Engeman was netting $200,000 per year. Late in 1879, Jerome organized the prestigious Coney Island Jockey Club (CIJC), which included Belmont, William K. Vanderbilt, and Pierre Lorillard, Jr. One year later the CIJC established the important Sheepshead Bay Track in Coney Island. Finally, in 1885, the politically astute Dwyer brothers, plungers who had made their fortune as butchers, opened Gravesend as a proprietary track. These three tracks were tolerated and protected by local politicians under the direction of Boss McKane, who permitted pool-selling to flourish. A political opponent, the Republican Kings County district attorney, secured fifty-seven indictments for penal code violations but could not obtain one single conviction. His Democratic successor never interfered during the racing season. McKane personally benefited from benign neglect because his construction company was awarded many lucrative contracts, including the building of the betting booths.[27]

In 1887 representatives of the racing interests passed the Ives Anti-Poolroom Law forbidding off-betting but permitting betting at the tracks during the May to October racing season. The state also levied a tax on the race courses to raise money for agricultural societies and county fairs. The new law resulted in a boom in racing and gambling. It led directly to the formation of the Metropolitan Turf Alliance (MTA) in 1888, an association of over sixty well-connected bookmakers who sought to monopolize the bookmaking privilege at the tracks and whose secretary was Timothy D. Sullivan. Another result was that, in 1889, John A. Morris constructed Morris Park Racetrack in Westchester to replace Jerome Park, which the city had purchased for a reservoir. Morris came from a wealthy New York family, but his reputation was not of the highest order because he had made his fortune operating the infamous Louisiana Lottery. He was politically influential, however, and his Tammanyite son was the district's assemblyman. Managed by the New York Jockey Club, Morris Park had the largest grandstand and the longest track in the United States. The facility cost several hundred thousand dollars and was regarded as palatial by contemporaries. It immediately became an important resort for the social set who traveled to the track in expensive carriages. Lesser folk had to be satisfied with a half-hour train ride from Grand Central Station.[28]

Poolroom operators learned to adapt and stay in business despite the Ives Anti-Poolroom Law. Poolrooms were mainly located in midtown or the Tenderloin, where clerks took bets on New York and New Jersey races. They attracted a lot of business, primarily from young clerks and artisans who could not afford the ninety-cent roundtrip and the two-dollar admission, much less the time to go to the tracks. Poolrooms not only made it unnecessary for gamblers to travel to the tracks, but they also took small, one-dollar bets that bookmakers at major New York tracks would not accept. Occasional raids were instigated by reformers like Anthony Comstock of the Society for the Suppression of Vice, but the poolrooms usually operated with impunity. The poolroom operators were well protected by Mayor Hugh Grant and other Tammany friends, by their contributions to Governor David B. Hill, and by payoffs to police and local political powers. Machine-appointed jurists were also supportive. In 1890, for instance, the courts ruled that poolrooms could operate as commission agents and transfer clients' money to the tracks. Immediately, all pool-sellers began to represent themselves as betting commissioners. They would accept bets right up to posttime, even though it was physically impossible to get the wagers to the track.[29]

The poolrooms got their race results from Western Union. The telegraph company paid about $1,600 per day to each New York track for the exclusive privilege of transmitting race results. Its racing department, which made $18,000 to $20,000 per week, was the most profitable unit in Western Union. These payments gave the racetracks a vested interest in the poolroom business. Early in the spring of 1893, the police instigated a major attack against local poolrooms, possibly at the instigation of Boss Richard Croker. The Tammany boss had recently purchased the famous Belle Meade stud and wanted New York tracks to prosper so he could race his horses there. In addition, Croker was a good friend of the Dwyers, who had often given him betting tips, and he hoped to protect their interests. With Croker's support, and despite the opposition of Tim Sullivan, the state legislature enacted the Saxton Anti-Poolroom Law making the keeping of a poolroom a felony.[30]

The status of horse racing was seriously threatened one year later by a coalition of social reformers, clergymen, and other Tammany opponents. This group used the September 1894 state constitutional convention as a forum to ban all horse-race gambling. There was widespread sentiment against betting, particularly at illegal poolrooms. Racing fans had become increasingly alienated against the sport by the activities of the Morrises and Dwyers, who seemed more interested in profits than improving the breed. Repeated rumors of fixed races also stimulated public outrage. The elite Jockey Club, organized in the summer of 1894, was expected to supervise carefully all aspects of the sport, but it did not assuage critics. Opponents were bolstered by the closing in December 1893 of New Jersey's tracks, which had been totally controlled by corrupt machine politicians. The New York State constitutional convention adopted a proposal banning horse-race betting completely. When the proposal was approved by voters in fall elections, the end of racing appeared imminent.[31]

Racing interests waged an all-out campaign to save the sport. Calmer minds recognized that the convention might have gone too far. Even the reform-minded *New York Times* sought to save racing, which it believed helped improve the breed. The turf had powerful friends in Albany. Racing advocates flexed their muscle in the passage of the Percy-Gray Act, establishing a state racing commission to supervise the sport. The new law permitted racing associations to race horses for a stake, but without wagering. Yet when the tracks reopened in the spring of 1895, betting was soon resumed by bookmakers, who instituted the English system of credit betting, in which no written records were kept and debts were paid off on an honor system. The courts ruled that the new system was legal, since bets were made on an individual basis and no odds were advertised.[32]

Offtrack betting was also back in business, even though a new law had been passed accompanying Percy-Gray that banned such betting. The enterprise now came under the protection of Big Tim Sullivan, and, under his patronage, offtrack betting soon reached its apogee. Sullivan's operation had Croker's approval. As many as 400 poolrooms belonged to the syndicate, each paying from $60 to $300 per month for the privilege of staying in business. New poolrooms paid Sullivan a $300 initiation fee. The poolroom operations were extraordinarily successful, and in 1902 the syndicate earned $3.6 million.[33]

Poolrooms operated openly in the backrooms of Tenderloin saloons, or under the guise of a bucket shop. Poolrooms were usually forewarned by police headquarters about occasional raids. Arrested clerks and telegraph operators generally were freed by sympathetic magistrates or fined a minimal amount. The poolrooms became a major issue during the 1901 city elections. Reform fusion candidates castigated Sullivan and the rest of the so-called Gambling Trust, which reputedly included Bill Devery, Frank Farrell, Police Commissioner Joseph Sexton, City Clerk J. F. Carroll, and Mayor Robert A. Van Wyck. Seth Low promised to clean up the gambling menace when elected, but other than firing Devery, he accomplished very little. DeLacey, Farrell, and Mahoney soon set up their own poolroom syndicates in cooperation with Sullivan, later described by journalist Josiah Flynt as "the most scandalous individual in the pool-room Griff in the United States."[34]

Thoroughbred racing's greatest crisis came in 1908, when Governor Charles Evans Hughes in his annual address to the state legislature called for the end of racetrack gambling. At first, the proposal attracted little public enthusiasm. The turf was popular, and its advocates had considerable political and economic clout. But the progressive governor believed that gambling on races was both a moral outrage and a flagrant violation of the state constitution. Hughes engaged in a major educational campaign to win public support for his views. He used his influence to get Republicans behind a bill to abolish on-site betting. The Agnew-Hart bill easily passed the assembly but failed on a tie vote in the Senate. Tammany and the state's eight jockey clubs seemed to have succeeded in saving the sport. The tracks purportedly raised a $500,000 defense fund, spending $162,000 for publicity and an untold amount for vote buying. Republican Otto Foelker claimed he had been offered $45,000 to vote for the racing interests, and at least one senator later admitted taking a $10,000 bribe.[35]

Disappointed with this defeat, Hughes persevered. He ordered a special election to fill a vacant Senate seat from the traditionally Republican Niagara-Orleans district. The governor put his prestige on the line by campaigning for the Republican candidate, who pledged to vote against racetrack gambling. Republican William C. Wallace won the seat in a surprisingly close contest. Hughes then convened a special session of the legislature, which passed the Agnew-Hart bill by a margin of one vote in the Senate. This victory was described by a Hughes biographer as his "most dramatic venture in the area of moral reform."[36]

The new law severely hampered the racing industry, a $75-million business nationwide. The major tracks tried to remain open by allowing oral betting, which the courts ruled was legal, but attendance declined by two-thirds. In 1910 the legislature passed the Agnew-Perkins Act, making racetrack owners liable for any gambling violations at their facilities. The result was that tracks still operating immediately went out of business. In 1911 and 1912 there was no thoroughbred racing in New York. However, in 1913, Judge Townsend Scudder ruled in the *Shane* case that track managers were liable only if they had wittingly permitted bookmakers to operate. As a consequence, Belmont Park and two minor tracks, Jamaica and Aqueduct, reopened. But such historic racetracks as Gravesend and Sheepshead Bay, each worth about $2.5 million, never reopened.[37]

IV

Unlike boxing and horse racing, which operated under severe legal restriction and social opprobrium, baseball was the national pastime. A clean, exciting sport, baseball epitomized the finest traditional American values like rugged individualism, hard work, and courage, as well as teamwork. Baseball owners were regarded as selfless, civic-minded men who sponsored teams out of a concern for the public welfare. But in reality, owners were not drawn from the "best people." New York baseball magnates included a heavy representation of machine politicians. They used their clout to benefit their teams, which provided patronage, financial and psychic rewards, and good public relations.[38]

Baseball in New York from its earliest days was closely tied to local politics. Tammany was an early sponsor of amateur baseball teams, the most important being the Mutuals, established in 1857. By the 1860s, when Tweed had become involved with the club, it was already one of the leading amateur nines. Players were subsidized with patronage jobs in the sanitation department and the coroner's office. In 1871, when the Mutuals joined the first professional league, the National Association of Professional Baseball Players (NA), its board of directors included the sheriff, several aldermen, two judges, and six state legislators. One of only three teams that played in all five NA campaigns, the Mutuals in 1876 joined the new National League (NL). But late in the 1876 season, after refusing to make a costly western trip, the Mutuals were expelled by the NL.[39]

New York City was without major league baseball until 1883, when Tammanyites John B. Day and Joseph Gordon and former minor leaguer John Mutrie were awarded franchises in both the NL and the year-old·American Association (AA). They devoted most of their attention to the Giants (NL), because the senior circuit charged fifty cents for tickets and the AA only twenty-five cents. In 1885, Day and his partners sold the AA team to Erastus Wiman, a Staten Island traction magnate who hoped to enrich his ferry business with fans traveling from Manhattan to Staten Island for ball games. His ball club, however, was a failure and lasted only two seasons. The Giants played at the old Polo Grounds at 110th Street until 1889, when political pressure forced them to move north to a new site at 157th Street. A competitor was established across the street in 1890 in the new Players' League, a cooperative venture of capitalists and players revolting against the reserve clause. The financial backers were prominent Republicans, who bought out the Giants in 1891 after the collapse of the Players' League. Tammany regained the Giants at the end of 1894, when Andrew Freedman, an intimate friend and business partner of Boss Croker, purchased the club for $48,000. Freedman held no elective office but wielded great influence through Croker and in his own right as a member of Tammany's powerful Finance Committee. In 1897, Freeman became treasurer of the national Democratic party.[40]

Brooklyn baseball was also heavily dominated by politicians. In 1884 the city got an AA franchise that played in the Red Hook section. The owners were gamblers Ferdinand Abell and Joseph J. Doyle (the latter a close friend of Tammany Boss John Kelly), realtor Charles Byrne, and editor George J. Taylor of the *Herald*—all typical members of the sporting fraternity. In 1890 the franchise was transferred to the NL and replaced in the AA by a club run by James C. Kennedy, a prominent sports promoter with important political connections. Brooklyn also had a team in the new Players' League owned by Brownsville boosters, including Wendell Goodwin, a politician who worked for a local traction line. But one year later, only the NL team remained, which Goodwin and his associates bought and moved to Brownsville. This shift did not work out well because of high rent, poor transportation, and the lack of neighborhood interest in the sport. In 1898 the Trolley Dodgers returned to South Brooklyn under a new president, Charles Ebbets, a former state assemblyman and future alderman. The switch was financed by Red Hook traction magnates who expected the presence of a baseball team to increase traffic along their routes.[41]

Freedman of the Giants used his clout to cower other owners, and sportswriters claimed that he ran his team as a Tammany appendage. The object of considerable abuse from fans, the press, and fellow owners for mismanagement and encouraging rowdy baseball, and disappointed with his profits, Freedman decided to sell out after the 1902 season. Besides, he had more important matters to attend to, principally the construction of the New York subway system. He sold most of his stock for $125,000 to John T. Brush, an Indianapolis clothier. Brush had just sold his Cincinnati Reds baseball team to a local syndicate consisting of Mayor Julius Fleischmann, Republican Boss George B. Cox, and Water Commissioner August Herrmann, Cox's right-hand man. According to one journalist, Brush had been forced to sell out to the machine, which threatened to cut a street through the ballpark.[42]

Despite the sale, the Giants remained the Tammany team. Still a minority stockholder, Freedman was more than willing to use his clout for the club. Brush died in 1912, and his heirs sold the team in 1919 for $1 million to Tammanyite Charles Stoneham, a curb-market broker of limited integrity. Other partners included baseball manager John J. McGraw, and Magistrate Francis X. McQuade, who was best known for his liberal handling of Sunday baseball cases. Stoneham's powerful political friends included Governor Al Smith and former sheriff Tom Foley, one of the machine's most powerful district leaders. Another important friend, along with McGraw, was the notorious Arnold Rothstein, partner in a rum-running deal and a Havana racetrack. Rothstein reputedly had been the middleman in Stoneham's purchase of the Giants.[43]

The Giants were enormously successful on the diamond in the early 1900s under McGraw's management. They won six pennants from 1904 to 1917 and became the most profitable team in organized baseball. From 1906 to 1910 the club annually earned over $100,000, and by 1913 earnings surpassed $150,000. After World War I, baseball experienced an enormous boom in the city, largely because of the legalization of Sunday baseball. In 1920 the Giants established a league record $296,803 in profits. Most of the revenue came from ticket sales, but profits also came from concessions, Western Union fees, and rents from such events as boxing matches, operas, and Yankee games played at the Polo Grounds from 1913 to 1922.[44]

The Giants had Manhattan to themselves until 1903, when the rival American League (AL) secured a New York franchise. The junior circuit had failed to organize a New York team earlier because Freedman controlled virtually all the potential playing sites through his political power and real estate interests. Even after Croker was exiled to England on the heels of Seth Low's election as mayor in 1901, Freedman and his Tammany friends still had enough power to stymie any interlopers. Late in 1902, AL President Ban Johnson convinced August Belmont II that the Interborough Rapid Transit Company (IRT) should purchase land at 142d Street on the East Side and lease it back to the league. However, the plan was vetoed by IRT Director Andrew Freedman.[45]

Johnson could not avoid dealing with Tammany Hall. In March 1903 the AL granted a franchise to a syndicate headed by Joseph Gordon, a figurehead for the real owners—poolroom king Frank Farrell and former Police Chief William Devery. They soon constructed a field on a rock pile at 165th Street that Freedman apparently had ruled out as unsuitable for baseball. Devery and Farrell paid the local district leader $200,000 for excavation and another $75,000 to build a grandstand. The site was inaccessible from downtown, but a subway with a nearby station was scheduled for completion one year later.[46]

The Highlanders (later known as the Yankees) failed to prosper, either on or off the field. After coming in second in 1904, they finished in the first division just twice between 1905 and 1914 and made a substantial profit only in 1910. By comparison, the Giants were first in the hearts of New Yorkers. They won four pennants and one world championship during the same period. Disappointed in the team's performance and estranged from each other, Devery and Farrell sold out in 1915 for $460,000 to brewer Jacob Ruppert, Jr., and C. Tillinghast Huston, a rich civil engineer. Ruppert was a prominent member of the sporting fraternity who bred and raced dogs and horses. A great fan of the Giants, he was a notable member of Tammany Hall, served on its Finance Committee, and had been selected personally by Croker in 1897 to run for president of the city council. But Ruppert's nomination raised jealousies among other brewers and Germans, and was withdrawn.

One year later he was chosen to run for Congress from a Republican district, was elected in an upset, and went on to serve four undistinguished terms. The Yankees struggled at first under new ownership but by 1920 had become the most profitable franchise in baseball, earning a record $373,862. Sunday baseball contributed to this, but the main reason was the new Yankee right fielder, Babe Ruth, who hit an astounding fifty-four home runs, nearly double the record twenty-nine he had hit one year before with the Red Sox. The team's attendance doubled from 1919 to 1920, a league record 1,289,422, which stood until 1946.[47]

New York owners took advantage of their political connections to enhance their baseball operations in valuable ways. Clout was used to deter interlopers from invading the metropolitan area. Influence at city hall provided access to the best possible information about property values, land uses, and mass transit, all essential matters when teams built new ballparks. This was especially crucial once teams began constructing permanent, fire-resistant ballparks that cost in excess of $500,000. In 1911 the Giants built their new Polo Grounds in Washington Heights on the site of the old field that had burned down. Two years later the Dodgers built Ebbets Field in an underdeveloped section of Flatbush known as "Ginney Flats," derided by most experts as a poor location far from the fans. But Charles Ebbets knew what he was doing, having purchased land cheaply in what would soon become a lovely and accessible residential community. A decade later the Yankees moved into their own ballpark in the Bronx, at a spot years before rejected for a ballpark as too distant. But when completed in 1923, Yankee Stadium was just sixteen minutes from downtown Manhattan via the Jerome Avenue extension of the East Side subway.[48]

Political connections facilitated various mundane but necessary business operations. Teams without such protection could find themselves vulnerable to political pressure and high license fees.[49] Cities also provided teams with a variety of municipal services, including preseason inspections to check for structural defects in the ballparks. Baseball men without influence might end up with an unusual number of expensive code violations. The most important ongoing service was police protection. Officers were needed to maintain order among those waiting to get into the park, keep traffic moving, and prevent ticket scalping. Inside the grounds, police prevented gambling and kept order among unruly spectators who fought with other fans, umpires, and even players. All cities provided protection outside the park, and in New York, teams got free police protection inside the grounds until 1907 when the reform commissioner Thomas A. Bingham stopped it. In Chicago that practice continued for years, saving the White Sox and Cubs thousands of dollars.[50]

New York was the center of the fight for professional Sunday baseball. Tammany led a long fight against the American Sabbath. The club owners wanted Sunday ball because they expected it to be popular with working-class fans who could not attend any other day. At the start of each season from 1904 to 1906, either the Giants or the Dodgers tried to use their political clout to stage Sunday games. They sought to circumvent the law by selling scorecards or magazines, or by asking for "donations" instead of selling tickets, which was against the law. However, each year the courts ruled against the ball clubs, and the Sunday experiments were halted.

In 1907 the scene of the battle shifted to Albany, but Tammany was unable to defeat upstate sentiment in favor of the American Sabbath. Support for Sunday recreation broadened during World War I. Many Americans believed that the doughboys fighting overseas for freedom should not have to return home to find their own liberty diminished by strict blue laws. Ebbets played a leading role in a reform coalition that included organized labor, progressives, journalists, veterans' organizations, women's groups, and Tammany. A local option measure nearly succeeded in 1918 but was blocked by Governor Whitman, who feared antagonizing conservative upstate voters. In 1919, however, a coalition of urban Republicans and Democrats passed, and Governor Smith signed, the Walker Bill permitting Sunday baseball on a local option basis. The city council promptly approved Sunday baseball, and it became a huge success, drawing crowds in excess of 20,000 to Ebbets Field and the Polo Grounds.[51]

V

Urban machine politicians and their closest associates played a crucial role in the rise of commercialized sports in New York. They were mainly Irish-American sports fans who seized the opportunity to promote spectator sports as a financial investment that might improve their political standing and social status. Professional sport was a business open to white men of ability, regardless of social background, much like the contemporary new movie industry shunned by old wealth and dominated by risk-taking Jewish entrepreneurs. Unlike amateur sports, dominated by distinctly old-stock Americans, commercialized sports had a prominent non-WASP composition. It was a field of enterprise in which professional politicians could utilize their clout to considerable advantage, much as they did in businesses like construction or real estate.[52]

Sports promoters used inside information to build their structures at the cheapest, most accessible sites. They employed political clout to protect their ballparks, racetracks, and boxing clubs from competition or police interference. This was especially crucial for betting parlors of the gambling syndicate, whose connections at police precincts and magistrate courts normally prevented strict enforcement of antigambling statutes. Political ties not only provided protection but also meant preferential treatment from municipal agencies. The machine's influence extended to Albany, but the legislature and governorship were usually in Republican hands. Nevertheless, the Democrats tried and occasionally succeeded in protecting urban sportsmen against new legal restrictions demanded by rural upstate constituents. They ultimately secured the legitimization of prizefighting and horse racing. Thus, politically connected sportsmen who promoted athletic contests, managed fighters, raced thoroughbreds, and owned or operated sports arenas, baseball franchises, and poolrooms profitably organized diversions for urban folk. Yet the politicians were not omnipotent and did not have the power to operate completely as they pleased. Pugilism was illegal until 1896 and then permitted only intermittently until 1920 when the Walker Bill was passed. Horse racing, and particularly turf betting, was always under severe scrutiny, and the sport actually was discontinued in 1911. Even in baseball, restrictions against Sunday games were not lifted until 1919.[53]

The manifest function of sponsoring commercialized sports was to make money, and politicians had considerable opportunity to profit handsomely from sporting enterprises. In addition, sponsorship had important latent functions, such as providing new sources of patronage and greater popularity with constituents, both of which could be translated into votes. Sporting activities gained politicians a leading position among the community of manly Americans, members of the bachelor subculture. Celebrity status enabled politicians to mix with sports heroes and social leaders. Sport, like politics, was a largely male preserve. It was perceived widely as a means of combatting the growing feminization of American culture. The politicians' sporting ventures proved that they were "one of the boys," offering vivid demonstration of their role in the neighborhood. They provided protection for local bookies and gave community youth a chance for fame, heroism, and wealth through boxing and baseball. Participation in sports raised self-esteem and provided an opportunity for individual accomplishment that working in a political machine might not bring. Sport also provided a nexus through which certain machine politicians became involved with syndicate crime. Politicians needed underworld money, power, and access to election workers, in return for which they provided protection for betting and other illicit operations.[54]

The politician-sportsmen discovered that leadership in sports did not guarantee instant respectability, even though they mingled with segments of the elite. Bosses like Richard Croker and other machine politicos like John Morrissey desperately sought acceptance and recognition by the social elite and tried to emulate their behavior. While the Belmonts, Lorillards, and Jeromes might race with the Crokers and gamble with the Morrisseys, they would never bring them home for dinner with the family. Unlike participation in boxing or horse racing, ownership of a baseball team was regarded as a civic contribution. Frank Farrell's image was markedly improved by his operation of the Highlanders, but that alone did not assure social acceptance. Baseball owners at the turn of the century seldom came from the social elite. Generally men of new wealth, they sought financial profits and social acceptance through a business largely shunned by old money.[55]

The prominence of professional politicians, particularly urban bosses, as promoters and facilitators of professional sports was not limited to New York. It was a nationwide pattern common to urban areas with a citywide machine and cities where the local ward machine model prevailed. In such major sporting centers as Chicago, Cincinnati, New Orleans, Philadelphia, and San Francisco, machine politicians were leading members of the sporting subculture. As political scientist Harold Zink reported in his classic *City Bosses in the United States* (1930), thirteen of his twenty subjects were well-known sportsmen.[56]

As befitted their venal reputations, the machine politicians were especially prominent in prizefighting and horse racing, sports that operated under severe moral disapproval and widespread legal restrictions. In New Orleans, the leading fan was probably John Fitzgerald, referee of the seventy-five-round bare-knuckle championship fight in 1889 between John L. Sullivan and Jake Kilrain. Fitzgerald was elected mayor in 1892 but was later impeached. After the sport was banned in New York in 1900, San Francisco became the major site of pugilism. Its leading promoters all were affiliated with Boss Abe Ruef, who received payoffs to guarantee licenses for staging bouts.[57]

In horse racing, it was commonplace for proprietary tracks to be affiliated with political machines. Offtrack betting operations were always closely allied to urban bosses for the necessary protection. In New Jersey, for instance, racing in the early 1890s at the state's six major tracks was controlled by machine politicians. Although horse-race gambling was nearly always illegal, notorious outlaw tracks like Guttenberg and Gloucester operated with impunity, servicing the sporting fraternity from New York and Philadelphia. Gloucester was owned by Bill Thompson, the local political boss, while Guttenberg received its protection from the notorious Hudson County machine that enabled it to operate year-round. In Chicago, the racing center of the Midwest, certain track officials were so closely allied to the local machines that the sporting press claimed its horsemen were outdoing Tammany. The most flagrant example in the early 1890s was Garfield Park, a proprietary track owned by West Side bookmakers. Their political clout emanated from Mike McDonald, reputed head of syndicate crime; Bathhouse John Coughlin, boss of the infamous Levee District; and Johnny Powers, "Prince of Boodlers" in the city council and boss of the Nineteenth Ward. These political connections were also important in Chicago's bookmaking circles, since nearly all the handbook operators were tied to local ward machines.[58]

The national pastime was not as tightly controlled by machine politicians as either prizefighting or horse racing, but nonetheless, professional baseball was dominated by notable politicos. Historian Ted Vincent has found that politicians made up nearly half of the 1,262 officials and stockholders of the nineteenth-century ball clubs he studied. Most teams outside New York were not organized and controlled by local political bosses. Several important teams did have such connections, most notably the Philadelphia Athletics, which until its demise in 1892 had always been run by members of the local Republican machine. Fifteen percent of the businessmen involved in baseball teams were also involved in traction, a highly politicized enterprise. The pattern established in the nineteenth century continued until 1920. Between 1900 and 1920 every American and National League team's ownership included professional politicians, traction magnates, or friends or relatives of prominent power brokers. A similar situation existed in the minor leagues, where traction executives often subsidized or sponsored baseball franchises to increase streetcar traffic. All the teams welcomed political connections as a means to protect the franchise against interlopers, to secure vital inside information from city hall, and to obtain preferential treatment from the municipal government.

Baseball best exemplified the pastoral world that white Anglo-Saxon

Americans sought to maintain and protect in the face of industrialization, immigration, and urbanization. The sport helped to certify the continuing relevance of traditional values. But, paradoxically, baseball was in large measure controlled by men who typified all that mainstream America detested in the immigrant-dominated cities.[5]

NOTES

[1]Frederick L. Paxson, "The Rise of Sport," *Mississippi Valley Historical Review* 4 (1917): 143–68; Arthur M. Schlesinger, Sr., *The Rise of the City, 1878–1898* (New York, 1933), 308–19; John R. Betts, *America's Sporting Heritage, 1850–1950* (Reading, MA, 1974); John A. Lucas and Ronald Smith, *Saga of American Sport* (Philadelphia, 1978); Benjamin G. Rader, *American Sports: From the Age of Folk Games to the Age of Spectators* (Englewood Cliffs, NJ, 1983); Stephen Hardy, "The City and the Rise of American Sport: 1820–1920," *Exercise and Sports Sciences Reviews* 9 (1981): 183–219. On the modernization of sport, see Allen Guttmann, *From Ritual to Record: The Nature of Modern Sports* (New York, 1978), chap. 2. On the link between urban political leadership and urban recreation, see Jon Teaford, "Finis for Tweed and Steffens: Rewriting the History of Urban Rule," *Reviews in American History* 10 (1982): 136, 141.

[2]Mark H. Haller, "Organized Crime in Urban Society: Chicago in the Twentieth Century," *Journal of Social History* 5 (Winter 1971–72): 212–18; Rader, *American Sports*, 32–33, 97–98; *Dictionary of American Biography*, s.v., "Croker, Richard"; *New York Times*, April 26, 1924 (hereafter cited as *NYT*).

[3]*NYT*, August 2, 1892, September 11, 1900; Schlesinger, *Rise of the City*, 408–9.

[4]Steven A. Riess, *Touching Base: Professional Baseball and American Culture in the Progressive Era* (Westport, CT, 1980), chap. 5. For Boss Croker's views on Sunday sport, see *NYT*, December 17, 1897.

[5]Ian R. Stewart, "Politics and the Park: The Fight for Central Park," *New-York Historical Society Quarterly* 61 (1977): 124–55; Frederick Law Olmsted, Jr., and Theodora Kimball, eds., *Frederick Law Olmsted: Landscape Architect, 1822–1903* (1922–28; reprint ed., New York, 1970), 196–97, 406–9, 424–25.

[6]Stewart, "Politics and the Park," 151–53; Ian R. Stewart, "Central Park, 1851–1871: Urbanization and Environmental Planning in New York City" (Ph.D. diss., Cornell University, 1973), 148–50, 225, 242, 347–48, 354; Laura Wood Roper, *FLO: A Biography of Frederick Law Olmsted* (Baltimore, 1973), 131, 139; Olmsted and Kimball, *Olmsted*, 90–91, 196–97. On the suburban parks, see Robert Knapp, "Parks and Politics: The Rise of Municipal Responsibility for Playgrounds in New York City, 1887–1905" (M.A. thesis, Duke University, 1968), 28.

[7]Knapp, "Parks and Politics," 27–32; Jerry Dickason, "The Development of the Playground Movement in the United States" (Ph.D. diss., New York University, 1979), 88–89, 102; Jeffrey Gurock, *When Harlem Was Jewish, 1870–1930* (New York, 1981), 35, 42.

[8]Michael P. McCarthy, "Politics and the Parks: Chicago Businessmen and the Recreation Movement," *Journal of the Illinois State Historical Society* 65 (1972): 158–72; Stephen Hardy, *How Boston Played: Sport, Recreation and Community, 1865–1915* (Boston, 1982), 67–68. See also Roy Rosenzweig, *Eight Hours for What We Will: Workers and Leisure in an Industrial City, 1870–1920* (Cambridge, 1983), chap. 5.

[9]Melvin L. Adelman, *A Sporting Time: New York City and the Rise of Modern Athletics, 1820–70* (Urbana, 1986), 230–37; Gustavus Myers, *The History of Tammany Hall* (New York, 1901), 189; Alfred H. Lewis, *Richard Croker* (New York, 1901), 42–44; Elliott J. Gorn, *The Manly Art: Bare-Knuckle Prize Fighting in America* (Ithaca, 1986), 125–27.

[10]Melvin L. Adelman, "The Development of Modern Athletics: Sport in New York City, 1820–1870" (Ph.D. diss., University of Illinois, 1980), 573–74; Alexander Callow, *The Tweed Ring* (New York, 1966), 7–8, 24; Martin Shefter, "The Electoral Foundations of the Political Machine: New York City, 1884–1897," in Joel H. Silbey, Allen G. Bogue, and William H. Flanigan, eds., *The History of American Electoral Behavior* (Princeton, NJ, 1978), 263–98.

[11]Dale A. Somers *The Rise of Sports in New Orleans, 1850–1900* (Baton Rouge, 1972), chap. 8.

[12]John F. Kasson, *Amusing the Million: Coney Island at the Turn of the Century* (New York, 1978); Raymond A. Schroth, *The Eagle and Brooklyn* (Westport, CT, 1974), 100; Henry I. Hazelton, *The Boroughs of Brooklyn and Queens and the Counties of Nassau and Suffolk, 1609–1924* (New York, 1925), 1083–85; "Arthur Lumley: Veteran Sportswriter, Manager, and Promoter," *Ring Magazine* 6 (May 1927): 23; *NYT,* September 24–26, 1893. For a detailed study of boxing in New York, see Steven A. Riess, "In the Ring and Out: Professional Boxing in New York, 1896–1920," in Donald Spivey, ed., *Sport in America: New Historical Perspectives* (Westport, CT, 1985), 95–128.

[13]*National Police Gazette,* December 13, 1890, February 16, 1895, January 25, 1896 (hereafter cited as *NPG*); *New York Clipper,* February 14, 1891; *NYT,* May 29, 1896.

[14]Werner, *Tammany Hall,* 344, 438–40; Roy Crandall, "Tim Sullivan's Power," *Harper's Weekly* 58 (October 18, 1913): 14–15; Theodore A. Bingham, "The Organized Criminals of New York," *McClure's* 34 (November 1909): 62–63; George K. Turner, "Tammany's Control of New York by Professional Criminals," ibid. 33 (June 1909): 117–34; Thomas M. Henderson, *Tammany Hall and the New Immigrants: The Progressive Years* (New York, 1976), 1–15.

[15]Somers, *Sport in New Orleans,* 187–89; *NPG,* May 18, June 1, 1895, December 5, 1896; *Brooklyn Eagle,* November 16, 17, 1896. For Roosevelt's comments, see *NPG,* December 5, 1896.

[16]Riess, *Touching Base,* 71–73; Richard J. Butler and Joseph Driscoll, *Dock Walloper: The Story of "Big Dick" Butler* (New York, 1928), 487–91; *NYT,* June 11, 1899.

[17]*NPG,* September 19, November 7, 14, 1896, May 12, 1900, March 16, 1901; *Brooklyn Eagle,* June 8, 1899; Robert Cantwell, *The Real McCoy: The Life and Times of Norman Selby* (Princeton, NJ, 1971), 97–100.

[18]*NPG,* April 21, 1900, March 16, May 11, 1901, May 13, September 2, 1905, *NYT,* April 2, 1907, November 2, December 18, 1908; "Scrapbooks on Boxing," vol. 1, pp. 87, 93, Chicago Historical Society, Chicago, Illinois; *New York Call,* October 26, 1908.

[19]*NYT,* April 13, June 8, 9, 22, September 29, October 27, 1911, February 15, 29, 1912.

[20]Ibid., October 5, 9, 1915, December 30, 1916, January 30, 31, February 1–3, 5, 6, April 24, 26, May 8, 11, 1917; *New York Herald,* November 30, 1915.

[21]Guy Lewis, "World War I and the Emergence of Sport for the Masses," *The Maryland Historian* 4 (1973): 109–22; *NYT,* March 14, 27, April 11, 12, 1918, February 4, 18, 27, March 13, 20, 27, April 10, 11, 17, 1919, February 23, March 25, April 2, 25, May 25, 1920; Gene Fowler, *Beau James: The Life & Times of Jimmy Walker* (New York, 1949), 100–3.

[22]*NYT,* September 18, 1920; Randy Roberts, *Jack Dempsey: The Manassa Mauler* (Baton Rouge, 1979), 95–99; Butler, *Dock Walloper,* 264; Mrs. Tex Rickard, *Everything Happened to Him: The Story of Tex Rickard* (New York, 1936), 274–75. On Dempsey as a symbol of the 1920s, see Roberts, *Dempsey,* 264–70.

[23]There is no American equivalent to Wray Vamplew's *The Turf: A Social and Economic History of Horse Racing* (London, 1976). The best accounts of thoroughbred racing are C. B. Parmer, *For Gold and Glory: The History of Thoroughbred Racing in America* (Englewood Cliffs, NJ, 1939); and William Robertson, *The History of Thoroughbred Racing in America* (Englewood Cliffs, NJ, 1964). On the sporting style of elite New York politicians, see David C. Hammack, *Power and Society: Greater New York at the Turn of the Century* (New York, 1982), 101, 103, 111, 315, 342n.109.

[24]Adelman, *Sporting Time,* 27–29, chap. 2; Robertson, *Thoroughbred Racing,* 103, 149. On Morrissey, see *Dictionary of American Biography,* s.v., "Morrissey, John;" Hugh Bradley, *Such Was Saratoga* (New York, 1950), 136–40; Henry Chafetz, *Play the Devil: A History of Gambling in the United States from 1492 to 1955* (New York, 1960), 271–84; and Herbert Asbury, *The Gangs of New York: An Informal History of the Underworld* (New York, 1970), 90–100.

[25]Adelman, *Sporting Time,* 80–89.

[26]Melvin L. Adelman, "Quantification and Sport: The American Jockey Club, 1866–1867: A Collective Biography," in Spivey, *Sport in America,* 52–63. On New Jersey Racing see, *NYT,* October 22, 1893; David R. Johnson, "A Sinful Business: The Origins of Gambling Syndicates in the United States, 1840–1887," in David H. Bayley, ed., *Police and Society* (Beverly Hills, 1977), 36–37; and Steven A. Riess, "The Politics of New Jersey Horse Racing, 1869–1894" (unpublished paper).

[27]*Spirit of the Times* (December 31, 1881): 607; Parmer, *Gold and Glory,* 124–25; Robertson, *Thoroughbred Racing,* 148–51; *NYT,* January 12, 1884; Anthony Comstock, "Pool Rooms and Pool Selling," *North American Review,* 157 (1893): 601–10; Harold C. Syrett, *The City of Brooklyn, 1865–1898* (New York, 1944), 182–86.

[28]*Spirit of the Times* (January 21, 1888): 872; (January 28, 1888): 16; *Chicago Times,* February 8, 1887, January 22, 25, 1888, August 21, 1889; *NYT,* October 1, 1892, October 1, 1893; Robertson, *Thoroughbred Racing,* 90–92; Parmer, *Gold and Glory,* 128; Chafetz, *Play the Devil,* 267; *New York World,* March 25, 1916.

[29]*Chicago Times,* May 11, 1888, April 20, 1889; *NYT,* January 4, 5, 1890, January 6, June 24, 1891. On political payoffs, see *NYT,* March 17, 18, 1891.

[30]*NYT,* May 30, October 2, 1891. By 1900 profits were reportedly $10 million. Ibid., March 10, 1900. See also Alvin F. Harlow, *Old Wires and New Waves: The History of the Telegraph, Telephone, and Wireless* (New York, 1936), 422. On periodic police enforcement of antipoolroom laws, see *NYT,* March–May, June 24, 25, 30, 1891, March 14, 15, 28, 1893. On Croker's racing interests, see *NYT,* February 4, March 18, 25, December 18, 1893, January 5, 1907; *Brooklyn Eagle,* January 22, 1893.

[31]*NYT*, September 24, October 21, November 9, 1894; *Brooklyn Eagle*, November 9, 1894. On New Jersey racing, see Riess, "Politics of New Jersey Racing"; William E. Sackett, *Modern Battles of Trenton* (Trenton, 1895), 383–88, 440–61; and Samuel T. McSeveney, *The Politics of Depression: Political Behavior in the Northeast, 1893–1896* (New York, 1972), 45–47, 56–59, 127.

[32]*NYT*, December 9, 1894, February 12, 15, 22, March 1, 22, April 1, 3, May 3, 10, 1895.

[33]Josiah Flynt, "The Men Behind the Pool-Rooms," *Cosmopolitan Magazine* 42 (April 1907): 39–48; John P. Quinn, *Gambling and Gambling Devices* (Canton, 1912), 275–77, 281. On Farrell, see *NYT*, December 25, 1899, December 23, 1900, October 13, December 27, 1901, August 31, December 2, 1902, February 11, 1926; and Herbert Asbury, *Sucker's Progress: An Informal History of Gambling in America from the Colonies to Canfield* (New York, 1938), 451–57.

[34]*NYT*, December 13, 1901; Flynt, "Men behind the Pool-Rooms," 46–47.

[35]*NYT*, January 2, 4, 5, April 9, 1908; "The Breed of Horses and the Breed of Men," *Independent* 64 (February 20, 1908): 428–29; "The Governor's Crusade," ibid. (March 12, 1908): 592–93; "Repulsed but Not Beaten," *Outlook* 88 (April 18, 1908): 845–46; Robert F. Wesser, *Charles Evans Hughes: Politics and Reform in New York, 1905–1910* (Ithaca, 1967), 189–203.

[36]"The End of Race-Track Gambling," *Outlook* 89 (June 20, 1908): 354–55; Daniel W. McGuire, "Governor Hughes and the Race Track Gambling Issue: The Special Election of 1908," *Niagara Frontier* 18 (Winter 1971): 66–72; Wesser, *Hughes*, 203–8.

[37]*NYT*, July 3, November 8, 21, 1908, November 10, 1909, March 22, 1911. On oral betting and the liability of track owners, see ibid., November 10, 1909; April 14, 21, 22, May 5, June 4, 16, 1910, October 14, 1912, February 22, 1913, and on the closing of the tracks, see ibid., October 14, 1911.

[38]On the social functions of baseball, see H. Addington Bruce, "Baseball and the National Life," *Outlook* 104 (May 1913): 103–7; Rollin L. Hartt, "The National Game," *Atlantic Monthly* 102 (August 1908): 220–31; McCready Sykes, "The Most Perfect Thing in America," *Everybody's Magazine* 25 (October 1911): 435–46; and Riess, *Touching Base*, 17–26, chap. 7. On the political connections of New York magnates and the advantages such ties gave them, see *Touching Base*, chaps. 2, 3.

[39]Ted Vincent, *Mudville's Revenge: The Rise and Fall of American Sport* (New York, 1981), 102–3; Riess, *Touching Base*, 66. Tweed is reported to have contributed $30,000 to the team's upkeep, but that seems an exaggeration. See *National Chronicle*, February 19, 1870, cited in Harold Seymour, "The Rise of Major League Baseball to 1891" (Ph.D. diss., Cornell University, 1956), 101.

[40]Riess, *Touching Base*, 66–68.

[41]Ibid., 70–71; Vincent, *Mudville's Revenge*, 175–78, 206–7.

[42]Riess, *Touching Base*, 69; Norman Rose to William Gray, April 29, 1911, August Herrmann Papers, National Baseball Library, Baseball Hall of Fame, Cooperstown, New York.

[43]Riess, *Touching Base*, 65, 70; Harold Seymour, *Baseball*, vol. 2, *The Golden Age* (New York, 1970), 389–90.

[44]Seymour, *Baseball*, 2:70, 106; Edward Mott Wooley, "The Business of Baseball," *McClure's*, 39 (July 1912): 251–55.

[45]Riess, *Touching Base*, 68, 71, 88, 90.

[46]Ibid., 90–91.

[47]Ibid., 70, 73.

[48]Ibid., 100–6.

[49]Ibid., 50–52, 56, 58–59.

[50]Ibid., 55–56, 59–63, 73–75.

[51]Ibid., 125–36.

[52]Ben B. Seligman, *The Potentates* (New York, 1971), 260–61; Robert Sklar, *Movie-Made America* (New York, 1975), 38–47, 141–52.

[53]Charles N. Glaab and A. Theodore Brown, *A History of Urban America* (New York, 1967), 197–98; David R. Goldfield and Blaine A. Brownell, *Urban America; From Downtown to No Town* (Boston, 1979), 285–86; Howard P. Chudacoff, *The Evolution of American Urban Society*, 2d ed. (Englewood Cliffs, NJ, 1981), 146–47, 160–64; Hammack, *Power and Society*, chap. 10.

[54]On the relationship between manly sport and the feminization of culture, see Joe L. Dubbert, *A Man's Place: Masculinity in Transition* (Englewood Cliffs, NJ, 1979), 178–80; Rader, *American Sports*, 150–51; and Adelman, "Modern Athletics," 684–86. On the relationship between the machine politician and his neighborhood youth, see Haller, "Organized Crime," 212–18, 225–28.

[55]Riess, *Touching Base*, 72, 76–77.

[56]Harold Zink, *City Bosses in the United States: A Study of Twenty Municipal Bosses* (Durham, 1930), 11, 30, 85–93, 138, 148–49, 258, 331, 355. For a colorful account of Chicago's sporting fraternity, see Herman Kogan and Lloyd Wendt, *Lords of the Levee* (Indianapolis, 1943), 21, 28–29, 50–54, 109–110.

[57]Joy J. Jackson, *New Orleans in the Gilded Age: Politics and Urban Progressivism, 1880–1896* (Baton Rouge, 1969), 270–72; Walton Bean, *Boss Reuf's San Francisco* (Berkeley, 1952), 85–88. On boxing and politics in Chicago, see Kogan, *Lords of the Levee*, 123–24; Charles H. Hermann, *Recollections of Life and Days in Chicago* (Chicago, 1945), 34; and George Siler, *Inside Facts on Pugilism* (Chicago, 1907), 34.

[58]*NYT*, October 22, 1893; Riess, "Politics of New Jersey Horse Racing." On Chicago horse racing, see *Spirit of the Times* (September 19, 1891): 330; Kogan, *Lords of the Levee*, 21, 28–29, 50–54, 109–10; Mark

Haller, "Bootleggers and American Gambling," in Commission on the Review of the National Policy toward Gambling, *Gambling in America*, Appendix 1 (Washington, DC, 1976), 102–6; Haller, "Organized Crime," 214–26, 218–19; John Landesco, *Organized Crime in Chicago*, pt. 3 of *The Illinois Crime Survey, 1929* (reprint ed.; Chicago, 1968), 45–83.

[59]Vincent, *Mudville's Revenge*, 28, 98–100, 106–8, 125–26, 175–77; Riess, *Touching Base*, 50–53.

The "Poor Man's Club": Social Functions of the Urban Working-Class Saloon

*Jon M. Kingsdale**

Historical studies of the period 1890 to 1920 generally refer to the saloon in connection with urban machine politics or Temperance, yet often ignore the saloon's social and cultural functions. But an analysis of the urban saloon is important to an understanding of working-class social history in this period. Saloons seem to have exercised a significant influence upon the values and behavior of the urban working class; certainly they were central to the workingman's leisure-time activities. The saloon provided him a variety of services and played three significant roles in a growing urban industrial environment: it was a neighborhood center, an all-male establishment and a transmitter of working-class and immigrant cultures.

In the middle of the nineteenth century, as America's cities were experiencing the first shocks of industrialization and "new-stock" immigration, the saloon came to replace colonial taverns and corner grocers as the urban liquor dispensary, par excellence. The saloon became an increasingly popular institution: by 1897 licensed liquor dealers in the United States numbered over 215,000, and unlicensed "blind pigs" or "blind tigers" represented an estimated 50,000 additional outlets.[1] Most brewers—the brewing industry being highly competitive at the close of the nineteenth century—sponsored as many outlets as possible, as exclusive retailers of their own beer, thus saturating cities with saloons. In Chicago, for instance, saloons were as numerous as groceries, meat markets and dry goods stores counted together.[2] Cities without effective restrictions were deluged with saloons: in 1915 New York had over 10,000 licensed saloons, or one for every 515 persons; Chicago had one licensed saloon for every 335 residents; Houston had one for every 298 persons; San Francisco had a saloon for every 218 persons.[3] The skewed

*Jon M. Kingsdale is vice president of planning for Tufts Associated Health Plan, Waltham, Massachusetts. Reprinted from American Quarterly 25 (October 1973): 472–89. Copyright 1973 by American Studies Association. Reprinted by permission of American Quarterly and Jon M. Kingsdale.

122

distribution of saloons within cities and the large number of unlicensed retailers meant that many an urban working-class district had at least one saloon
for every 50 adult males (fifteen years of age and older). Reflecting both the
growing popularity of saloons and a switch from distilled spirits to beer,
alcoholic beverage consumption increased steadily after 1850. While consumption of distilled spirits fell by half, adult per capita consumption of beer
rose from 2.7 gallons at midcentury to 29.53 gallons per year in the period
1911–15.[4]

Of the saloon's popularity there can be little doubt: in one day half the
population of a city might visit its saloons. A survey of Chicago found that
on an average day the number of saloon customers equaled half the city's
total population.[5] In Boston, with a total population of less than half a million
in 1895—including women and children, most of whom did not frequent
saloons—a police count numbered 227,000 persons entering the city's saloons.[6]
Many of those counted were suburban commuters not included in the city's
population, as well as customers entering for a second or third time that day;
nevertheless, considering the size of Boston's adult male population, the count
is surprisingly high.

Part, but not all, of the saloon's attraction was alcoholic. Certainly the
liquor was an integral and necessary element, as the failure of most temperance substitutes in America proved. But saloons did a great deal more than
simply dispense liquor. The alcoholic "stimulation"—the neurological effects
of alcohol are actually depressant, producing a diminution of inhibitions and
thus a reduction in reserve and distance in social gatherings[7]—cannot readily
be distinguished from the social aspects of the saloon. The bartender, as
"host" in his saloon, knew as well as the middle-class hostess of today that
alcohol is an excellent icebreaker. As Raymond Calkins concluded after an
extensive survey, the saloon, with its absence of time limit and its stimulus
to self-expression and fellowship, was a natural social center.[8]

Despite city ordinances regulating location and levying high license fees,
it was relatively easy to open a saloon. With $200 to start, one could easily
find a brewer willing to provide financial backing and find a location. The
brewer paid the rent, the license fee, a bond if necessary, and supplied the
fixtures and the beer. The saloon-keeper agreed to sell no other brand of beer
and reimbursed his brewer by means of a special tax added on to the normal
price of each barrel of beer. Four-fifths of Chicago's saloons were estimated
to be under such an arrangement with brewers in 1907, as were 80 to 85
percent of New York's saloons in 1908.[9]

Although an appealing and easily accessible occupation, saloon-keeping
was often an unprofitable business enterprise. The competition was tremendous; many saloons closed after only a few months in operation. In the lean
years, 1897–1901, a third of Chicago's saloons closed down or sold out—in
one and a half blocks of Chicago's 17th ward eighteen saloons opened and
closed in as many months.[10] Some saloons flourished as fancy establishments
or well-known hangouts for politicians, athletes and other notables. But many
saloons failed, and of those which stayed on, most merely continued to do a
steady quiet business with neighborhood regulars.

Urban saloons of the late nineteenth and early twentieth centuries did not conform to a single pattern. Saloons varied greatly in appearance, atmosphere and character of the clientele they served. Yet a majority of urban saloons may be subsumed under a single prototypic description. Usually situated on a corner for maximum visibility, the typical workingman's saloon was readily recognizable by its swinging shuttered doors and wrought iron windows cluttered with potted ferns, posters and bottles of colored water. Inside was a counter running almost the length of the room, paralleled by a brass footrail. The floor was covered with sawdust. Across from the bar were perhaps a few tables and chairs backed up by a piano, pool table or rear stalls. Behind the bar and over an assortment of lemons, glasses and unopened magnums of muscatel, port and champagne hung a large plate-glass mirror. The other walls would sport a number of murals, posters, photographs and brewers' advertisements. As common as the plate-glass mirror was the presence of at least one chromo reproduction of a disrobed siren reclining on a couch. The posters and photographs were often of sports heroes: about 1890 a picture of John L. Sullivan would have been found in most saloons. A few men might be leaning over the bar, clustered about the saloon-keeper—in his white starched coat or vest, moustache and well-oiled hair; a few more might be playing pool or sitting at tables talking over a beer, reading or playing cards. Beer for five cents and whiskey for ten or fifteen were the staples. The whiskey was drunk straight—to do otherwise would be considered effeminate—followed by a chaser of water or milk to put out the fire.

The typical workingman's saloon experienced rather slow business through the day until about seven or eight o'clock, except on weekends when it was generally crowded from Saturday noon to early Monday morning. The morning in most saloons began at about five or six o'clock and was spent mostly in cleaning up and preparing the free lunch for the noontime crowd and teamsters who would drop in throughout the afternoon. But in the evenings things picked up as workingmen gathered in saloons to enjoy each other's company.

Though by far the most common, the working-class saloon described above was not the only type of urban saloon. There were suburban beer gardens, downtown businessmen's saloons, and waterfront dives and barrelhouses serving sailors, tramps, petty criminals and the very poor. Jacob Riis, in *How the Other Half Lives*,[11] described the lowest of the low in a New York tenement slum: in a dark clammy hovel were grouped ten or fifteen tramps and petty criminals seated on crates and broken chairs around a keg of stale beer. The dregs from used beer barrels lying out on the sidewalk awaiting the brewer's cart were drained off and doctored up to be served in old tomato cans to the less than distinguished clientele. But this was an extreme case. William Cole and Kellog Darland of the South End House in Boston described a typical waterfront dive as small, dirty and inhospitable.[12] It was lighted by unshaded flickering gas jets revealing a gaudy mirror, foul beer-soaked sawdust on the floor, and no tables, chairs or inviting free lunch to encourage patrons to linger at their ease.

At the other end of the spectrum, the business districts contained a large number of well-appointed saloons catering to professionals, businessmen and the middle and upper classes in general. Here the bars were of mahogany, the pictorial art of a better class, and some even had orchestras. These saloons were often used as meeting places for business purposes, especially by sales representatives and buyers who might complete a transaction over a beer in an oak table alcove. In the suburbs could be found old homes of solid decor, converted to roadhouses for the use of travelers and suburban residents. Also in the suburbs as well as in town were German-model beer gardens providing good food and open spaces in which to relax while listening to a symphony orchestra.

With this perspective in mind, let us turn to an analysis of the social functions of the working-class urban saloon. The workingman's saloon was a leisure-time institution playing a large part in the social, political, even the economic, aspects of his life. It performed a variety of functions, major and minor: furnishing the cities' only public toilets, providing teamsters with watering troughs, cashing checks and lending money to customers, in addition to serving as the political and recreational focus of the workingman.

In its most encompassing function the saloon served many workingmen as a second home. If the middle-class male retired to his living room after dinner to relax, the workingman retired to the corner saloon to meet his friends, relax and maybe play a game of cards or billiards. Many workingmen thought of and treated the corner saloon as their own private club rather than as a public institution. They used it as a mailing address; leaving and picking up messages, and meeting friends there; depositing money with, or borrowing from, the saloon-keeper. Workingmen played cards, musical instruments and games, ate, sang and even slept there. Even today, "home territory" bars are characterized by a familiarity among patrons and hostility or suspicion toward newcomers.[13]

For slum residents, especially in immigrant ghetto and tenement districts, the neighboring saloons were inevitably more attractive than their own over-crowded, dirty, noisy, ugly, poorly lighted and ventilated flats. For many immigrants their new homes in America were merely places to sleep and eat—life moved out of the flats into the streets and saloons.[14] Large numbers of lodging-house boarders adopted saloons as surrogate homes, their own quarters being cramped, filthy and dull.[15] Compared to cheap boarding houses that slept men dormitory style in long rows of bunks, the corner saloon was by far the more hospitable place to spend the evenings. Some saloon habitués even slept there—a place on the floor at night cost five cents.

Saloons also functioned as food suppliers. The "free lunch" fed thousands of men in each city. There was usually something on hand in saloons to munch on at any time, but from about eleven o'clock in the morning to three in the afternoon a special buffet lunch was served free to customers—who were, of course, expected to buy at least one beer. If a saloon did not serve a free lunch it often served a "businessman's lunch," which for ten to twenty-five cents was better than most restaurants could offer. The accent in the free lunch was on salty and spiced foods to provoke a thirst, but for five cents the workingman got a better lunch than most ten-cent restaurants served, plus a beer and more attractive surroundings in which to enjoy it. Saloons could afford the free lunch because the brewer supplied the food at cost, having purchased it cheaply in quantity.

Saloons that sold lunches and some large saloons that offered free lunches provided quite a feast. One saloon in the 17th ward of Chicago, a working-class district, offered in its free lunch a choice of frankfurters, clams, egg sandwiches, potatoes, vegetables, cheeses, bread, and several varieties of hot and cold meats. Employing five men at the lunch counter, it gave away between thirty and forty dollars' worth of food a day: 150 to 200 pounds of meat, 1 to 2 bushels of potatoes, 50 loaves of bread, 35 pounds of beans, 10 dozen ears of corn and $2 worth of other vegetables.[16] This was not the typical fare in a workingman's saloon, but even the average free lunch in an Eastern city—the free lunches in the East were usually less generous than those of the West and South, due perhaps to higher food prices and less competition among saloons of the East—was sufficient for noontime needs. In Boston, New York, Philadelphia or Baltimore a typical free lunch would consist of bread or crackers, bologna or weinerwurst, sliced tomatoes, salad, pickles, onions, radishes and perhaps soup or a hot meat stew.[17] But even this, considering that cheap restaurants in Boston charged five cents for a sandwich, a piece of pie, two doughnuts, or a glass of milk, ten cents for a meat pie and twenty-five cents for a full dinner, was a bargain.[18]

The free lunch fed a large portion of the working class and the middle class. Probably half or more of the cities' saloons offered a free lunch. In some cities, such as Boston, saloons were required by law to offer free food, if not exactly a meal, though in others, Atlanta for instance, they were forbidden by law to offer food. In Chicago, at the end of the nineteenth century, 92 of the 157 saloons in the 19th ward, and 111 of the 163 saloons of the 17th ward, both working-class districts, offered a free lunch.[19] Along a distance of four miles on Madison Street, which ran through working-class residential and business districts of Chicago, 115 saloons offered a free lunch, compared to three restaurants offering a 5¢ lunch, five 10¢ restaurants, twenty 15¢ restaurants and twenty-five restaurants charging 20¢ to 35¢.[20]

Saloons were also the most important source of recreation and amusement for the urban working class. They provided both recreational facilities and a general atmosphere which encouraged informal, spontaneous group activities. They catered to a larger clientele in a greater variety of ways than any other leisure-time institution, until athletics, films, the automobile and radio achieved a dominant position in recreational activities in the 1920s. In Boston,[21] to take one example, the relatively extensive system of outdoor swimming facilities drew an attendance of just over 2 million in 1899—an attendance which Boston's saloons surpassed in nine days. Poolrooms in Boston drew a daily attendance one-tenth as large as the saloons attracted; coffee rooms did less well than poolrooms; and reading rooms in Boston drew a daily attendance less than one-twentieth of the saloons' patronage. While there was always a saloon just down the street or around the corner, city parks were usually located at such a distance from working-class residential districts that they were of little value to workers except on Sundays and holidays. In Boston the parks nearest working-class areas were far beyond walking distance.[22] In Manhattan parks were conspicuous by their absence from tenement areas.[23] Chicago's fine system of parks was located primarily in the suburbs.[24] Public and private athletic facilities, reading rooms, clubs, and labor union recreational halls were not plentiful at the turn of the century, nor were they desired by the working class nearly so much as saloons. They often catered to the values of a sponsoring philanthropist, whereas saloons tried to give the workingman exactly what he wanted.

Saloons offered a variety of amusements and recreational facilities, such as newspapers, cards, movies, a gramophone or live entertainment—usually a violinist, singer or vaudeville show—billiards, bowling, and sporting news relayed by ticker tape. Tables and chairs, cards and billiards were the most common and widely used facilities, though for an evening's entertainment at least one saloon offering a burlesque show was usually within easy reach of any working-class neighborhood.[25]

The quality and quantity of amusements varied from one city to the next, and from one section of the country to another. In the East facilities were often limited due to strict government regulations which either explicitly prohibited certain forms of recreation in saloons, or kept the number of saloons in a city low enough that there was little competitive incentive to sponsor amusements in order to attract customers. In Boston, for example, pool tables in saloons were permitted only in rare instances; tables, chairs and cards were rare; prostitution and gambling were totally divorced from the saloons.[26] Gambling machines, billiards, bowling and similar games were prohibited in Philadelphia's saloons.[27] Recreational facilities were more plentiful in the West. The great majority of saloons in St. Louis had tables, chairs and cards; many had billiard tables, and some had pianos.[28] Tables, chairs, cards, billiards, gambling machines and games, and prostitution were common in the saloons of San Francisco.[29] In Chicago, of the 320 saloons in the 17th and 19th wards, 183 had tables and chairs, 209 provided newspapers, 102 had pool tables and several saloons ran small gymnasiums, provided handball courts, music halls and/or gambling.[30]

More important than the actual facilities was the air of relaxed, informal sociability which pervaded saloons. Saloon names like "The Fred," "Ed and Frank's," "The Club" and "The Poor Man's Retreat" promised a warm, friendly atmosphere.[31] Patrons of a saloon often had something in common with each other—neighborhood ties, similar interests or a common occupation or ethnic background—to stimulate group feelings and camaraderie. Neighborhood ties and a common ethnic background most often united the group. Sometimes formal groups patronized saloons: singing societies, lodge chapters and neighborhood committees often met in saloons or adjoining rooms.[32] Boxers and other athletes opened saloons which attracted fellow sportsmen and spectators. Saloons such as the "Milkmen's Exchange" and the "Mechanic's Exchange" attracted workingmen of the same occupation.[33]

Alcohol, by virtue of its inhibition-releasing effect, stimulated feelings of social familiarity, group identification and solidarity and was itself a focus of group activity. The custom of treating was nearly universal: each man treated the group to a round of drinks and was expected to stay long enough to be treated in turn by the rest of the group—which made for much happy back-slapping, sloppy singing and drunken exuberance. If things were going slowly, the saloon-keeper might treat the house to a round in order to stimulate fellowship and, hopefully, a few more paying rounds. The saloon-keeper often played the part of a host, keeping the "guests" happy—and somewhat orderly—and keeping the "party" going.

Singing seems to have been fairly common, both by groups and arising spontaneously.[34] The songs, like the conversation, were often highly senti-mental, lamenting the fallen girl or the drunk, idolizing motherhood, patri-otism, the nobility of the workingman, the righteousness of working-class causes, or almost any other highly emotional subject. Such songs as "A Boy's Best Friend is His Mother," "Always Take Mother's Advice" and "A Flower From My Angel Mother's Grave" typify the sentimentality of saloon singing.[35] But the saloon could be subdued and relaxed as well as loud and exuberant. Men might sit over a single beer for hours in earnest conversation, quietly playing cards or discussing politics.

Being central to the workingman's leisure-time activities, saloons came into contact with almost all aspects of his life; they touched the life of the cities at many points, from crime and poverty to politics and work. Crime, poverty, prostitution and machine graft flourished in the city and fed off saloons. Though the causes of these evils were deep-rooted and complex, the saloon was often pictured—in an overly simplified view—as the sole or main force responsible for the cities' problems. The saloon symbolized that threat which the lower-class immigrant, caught up in the harsh urban-industrial explosion after the Civil War, posed to traditional American morality.

Evils were ascribed all too simply to saloons, and the evils manifest in saloons were often exaggerated. As E. C. Moore, professor of sociology and social worker at Hull House, testified, saloons generally did not stand for intemperance and vice.[36] In two hundred visits to saloons in Chicago's working-class districts he saw only three drunken men. Only 2 of the 157 saloons in Chicago's 19th ward were known to police as hangouts for thieves; one was known as a house of assignation. In Boston and Philadelphia gambling and prostitution were completely divorced from the saloons. But in many cities the connection did exist. The Raines Law in New York, prohibiting all liquor retailers except hotels from opening on Sunday, the biggest day of business, turned hundreds of saloons into brothels, or so-called Raines Law hotels. In certain well-defined sections of Chicago, St. Louis, San Francisco, Denver, Buffalo, Baltimore and many more cities prostitution and gambling were rife in the saloons.[37] Chicago's Vice Commission of 1911 found saloons to have been the most conspicuous and important element in connection with pros-titution aside from the brothels themselves.[38] Prostitutes were tolerated by some saloon-keepers for the added business they were expected to attract. Sometimes the proprietor contracted with the girls to pay them a commission on drinks bought for them—a commission the saloon could well afford since it charged twenty-five cents for a beer in the rear stalls, and often served the girls soft drinks when they ordered distilled liquor. Sometimes waiters were expected when they took a job to bring their own prostitutes or bar girls with them to solicit drinks. Most saloons in almost every city were also guilty of consistently breaking laws regulating their closing hours and forbidding sales on Sunday. The fighting and drunkenness endemic to slum life was found as much in the saloons as on the streets and in tenements—perhaps more so, despite the fact that most saloon-keepers refused to serve drunks and tried to maintain order in their saloons, out of self-interest if for no other reason.

In assessing the relationship of crime, poverty and insanity to saloons, one is handicapped not so much by a lack of information as by a plethora of contradictory statistics, reflecting the bias of the surveyor as well as the reluctance of subjects to be completely frank. When data do seem reliable and statistical correlations are strong and positive, still, nothing is revealed of the causal relationship. Nevertheless, for what it is worth, the correlation of intemperance with pauperism, crime and insanity seems to have been very high.[39] What this says about saloons is unclear since intemperance was not dependent solely upon saloons, nor did it disappear with Prohibition. As for the allegation, commonly made by temperance advocates, that the liquor bill was a drain on the family budget, it would seem to have been the cause, in itself, of very few cases of poverty. Liquor consumption averaged not more than 5 percent of a workingman's family budget.[40]

Saloons became involved even in the occupational concerns of the working class. Men of the same occupation would gather at certain saloons, and unemployed coworkers would go there for news of job openings and perhaps some relief. Employers in need of laborers might apply to the saloon-keeper. Prior to the existence of the International Longshoremen's Association dockworkers were usually hired by saloon-keepers—and sometimes forced to spend their wages in the contractor's saloon.[41]

The unions had mixed feelings about saloons. Though union members were overwhelmingly antiprohibitionist, union organizers and officers often feared the dulling effect of alcohol on working-class consciousness. Thus, although locals of the Union of Bakers and Confectioners met in saloons before the establishment of a national office, an officer of the national union stated his opposition to saloons, "especially when a 'Baker's Home' is connected therewith. When possible we establish employment offices ourselves, to give work free of charge to our members."[42] The Knights of Labor and the Brotherhood of Locomotive Firemen refused membership to saloon-keepers. The United Garment Workers, the Journeymen Tailors and the United Mine Workers, to name only a few, tried whenever possible not to hold meetings in halls connected with saloons. But saloons welcomed unions and offered their rooms at prices below market level for chapter meetings, at a time when many unions were hard pressed to find any halls open to them. At the turn of the century half or more of the United Brewery Workers, the Wood Carvers' Association, the Amalgamated Wood Workers, and the Brotherhood of Boiler Makers and Iron Shipbuilders met in saloons or halls connected with them.[43] In Buffalo, at the turn of the century, 63 of the city's 69 labor organizations held their meetings in halls connected with saloons, and in many other cities the dependence on saloons was nearly as great.[44]

In politics, too, saloons played a major role. The liquor industry as a whole was thoroughly involved in politics, and saloons in particular were often associated with urban machine politics. Saloons provided politicians a means to contact and organize workingmen, and the political machine sold favors to saloons. In the former case, saloons were especially useful at the ward level. The ward leader was the backbone of the political machine, his club the bastion of political power in the ward. He built his following out of the ward club, called them together at the club for special occasions and kept them happy there. The club was a pleasant place where leaders and followers could find relaxation at a billiard table or a bar, and chew the political fat. It served as a social institution, a center for recreation and camaraderie, and a refuge from wife and family. The ward leader needed to be friendly, generous and thoroughly knowledgeable about his neighborhood. Saloons fitted the needs of the machine politician perfectly. Saloons could, and did, easily double as ward clubs, and the type and extent of the saloon-keeper's contact with his neighborhood was a valuable political asset. Being a working-class social center, the saloon provided a natural stage for politicians and an excellent base for organizing the vote. Plus, saloons were a good source of bums, drunks, petty criminals, hoboes and anyone else who might sell his vote for a few dollars in cash or in liquor. Half the Democratic captains of Chicago's first ward at the beginning of the twentieth century were saloon proprietors.[45] One-third of Milwaukee's 46 city councilmen in 1902 were saloon-keepers, as were about a third of Detroit's aldermen at the end of the nineteenth century.[46] Tweed's "Boodle Board" of aldermen was composed in half of saloon-keepers or ex-saloon-keepers; in 1884 nearly two-thirds of the political conventions and primaries in New York City were held in saloons; and in 1890 eleven of New York City's 24 aldermen were saloon-keepers.[47]

If the saloon was a natural center for political activity and a boon to the machine politician, the combination of early-hour closing laws and strong competition among saloons made the crooked politicians and his favors indispensable to saloon-keepers. Proprietors were forced to pay the police and the political machine in order to stay open late at night, as well as for prostitution and gambling. In Chicago's first ward the annual Democratic Club Ball cost every saloon-keeper fifteen to twenty-five dollars in fifty-cent tickets, not to mention the routine monthly payments.[48] Thus was cemented the bond between saloon and politician. The saloon was as often the victim as it was the springboard of the machine politician—in either case the relationship was intimate.

Not surprisingly, the saloon was itself a major, perhaps the major, issue in urban politics and reform. Sunday closing laws and their enforcement were a perennial, often highly emotional and important, campaign issue, which elicited from saloons an active and organized response. For instance, the Keep Your Mouth Shut Organization, centered in Detroit, supported, out of assessments on its member saloons, political candidates favorable to the liquor interests. The Detroit Liquor Dealers Protective Association was founded in 1880 with the intention of challenging "unfair" liquor legislation in the courts and aiding any of its 400 members charged with violations of the closing laws. At the end of the nineteenth century both retailers and brewers organized fraternal orders to promote their interests and protect themselves from temperance legislation. The Royal Ark organized Detroit's saloons into wards, each with a captain to look after the interests of the saloons in his ward. It also distributed to its members a list of endorsed candidates who would not enforce Sunday, holiday and early-hour closing laws. This was known as the "Saloon Slate."[49]

If, then, the saloon affected the workingman's life in a variety of ways, what significant role did it play for the working class? The urban working-man's saloon served three major functions. First, saloons served as a major social focus of the neighborhood. The saloon was a local institution in an economy well on its way to production and consumption en masse. It was a neighborhood center in an urban environment which denied its residents that sense of community and stability inherent in an earlier, small-town America. Although some working-class saloons clustered about industrial enterprises, feeding off factory workers during the day, or depended on nightly enter-tainment and prostitution to draw patrons from a wide radius, these types were common only in certain slum, business and industrial areas of a city. Most saloons in residential districts—urban and suburban—drew a steady crowd of neighborhood regulars. And most city blocks had at least one "neigh-borhood" saloon. Indeed, the corner saloon may have been the most neigh-borly institution in the city. While children played in the street and women talked on tenement stoops, the men went to a saloon.

The saloon-keeper himself was often an important figure in the neigh-borhood and claimed a large place in the hearts of his regular customers. If a new saloon opened or an old one changed management, the whole neigh-borhood would know of it in a matter of hours and come in to size up the new proprietor.[50] The saloon-keeper often fostered community ties, for com-mercial reasons or otherwise. He might open connecting rooms for the enter-tainment of a local boys' club, or provide them with a club room for a small price.[51] He might be the favorite local "pharmacist," prescribing stale beer for a gaseous stomach, a sloe gin fizz for clearing morning-after headaches, and other mixtures for chest colds or cramps.

Saloons mirrored the character of the surrounding neighborhood, helped to shape it, and tried to serve it. One could speak of the typical Jewish saloon on the lower East Side where the signs and conversation were all in Yiddish, of an Italian café-style saloon, the Irish-American stand-up saloon, or the German beer garden which attracted not only neighboring males, but their families as well.[52] Whatever the ethnic background, saloons offered their services to the community. In a survey of Chicago's saloons they were noted to offer furnished rooms free or for a small charge to local men's clubs, musical societies, fraternal orders, small wedding parties and neighborhood meetings. As the surveyor stated, "The saloon is, in short, the clearing house for the common intelligence—the social and intellectual center of the neighborhood."[53]

In a second aspect of its role, the saloon was a male institution in a culture still predominantly male-oriented, but loosing ground quickly to the concept of female emancipation and equality. Although some women drank in res-taurants and beer gardens, the social and legal injunction against women drinking in, or even entering, working-class saloons was generally observed, except by prostitutes.[54] The saloon was a thoroughly male institution with the appropriate atmosphere, from the sawdust on the floor to the pictures of athletes on the walls to the prostitutes in the backroom stalls. The saloon supported and reinforced a stereotypically masculine character and a self-sufficient, all male culture separate from the prissy world of women and the constraints of family. Judging from barroom conversation and behavior, women were valued primarily as sexual objects. Otherwise they were pictured as a nuisance, superfluous at best, downright troublesome at worst. The ideal as represented in the decor and personified by the saloon-keeper was the strong male, unfettered by domestic chains and enjoying the camaraderie of his fellows with a carefree sociability. As children often gathered at saloon door-ways, excited by the noisy scene within, the saloon probably played a part in the process by which many boys formed their values as American males. That happy, boisterous, uninhibited scene was a powerful model for the American male. As Jack London put it: "In the saloons life was different. Men talked with great voices, laughed great laughs, and there was an atmosphere of greatness. . . . Terrible they might be, but then that only meant they were terribly wonderful, and it is the terribly wonderful that a boy desires to know."[55] Drink was the badge of manhood, the brass rail "a symbol of masculinity emancipate."[56]

It seems likely that some sort of bachelor subculture existed prior to Prohibition and has since waned. The proportion of singles among the male population has declined significantly since the end of the nineteenth century: of males aged fifteen and over, the proportion single declined from 42 percent in 1890 to 33 percent in 1940, and to less than 25 percent in 1950.[57] The thousands of men in any large city who lived in lodging houses, spending their days at work and their evenings in saloons and pool halls, had little real contact with women other than prostitutes. The saloon was particularly important as a social center for this group of workingmen. Many saloon-goers were, of course, married, but in some saloons the patrons were noted to be mostly over thirty and single.[58] Clark Warburton, in his study of the effects of Prohibition, estimated that more than half of working-class drinking was done by single men.[59] Certainly many of the heavy drinkers, saloon regulars, were bachelors: although only 45 percent of Boston's male population aged fourteen or over was single, 60 percent of a study sample of arrested drunks in Boston in 1909 were unmarried.[60]

For married men the saloon was an escape from wife and family. The workingmen at McSorley's—of John Sloan's painting, "McSorley's Saloon"—looked "as if they never thought of a woman. They were maturely reflecting in purely male ways and solemnly discoursing, untroubled by skirts or domesticity."[61] For married men, free for only a few hours, as well as for young "stags" and older bachelors, the saloon was an escape, a bastion of male fellowship and independence.

Abstainers, too, seem to have understood the self-sufficient masculine character of saloons. Saloons were often pictured by Prohibitionists and middle-class women as competitors to home and family.[62] Feminists heartily supported the Temperance movement. The Women's Christian Temperance Union was a leading temperance organization, also strongly committed to female suffrage and feminism. The Anti-Saloon League, though it tried to stay clear of all causes other than Temperance, apparently felt that the link between Prohibition and woman suffrage was so strong that the League could hardly afford to ignore the latter. For the Temperance movement was in part a reflection of a public desire, especially strong among women, to curb the self-assertive, boisterous masculinity of the saloon, to support and protect the family, and to return the husband—immigrant workingmen in particular— to the home. Even moderate temperance advocates felt that the nation needed and Prohibition might start "a new awakening to the values of the home . . . broadened into a contagion that shall cover the country."[63]

Third, the saloon was symbolically and functionally alien to that traditional American ethic rooted in a largely Anglo-Saxon, Protestant population heavily influenced by its Puritan antecedents. The Yiddish saloon on the lower East Side, as much as the intoxicated "nigger" in the South, was perceived as a threat to the traditional culture and social fabric. The saloon was not only the symbol of a predominantly urban, new-immigrant, working-class life-style alien to the traditional American ascetic ethic of work, frugality, self-control, discipline and sobriety; it served as an alternative, a competitor to the traditional pattern. Content to waste his time and money in saloons and take his sodden pleasures in near absolute leisure, the urban immigrant worker lacked the ability and incentive to bootstrap himself up into the middle class. In the eyes of the temperance advocate, it was the saloon that kept him down, thus impeding the process of cultural assimilation and slowing down America's march to material bliss.

Rather than aid immigrant groups to assimilate, rather than encourage the working class to adopt middle-class manners and aspirations, the workingman's saloon tended to conserve and reinforce ethnic and class ties. Saloons in immigrant districts usually attracted and catered to a single ethnic group, according to the character of the neighborhood and the nationality of the saloon-keeper. As a highly adaptive local institution, the saloon tended to reflect and serve the character of its clientele: drinking habits, games, newspapers, language—all reflected the ethnic milieu. Immigrants also used their saloons for ethnic group meeting halls and for the celebration of their national occasions. Moreover, the saloon provided immigrants, Eastern and Southern Europeans especially, the kind of informal, relaxed, slow-moving social setting many had been accustomed to in the old country. As for class ties, the workingman's saloon was oriented toward relief from work and toward the weekend binge. The absence of time limits, the stimulus to uninhibited self-expression, the lack of any goal-oriented activity in saloons made them a purely nonproductive leisurely institution, reflecting working-class values in general and a lower-class tendency to divorce work and enjoyment in particular.

The ethnic and class orientation of saloons was clear. They were most dense in immigrant neighborhoods and most frequented by the working class. The working-class saloon was central to a way of life engendered by large-scale immigration and a growing urbanism and industrialism, and appropriate to a relatively newly formed proletariat. Providing ample opportunity for relaxation, supporting immigrant groups in their efforts to retain ethnic identity, harboring vice, gambling, criminals and machine politicians, the saloon was alien to Puritan America and efficiency-minded Progressives alike.

The saloon, then, was a community center tending to give some coherence to neighborhoods by focusing the attention of male residents upon the people and events of the area. It was a male institution reinforcing stereotypically masculine qualities and catering to the social needs of that large segment of men who remained bachelors. It was a form of amusement that encouraged the working class, immigrants especially, in the retention of their cultural identity and retarded the movement to assimilation into the American middle class.

The character of the urban workingman's saloon as depicted above suggests some interesting questions, the answers to which lie beyond the scope of my own research. An understanding of the role of saloons suggests that Temperance may have been a practical, politically goal-oriented movement. Temperance sentiment in the late nineteenth and early twentieth centuries is often ascribed to an excess of reactionary populism or status-group concern for symbolic cultural victories. Rarely is it viewed today as a practical measure designed primarily to achieve tangible results.[64] But if the saloon itself was not merely a liquor dispensary—if, as I have claimed, it actually played a significant role in the life of workingmen, immigrants especially—then why should the Temperance movement, which was in part a battle against saloons per se, be seen primarily as a symbolic issue? If the saloon functioned as an institutional support of working-class and ethnic values, an obstacle to assimilation, and a competitor or alternative to the traditional ideal of family, then perhaps Prohibition was a logical measure in line with immigration restriction to preserve the Anglo-Saxon Protestant character of America, and in line with child labor laws to preserve and protect the family. Perhaps we ought to ask what effect Prohibition actually had on family structure and working-class values.

The saloon study also raises some questions about the concept of community in twentieth century America. If saloons imparted a focus and some meaning to working-class neighborhoods, did they also give male residents a real sense of community? Can we look to corner saloons and pool halls, neighborhood theaters and local chapters of labor unions, women's clubs and fraternal organizations for at least a watered-down sense of belonging and identity? What other local institutions may have contributed in a similar manner to a sense of community? And what was the effect of the waning of neighborhood recreational institutions in the 1920s? Social historians might profitably look to the neighborhood, as well as to the city, for a basic social unit.

Finally, the social functions of urban working-class saloons suggest some interesting questions concerning the existence and nature of a male ethic and a bachelor subculture. If a special image of the American male shaped his values and behavior, what exactly was that image, what were its effects and what other institutions besides the saloon were intimately tied to it? Perhaps labor unions, amateur athletics, family structure and other organizations and activities should be looked at with reference to the needs and motives arising out of a male ethic. Certainly the existence of a bachelor subculture should be of interest to social historians. Census statistics indicate that there was a substantially larger proportion of single men before World War II than at present—due perhaps to an inordinately large number of single males among

first-generation immigrants. The only reference I have found to this phenomenon is in one of a series of sociological sketches by Ned Polsky, which ascribes
the decline of pool halls since the 1920s to the disappearance of a subculture
of professional bachelors.[65] Polsky is referring to lower-class bachelors for the
most part: hustlers, petty gamblers and criminals, saloon-keepers and probably a good number of workingmen. With urban modernization, growing
national wealth and an increased tendency among men to marry, this component of the urban scene has waned. We might ask if this was actually a
subculture with a distinctive value set and a measure of continuity. If so,
what institutions besides saloons, pool halls and lodging houses were intimately connected with it? What has happened to them and to the subculture
itself? It is, I think, the proper vocation of the social historian to delve into
these subtler aspects of history in order to comprehend the texture of life in
the past.

NOTES

[1]U.S. Congress, House, *Twelfth Annual Report of the Commissioner of Labor*, House Doc. 564, 55th Cong.,
2d sess., 1897, p. 41; Andrew Sinclair, *Prohibition, the Era of Excess* (Boston: Little, Brown, 1962), p. 77.

[2]Francis G. Peabody, ed., *The Liquor Problem: a Summary of Investigations Conducted by the Committee of
Fifty* (Boston: Houghton Mifflin, 1905), p. 147. The reports of the Committee of Fifty, as well as a number
of other sources on which I relied heavily, reflect the progressive reformer's point of view. By and large,
the members of the Committee were academics, clergymen and other professionals who proposed to dispel
the confusion caused by a welter of contradictory claims put out by wet and dry propagandists. They
concluded that what was needed were saloon substitutes rather than the all too simple solution of legislative
prohibition. Recognizing that saloons were attractive because they performed necessary services, the
Committee of Fifty suggested that those services be taken over by temperate enterprises. Their accounts
represent the honest and, on the whole, successful effort of socially concerned and well-educated men to
comprehend the dynamics of a difficult problem.

[3]U.S. Department of Commerce, Bureau of the Census, *General Statistics of the Cities: 1915*, p. 37.

[4]E. M. Jellinek, "Recent Trends in Alcoholism and Alcohol Consumption," *Quarterly Journal of Studies
on Alcohol*, 8 (June 1947), 2.

[5]Peabody, ed., *The Liquor Problem*, p. 147.

[6]Francis G. Peabody, "Substitutes for the Saloon," *Forum*, 21 (1896), 598.

[7]J. N. Cross, *Guide to the Community Control of Alcoholism* (New York: American Public Health Assoc.,
1968), pp. 21–24.

[8]Raymond Calkins, *Substitutes for the Saloon* (Boston: Houghton Mifflin, 1901), pp. 2–5.

[9]George K. Turner, "The City of Chicago," *McClure's Magazine*, Apr. 1907, p. 577; Arthur H. Gleason,
"The New York Saloon," *Collier's Weekly*, Apr. 25, 1908, p. 16.

[10]Turner, "Chicago," p. 579.

[11]Jacob Riis, *How the Other Half Lives* (1890; rpr. Cambridge: Harvard Univ. Press, 1970), p. 139.

[12]William I. Cole and Kellog Darland, "Substitutes for the Saloon in Boston," in *Substitutes for the
Saloon*, ed. by Raymond Calkins (Boston: Houghton Mifflin, 1901), p. 321.

[13]Sherri Cavan, *Liquor License, an Ethnography of Bar Behavior* (Chicago: Aldine, 1966), pp. 211–13.

[14]Robert W. DeForest and Lawrence Veiller, eds., *The Tenement House Problem* (New York: Macmillan,
1903), Vol. I; Oscar Handlin, *The Uprooted* (Boston: Little, Brown, 1951), pp. 153–62.

[15]Royal L. Melendy, "The Saloon in Chicago, II," *American Journal of Sociology*, Jan. 1901, pp. 450–
54.

[16]Melendy, "The Saloon in Chicago, I," *American Journal of Sociology*, Nov. 1900, p. 295.

[17]Calkins, *Saloon Substitutes*, pp. 15–18; "The Experiences and Observations of a New York Saloon-
Keeper as Told by Himself," *McClure's Magazine*, Jan. 1909, p. 305.

[18]Cole and Darland, "Saloon Substitutes in Boston," in *Saloon Substitutes*, ed. Calkins, p. 329.

[19]E. C. Moore, chap. 8, in *Economic Aspects of the Liquor Problem*, ed. John Koren (Boston: Houghton
Mifflin 1899), p. 219.

[20]Melendy, "Saloon in Chicago, II," p. 455.

[21]Peabody, "Saloon Substitutes," p. 598.

[22]"Saloon Substitutes in Boston," in *Saloon Substitutes*, ed. Calkins, p. 333.

[23]DeForest and Veiller, *Tenement Problem*, Vol. 2, chap. 1.

[24]Melendy, "Saloon in Chicago, II," p. 448.

[25]Melendy, "Saloon in Chicago, I," p. 298.

[26]Chicago Commission on the Liquor Problem, Chicago City Council, *Preliminary Report to the Mayor and Aldermen*, 1916.

[27]U.S. Brewer's Association, *Proceedings of the 49th Annual Convention* (Atlantic City, N.J., 1909), p. 121.

[28]Frederic H. Wines and John Koren, *The Liquor Problem in Its Legislative Aspects* (Boston: Houghton Mifflin, 1898), p. 329.

[29]*Economic Aspects*, ed. Koren, chap. 8, p. 233; Calkins, *Saloon Substitutes*, p. 381.

[30]*Economic Aspects*, ed. Koren, chap. 8, p. 214; Melendy, "Saloon in Chicago, I," p. 293.

[31]Calkins, *Saloon Substitutes*, pp. 8, 9.

[32]Melendy, "Saloon in Chicago, II," pp. 435, 437.

[33]Calkins, *Saloon Substitutes*, pp. 8, 9.

[34]George Ade, *The Old-Time Saloon, Not Wet–Not Dry, Just History* (New York: R. Long & R. R. Smith, 1931), pp. 126–29.

[35]Ibid.

[36]*Economic Aspects*, ed. Koren, chap. 8, p. 213.

[37]Melendy, "Saloon in Chicago, I," p. 303; Calkins, *Saloon Substitutes*, Appendix IV.

[38]The Vice Commission of Chicago, *The Social Evil in Chicago* (Chicago: Gunthorp-Warren, 1911).

[39]For some reliable studies done before Prohibition on crime, poverty and insanity in connection with alcohol and intemperance in America, see: Koren, ed., *Economic Aspects*; U.S. Department of Commerce and Labor, *Bulletin of the Bureau of Labor*, S. E. Forman, "Charity Relief and Wage Earnings" (Washington, D.C.: GPO, 1908); Mass., Bureau of Statistics of Labor, *The Twenty-Sixth Annual Report*, by Horace G. Wadlin (Boston: Wright & Potter, 1896).

[40]Robert C. Chapin, "The Standard of Living Among Workingmen's Families in New York City" (New York, 1909), quoted in Clark Warburton, *The Economic Results of Prohibition* (New York: Columbia Univ. Press, 1932), p. 138.

[41]James H. Timberlake, *Prohibition and the Progressive Movement, 1900–1920* (Cambridge: Harvard Univ. Press, 1963), p. 83.

[42]Edward M. Bemis, appendix, "Attitude of Trade Unions," in *Substitutes for the Saloon*, ed. Raymond Calkins (Boston: Houghton Mifflin, 1901), p. 304.

[43]Ibid., pp. 307–13.

[44]Calkins, *Saloon Substitutes*, p. 61.

[45]Turner, "Chicago," p. 584.

[46]John M. Barker, *The Saloon Problem and Social Reform* (Boston: Everett Press, 1905), p. 32; Lawrence D. Engelmann, "O, Whiskey: The History of Prohibition in Michigan," Diss. University of Michigan 1971, p. 78.

[47]Peter Odegard, *Pressure Politics* (New York: Columbia Univ. Press, 1928), p. 247.

[48]Turner, "Chicago," p. 587.

[49]Engelmann, "O, Whiskey," pp. 71–75.

[50]"Experiences of a Saloon-Keeper," p. 310.

[51]Calkins, *Saloon Substitutes*, pp. 51, 52.

[52]Robert A. Stevenson, "Saloons," *Scribner's Magazine*, May 1901, pp. 573–75.

[53]Melendy, "Saloon in Chicago, I," p. 295.

[54]U.S. Department of Commerce, *Cities: 1915*, p. 35.

[55]*John Barleycorn* (New York: Century, 1913), pp. 30, 31.

[56]Travis Hoke, "The Corner Saloon," *American Mercury*, Mar. 1931, p. 311.

[57]Paul H. and Pauline F. Jacobson, *American Marriage and Divorce* (New York: Rinehart, 1959), p. 35.

[58]*Economic Aspects*, ed. Koren, p. 219.

[59]*The Economic Results of Prohibition* (New York: Columbia Univ. Press, 1932), p. 138.

[60]Maurice F. Parmelee, *Inebriety in Boston* (New York: Columbia Univ. Press, 1909), pp. 25–41.

[61]Hutchins Hapgood, "McSorley's Saloon," *Harper's Weekly*, Oct. 25, 1913, p. 15.

[62]Typical of temperance propaganda pitting the saloon against family and home is a cartoon in the Anti-Saloon League's weekly newspaper, *American Issue*, Jan. 17, 1914, p. 1, in which the saloon-keeper is portrayed as battling the housewife for the workingman's paycheck. The caption reads, "Which Needs It Most?"

[63]The Rev. Robert A. Woods, "A New Synthesis After the Saloon," in *Substitutes for the Saloon*, ed. Francis G. Peabody, 2nd ed., rev. (Boston: Houghton Mifflin, 1919), p. 325.

[64]Typical of today's critical perspective on Temperance and Prohibition are: Joseph R. Gusfield, *Symbolic Crusade: Status Politics and the American Temperance Movement* (Urbana: Univ. of Illinois Press, 1963);

Andrew Sinclair, *Prohibition, the Era of Excess* (Boston: Little, Brown, 1962). For a sympathetic modern interpretation of Prohibition as a Progressive reform which, at least initially, advanced the status and living conditions of the American working class, see: J. C. Burnham, "New Perspectives on the Prohibition 'Experiment' of the 1920's," *Journal of Social History*, 2 (Fall 1968), 51–68.

[65]*Hustlers, Beats, and Others* (Chicago: Aldine, 1967).

Leisure and Labor

*Kathy Peiss**

After ten or twelve hours a day bending over a sewing machine, standing at a sales counter, or waiting on tables, what energy could a turn-of-the-century working woman muster to attend a dance hall or amusement park? Quite a lot, according to the testimony of employers, journalists, and the wage-earners themselves. "Blue Monday" plagued employers. The head of a dressmaking shop, for example, observed that her employees "all took Sunday for a gala day and not as a day of rest. They worked so hard having a good time all day, and late into the evening, that they were 'worn to a frazzle' when Monday morning came." On week nights, working women hurriedly changed from work clothes to evening finery. Said one saleswoman, "You see some of those who have complained about standing spend most of the evening in dancing." The training supervisor at Macy's agreed, noting in exasperation, "We see that all the time in New York—many of the employees having recreation at night that unfits them for work the next day."[1]

Young, unmarried working-class women, foreign-born or daughters of immigrant parents, dominated the female labor force in the period from 1880 to 1920. In 1900, four-fifths of the 343,000 wage-earning women in New York were single, and almost one-third were aged sixteen to twenty. Whether supporting themselves or, more usually, contributing to the family economy, most girls expected to work at some time in their teens. Nearly 60 percent of all women in New York aged sixteen to twenty worked in the early 1900s. For many young women, wage-earning became an integral part of the transition from school to marriage.[2]

Women labored for wages throughout the nineteenth century, but by the 1890s, the context in which they worked differed from that of the Victorian era. New jobs in department stores, large factories, and offices provided alternatives to domestic service, household production, and sweated labor in small shops, which had dominated women's work earlier. These employment opportunities, the changing organization of work, and the declining hours of

*Kathy Peiss is assistant professor of American studies at the University of Maryland. Reprinted from Cheap Amusements: Working Women and Leisure in Turn-of-the-Century New York by Kathy Peiss. Copyright 1986 by Temple University. Reprinted by permission of Temple University Press.

138

labor altered the relationship between work and leisure, shaping the way in which leisure time was structured and experienced. The perception of leisure as a separate sphere of independence, youthful pleasure, and mixed-sex fun, in opposition to the world of obligation and toil, was supported by women's experiences in the workplace. Far from inculcating good business habits, discipline, and a desire for quiet evenings at home, the workplace reinforced the wage-earner's interest in having a good time. Earning a living, an economic necessity for most young working-class women, was also a cultural experience organizing and defining their leisure activities.

Women's Work in the Victorian City

In the late nineteenth century, New York's economic landscape was crowded with flourishing commercial enterprises, a thriving port, manufacturing lofts, and workshops. New York achieved prominence early in the century as the leading mercantile city in the United States, ensuring its primacy in commerce, shipping, and finance by dominating the Atlantic trade and developing transportation links to the hinterlands. By the Civil War, New York led the country in manufacturing, its strength lying in the garment trades, tobacco-processing and cigar-making, printing and publishing, metal-working, and furniture- and piano-making. Manufacturing was spurred by commercial trade, with merchant capitalists developing products such as ready-made clothing for the national market. Other types of business were developed to answer the clamor for goods and services arising from the city's burgeoning population. Unlike many American cities, where the age of industry was characterized by huge, mechanized factories, the city's high rental costs, cheap immigrant labor supply, and lack of a good energy source led to a myriad of small, highly specialized shops.[3]

This expanding mercantile and manufacturing economy brought many young women into the labor force after 1840, but not primarily as "mill girls" or factory hands, as was the case in cities where capital-intensive industries flourished. The majority of women workers in Victorian New York labored as domestic servants, needlewomen, laundresses, and in other employments seemingly marginal to an industrial economy.[4] As late as 1880, 40 percent of all New York working women were in domestic service, an experience particularly common among adolescent Irish and German girls. Home-based occupations and street trades, such as keeping boarders, washing laundry, cleaning, ragpicking, and peddling, provided necessary income for poor working-class wives and widows. In manufacturing, New York women were concentrated in the needle trades, with over one-fifth working as dressmakers, tailors, and milliners in 1880. In these years, garments were produced in small workshops or in the home. Even after the introduction of the sewing machine, much of the clothing trade was contracted to tenement sweatshops, often conducted as a family-based enterprise. A similar scale of production characterized cigar-making, a common employment among women.[5] Relatively few women, married or single, were engaged in the type of large-scale, mechanized factory production considered the vanguard of an industrial society.

Much of women's wage work was centered in the home and followed household routines, or fitted into them without serious difficulty. This was especially true for married women, whose productive labor was often ignored by census enumerators. Keeping boarders, for example, a common occupation of working-class wives, involved the same tasks of cooking, washing, and cleaning that women performed for their families. Sewing and other forms of industrial homework, which endured among southern and eastern European immigrants well into the twentieth century, filled the days of mothers already occupied with child care and housework. As the daughter of an Italian home-worker observed in 1913, "My mother works all the time—all day, Sundays and holidays, except when she is cooking or washing. She never has time to go out or she would get behind in her work."[6] The task-oriented rhythms of such work, its lack of clear-cut boundaries, and the sheer burden of the "double day" left little time for leisure.

With greater job opportunities and limited household concerns, single women had fewer restrictions on their time than did working mothers. Indeed, by the mid-nineteenth century, some young working girls achieved notoriety in the city as pleasure seekers. While their mothers turned increasingly toward domestic pursuits, young factory hands, domestic servants, and prostitutes sought a life of finery, frolics, and entertainment. Industrial workers in particular found possibilities for leisure, sociability, and fun affirmed in the workplace. These Victorian "rowdy girls"—controversial figures within working-class communities—prefigure the broader trend toward a pleasure-oriented culture that swept working women's lives at the turn of the century.[7]

At the same time, women's access to a world of leisure at midcentury was limited by their work situations, as well as by poverty and social disapprobation. Single women who labored as domestic servants found that middle-class mistresses encroached upon their opportunities for leisure. Servants' desire to wear fine clothes and attend entertainments collided with employers' edicts limiting their time off. Maids were often on call twelve or thirteen hours a day and generally had only one afternoon and evening a week free.[8] Similarly, the exploitative conditions in the dominant manufacturing industries often permitted little free time. Grueling hours of labor for small wages in sweatshops and tenements characterized the work of seamstresses and needlewomen, cigar-makers, and others. Many of them labored fifteen to eighteen hours daily, working by gaslight late into the evening to earn enough for food and rent. Fatigue and poor health were more often their lot than finery and entertainments.[9]

Periods of sociability and amusement were often snatched within the rhythms of work. Domestic servants, for example, would meet together in the street or park to gossip and socialize while tending their mistresses' children. Yet for many, the relatively isolated nature of their labor, its long hours, and task-oriented rhythms did not reinforce a concept of leisure as a separate sphere of social life. One important exception to this pattern lay in the experience of female factory workers, whose work involved the segmentation of time and sociability among peers. By the end of the century, the distinction between household-based work and new forms of labor located in centralized production widened. While married women continued to do home-based work, single women increasingly entered an array of jobs not only in factories but in department stores, restaurants, and offices.

Changes in Women's Labor

By 1900, important changes in the social organization of labor and expanding job opportunities in New York created new work experiences for women. Small shops, lofts, and trading companies still crowded lower Manhattan, but the city's economic landscape was rapidly changing. The wards at the southern tip of Manhattan were increasingly given over to corporate head-quarters, banking and investment firms, and specialized business offices. Towering skyscrapers and the canyons of Wall Street symbolized New York's transformation from a mercantile city to the nation's center for corporate industry. This expanding office complex created a demand for workers increasingly filled by female clerks, "typewriters," secretaries, and telephone operators. The explosive growth of the white-collar sector in the twentieth century, and women's participation in it, was anticipated in New York a decade before it affected the rest of the country. A negligible number of New York's clerks, typists, and bookkeepers were female in 1880; in 1900, 7 percent of all New York working women were filling such positions; and by 1920, this number had increased to 22 percent. These were native-born women who had received a public school education, primarily daughters of American, German, and Irish parents.[10]

Women's opportunities for jobs in trade and services expanded as consumers, travellers, and businesses demanded a range of urban amenities. Retail trade grew substantially, symbolized by the emergence of such large department stores as Macy's, Bloomingdale's, and Lord and Taylor's. The center for retail business moved uptown, near Fifth Avenue, Broadway, and 34th Street, close to an emerging commercial center, railroad connections, and middle-class residents. This expansion coincided with a shift in the sex-typing of store work. Retail sales had been a predominantly male occupation as late as the 1880s, when only 12 percent of clerks and salespersons in New York stores were women. By 1900, the saleslady had become a fixture of the retail emporium, a much coveted position for young working women. Working as a saleswoman or store clerk was the second most common occupation of native-born single wage-earners, whether "American girls" or daughters of immigrants.[11] Other businesses catered to the work routines and pleasures of a mobile, hectic population. Restaurants and lunchrooms, laundries, hotels, beauty parlors, drugstores, and theaters offered young women desirable alternatives to domestic service.

Although small workshops and households continued to play an important role in manufacturing, the production process increasingly turned toward larger factories. In the complex world of garment-making, conditions varied in the different branches of the industry. Generally, however, production shifted from isolated homework toward small sweatshops housed in tenements by the 1880s; by 1910, as the demand for ready-made clothing grew and further mechanization of the industry occurred, it was increasingly based in large-scale factories. John Commons estimated that, while 90 percent of ready-made garments had been produced in sweatshops in 1890, 75 percent were made in factories after 1900. While the clothing trades dominated New York industry, women also found work in a variety of light assembling and operative jobs producing consumer goods. Artificial flower-making, box-making, confectionary dipping, jewelry work, and bookbinding were typical female occupations.[12]

These new patterns of labor fostered differing work expectations across generations, expectations that particularly affected the American-born daughters of immigrant parents. Although domestic service remained the foremost occupation of single women, the daughters of immigrants increasingly refused to don the maid's uniform. In her 1914 study of 370 working mothers, Katharine Anthony found that almost half had been employed in domestic service and one-third in manufacturing before marriage; as working mothers, 70 percent of them labored in domestic and personal service. In contrast, most of their daughters worked in stores, offices, and factories, with only a small fraction going into service. "The German-American child wants a position in an office," noted anthropologist Elsa Herzfeld. "The daughter refuses to go into domestic service although her mother had formerly taken a 'position.'"[13] New immigrant groups from southern and eastern Europe repeated this pattern. As Thomas Kessner has shown for the years between 1880 and 1905, Italian and Jewish wives rarely worked outside the home, but depended on homework to supplement the family income. Their daughters' work patterns changed significantly in the twenty-five year period. Italian girls' occupations shifted from unskilled labor and street trades to factory work. Jewish girls throughout the period worked in the small shops of the garment industry, but by 1905 were also finding positions in schools, offices, and department stores.[14]

Women flocked to these jobs in part because they allowed more free time and autonomy, splitting the realms of work and leisure more clearly than household-based labor. A bitter complaint about domestic service was its lack of leisure time. One woman, for example, who had turned to service after working in manufacturing, asserted, "as long as I had a trade I was certain of my evenings an' my Sundays. Now I'm never certain of anything." An investigation into the "servant question" agreed with this assessment: "Especially is objection made to the fact that her evenings are not her own, so that she may go out at will with her friends or may attend places of amusement."[15]

Among working women, leisure came to be seen as a separate sphere of life to be consciously protected. Whether their employer was exploitative or well-intentioned, women resented interference with their "own" time. Non-unionized bindery workers, for example, tried to protest overtime work that kept them on the job through Christmas Eve. Shopgirls, too, who had been urged at a public hearing to state their grievances over working conditions, complained chiefly about not getting out of work on time. "Make them close at 6 o'clock," one exclaimed, testifying that her employer rang the closing bell late, causing store workers to labor an extra fifteen to thirty minutes: "Q. And that really has the result of depriving you of your evenings—of getting to places of entertainment in time, does it not? A. Yes, sir; that is right." Another store clerk observed that all the workers took turns closing up the department, so that each night one could leave early at 5:45 P.M.[16]

Those who could—predominantly the young, unmarried, and American-born—rejected the household-based, task-oriented employments that had traditionally been women's work. They preferred to labor in stores and factories, where they sold their labor and submitted to employers' work discipline for a specified portion of time. The remainder of the day, while often limited by exhaustion and household obligations, they could call their own. This distinctive sphere of leisure, demarcated in new forms of wage-earning, grew as the hours of labor decreased from 1880 to 1920.

The Declining Hours of Labor

The actual time working women had for relaxation and amusement is difficult to assess, since women's occupations rarely conformed to a single standard. Variations in the size and scale of industries, the seasonal nature of many jobs, differences between piecework and hourly wages, and low levels of unionization contributed to the nonuniformity of women's workdays. The New York State Bureau of Labor Statistics in 1885, for example, in cataloguing hundreds of industrial concerns, found that women's working days ranged from eight to seventeen hours. Even within a single industry, vast differences among workers are apparent. In the cigar industry, for example, some cigar-makers, presumably unionized, worked only eight hours, while bunch-makers regularly worked fifteen to seventeen hours daily. Moreover, women doing piecework often felt compelled to labor extra hours in the factory or at home in the evening.[17]

For many, the seasonal demand for consumer goods and services created an alternating pattern of intense labor and slack work. Garment manufacturers made heavy demands on employees in the fall and spring, but laid off workers in the dull seasons after Christmas and in the summer. The work history of one milliner typifies the casual employment many women faced: from February to May she had steady work; she was then laid off and hunted for a job in June and July; from August to December, she worked a total of fourteen weeks at four different establishments. During intermittent layoffs and the month-long slack period after Christmas, she sold candy. Cigarette-makers, carpet weavers, candy-makers, and bookbinders all experienced the seasonal rush to produce goods, and department store clerks put in ten- to sixteen-hour stints during the Christmas and Easter holidays. While posted hours in New York City factories were usually less than those upstate, many women regularly worked overtime as many as three or four nights a week during the busy season.[18] These spells allowed little time for leisure, while the slack season left women with time on their hands. Many looked for employment and filled in at other jobs, but others "took it easy" during the layoffs and, like Maria Cichetti, spent their hard-earned money going to vaudeville shows and movies.[19]

The contracting of jobs in some trades created a peculiar weekly rhythm of heavy labor and slack work. In many small task shops, garment-makers worked a fourteen-hour stretch for three days and then were idle the rest of the week. Similarly, laundries often had little work on Saturdays and Mondays, but might keep their employees at labor sixteen or seventeen hours on other days. In some jobs, labor intensity varied widely during the day. Waitresses, for example, often worked "split tricks"—on duty during the busy hours of lunch and dinner, relieved in the afternoon, hardly the best time for social engagements.[20]

Despite the irregularity of women's labor, the general trend of the period from 1880 to 1920 was toward shorter working days for female wage-earners in factories and stores. In 1885, women's workday ranged from ten to seventeen hours, but by the 1910s the long stints were much less common. Millinery workers, for example, who typically worked fourteen hours in 1885, put in only nine to ten hours in 1914. Similarly, a 1911 study of workers in lower Manhattan found that almost two-thirds of the female wage-earners worked less than ten hours daily. In addition, growing numbers of businesses closed early on Saturdays, particularly in the slow summer months, to give their workers a half-holiday.[21] The movement for protective legislation, greater union activity among working women, the increased rationalization of production, and changing attitudes toward workers' leisure contributed to this overall decline.

Protective legislation to lower women's work hours was pushed by middle-class reformers seeking to safeguard women's health and reproductive capacities, and by craft unions anxious about women's growing role in the workforce. Under pressure from these groups, New York's state legislature enacted a series of laws limiting the hours of labor, beginning in 1886 with the restriction of minors and women under twenty-one from working in manufacturing more than ten hours a day or sixty hours a week. This ceiling was extended to all female factory workers in 1899. In 1912, a revised statute curtailed the working day for women in manufacturing to nine hours, and two years later, this limit covered women's work in the city's mercantile stores. The nine-hour day and fifty-four hour week continued to be the legal standard in New York well into the 1920s.[22]

Generous loopholes and ineffective enforcement limited the efficacy of these laws, however. The legislation failed to cover women who did not work in factories and stores. It also permitted mercantile and industrial employers to demand irregular hours and overtime on a daily basis, as long as they obeyed the weekly limit. Enforcement was hampered by the hostility of employers, the limited number of factory inspectors, and the perfunctory penalties for violations. Mary Van Kleeck echoed the criticism of many reformers in observing that "the limit of the law is exceeded in numerous instances and in many trades—so that it is by no means uncommon to find young girls in the factories of New York working twelve, thirteen, even fourteen hours in a day." Despite these limitations, protective legislation contributed to the gradual decline in hours by setting legal limits and popularizing the notion of the "right to leisure." Major employers of women, including large clothing manufacturers and department stores, generally adhered to the labor laws.[23]

For some women, the labor movement's demand for the eight-hour day held the most promise of greater leisure. Although the vast majority of working women were not organized in this period, the union movement made important inroads after 1905 in industries with high female employment, such as garment-making and bookbinding. Bookbinders successfully struck for the eight-hour day in 1907, while waist-makers and other clothing workers achieved shorter hours in the settlements following the famous garment strikes of the 1910s.[24] Workers in unionized shops experienced a dramatic increase in their leisure time, as this young woman attested:

> The shorter work day brought me my first idea of there being such a thing as pleasure. It was quite wonderful to get home before it was pitch dark at night, and a real joy to ride on the cars and look out the windows and see something. Before this time it was just sleep and eat and hurry off to work. . . . I was twenty-one before I went to a theater and then I went with a crowd of union girls to a Saturday matinee performance. I was twenty-three before I saw a dance and that was a union dance too.[25]

Changes in the scale and organization of industry also hastened the decline in hours. As they achieved greater worker productivity through scientific management and mechanization, many major employers yielded to the shorter workday. Thus the trend in New York City toward larger mercantile establishments and factories had a salutary effect on lowering working hours. The reorganization of the garment trades, for example, sharply reduced hours. When the industry was dominated by home-sewing, there were no limits placed on the hours women might work. Workers in small task shops continued to be plagued with irregular employment and fourteen-hour workdays, while large clothing factories offered more steady work and a ten- to eleven-hour day. These establishments stopped work at 6:00 P.M., giving workers their evenings for rest and recreation. Similarly, the large department stores required only nine hours of labor except in the pre-Christmas season, in contrast to smaller neighborhood stores, which kept late hours to serve the working-class trade.[26]

Finally, liberalized attitudes toward workers' leisure began to take hold by the 1910s. The philanthropic bent of some large industrialists and retail merchants, joined with their desire to forestall unionization drives, led to welfare programs and practices designed to improve workers' health and well-being, in part by reducing hours. Josephine Goldmark's influential study of workers and efficiency, Louis Brandeis' brief on the hazards of long hours and night work for women, and the publicity campaigns of the Consumer's League contributed to the growing cultural legitimacy of the short day for women.[27]

By 1920, the hours of labor had declined sharply for many urban working women. In 1923, three-quarters of the women surveyed by the New York State Department of Labor worked only forty-eight hours or less in New York City, in contrast to their upstate sisters, of whom fewer than one-third worked such a short week. The memories of Nathan Cohen and Ruth Kaminsky, brother and sister, suggest the dimensions of change in the hours of labor. Nathan, a Russian immigrant who arrived in the United States in 1912, remembers doing little at night other than working, but his sister Ruth, who came to this country in 1921, had time to go to night school: "When I came over, they didn't work ten, twelve hours a day anymore. Tops was eight, nine, unless it was a small business, or some factories." Although she worked nine hours daily with a Saturday half-holiday in the 1910s, observed another immigrant woman, "at that time, we didn't consider it long."[28]

Work Cultures and Women's Leisure

While the shortened workday allowed more leisure time, women's experiences in the workplace reinforced the appeal of pleasure-oriented recreation in the public sphere. On one level, the desire for frivolous amusement was a reaction against the discipline, drudgery, and exploitative conditions of labor. A woman could forget rattling machinery or irritating customers in the nervous energy and freedom of the grizzly bear and turkey trot, or escape the rigors of the workplace altogether by finding a husband in the city's night spots. "You never rest until you die," observed one young box-maker, "but I will get out by marrying somebody." Indeed, factory investigators recorded the "widespread belief of the girls that marriage is relief from the trouble and toil of wage labor."[29]

At the same time, women's notions of leisure were reaffirmed through their positive social interactions within the workplace. In factories, stores, and offices, women socialized with other women and informally cooperated to affect working conditions. Their experience of work in a group context differed sharply from the home-bound, task-oriented, and isolated situation of domestic servants, outworkers, and housewives. There developed in this setting a shared and public culture, which legitimized the desires and behaviors expressed in young women's leisure.

Like other work groups, women workers developed degrees of autonomy and control in their relationship to managers and the work process by enforcing informal work rules and production quotas, socializing new employees into these patterns of behavior, and protecting their job skills from the bosses' encroachment. Given their status as low-skilled and easily replaced workers, wage-earning women rarely commanded the control over the work process that men in the skilled trades could exert, but neither were they merely victims of capitalist discipline.[30] Department store saleswomen, for example, used their selling skills to manipulate managers, supervisors, and customers, enforcing work rules among the women to sell only so many goods each day and employing code words to warn coworkers of recalcitrant customers. Bookbinders too employed the notion of a "fair day's work," controlling the output during each stint, while other factory hands orchestrated work stoppages and job actions over such issues as sexual harassment and pay cuts. Even waitresses worked out their resentment toward employers by pilfering pins and small objects, supplying themselves liberally with ice water and towels, and eating desserts ordered for imaginary customers.[31]

In mediating the relationship between the wage-earner and the labor process, work cultures involved not only informal efforts to control work but also the daily interactions that helped pass the long hours. While women characterized the workplace as tedious and demanding, a necessity to be endured, most tried to create places of sociability and support on the shop floor. Women sang songs, recited the plots of novels, argued politics, and gossiped about social life to counteract the monotony and routine of the workday. One feather-maker, for example, described her coworkers' conversations: "We have such a good time. We talk about books that we read, . . . the theatres, and newspapers, and the things that go on about town." Pieceworkers, who had more control over their time than hourly hands, could follow their own rhythms of intense work mixed with periods of sociability. "When I was a pieceworker," recalled one garment worker, "I would sing, I would fool around, say jokes, talk with the girls."[32] Singing helped pace the work, as in one box-maker's shop where songs would rise and fall while the workers sped through their tasks:

> Three o'clock, a quarter after, half-past! The terrific tension had all but reached the breaking point. Then there rose a trembling, palpitating sigh that seemed to come from a hundred throats, and blended in a universal expression of relief. In her clear, high treble Angelina began the everlasting "Fatal Wedding." That piece of false sentiment had now a new significance. It became a song of deliverance, and as the workers swelled the chorus, one by one, it meant that the end of the day's toil was in sight.[33]

Even in factories with loud machinery, women would try to converse above the noise, while lunch hours and the after-work walk home also afforded time to socialize with workmates. At Macy's, employees were "fond of sitting down in a corner and eating a pickle and pastry and a cup of tea; they can do that very quickly and can then visit for quite a long time during the rest of the noon hour."[34]

Women's work cultures varied according to type of employment, ethnic and religious affiliation, and larger cultural traditions. American-born union women, believing in self-education and uplift, often mirrored their male counterparts' behavior in the shop. In one New York cigar factory, for example, female trade unionists would pay one of their members to read aloud while they worked: "First the newspaper is read, then some literary work, such as for instance Morley's 'Life of Gladstone.'"[35] Even among nonunionized workers, the rituals, rules, and interactions governing work in stores and restaurants, where interpersonal skills were utilized, differed from semiskilled production, where machinery dominated the shop floor. The women themselves had a firm understanding of the occupational hierarchy indicated by language, mores, and "tone." The saleslady's patina of style and refinement differentiated her from the rougher manner of many tobacco or garment workers. Within a single industry, ethnic patterns also shaped different work cultures; cultural and political traditions, for example, contributed to the Jewish waist-makers' readiness to organize and strike, unlike their more hesitant Italian workmates.[36] Despite these distinctive differences, we can discern important commonalities in the work cultures of women that shaped and defined their attitudes toward leisure.

In the workplace, young women marked out a cultural terrain distinct from familial traditions and the customary practices of their ethnic groups, signifying a new identity as wage-earners through language, clothing, and social rituals. "Learners" might adopt new names from storybook romances when they entered a workplace for the first time, and greenhorns shed their Old World names for Anglicized ones. Fads, modish attire, and a distinctive personal style were also encouraged, as wage-earners discussed the latest fashions, learned new hairstyles, and tried out cosmetics and cigarettes. Indeed, employers often found it necessary to proscribe the unseemly behavior of working women: "At Koch's there is a splendid system of rules prohibiting the chewing of gum, rougeing and excessively using face powder."[37]

For factory hands, talking and socializing forged links between the world of labor and the pleasures of leisure. Some working girls, noted Lillian Betts, "dance[d] on the street at lunch-time, in front of their factory, singing their own dance music."[38] Part of the enjoyment inherent in the evening's entertainment lay in recounting the triumphs of the ball or party to one's workmates. Moreover, coworkers became a circle of friends apart from neighborhood or ethnic group ties. One Jewish garment worker observed, for example, that "while working, [I] used to have friends—Gentile girls. Sometimes we used to go out, we used to attend weddings, [I] was in their homes a few times."[39] Others formed social clubs comprised of coworkers and school friends.

Department store workers too were irrepressible in integrating work and social life through their use of language, special events, and organizations. When extra employees were laid off at the end of the holiday season, for example, they referred to the mass exodus as the "cake walk," after the popular Afro-American dance and strut. Holidays and engagements were constant excuses for parties, suppers, and celebrations. A popular ritual involved cutting a Halloween cake, wherein one lucky saleswoman found a ring, forecasting marriage, while an unfortunate coworker discovered a button or thimble, threatening spinsterhood. Numerous social clubs formalized the relationship between work and leisure. At the Siegel-Cooper department store, the workers banded together by department, forming, for example, the Foot Mould Social Club, comprised of women in the shoe department, and the Bachelor Girls Social Club, organized by the mail order clerks. These associations of women workers typically sponsored dances, entertainments, and excursions to Coney Island.[40]

In the workplace, women's conversations, stories, and songs often gravitated to the subject of dating and romantic entanglements with men, a discourse that accentuated the mixed-sex character of their leisure. During free moments, waitresses relished gossip about "the ubiquitous 'gentleman friend,' the only topic of conversation outside of the dining room interests." Women's socialization into a new workplace might involve a ritualistic exchange over "gentlemen friends." In one steam laundry, for example, an investigator repeatedly heard this conversation:

> 'Say, you got a feller?'
> 'Sure. Ain't you got one?'
> 'Sure.'[41]

One Jewish garment worker recalled daydreaming about love and marriage in the shops: "We used to even sing the songs . . . Yiddish naturally, singing the dream songs, the love songs, and this is how we dreamed away our youth and go out gay and happy."[42]

In department stores, the mixed-sex workplace became a setting for romance, trysts, and discussion of male-female relations. *Thought and Work*, the in-house magazine of the Siegel-Cooper department store, which was written by workers, evinced little interest in selling skills and business news, but resonated with gossip about eligible bachelors, intra-store courtships, wedding notices, and entertainments about town. Personal popularity, beauty, hair styles, clothing, and dancing ability were newsworthy items. Cultural practices among department store workers emerge from the breathless commentary of the newsletter: the saleslady who changes her hair color because, the gossip speculates, she "wants a man"; the competition between departments for the most engagements and marriages; the delivery of roses and mash notes to young women; the debates among idle saleswomen on such topics as kissing mustachioed men. Some department managers were portrayed more as popular matchmakers than enforcers of work discipline. "Mr. Eckle is a past master at securing husbands for the young ladies in his department," noted *Thought and Work*. "He'd rather do that than sign time cards."[43] While doubtlessly the magazine embellished the business of romance at the store, management eventually reined in its editors, ordering less copy on personal life and more articles on the business of selling.[44]

Bound to the language of romance was the frank discussion of sexuality among laboring women, a practice in the workplace that mirrored that of popular amusements. Risqué jokes, swearing, and sexual advice were a common part of the work environment in restaurants, laundries, factories, and department stores. Waitresses bandied obscenities and engaged in explicit discussion of lovers and husbands before work and during breaks. As one surprised middle-class observer described the scene in a restaurant: "They were putting on their aprons, combing their hair, powdering their noses, . . . all the while tossing back and forth to each other, apparently in a spirit of good-natured comradeship, the most vile epithets that I had ever heard emerge from the lips of a human being."[45] Despite their image of gentility and upward mobility, department store workers relished a similar freedom in language and behavior. At Macy's, a store that sought to maintain strict standards of employee respectability, investigators found "salacious cards, poems, etc., copied with avidity and passed from one to another, not only between girls and girls, but from girls to men." While many workers remained aloof from such vulgarities, there was "more smutty talk in one particular department than in a dance hall."[46]

Sexual knowledge was communicated between married and single women, between the experienced and the naive. A YWCA study of the woman worker observed that "the 'older hands' initiate her early through the unwholesome story or innuendo. She is forced to think of sex matters in relation to herself by the suggestions made to her of what she may expect from suitors or find in marriage." Examples of such initiation abound in the reports of middle-class investigators and reformers. In one department at Macy's dominated by married women, for example, "there was enough indecent talk to ruin any girl in her teens who might be put at work on that floor."[47] Stripped of their moralistic overtones, such observations reveal the workplace as an arena in which women wage-earners articulated their sexual feelings and shared their acquired wisdom about negotiating the attentions of men, both on the job and in their leisure time.

It was also an arena in which they experienced sexual vulnerability, a world of harassment as well as the give-and-take of humor and conversation. Then as now, sexual harassment limited women's position in the workforce and maintained male privilege and control. Wage-earning women were perceived by bosses and male workers alike to be outside the realm of parental or community protection. As one cigar-maker observed, behavior that in another context would not be tolerated was given free rein on the shop floor:

> Many men who are respected—when I say respected and respectable, I mean who walk the streets and are respected as working men, and who would not, under any circumstances, offer the slightest insult or disrespectful remark or glance to a female in the streets, . . . in the shops, will whoop and give expressions to "cat calls" and a peculiar noise made with their lips, which is supposed to be an endearing salutation.[48]

Women learned to tread a fine line between participating in acceptable workplace practices and guarding their integrity and respectability. Macy's clerks, who could trade obscenities and *double entendres* with the salesmen, knew "just how to be very friendly, without permitting the least familiarity," when conversing with male customers. As one factory investigator observed, "such women learn to defend themselves and to take care of themselves."[49] As we shall see in later chapters, this sexual knowledge gained in the workplace informed women's relations with men in the world of leisure.

Women's Wages and Treating

The work culture of women encouraged an ideology of romance that resonated with explicit heterosexual pleasures and perils at the same time that it affirmed the value of leisure. Still, working women's lack of financial resources posed a problem to their participation in an active social life, particularly in the world of commercial amusements. On the surface, low wages and little spending money would seem to have limited women's access to leisure, thus undercutting the heterosocial, pleasure-oriented culture of the workplace. Paradoxically, the material conditions of their lives at work and at home served instead to strengthen that culture.

Working women in New York typically earned below the "living wage," estimated by economists to be nine or ten dollars a week in 1910. Employers and workingmen alike justified women's low wages and their exclusion from higher-paying skilled trades by claiming that women were temporary wage-earners who worked only until marriage. Occupational segregation of the labor market was deeply entrenched, and women were concentrated in semi-skilled, seasonal employment. As cashgirls and salesclerks, assemblers and machine-tenders, waitresses and servants, their average earnings were one-half of those received by men in their employments. In New York factories in the early 1910s, 56 percent of the female labor force earned under $8.00

a week. Despite their higher social status, the majority of women in retail stores earned under $7.50, although the large emporia offered higher wages than neighborhood stores and five-and-tens. Deductions for tardiness, poor workmanship, and other violations further depleted wage-earners' already meager earnings.[50]

Relatively few women were able to live alone in comfort. Among the large industrial cities of the United States, New York had one of the highest percentages of wage-earning women residing with parents or relatives, from 80 to 90 percent. Self-supporting workers lodging in boardinghouses or renting rooms tended to be older, native-born women who earned higher wages than those living at home.[51] Most found, nevertheless, that their earnings were consumed by the cost of room, board, and clothing, leaving little for recreation.

To make ends meet, self-supporting women would scrimp on essential items in their weekly budgets. Going without meals was one common strategy, as was sleeping three to a bed to reduce the rent. "Some never boarded a street car for an evening's ride without planning days ahead how they could spare the nickel from their lunch or clothes money," noted reformer Esther Packard, describing women who lived on six dollars a week.[52] After work, the self-supporting woman sewed and washed her own clothing, cooked meals, and prepared for the next workday. Such scheduling and scrimping often left little time or money for evening amusements: "When the women or girls were visited at night, they were more likely to be found at home busy at the wash tub or ironing board than out at a dance or the theater." A movie and occasional ball were their only forms of leisure.[53]

By scrimping and making do, young women could provide some recreation for themselves. Yeddie Bruker, a factory worker earning seven dollars a week, spent almost two dollars of that on clothing and four dollars on room and board. A union member, she spent sixteen cents weekly for union dues and a benefit association, while for recreation she allocated ten cents a week for theatre tickets. Katia Markelov, a corset maker earning ten dollars, saved thirty dollars yearly for outings, while Rita Karpovna's low wages, six to seven dollars weekly, forced her to sacrifice essential items for union dues and the "Woman's Self-Education Society": "The Union and this club meant more to Rita than the breakfasts and luncheons she dispensed with, and more, apparently, than dress, for which she spent only $20 in a year and a half."[54]

For women living at home, recreation was limited not so much by the size of their income as by access to it. In exchange for their wages, most parents gave their daughters small sums of spending money, averaging twenty-five to fifty cents each week, in addition to lunch money and carfare. Like self-supporting women, those who lived at home necessarily scrimped and depended on others for recreation. They commonly saved their allowances for lunch by eating the free food served in saloons or skipping the meal altogether. Many, like Maria Cichetti, saved carfare by walking to or from work. Maria received ten cents for the roundtrip trolley ride to her shop; by walking home with friends at night, she could save a nickel for the movies. As one investigator of West Side girls observed, "A carfare saved by walking to work is a carfare earned for a trip to a dance hall 'away out in the Bronx.'"[55]

Women also relied on coworkers and female friends to help them out with food, clothing, and recreation. The low-wage cashgirl or salesclerk was "helped by those about her in the store with gifts of clothing or even with money," observed one salesgirl. In factories, older wage-earners would aid the youngest by paying her a dime to fetch tea or lunch. A tradition of mutual aid and support can be seen in the frequency of raffles and events to raise money for less fortunate workmates.[56]

Typically, however, young women looked to men for financial assistance and gifts. "If they didn't take me, how could I ever go out?" observed a young department store worker. Treating was a widely accepted practice, especially if the woman had a fiancé, or "steady," from whom she could accept food, clothing, and recreation without compromising her reputation. One woman, for example, counted on her steady for Sunday meals, exclaiming, "Why! if I had to buy all of my meals I'd never get along." Unable to save a penny of her seven-dollar weekly wage, Clara X. depended on her beau, who earned more than twice her income, to occasionally purchase her clothes and take her on vacation.[57] Rose Pasternak paid for an overcoat on installments until she was "keeping company": "I paid and paid and paid, till I got with the company with my fella. He paid eight dollars. After I was a long time married, he used to throw it in my face, 'you made so much money that I had to pay for the plush coat.'"[58] Other self-supporting women had no qualms about accepting treats from unknown men or chance acquaintances. As one observer concluded, "the acceptance on the part of the girl of almost any invitation needs little explanation when one realizes that she often goes pleasureless unless she does accept 'free treats.'"[59]

The culture of treating was reinforced in the workplace through women's interactions with employers, male workmates, and customers, particularly in service and sales jobs. In department stores, managers were said to advise shopgirls to find gentleman friends who could buy them the clothing and trinkets that their salaries could not cover. At a government hearing, one saleswoman testified: "One of the employers has told me, on a $6.50 wage, he don't care where I get my clothes from as long as I have them, to be dressed to suit him."[60] Some investigators denied the accuracy of these reports, but their widespread currency among saleswomen suggests the tacit legitimacy of treating as a means of gaining access to the world of amusements. Waitresses knew that suggestive familiarity with male customers often brought good tips, and some used their skills and opportunities to engage in an active social life with chance acquaintances. "Most of the girls quite frankly admit making 'dates' with strange men," observed a Consumer's League study. "These 'dates' are made with no thought on the part of the girl beyond getting the good time which she cannot afford herself."[61] These working women sought a way to negotiate dependency and claim some choice, autonomy, and pleasure in otherwise dreary lives. They understood, albeit hazily, that leisure was the realm in which that quest could most easily be achieved.

NOTES

[1] [Siegel-Cooper Department Store], *Thought and Work*, Dec. 1904, p. 15; "A Salesgirl's Story," *Independent* 54 (31 July 1902): 1821; Harry B. Taplin, "Training for Store Efficiency," 17 March 1915, p. 2, Box 118, Welfare Department Subject File, National Civic Federation Papers, Rare Books and Manuscripts Division, New York Public Library, Astor, Lenox and Tilden Foundations.

[2]U.S. Bureau of the Census, *Statistics of Women at Work* (Washington, D.C., 1907), pp. 270–271, 148–151; New York State Factory Investigating Commission, *Fourth Report Transmitted to Legislature, Feb. 15, 1915* (S. Doc. no. 43; Albany, N.Y., 1915), vol. 1, p. 37, and vol. 4, p. 1478–1489. See also U.S. Bureau of the Census, *Women in Gainful Occupations, 1870–1920*, by Joseph A. Hill (Washington, D.C., 1929). Women's role in the labor force is surveyed in Leslie Woodcock Tentler, *Wage-Earning Women: Industrial Work and Family Life in the United States, 1900–1930* (New York, 1979); Alice Kessler-Harris, *Out to Work* (New York, 1982); Susan Estabrook Kennedy, *If All We Did Was to Weep at Home: A History of White Working-Class Women in America* (Bloomington, Ind., 1979); Miriam Cohen, "Italian-American Women in New York City, 1900–1950: Work and School," in *Class, Sex, and the Woman Worker*, ed. Milton Cantor and Bruce Laurie (Westport, Conn., 1977), pp. 120—143.

[3]David C. Hammack, *Power and Society: Greater New York at the Turn of the Century* (New York, 1982), pp. 31–58; Sean Wilentz, *Chants Democratic: New York City and the Rise of the American Working Class, 1788–1850* (New York, 1984), especially pp. 107–142; Bayrd Still, *Mirror for Gotham* (New York, 1956).

[4]Mary Christine Stansell, "Women of the Laboring Poor in New York City, 1820–1860" (Ph.D. diss., Yale University, 1979); Amy Srebnick, "True Womanhood and Hard Times: Women and Early New York Industrialization, 1840–1860" (Ph.D. diss., State University of New York at Stony Brook, 1979); Carol Groneman, "'She Earns as a Child, She Pays as a Man': Women Workers in a Mid-Nineteenth-Century New York City Community," in *Class, Sex, and the Woman Worker*, ed. Cantor and Laurie, pp. 83–100; U.S. Senate, *Report on the Condition of Woman and Child Wage-Earners in the United States, Vol. 9: History of Women in Industry in the United States* (S. 645, 61st Cong., 2d sess.; Washington, D.C., 1910), pp. 115–155.

[5]U.S. Bureau of the Census, *Statistics of the Population at the Tenth Census, 1880*, vol. 1 (Washington, D.C., 1883), p. 892; U.S. Bureau of the Census, *Social Statistics of Cities, 1880* (Washington, D.C., 1883), pp. 594–596; Christine Stansell, "The Origins of the Sweatshop: Women and Early Industrialization in New York City," in *Working-Class America*, ed. Michael H. Frisch and Daniel J. Walkowitz (Urbana, Ill., 1983), pp. 78–103.

[6]Mary Van Kleeck, *Artificial Flower-Makers* (New York, 1913), p. 235. On the prevalence of homework in New York, see Thomas Kessner, *The Golden Door: Italian and Jewish Immigrant Mobility in New York City, 1880–1915* (New York, 1977), pp. 72–77; Mabel Hurd Willett, *The Employment of Women in the Clothing Trades* (Studies in History, Economics and Public Law, vol. 16, no. 2; New York, 1902), pp. 102, 108; New York State Legislature, Special Committee of the Assembly Appointed to Investigate the Condition of Female Labor in the City of New York, *Report and Testimony* (Albany, N.Y., 1896), vol. 1, pp. 17–19, and vol. 2, pp. 1024–1025. See also John Modell and Tamara K. Hareven, "Urbanization and the Malleable Household: An Examination of Boarding and Lodging in American Families," *Journal of Marriage and the Family* 35 (Aug. 1973): 467–479; Joan M. Jensen, "Cloth, Butter and Boarders: Women's Household Production for the Market," *Review of Radical Political Economics* 12, no. 2 (Summer 1980): 14–24; Margaret F. Byington, *Homestead: The Households of a Mill Town* (1910; rpt. Pittsburgh, 1974), pp. 138–157.

[7]Stansell, "Women of the Laboring Poor," pp. 105–108, 204.

[8]*Ibid.*, pp. 139–159; David M. Katzman, *Seven Days a Week: Women and Domestic Service in Industrializing America* (Urbana, Ill., 1981).

[9]Stansell, "Women of the Laboring Poor," p. 73; James McCabe, *Lights and Shadows of New York Life* (Philadelphia, 1872), p. 822.

[10]Percentage changes in women's employment are derived from U.S. Bureau of the Census, *Tenth Census, 1880*, vol. 1, p. 892; U.S. Bureau of the Census, *Statistics of Women at Work*, pp. 270–271; U.S.Bureau of the Census, *Women in Gainful Occupations*, pp. 204, 206. The demand for women clerical workers is discussed in Margery Davies, *Woman's Place Is at the Typewriter: Office Work and Office Workers, 1870–1930* (Philadelphia, 1982). New York's economy in the early twentieth century is discussed in Hammack, *Power and Society*, pp. 39–51.

[11]See note 10, and Susan Porter Benson, "'The Customers Ain't God': The Work Culture of Department-Store Saleswomen, 1890–1940," in *Working-Class America*, ed. Frisch and Walkowitz, pp. 185–211.

[12]John Commons quoted in U.S. Senate, *Woman and Child Wage-Earners*, vol. 9, p. 143; see also Willett, *Women in the Clothing Trades*. Women's industrial jobs underwent extensive examination by New York reformers and social workers; see especially Annie M. MacLean, *Wage-Earning Women* (New York, 1910); Louise C. Odencrantz, *Italian Women in Industry: A Study of Conditions in New York City·*(New York, 1919); Mary Van Kleeck, *Artificial Flower-Makers*; Van Kleeck, *A Seasonal Industry: A Study of the Millinery Trade in New York* (New York, 1917); Van Kleeck, *Women in the Bookbinding Trade* (New York, 1913).

[13]Elsa G. Herzfeld, *Family Monographs: The History of Twenty-four Families Living in the Middle West Side of New York City* (New York, 1905), p. 12; Katharine Anthony, *Mothers Who Must Earn* (New York, 1914), pp. 49, 59, 62.

[14]Kessner, *Golden Door*, pp. 71–99.

[15]Helen S. Campbell, *Prisoners of Poverty: Women Wage-Earners, Their Trades and Their Lives* (1887; rpt. Westport, Conn., 1970), p. 148; Gail Laughlin, "Domestic Service," in U.S. Industrial Commission, *Report of the Industrial Commission on the Relations and Conditions of Capital and Labor Employed in Manufacturing and General Business*, vol. 14 (Washington, D.C., 1901), pp. 758, 756–757. See also Katzman, *Seven Days a Week*, pp. 236–243.

[16]Special Committee to Investigate Female Labor, *Report and Testimony*, vol. 2, pp. 989–990, 994, 1083; Van Kleeck, *Women in the Bookbinding Trade*, p. 173.

[17]New York State Bureau of Labor Statistics, *Third Annual Report* (Albany, N.Y., 1885), pp. 32–59, 169, and *Fourteenth Annual Report* (Albany, N.Y., 1896), pp. 918–919.

[18]Alice P. Barrows, "The Training of Millinery Workers," in *Proceedings of the Academy of Political Science in the City of New York*, vol. 1 (Oct. 1910): 43–44. Testimony on irregular working hours by reformers and working women is extensive; see in particular New York Bureau of Labor Statistics, "Unorganized Workingwomen," *Fourteenth Annual Report* (1896); New York State Factory Investigating Commission, *Preliminary Report Transmitted to Legislature, March 1, 1912* (Albany, N.Y., 1912), vol. 1, p. 296, and *Fourth Report*, vol. 2, pp. 252, 516–517, 592–595; and studies cited in note 12.

[19]Tapes I–116 (side A) and II–30 (side B), New York City Immigrant Labor History Collection of the City College Oral History Project, Robert F. Wagner Archives, Tamiment Institute Library, New York University.

[20]Consumer's League of New York City, *Behind the Scenes in a Restaurant: A Study of 1017 Women Restaurant Employees* (n.p., 1916), p. 15; Willett, *Women in the Clothing Trades*, p. 74; Sue Ainslie Clark and Edith Wyatt, *Making Both Ends Meet: The Income and Outlay of New York Working Girls* (New York, 1911), p. 190.

[21]Cf. New York Bureau of Labor Statistics, *Third Annual Report* (1885), pp. 32–59, and New York Factory Investigating Commission, *Fourth Report*, vol. 2, pp. 424–425, 209–210, 320; Edward Ewing Pratt, *Industrial Causes of Congestion of Population in New York City* (Studies in History, Economics and Public Law, vol. 43, no. 1; New York, 1911), p. 124. The growing acceptance of the half-holiday may be followed in New York State Bureau of Labor Statistics, *Fifth Annual Report* (Albany, N.Y., 1887), p. 555; New York State Bureau of Labor Statistics, *Eighth Annual Report* (Albany, N.Y., 1890), pt. 1, p. 448; New York Bureau of Labor Statistics, *Fourteenth Annual Report* (1896), p. 935; New York Factory Investigating Commission, *Fourth Report*, vol. 2, p. 88.

[22]Elizabeth Faulkner Baker, *Protective Labor Legislation* (Studies in History, Economics and Public Law, vol. 116, no. 2; New York, 1925), pp. 113–114, 133–138.

[23]Mary Van Kleeck, "Working Hours of Women in Factories," *Charities and the Commons* 17 (6 Oct. 1906): 13; Baker, *Protective Labor Legislation*, pp. 151, 309–313. For an example of employers' maneuvers around the law, see Van Kleeck, *Women in the Bookbinding Trade*, pp. 134, 144–145. Oral testimony of working women confirms large employers' observance of the law, particularly with respect to minors; see, for example, tape II–30 (side A), Immigrant Labor History Collection.

[24]Van Kleeck, *Women in the Bookbinding Trade*, pp. 177–181. On unionization in the garment industry, see Nancy Schrom Dye, *As Equals and as Sisters: Feminism, the Labor Movement and the Women's Trade Union League of New York* (Columbia, Mo. and London, 1980); Meredith Tax, *The Rising of the Women* (New York, 1980), pp. 205–240.

[25]"Making Ends Meet on the Minimum Wage," *Life and Labor* 3 (Oct. 1913): 302. See also tape I–105, Immigrant Labor History Collection.

[26]Kessler-Harris, *Out to Work*, pp. 180–202; Baker, *Protective Labor Legislation*, p. 331; New York Factory Investigating Commission, *Fourth Report*, vol. 2, pp. 123; New York State Department of Labor, *Hours and Earnings of Women in Five Industries* (Special Bulletin no. 121; Albany, N.Y., Nov. 1923), p. 13; Willett, *Women in Clothing Trades*, p. 74; New York Bureau of Labor Statistics, *Third Annual Report* (1885), p. 169; New York Special Committee to Investigate Female Labor, *Report and Testimony*, vol. 1, pp. 60, 86–87; Irving Howe, *World of Our Fathers* (New York, 1976), p. 82.

[27]Daniel T. Rodgers, *The Work Ethic in Industrial America, 1850–1920* (Chicago and London, 1974); Alice Kessler-Harris, *Out to Work*, pp. 200–201; Florence Kelley, "Right to Leisure," *Charities* 14 (2 Sept. 1905): 1055–1062.

[28]Tapes I–51 (side B) and I–21 (transcript), Immigrant Labor History Collection; New York Department of Labor, *Women in Five Industries*, p. 13.

[29]New York Factory Investigating Commission, *Fourth Report*, vol. 4, pp. 1577–1578; Frances R. Donovan, *The Woman Who Waits* (1920; rpt. New York, 1974), p. 50. For an elaboration of this argument, see Tentler, *Wage-Earning Women*.

[30]Pathbreaking studies of work cultures include David Montgomery, *Workers' Control in America* (Cambridge, Eng., 1979); Susan Porter Benson, "The Customers Ain't God"; Barbara Melosh, *'The Physicians' Hand': Work Culture and Conflict in American Nursing* (Philadelphia, 1982). See also Karen Brodkin Sacks and Dorothy Remy, eds., *My Troubles Are Going to Have Trouble with Me* (New Brunswick, N.J., 1984), pp. 193–263.

[31]Benson, "The Customers Ain't God"; Mary Bularzik, "Sexual Harassment at the Workplace, Historical Notes," in *Workers' Struggles, Past and Present*, ed. James Green (Philadelphia, 1983), pp. 117–135; Amy E. Tanner, "Glimpses at the Mind of a Waitress," *American Journal of Sociology* 13 (July 1907): 50; Van Kleeck, *Women in the Bookbinding Trade*, p. 83.

[32]Mary Gay Humphreys, "The New York Working Girl," *Scribner's* 20 (Oct. 1896): 505; tape II–30, Immigrant Labor History Collection.

[33]Dorothy Richardson, *The Long Day: The Story of a New York Working Girl* (1905) in *Women at Work*, ed. William L. O'Neill (New York, 1972), pp. 105–106. Although colored by middle-class moralisms,

Dorothy Richardson's autobiographical novel gives a particularly rich portrait of young, unskilled female wage-earners' interactions in the workplace.

[34]Taplin, "Training for Store Efficiency," p. 2; MacLean, *Wage-Earning Women*, p. 35; Bessie and Marie Van Vorst, *The Woman Who Toils* (New York, 1903), p. 25.

[35]Conference on Welfare Work at Chicago Commons, Minutes of Seventh Meeting, 15 May 1906, p. 3, Box 121, Welfare Conferences, National Civic Federation Papers.

[36]New York Factory Investigating Commission, *Fourth Report*, vol. 4, p. 1588; Anthony, *Mothers Who Must Earn*, p. 51.

[37]Department Store Study, *Civic Federation Review*, galley 20B, box 116, Department Store Subject File, National Civic Federation Papers; Clark and Wyatt, *Making Both Ends Meet*, p. 184; Richardson, *Long Day*, pp. 96–97.

[38]Lillian W. Betts, "Tenement-House Life and Recreation," *Outlook* 61 (11 Feb. 1899): 365.

[39]Tapes I–51 (side B) and I–132 (side A), Immigrant Labor History Collection.

[40]*Thought and Work*, Dec. 1903, p. 9; Jan. 1904, pp. 10, 15; and Jan. 1905, pp. 1, 3; Department Store Study, draft typescript, p. 38, box 116, Department Store Subject File, National Civic Federation Papers.

[41]Tanner, "Glimpses," p. 52; Clark and Wyatt, *Making Both Ends Meet*, pp. 187–188; see also Richardson, *Long Day*, pp. 94–95.

[42]Tape I–59 (side A), Immigrant Labor History Collection.

[43]*Thought and Work*, June 1903, p. 7; Sept. 1904, p. 5; Jan. 1904, pp. 10, 15; 15 April 1904, p. 6; Nov. 1904, p. 5; April 1905, p. 11; and Jan. 1905, p. 11.

[44]*Thought and Work*, Feb. 1905, p. 1.

[45]Donovan, *Woman Who Waits*, pp. 20, 26, 80–81; Clark and Wyatt, *Making Both Ends Meet*, p. 188.

[46]Committee of Fourteen in New York City, *Department Store Investigation: Report of the Sub-committee* (New York, 1915), p. 10. See also Committee of Fourteen in New York City, *Annual Report* (New York, 1914), p. 40.

[47]"Report of the Commission on Social Morality from the Christian Standpoint, Made to the Fourth Biennial Convention of the Young Women's Christian Associations of the U.S.A., 1913," Pamphlets on Marriage and Family Relations, Archives of the National Board of the Young Women's Christian Association of the U.S.A., New York City; Committee of Fourteen, *Department Store Investigation*, p. 10. Cf. Sharon Hartman Strom, "Italian American Women and Their Daughters in Rhode Island: The Adolescence of Two Generations, 1900–1950," in *The Italian Immigrant Woman in North America*, ed. Betty Boyd Caroli et al. (Toronto, 1978), p. 194, in which one informant explained: "You found out about sex through the shop where you worked. The mother don't tell you nothing. The married women would put us wise."

[48]New York State Bureau of Labor Statistics, *Second Annual Report* (Albany, N.Y., 1884), pp. 153, 158. Examples of sexual harassment abound; see, New York Bureau of Labor Statistics, *Third Annual Report* (1885), pp. 150–151; Clara E. Laughlin, *The Work-a-Day Girl: A Study of Some Present-day Conditions* (New York, 1913), p. 112; Richardson, *Long Day*, p. 260; U.S. Industrial Commission, *Report of the Industrial Commission on the Relations and Conditions of Capital and Labor Employed in Manufacturing and General Business*, vol. 7 (Washington, D.C., 1901), pp. 389–390. See also Bularzik, "Sexual Harassment."

[49]Committee of Fourteen in New York City, *Department Store Investigation*, p. 10; U.S. Industrial Commission, *Report*, vol. 7, p. 59.

[50]Wage differentials in New York City according to sex may be seen in U.S. Bureau of the Census, *Report on Manufacturing Industries in the U.S. at the Eleventh Census* (Washington, D.C., 1895), pp. 390–407, 708–710; New York Factory Investigating Commission, *Fourth Report*, vol. 4, pp. 1507–1511, 1081, and vol. 1, pp. 35–36. Estimates for the living wage of self-supporting girls varied; see, for example, Clark and Wyatt, *Making Both Ends Meet*, p. 8.

[51]The exact percentage of women living alone varies in different reports. U.S. Senate, *Report on the Condition of Woman and Child Wage-Earners in the United States, Vol. 5: Wage-Earning Women in Stores and Factories* (S. 645, 61st Cong., 2d sess.; Washington, D.C., 1910), p. 15, indicates that 87 percent of factory workers and 92 percent of retail clerks lived at home. Cf. New York Factory Investigating Commission, *Fourth Report*, vol. 5, p. 2561, which stated that 85 percent of women wage-earners lived with families, friends, or relatives. For testimony on women's inability to live alone on low wages, see New York Bureau of Labor Statistics, *Fourteenth Annual Report* (1896), pp. 913–945. For a fictional account of the controversy surrounding a young woman who chooses to live alone, see Anzia Yezierska, *Bread Givers* (1925; rpt. New York, 1975).

[52]New York Factory Investigating Commission, *Fourth Report*, vol. 4, p. 1685. For an excellent discussion of the survival strategies of self-supporting women, see Joanne J. Meyerowitz, "Holding Their Own: Working Women Apart from Family in Chicago, 1880–1930" (Ph.D. diss., Stanford University, 1983).

[53]Odencrantz, *Italian Women in Industry*, p. 235; Lillian D. Wald, *The House on Henry Street* (1915; rpt. New York, 1971), p. 211; New York Factory Investigating Commission, *Fourth Report*, vol. 4, pp. 1675–1692; Clark and Wyatt, *Making Both Ends Meet*, p. 10.

[54]Clark and Wyatt, *Making Both Ends Meet*, pp. 97, 103–104, 108.

[55]Ruth S. True, *The Neglected Girl* (New York, 1914), p. 59; New York Factory Investigating Commission, *Fourth Report*, vol. 4, pp. 1512–1513; tape II–30 (side A), Immmigrant Labor History Collection.

[56]"Salesgirl's Story," p. 1818; New York Factory Investigating Commission, *Fourth Report*, vol. 4, p. 1576, 1585; Clark and Wyatt, *Making Both Ends Meet*, p. 189.

[57]New York Factory Investigating Commission, *Fourth Report*, vol. 4, pp. 1698, 1678 (quotations), 1577, 1675–1678, 1695–1714.

[58]Tape I–132, Immigrant Labor History Collection.

[59]New York Factory Investigating Commission, *Fourth Report*, vol. 4, pp. 1685–1686.

[60]New York Factory Investigating Commission, *Fourth Report*, vol. 5, p. 2809; U.S. Industrial Commission, *Report*, vol. 7, p. 59; Laughlin, *Work-a-Day Girl*, pp. 60–61; "Salesgirl's Story," p. 1821; Clark and Wyatt, *Making Both Ends Meet*, p. 28.

[61]Consumer's League, *Behind the Scenes*, p. 24; Donovan, *Woman Who Waits*, p. 42.

The Formation of Chicago's "Little Italies"

*Rudolph J. Vecoli**

Two decades ago Frank Thistlethwaite admonished us not to think of immigrants as "an undifferentiated, mass movement of 'peasants' or indeed 'artisans' thronging towards immigrant ports from vaguely conceived 'countries of origin' like 'Italy,' 'Germany,' or even 'Poland' or 'Ireland.'" "Seen through a magnifying glass," he observed, "this undifferentiated mass surface breaks down into a honeycomb of innumerable particular cells, districts, villages, towns, each with an individual reaction or lack of it to the pull of migration."[1] Thistlethwaite's advice has been taken to heart and fruitfully applied in microstudies of immigrant origins. However, once the immigrants are safely transported across the Atlantic they appear to assume the uniform national identity which they lacked at the moment of embarkation. Our literature on ethnic groups is replete with generalizations about Irish Americans, Polish Americans, and Italian Americans as if these were homogeneous entities. In fact such labels often disguise at least as much as they reveal. To assume that a Swabian becomes a German, a Gorali a Pole, or a Calabrian an Italian through a sea change is as unjustified as to assume that they instantaneously become Americans upon landing.

If we are to advance the study of immigration beyond the level of facile generalizations, we need a series of microstudies which trace particular contingents of immigrants from their specific origins to their specific destinations. And we need to ask what bearing those specific origins and the characteristics associated with them had upon outcomes in terms of settlement, employment, politics, mobility, ethnicity and assimilation. This study seeks to analyze the process of formation of Chicago's "Little Italies" in terms of such specific origins. Seen from this perspective the history of the Italians in Chicago becomes the sum of the collective histories of the dozens of village groups which comprised this migration.[2]

Rudolph J. Vecoli is professor of history at the University of Minnesota and director of the Immigration History Research Center. Reprinted from Journal of American Ethnic History 2 (Spring 1983): 5–20. Reprinted by permission of the Immigration History Society and Rudolph J. Vecoli.

When the Italians arrived in Chicago they found a tough and raw, but fluid urban environment. In the formation of their neighborhoods, the Italians did not conform to the neat model of the Chicago school of urban sociology. According to Robert E. Park and Ernest W. Burgess, the city could be conceived of as being divided by concentric rings in which land use was determined by the competition of business, industrial, and residential needs.[3] By analogy to natural ecology, this theory portrayed the city as an organic whole consisting of natural areas which existed in symbiotic relationship with each other. In the Parkian model, arriving immigrants established their area of first settlement in the central ring, adjacent to the downtown business district. As they assimilated socially and economically they migrated outward to areas of second and third settlement. This intraurban migration became a yardstick for measuring the rapidity and degree of assimilation. Such a deterministic model, however, does not allow for the influence of human agency, cultural preferences, and chance. All of these in my analysis had a great deal to do with the particular pattern of Italian settlement in Chicago.

Contrary to the concentric ring theory, the most important factor in shaping Chicago's cultural and industrial geography was the lakeshore and the Chicago River with its north and south branches. Providing means of water transport and waste disposal, the river banks became choice industrial locations. Consequently the river wards became the districts housing the immigrant workers who manned the city's factories, mills, and packinghouses. Meanwhile, the "Loop" emerged as the central business district at the mouth of the Chicago River. While the ethnic map of the city was shaped in part by this industrial ecology, it also reflected the distinctive histories and characters of the various immigrant groups.

Although the majority of the Italians did settle in the river wards, the imposition of the Parkian model ignores significant internal differences such as time of arrival and Old World origins which had a great deal to do with the location of their neighborhoods. A large proportion of the Italians *initially* settled in outlying areas of the city and even the suburbs. For there was not one "Little Italy" in Chicago but at least sixteen discrete settlements each with its own particular history, character, and reputation.

The Genoese (actually from the region of Liguria and not the city of Genoa) were the pioneers of the Italian immigration to Chicago. From the 1850s on they were conspicuous as fruit peddlers, confectioners, saloon-keepers, and restaurateurs. Living in rooms behind or above their stores, they clustered on the busy streets of the downtown district. A distinctive Genoese settlement developed on the Near North Side in the angle of the Chicago River and its north branch (A).[4] After the great fire of 1871, a general migration of Genoese to this area, which had escaped the conflagration, occurred. As they prospered, many built two- and three-story structures with business premises on the ground floor and living quarters above. By 1884, 455 Italians were living in the district, and the number never increased much beyond 1,000. The neighborhood remained solidly Genoese, and was shunned by the southern Italians who were not welcome. The first Italian church, the Church of the Assumption, was established here in 1881. Although frequented by Italians from other neighborhoods, it was always known as *"la chiesa degli Genovesi."*[5]

From the 1870s on, Chicago's role as the railroad labor market for the central and western United States drew increasing numbers of Italians, especially those from the southern regions. At any given time, the city's Italian population was composed to a large extent of these migrant laborers. Gradually permanent settlers ensconced themselves in emerging Italian neighborhoods. By 1900 practically all of Italy's regions were represented in Chicago, and the predominance of the *meridionali* was already pronounced. It would become increasingly so in the succeeding decades. Chicago's Italian-born population grew dramatically during a half century: from 552 in 1870 to 16,008 in 1900 to 59,215 in 1920. By the latter year, it was estimated that over 75 percent were from the *Mezzogiorno*.[6]

The province of Potenza in Basilicata sent a major contingent of its sons and daughters to Chicago. From the *paesi* of Trivigno, Corleto, and Calvello, but above all from Laurenzana, they began arriving in the 1870s. Settling south of the Loop in the midst of the city's vice district, they formed an early distinctive Italian settlement (B). Since the Dearborn Station where the immigrant trains arrived was nearby, the Italians called the area "Polk Depot." Others came from the province of Salerno in Campania, especially from the hilltowns of Senarchia, Oliveto Citra, Teggiano, and Ricigliano. This last *paese* was said to have lost half of its population to emigration by 1890, the majority coming to Chicago. Meanwhile, from Calabria, immigrants from Cosenza and the nearby *paesi* of Rende, San Fili and Fiumefreddo and from Nicastro and other villages in the province of Catanzaro augmented the

Table 1

Italian Population of Chicago in 1910 by Major Wards of Residence

Ward	Born in Italy	Native of Italian Parentage	Total
1	3,045	1,853	4,898
4	1,892	1,242	3,134
12	813	348	1,161
14	1,652	1,402	3,054
17	4,910	3,593	8,503
19	14,649	8,757	23,406
22	8,216	4,564	12,780
31	638	637	1,275
33	2,963	1,091	4,054
Total for These Wards	38,778	23,487	62,265
Total for the City	45,169	27,737	72,906

Source: United States Bureau of the Census, *Thirteenth Census: 1910, Population*, II (Washington, DC, 1913), 512–14. All references to population statistics for 1910 in the text are drawn from this source.

Note: Of Chicago's thirty-five wards, these nine reported a total of over one thousand Italians, first and second generations combined.

growing colony. Others were arriving from Abruzzi-Molise, particularly from the provinces of L'Aquila and Campobasso. By the 1880s, the Polk Depot embodied the spectrum of the southern regions, but true to the spirit of *campanilismo*, the *paesani* clustered along the streets and alleys of the district. The Laurenzanesi preempted the more substantial buildings along South Clark Street, those from Ricigliano settled along Plymouth Court, those from Senarchia on Sherman, and so on. The Polk Depot settlement was a mother colony which spawned a number of other settlements. The conversion of the land to commercial purposes eventually drove the Italians elsewhere. However, this First Ward settlement which became known as the "Dago District" was influential in shaping enduring prejudices against the Italians.[7]

As their numbers increased, the Italians expanded from the South Side westward across the Chicago River. Their coming, however, was violently opposed by the Irish, and it was only after many a bloody battle that they were able to establish a beachhead on the Near West Side. By the mid-1890s, however, they had advanced as far west as Halsted Street which became the frontier between Irish and Italians for some years. In time this Near West Side settlement became by far the largest of the city's Italian colonies (C). In 1910, almost 25,000, approximately one-third of Chicago's Italians, resided here in the Nineteenth Ward. This river ward contained some of the city's oldest and cheapest housing; it was also convenient to the Loop where many Italians worked as peddlers and streetsweepers and to the railroad depots from which the labor gangs left the city.[8]

By 1900, this "Little Italy" extended from Polk Street on the north to Taylor Street on the south and Halsted and Canal Streets on the west and east. An Italian parish, the Church of the Guardian Angel, was established on Forquer Street in 1899, but by 1911 a new church, Our Lady of Pompei, was built a mile farther west for the Italians now living in the vicinity of Racine Avenue. The westward movement continued until by 1915 the more prosperous Italians had breached the exclusive neighborhood of Ashland Avenue. "Ascellando," as the Italians called it, became known as the Royal Italian Boulevard.[9]

This Near West Side colony was predominantly South Italian in character, drawing upon all the regions of the *Mezzogiorno*. As Father Edmund N. Dunne, the pastor of the Guardian Angel Church, commented, "The natives from Naples, Salerno, Bari, Basilicata, Abruzzi, Calabria, Catanzaro, le Marche, Lucca, Messina, and Palermo are as plentiful as the English sparrow." Their neighbor, Jane Addams, observed that the *contadini* sought to fill "an entire tenement house with people from one village." It was said that if a few teams of oxen had been added to Forquer Street the illusion of a *paese* in Campania would have been complete.[10]

While the movement out of the South Side was primarily to the west, the Riciglianesi particularly migrated southward into the Fourth Ward. The removal of the segregated vice district to the Near South Side diverted their march southwest along Archer Avenue and then south again along Wentworth and Princeton Streets. They settled thickly in the Armour Square district between Twenty-second and Twenty-fifth Streets with the New York Central railroad tracks to the east and the Pennsylvania tracks to the west (D). The

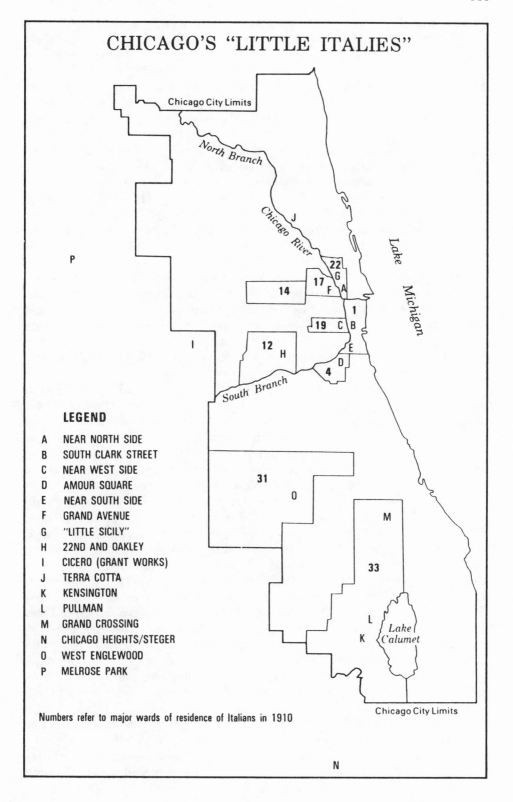

CHICAGO'S "LITTLE ITALIES"

LEGEND

A   NEAR NORTH SIDE
B   SOUTH CLARK STREET
C   NEAR WEST SIDE
D   AMOUR SQUARE
E   NEAR SOUTH SIDE
F   GRAND AVENUE
G   "LITTLE SICILY"
H   22ND AND OAKLEY
I   CICERO (GRANT WORKS)
J   TERRA COTTA
K   KENSINGTON
L   PULLMAN
M   GRAND CROSSING
N   CHICAGO HEIGHTS/STEGER
O   WEST ENGLEWOOD
P   MELROSE PARK

Numbers refer to major wards of residence of Italians in 1910 construction of the Church of Santa Maria Incoronata on Alexander Street in 1904 attracted other *paesani* to the neighborhood. Since many of the Riciglianesi plied the trades of newsvender, bootblack, and streetsweeper in the Loop, easy access to downtown was an important consideration. This solid settlement of several hundred families exhibited the spirit of *campanilismo* par excellence. Among the Riciglianesi it was considered a scandal for anyone to marry out of the village group even unto the second géneration of American born.[11]

The Near South Side also attracted immigrants from Termini Imerese in Sicily. While the Terminesi could be found in other parts of the city, this settlement at the juncture of Archer Avenue, Clark and Twentieth Streets in the First Ward became their most distinctive colony (E). The only other Sicilians on the Near North Side hailed from Nicosia, province of Catania. Although the Terminesi and the Nicosiani lived in close proximity along South Clark Street, they retained their separate identities, holding "tenaciously to their sacred, ancestral traditions." Those from Termini were for the most part fruit peddlers while those from Nicosia were mainly laborers. Although the Sicilians in time outnumbered the Riciglianesi, their neighborhoods remained quite distinct with Twenty-second Street as the dividing line. While sharing the Church of Santa Maria Incoronata, each group of *paesani* had its own religious sodality and celebrated the feast of its patron saint. Together the Near South Side and Armour Square districts by 1910 encompassed the city's fourth largest concentration of Italians.[12]

Another major settlement took shape in the Seventeenth Ward in an area bounded by the North Branch of the Chicago River on the east and railroad tracks on the south (F). The earliest settlers, Genoese and Tuscans, were soon outnumbered by southern Italians. Situated along Grand Avenue and adjacent streets, the immigrants congregated by village and regional groups: several hundred *paesani* from Calvello resided on Sangamon Street; other Potenzanesi were on Peoria Street; Luccesi along with Veneziani and Romani located on Hubbard, Racine and May Streets, while those from Campania and Abruzzi were strung out along Grand Avenue and Ohio and Erie Streets. After 1900, newcomers from Apulia and Sicily poured into the Seventeenth Ward; the former from Nola di Bari, Triggiano and Modugno settled along Grand Street, while the latter from Termini Imerese and the province of Palermo established a "Little Sicily" in the southeastern corner of the ward. Their influx resulted in the withdrawal of the former residents, Norwegians, Germans and Irish. In 1899 the Norwegian Church at Peoria and Grand was rededicated as the Church of Santa Maria Addolorata. Although the Seventeenth Ward was industrial in character, few Italians were employed in its factories. Rather they worked in the adjacent railroad yards or produce markets. The Grand Avenue colony in the Seventeenth and Fourteenth Wards comprised the third largest agglomeration of Italians in the city, over 11,500 in 1910.[13]

The Near North Side had early sheltered a Genoese neighborhood; later Tuscans had fruit stores and saloons along Franklin, Wells and Orleans Streets between Grand Avenue and Chicago Avenue. To the north, plaster workers from Lucca employed in statuary shops centered about Division

Street and Clybourne Avenue. In the first decade of the twentieth century, a wave of immigration from Sicily swept over the Near North Side. By 1910, the Twenty-second Ward's Italians (now predominantly Sicilian) numbered almost 13,000, placing it second only to the Nineteenth Ward (G). The Terminesi were the earliest Sicilians in this part of the city as well. However, the major source became the villages in the hinterland of Palermo: Monreale, Bagheria, Alta Villa-Milica, Vicari, Ventimiglia, and Cimminna. Among these Palermitani were *contadini* who had worked on the sugar plantations in Louisiana and had subsequently migrated north. In 1904, the Church of St. Philip Benizi was built at the corner of Oak and Cambridge as "*la chiesa degli Siciliani*." Described as a "mosaic of Sicilian villages," the colony extended from Chicago Avenue to Division Street and from Sedgwick Street to the river. In the heart of industrial Chicago, the *paesani* "retained their identity, living together as far as possible, intermarrying, and celebrating the traditional feasts." On Larabee Street were those from Alta Villa, on Townsend those from Bagheria, on Milton those from Sambuca-Zabat, and so on. This "Little Sicily" became notorious because of the frequency of murders and bombings. Such was its sinister reputation that its residents were often barred from employment and had difficulty moving into other neighborhoods.[14]

In 1910, two-thirds of the city's Italians resided in these five river wards. Arranged in a semicircle around the downtown business district, a three-mile radius using the corner of State and Madison Streets as a pivot would have included all of the settlements. Still, a considerable and growing number of Italians lived in outlying districts and suburbs. Several thousand were scattered about the city engaged in petty commerce for the most part. A number of settlements, however, emerged in response to localized employment opportunities. One of the few industries hiring Italians in the 1890s was the McCormick Reaper Works on Blue Island Avenue. A colony of Tuscans from Ponte Bugianese, Altopiano, San Gennaro, Ciesina, and Borgo Abuszarma took shape between Twenty-second Street and Blue Island Avenue running from Leavitt Street to Western Avenue (H). Although most had been *ortolani* (truck farmers), the Tuscans worked at "McComio" (as they called it) or the nearby National Malleable and Casting Works. By 1910, the Italians in the Twelfth Ward totaled over one thousand. Having displaced the Swedes, the Lutheran Church on Twenty-Fourth Place was converted to the Church of San Michele Arcangelo. The Tuscan colony, a stronghold of the Italian Socialist Federation, was known for its fierce anticlerical sentiment, and the church languished. When National Malleable opened its Grant Works in Cicero in 1910, many migrated from the Twenty-second and Oakley area to the new plant (I). Here they formed a small settlement of a few hundred persons between Laramie Avenue and Fiftieth Avenue and Twelfth and Fourteenth Streets. Noted for its fiery radical spirit, the neighborhood had a cooperative store, recreation hall, and saloon, but no church.[15]

Another pocket of Tuscans, these Luccesi from Bagni di Lucca, Camaiore, and Barga, established themselves on the North Side between Fullerton and Diversey along the North Branch (J). Having a long tradition of working with ceramics, they found jobs with the Northwestern Terra Cotta Works, especially after a Luccese became a foreman. Known among themselves as

"Terra Cotta," several hundred had settled in this part of the Twenty-fourth Ward by 1910.[16]

Work of a similar character attracted other Italians to Kensington on the west shore of Lake Calumet. As early as 1892 immigrants from Altipiano di Asiago, province of Vicenza (Veneto) worked here for the Illinois Terra Cotta and Lumber Company. Recruits from other provinces soon formed a substantial colony of Veneziani. After 1900 a large number of Calabresi and Piemontesi as well as smaller contingents from Lombardy, Tuscany and Sicily also converged on Kensington. While many worked in the brick yards, an increasing percentage were hired by the nearby Pullman Works and the Burnside shops of the Illinois Central. In 1902, The Kensington Italians numbered about a thousand persons, concentrated in an area east of Michigan Avenue to the Illinois Central tracks and from 115th to 120th Streets (K). Reflecting an intense spirit of *regionalismo*, the various groups settled along certain blocks and formed their own mutual aid societies. Regional differences came out forcefully on the issue of religion. The Piemontesi tended to be strongly anticlerical while the Veneziani and *meridionali* were more church-oriented. Immediately to the north of Kensington was the company town of Pullman. By 1912, some nine hundred Italians worked at the Pullman Palace Car Company and lived in the brick rowhouses (L). In the Thirty-third Ward, which included both Pullman and Kensington, the Italians, numbering over four thousand made up one of the largest nationality groups by 1910.[17]

One other small neighborhood in the Thirty-third Ward in the district known as Grand Crossing was composed completely of Calabresi from the provinces of Cosenza, Catanzaro, and Reggio Calabria (M). The first settlers were laborers in section gangs who purchased lots and built houses. Later some worked in the Illinois Central shops at Burnside, others in a factory on Seventy-ninth Street, still others commuted to Pullman. The area had a semirural aspect with ample room for vegetable gardens. The only business establishments were a few groceries, a saloon, and a barber shop. Several hundred Calabresi settled compactly on Dobson and Greenwood Avenues between Seventy-fifth and Seventy-ninth Streets. They formed mutual aid societies, and in 1911 the Church of St. Francis de Paula was established. It was said of the Grand Crossing colony that "if one were to remove a single family with all its cousins, the whole neighborhood would be practically wiped out."[18]

Meanwhile ten miles south of Kensington, other Italian immigrants were congregating in the industrial satellite city of Chicago Heights (N). The first were Marchegiani, particularly from the fishing village of San Benedetto del Tronto. Subsequently a large number of Abruzzesi from Castel di Sangro and Sulmona and smaller groups from Calabria, Sicily and Lazio arrived. By 1910, numbering 3,224, the Italians were by far the largest nationality in the city. Initially employed on the railroads, the opening of the Inland Steel Plant in 1894 offered new opportunities, particularly after an Italian became foreman of the railcutting department. Some had worked in steel mills in France and Germany, but most of the Italians had been farmers or fishermen. Settling on Chicago Heights' East Side between Fourteenth and Twenty-sixth

Streets, each of the regional groups appropriated certain blocks: the Marchegiani on Hanover and Wentworth, the Abruzzesi on Twenty-third, the ·Calabresi on Sixteenth and Seventeenth Streets. Mutual aid societies were formed along regional lines, and a section of the Italian Socialist Federation, in which the Abruzzesi and Marchegiani were especially active, was organized. The conflict between pro- and anticlerical elements was especially heated, but the Church of San Rocco was nonetheless dedicated in 1906.[19]

Three miles south of Chicago Heights, quite a number of Italians worked in the Steger Piano Company and lived in the company town of Steger. They were for the most part from Amaseno in the province of Frosinone (Lazio). A cabinetmaker from that *paese* had become foreman in the rubbing and finishing department, and whenever there was an opening he hired a *paesano*. In this fashion, the Amasenesi, most of whom had been day laborers on large estates, developed an occupational specialization in piano and furniture factories. So many of them settled in Chicago Heights that it became known as "Amaseno the Second."[20]

These outlying settlements were not created by immigrants seeking to escape from the inner city "ghetto." Rather they originated independently of the downtown Italian neighborhoods and grew through direct chain migration from specific *paesi* in Italy. Two major colonies, however, were initially formed by outmigrations from the river ward "Little Italies." West Englewood, located about seven miles southwest of the Loop, attracted its first Italians from the South Clark Street settlement in the 1880s (O). Attracted by the low price of land, the early settlers from Oliveto Citra transformed the prairie into bountiful truck gardens. Because of their livestock, the area earned the nickname of Goatsville. The Olivetani formed a sodality in 1891 to celebrate the feast of *la Madonna del Carmine*. The widespread cult of the madonna and the rustic setting attracted thousands from the city to this annual *festa*. This in turn stimulated the growth of the settlement. Work was available on the railroad and streetcar lines and in building construction. The newcomers were also for the most part Salernitani from the *paesi* of Contursi, Campagna, and Senarchia. By 1910 the Italian population in the Thirty-first Ward, centering about Hermitage Avenue and Sixty-ninth Street, was over 1,200.[21]

A second garden community developed in Melrose Park, some eleven miles west of downtown Chicago (P). In 1890, the suburb was already the scene of real estate promotion among the Italians with excursions featuring balloon ascensions, fireworks and Professore Ernesto Libonati's orchestra. Emilio de Stefano, leader of the Laurenzanesi in the South Clark Street quarter, was a promoter of this development. When he recovered from a serious illness, his wife in thanksgiving erected a chapel with a replica of the statue of the *Madonna del Carmine* which stood in the church in Laurenzana. In 1894 the first *festa della Madonna* was held on the De Stefano farm in Melrose Park. This became the most popularly attended of the Italian *feste*, and many who came decided to settle here. As in West Englewood, the Italians built wooden shacks and established gardens on the virgin prairie. Because of the abundance of this crop, the settlement became known as Pepper Town. While the families engaged in subsistence farming, the men worked in nearby steel mills and foundries, on section gangs, and in construction. By 1910, the Italian community numbered over a thousand and was rapidly growing. Two groups heavily represented in the colony were the Trivignesi and the Riciglianesi from Basilicata and Campania respectively. Siciliani, Calabresi, and Marchegiani were later arrivals. Regional lines appear to have been less sharply drawn in Melrose Park than in the other settlements. Such was the intermingling that it was said an outsider could not identify what part of Italy a Melrose Park Italian came from by his dialect.[22]

This panoramic view of the Italian neighborhoods of Chicago during the period of formation sketches their Old World origins, their economic base, and something of their social and cultural character. Of course, each of these settlements had a history dense with life and deserving of study. If we had histories of the Tuscans at Twenty-second Street and Oakley or of the Riciglianesi of Armour Square or of the Amasenesi of Chicago Heights, we would know much more about the Italian immigration than we do now. However, even this broad overview suggests the dangers of generalizing about the Italian experience in Chicago (or elsewhere for that matter). Unless we are willing to deal with the Italian immigration in all its complexity, we run the risk of arriving at gross and erroneous conclusions. Certainly the crude North Italian-South Italian dichotomy which is employed by even recent studies is misleading as an interpretive scheme for understanding that immigration.[23]

In sum, this analysis of Italian settlement in Chicago suggests several conclusions—or better hypotheses to be tested in further research. First of all, the ecological model does not adequately explain the peculiarities of the spatial distribution of the Italian neighborhoods. Land use patterns, industrial location, labor market, and housing market did not in themselves *determine* where the Italians finally lighted. For example, one needs to explain the absence as well as the presence of the Italians. Why were they not to be found in significant numbers in the "Back-of-the-Yards" district or in South Chicago? Because they were not employed in the meatpacking plants or steel mills. But why were they not? Clearly the immigrants were not responding blindly to economic forces. They were able to exercise some choices in a "free labor" market, to express preferences for type of work and living environment. One must allow for the play of contingency, cultural preference, and human agency.

I have been particularly struck by the role of the pioneer who is the pathfinder, who chooses this rather than that fork in the road. For each of the *paesani* groups, one finds such a trailblazer at the beginning of the migration process. Francesco Lagorio served such a function for the Genoese. Arriving in the early 1850s, realizing a modest success, he sent for family and friends. It was about his restaurant on the Near North Side that the Genoese colony coalesced. In the case of the Laurenzanesi, Emilio de Stefano who came to Chicago in 1873 became the acknowledged leader. It was De Stefano who was instrumental in bringing many from the province of Potenza first to the Polk Depot area and then to Melrose Park. A similar role was played among the Calabresi by Luigi Spizziri who also arrived in the early seventies and became an important padrone among his *paesani*. Lending money to would-be immigrants from Calabria, he was reputed to have brought more Italians than anyone else to Chicago and specifically to the South Clark Street settlement. For the immigration from Termini Imerese, Andrea Russo served as a guide and catalyst. Coming in 1882, he began as a peddler and ultimately became a large importer of Italian food products. Bringing relatives and *paesani*, he initiated a general immigration to the Grand Street colony of the Terminesi. Or one can cite the role of the anonymous foremen who secured jobs for their *paesani* with the Northwestern Terra Cotta Works and the Steger Piano Company. These "founding fathers" had a great deal to do with directing the migrations from specific villages and provinces to particular destinations.[24]

Finally one cannot help but be impressed by the force of group solidarity in shaping the Italian neighborhoods of Chicago. *Campanilismo* and *regionalismo* expressed through the process of chain migration, mutual assistance, and cultural affinity exerted a profound influence upon the settlement patterns among and within the "Little Italies." Of course, not all of the residents of a particular street or district came from specified villages, nor were all of the residents of these neighborhoods Italian. We are not arguing here the ethnic homogeneity of these settlements, but rather for a recognition of this powerful tendency of reconstitute community in accordance with Old World origins. Certainly the neighborhoods which were formed during the period of mass immigration remained intact for several decades. A map for 1930 plotting the Italian-born population of Chicago by census tracts reveals the persistence of these settlements over time. Although conversion of land to nonresidential uses and the influx of new migrant groups had resulted in certain population movements, the continuity of ethnic concentration over the period of two decades is remarkable. What this suggests is the enormous cohesive force of these neighborhoods.

While conducting research in Chicago during the late fifties and early sixties, I visited the sites of all of these settlements. By then, some were in an advanced stage of disintegration, while others retained a remarkable vitality. Today some are gone altogether as in the case of the Near West Side neighborhood and the "Little Sicily" of the Near North Side. They were completely wiped off the face of the city by "urban renewal." But certain districts such as Melrose Park and Kensington remain even today strongholds of Italian-American communities. As part of our agenda for the study of "Little Italies" and ethnic neighborhoods in general we need analyses of those factors which make for the persistence of some and the disappearance of others. The history of particular communities from their genesis to their demise would contribute to our understanding of the role of ethnicity in shaping the cultural geography of our cities.

NOTES

[1]Frank Thistlethwaite, "Migration from Europe Overseas in the Nineteenth and Twentieth Centuries," in XIe Congrès International des Sciences Historiques, Stockholm 1960, *Rapports*, 5: *Historiques Contemporaine* (Göteborg-Stockholm-Uppsala, 1960): 32–60.

[2]For an effort to write the history of the Italians in Chicago from this perspective see my doctoral dissertation, "Chicago's Italians prior to World War I: A Study of their Social and Economic Adjustment" (University of Wisconsin, 1963).

[3]Robert E. Park, Ernest W. Burgess, and Roderick D. MacKenzie, *The City* (Chicago, 1925), pp. 1–62; Fred H. Matthews, *Quest for an American Sociology: Robert E. Park and the Chicago School* (Montreal, 1977), pp. 121–56.

[4]The letters refer to location symbols on map: Chicago's "Little Italies."

[5]Tanner, Halpin and Co., comp., *D. B. Cooke & Co.'s Directory of Chicago for the Year 1858* (Chicago, 1858); Richard Edwards, comp., *Chicago Census Report; and Statistical Review Embracing a Complete Directory of the City* (Chicago, 1871); Local Community Research Committee, University of Chicago, "Documents: History of the Lower North Side" no. 28, 29 (transcript in Chicago Historical Society); Chicago Board of Education, *School Census of the City of Chicago, 1884* (Chicago, 1884); and *School Census of 1898* (Chicago, 1899); *Diamond Jubilee of the Assumption Parish, 1881–1956* (Chicago, 1956). In addition, interviews conducted by the author in the various Italian neighborhoods of Chicago between 1957–1960 constitute one of the basic sources for this study.

[6]United States Commissioner of Labor, *Ninth Special Report: the Italians in Chicago, a Social and Economic Study* (Washington, D.C., 1897), p. 21; Frank O. Beck, "The Italians in Chicago," *Bulletin of the Chicago Department of Public Welfare*, 2 (February 1919): 7.

[7]Chicago Board of Education, *School Census, 1884*; Edith Abbott, *The Tenements of Chicago, 1908–1935* (Chicago, 1936), p. 110; *Golden Anniversary, 1904–1954, Santa Maria Incoronata Church* (Chicago, 1954); *L'Italia* (Chicago), 14 February, 18 April 1903; *Chicago Daily News*, 15 July 1887, *Chicago Tribune*, 26 July 1885, 24 July 1887, 2 June 1888, 23 February 1890; *Chicago Record-Herald*, 14 June 1903; Agnes S. Holbrook, "Map Notes and Comments," in *Hull House Maps and Papers* (New York, 1895), pp. 15–23.

[8]Emilio Grandinetti, "50 anni di lotte e di aspirazioni fra gli Italiani di Chicago," *La Parola del Popolo* (Chicago), 9 (December 1958-January 1959): 87; United States Commissioner of Labor, *Seventh Special Report: The Slums of Baltimore, Chicago, New York and Philadelphia* (Washington, D.C., 1894), p. 38; Abbott, *Tenements of Chicago*, pp. 77, 95.

[9]*Chicago Record-Herald*, 14 June 1903; *Diamond Jubilee of the Archdiocese of Chicago* (Des Plaines, Ill., 1920), pp. 578, 645.

[10]Edmund M. Dunne, *Memoirs of "Zi Pre"* (St. Louis, 1914), p. 2; Jane Addams, *Newer Ideals of Peace* (New York, 1911), p. 67.

[11]*Golden Anniversary, 1904–1954, Santa Maria Incoronata Church*; Abbott, *Tenements of Chicago*, p. 113; Local Community Research Committee, "Documents: History of Armour Square," no. 1, 2, 10; Evelyn B. Espey, "Old World Customs Continued in Chicago," *By Archer Road*, 1 (September, 1907).

[12]Espey, "Archer Road," and "One of Our Neighbors," *By Archer Road*, 1 (May 1906), 4 (May 1910); *L'Italia*, 12 August 1894, 15–16, 22–23 August 1896, 16 March 1901, 21 March 1903.

[13]Chicago Department of Public Welfare, "Housing Survey in Italian District of the 17th Ward," *First Semi-Annual Report* (Chicago, 1915), p. 74; *Chicago Commons, 1894–1911* (n.p., n.d.); Abbott, *Tenements of Chicago*, p. 102; *L'Italia*, 24 February 1894; G. Sofia, ed., *Missioni Scalabriniane in America* (Rome, 1939), p. 115.

[14]Local Community Research Committee, "Documents: History of the Lower North Side," no. 27, 30, 36, 61; Harvey W. Zorbaugh, *The Gold Coast and the Slum: A Sociological Study of Chicago's Near North Side* (Chicago, 1929), pp. 165–73; *Chicago Daily News*, 11 November 1922; *L'Italia*, 18, 25 November, 9 December 1905.

[15]Armando Pierini, "Provincia 'S. Giovanni Battista,' Canada," *Cinquantesimo: Numero Speciale de' L'Emigrato* (Monza, Italy), 49 (May-June 1953): 60; United States Immigration Commission, *Reports*, 26 (1911): 307–311; *Diamond Jubilee of the Archdiocese of Chicago*, p. 599; *La Parola dei Socialisti* (Chicago), 17 February 1908; "The Development of Cicero," (typescript, Chicago Community Inventory, University of Chicago).

[16]Interviews.

[17]Sofia, *Missioni Scalabriniane*, pp. 103–106; *L'Italia*, 14–15 December 1895, 4 October 1902; Abbott, *Tenements of Chicago*, pp. 151, 154; Alice Anderson, "Kensington," (ms., Chicago Community Inventory, 1924); Graham R. Taylor, "Satellite Cities: Pullman," *The Survey*, 29 (2 November 1912): 121–26.

[18]Abbott, *Tenements of Chicago*, pp. 154–55; Local Community Research Committee, "Documents: History of Grand Crossing," no. 1, 10; Frieda Bachmann, "Grand Crossing," (ms., Chicago Community Inventory, 1924); *Diamond Jubilee of the Archdiocese of Chicago*, p. 651.

[19]*The New World* (Chicago), 15 December 1906; *La Parola dei Socialisti*, 5, 12 March 1908.

[20]*La Parola dei Socialisti*, 5 March 1908.

[21]*Souvenir of the Golden Jubilee of the Parish of St. Mary of Mt. Carmel, 1892–1942*; Local Community Research Committee, "Documents: History of Englewood," no. 1, 3, 4, 7; *L'Italia*, 28–29 July 1894; 1–2 August 1896; 8 June, 24, 31 August 1901.

[22]Melrose Park Village Board, *Souvenir, The Village of Melrose Park, Illinois* (Chicago, 1907); *Golden Jubilee of the Feast of Our Lady of Mt. Carmel, Melrose Park, Illinois, 1894–1944*; Sofia, *Missioni Scalabriniane*, p. 122; *L'Italia*, 3 July, 13 September 1890; 4–5 August 1894.

[23]A particularly crude use of the North-South Italian dichotomy is Humbert Nelli, *The Italians in Chicago, 1880–1930* (New York, 1970).

[24]Local Community Research Committee, "Documents: History of the Lower North Side," no. 28; *Chicago Tribune*, 28 February, 4 March 1886; 23 February 1890; *L'Italia*, 4, 11 June 1892; 30 June 1894; 15–16 February 1896; 2 April 1904; W. A. Goodspeed and D. D. Healy, eds., *History of Cook County, Illinois*, 2 vols. (Chicago, 1909), 1:812–13.

Migration, Kinship, and Urban Adjustment: Blacks and Poles in Pittsburgh, 1900–30

*John Bodnar, Michael Weber, and Roger Simon**

T he early decades of the twentieth century witnessed the initial confrontation on a large scale of Afro-Americans and European immigrants with the American city. Since both of these groups migrated primarily from rural to urban areas, historians and sociologists have compared their experiences. Many have concluded that any economic disadvantages endured by blacks took place simply because they were "the last of the immigrants." Eventually they would experience the same economic advancement all immigrant groups were assumed to have made. Like most generalizations, however, this one was seldom based on detailed, systematic analysis, especially at a disaggregate level. This view, moreover, did a disservice to the historical interpretation of both the black and immigrant encounters with urban life, for it obscured the variety of adaptive measures different ethnic groups assumed in the urban milieu and it underestimated the impact of established racial and ethnic stereotypes which affected both groups of newcomers.

Existing interpretations of urban migration and adaptation for blacks and immigrants usually fall between two extremes. For some historians the urban environment was essentially destructive and resulted in poverty, familial disorganization, a separation between work and family interests, and the abandonment of premigration behavioral patterns. The theory of "ethnic succession," a widely employed model in explaining the adaptation of various ethnic groups to urban America, rested partially upon this assumption. It saw a direct correlation between adaptation and length of residency in the city. Recent arrivals would fill the lower jobs and homes of older residents who moved upward and outward.[1] In time urbanization would inevitably

John Bodnar is professor of history at Indiana University, Bloomington, Michael Weber is professor of history and graduate dean at Duquesne University, and Roger Simon is professor of history at Lehigh University. Reprinted from Journal of American History *66 (December 1979): 548–65. Reprinted by permission of the Organization of American Historians.*

eradicate premigration cultures and effect an accommodation of the migrant with the urban society. This model implied that adjustment and integration were inevitable. Sociologists who accepted this model frequently noted the special difficulties of Afro-Americans but resorted to the recency of their arrival from preurban settings as an explanation. Some felt Afro-Americans would eventually experience the same accommodation that previous immigrants had. More recently, however, historians have suggested that the earlier immigrants benefited from the pervasive racism of society and advanced occupationally and socially in American cities only at the expense of Afro-Americans.[2] The findings of the Philadelphia Social History Project have especially emphasized the destructive impact of the urban experience as an explanation of black behavior and persistence in poverty. The project's publications have denied the significance of such variables as preurban culture. Black families suffered in the city, for instance, because of high mortality rates among males. Black workers, moreover, were unable to overcome racial hostility and pass job skills to their children. Urban racism and structural inequality were also found to have had a greater impact on blacks than the preindustrial legacy of slavery.[3]

An alternative interpretation of movement and adaptation to urban America rests upon the assumption that premigration culture and values persisted in the cities and withstood the disintegrating impact of city life. This widely held approach emphasized race and ethnicity as independent variables which accounted for dissimilar patterns of urban adaptation. Josef Barton, in a recent study of Cleveland, explained the divergent patterns of immigrant mobility among Slovaks, Rumanians, and Italians in terms of their respective ethnic backgrounds and orientations. Victor Greene's account of Poles in Chicago interpreted Polish behavior on the basis of a search for traditional objectives of religion and land. Helena Lopata argued that Polish behavior in America is to be understood in terms of status competition which originated in peasant Poland. Thus, young Poles would be eager to get a mill job because of the value placed upon hard work within the Polish community. Herbert Gutman has emphasized the continuity in the black family during migration from the rural South to the urban North. Gutman in particular stressed the persistence of black kinship ties, but neither he nor the others closely examined the manner in which immigrants and their families functioned during migration and initial settlement in the city. Similarly, a study of New York City concluded that the cultural backgrounds of Italian and Jewish immigrants explained their differential patterns of mobility.[4]

A more balanced portrait of urban adaptation—one which acknowledges the complexity of the process—is found in the work of Robert L. Crain and Carol Sachs Weisman. Basing their analysis on detailed survey interviews, they found that the view of the unstable black family in northern ghettos was overly simplistic. To be sure, a high rate of marital instability was found among blacks, but no evidence of intergenerational transfer of such instability was discovered. For instance, daughters from broken homes were not more likely to initiate divorce in their own homes. In other words, the urban experience, at least for blacks, was not simply a question of destruction or cultural persistence but involved complex and specific reactions to particular circumstances. Data in recent historical works further suggests that adaptation was considerably more involved than the sweeping generalizations of the past have indicated. Research has demonstrated that Jews were more upwardly mobile than Italians, Rumanians manifested higher educational aspirations than Slovaks, and women were less likely to work outside the home in an Italian than in a Polish family. Dissimilarity was never more evident than when immigrants were compared with blacks. The intensity of racism directed toward blacks was unparalleled. Immigrants encountered a degree of hostility themselves. Precisely how both these groups interacted with a racially biased urban society is still unclear, however. Few examinations exist which attempt to go beyond "ethnic succession" or "premigration culture" as explanations for the process of urban adaptation and confront the complex interplay between migrants and the city they encountered.[5]

This essay examines the differential pattern of urban adaptation by concentrating on the actual process of moving to the city and securing work. Premigration backgrounds and the harsh effects of lower-class urban life were certainly important, but until the actual mechanics of migration and settlement are clarified, dissimilar patterns of behavior and adjustment for various ethnic groups cannot be fully explained. Urban adaptation will be analyzed by comparing the migration experiences, socialization practices, and occupational mobility patterns of Poles and blacks in Pittsburgh between 1900 and 1930. Explanations for their respective patterns will be offered not only to explain the difference between immigrant and black patterns of adjustment but also to suggest the pernicious effects of urban racism.

This analysis is based upon ninety-four oral history interviews conducted among Polish immigrants and black migrants in Pittsburgh who came before 1917. In addition, we have taken a 20 percent random sample of Christian Polish and black families in Pittsburgh from the 1900 United States census manuscripts. All wards were sampled except for several with extremely small numbers of immigrants or blacks. Although the census did not give information on religion, it was possible to separate Jewish and Christian Poles by using first names and known information about wards which were heavily Jewish. Other sources clearly suggest that Jews did not name their children John, Stanislaus, Cazimir, or Thaddeus. Even more strikingly, Christian Poles did not name their children Abraham, Isaac, Moses, Rebecca, Miriam, or Ruth. A few names, such as Joseph, were common to both groups, but the manuscripts listed entire families. Thus it was not difficult to determine which were the Jewish families. This method is similar to that used by Thomas Kessner in his recent study of Jews and Italians in New York.[6]

Opinion concerning early black migration from the South is diverse. According to observers such as Carter Woodson, the initial wave of black migrants was composed mostly of "talented" blacks who were "higher" in education and aspirations than the mass of poor Afro-Americans who composed the bulk of migrants before World War I. A study of Detroit concluded that early migrants were primarily those disillusioned by the deprivation of black political rights in the South. Some investigators have modified Woodson's views, but nearly all have agreed with Gunnar Myrdal that a desire for economic and social betterment was the chief motive for migration.[7]

Black movement from the South followed a classic migratory pattern of increasingly widening circles away from home in search of cash employment. At first the migration was brief; then it became seasonal, and eventually permanent, as the migrants strayed farther and farther from home. Clyde Kiser discovered that permanent migration from St. Helena Island, South Carolina, to New York City was preceded by temporary migration to nearby cities such as Savannah. Usually a father or other family member would seek temporary work outside the island in order to supplement agricultural income and allow most of the family to remain intact at home. These short-term movements not only provided additional income but familiarized blacks with wage labor and broader possibilities beyond farming.[8]

That early black migration is explained by the gradual movement of southern blacks from farms rather than an escape of the "talented tenth" was confirmed in oral interviews conducted between 1974 and 1976 among forty-seven migrants who came to Pittsburgh before 1917. Most Afro-Americans interviewed in Pittsburgh were raised on small farms in Alabama, Georgia, and Virginia. Migrants recalled their parents working as sharecroppers for larger farmers, who were in a few instances black. About one-fifth of the respondents came from farms owned by their fathers.

Common to most personal histories was the temporary departure of the male from the household in search of supplemental wages. Carrie J. recalled that a white owner frequently cheated her sharecropper father. Several times he was even denied his extra bale of cotton at Christmas. Such exploitation created economic difficulties which forced him to obtain a garbage collection job in Fitzgerald, Georgia.[9] The father of Olive W. first left sharecropping in Georgia to tap turpentine. Several years later he moved to a neighboring town to work in a sawmill. William H. recalled that his father, who owned his own farm, traveled from Alabama to a Georgia sawmill when farm work was "slack." Floyd T. had a father who left their family-owned Virginia farm to earn wages "driving" in Roanoke. Ben E. remembered his father leaving their Alabama farm to work on the railroad for "long periods of time." His father even spent some time in Pittsburgh before returning from one trip. It was no accident that Ben, who moved to the Steel City at age eighteen, or other respondents eventually came North. Their parents had already provided a glimpse of industrial wages and broader horizons.[10]

Often temporary toil stretched into periods of longer duration. Hezikiah M. was born in Louisa County, Virginia, in 1886. His parents had been slaves in Louisa County and by 1880 had only twenty acres of "poor land" growing mostly vegetables for the consumption of their fourteen children. When his father heard of "higher and regular" wages in West Virginia coal mines, he temporarily left his wife and children. Hezikiah recalled that his father returned about twice annually to bring much needed wages. In the meantime, his mother raised the children and earned extra money by taking in laundry work. When he was thirteen, Hezikiah and his brothers were taken by their father to Sunswitch, West Virginia, to load coal. Living in shanties with older men, Hezikiah worked the mines for four years and then left for a series of jobs in hotel kitchens which eventually brought him to Pittsburgh.[11]

Essential to the process of migration was information on job availability and wages. As with other immigrant groups, blacks relied on informal net-works of kin. This continued reliance on family supports Gutman's notion that various aspects of black kinship endured during slavery and later urban-ization. He argued that the adversity which blacks faced during the late eighteenth and early nineteenth centuries continued to nurture a reliance on kin. A similar dependency upon kin was clearly evident in at least the initial phase of the migration process.[12]

The movement of friends and kin from southern farms generated informal dissemination of knowledge about industrial employment. As a teenager Jean B. began working at a sawmill near Mobile, Alabama, while living on his parents' farm. It was at the sawmill that he heard mention of Philadelphia, New York, and Chicago. Such conversation prompted him to come north. He decided upon Pittsburgh because of information supplied by two friends already living there. After saving forty-five dollars, he took a train from Mobile through Cincinnati to Pittsburgh, where his friends obtained a room for him.[13] William H. was working for a railroad in Alabama. His wife's uncle, who had worked in coal mines near Pittsburgh, informed him of higher wages. Although he initially intended to seek employment in the mines, a friend in Pittsburgh drew him to the Jones and Laughlin Steel plant where wages appeared even "better." Another black, who preferred to remain anonymous, told how his father became dissatisfied with his career of "hiring out" from farm to farm in Virginia. He decided to come to Pittsburgh in 1902, where he gained "permanent" work and later brought his family. Several relatives "on his mother's side" followed his father to Pittsburgh, lived with him until they found work, and then moved out.[14] Similar experiences were related by other migrants. James N. learned of larger opportunities and wages while periodically working as a "sawmill man" and in an Alabama steel mill. James eventually followed a younger brother to Pittsburgh's Hill District where he correctly recalled a neighborhood teeming with Jews, Italians, and blacks. Another black woman recalled following brothers to Pittsburgh and settling in "Jewtown."[15] Olive W. settled in the Mount Washington section because her husband had relatives there. She eventually brought a sister to Pittsburgh to live with her in 1920.[16]

Kinship and friendship ties, however, were considerably less effective in helping newly arrived Negroes acquire industrial jobs. This is not to say that blacks were completely unable to offer assistance in getting work. The Pitts-burgh Survey (1907–08) described an exceptional cluster of black steelworkers at the Clark Mills of the Carnegie Steel Company. This group had worked as hod carriers or on the railroad before coming to Pittsburgh. The fact that over 61 percent of the group was from Virginia suggested the existence of a form of chain migration. However, these incidents were rare.[17]

In fact, a key role in hiring newcomers in Pittsburgh mills and plants, as elsewhere in American industry, was performed by white foremen, usually of English, Scottish, Irish, or German extraction. Furthermore, nearly every investigation of early twentieth-century Pittsburgh depicted the stereotypical outlooks of these influential men. Southern-born blacks were particularly unwanted because they were thought to be "inefficient," "unstable," and unsuitable for the heavy pace of mill work.[18] By contrast, Slavs were actually preferred to both blacks and native whites because of their assumed docility and "habit of silent submission, their amenability to discipline, and their willingness to work long hours and overtime without a murmur." One foreman, interviewed by the Pittsburgh Survey, commented about Slavs: "Give them rye bread, a herring, and beer, and they are all right." Whether any validity could be attached to these views is not as important as their existence. Both groups were the objects of a condescending racism, but Slavic newcomers such as the Poles benefited from this discrimination in that they were able to secure work not only for themselves but for their children. By 1910 they were no longer depending on the American foremen for work; superintendents routinely allowed immigrants to hire their own relatives and friends.[19]

Largely as a result of the foremen's hostility, the black work force in Pittsburgh before 1917 was widely distributed throughout various industries and was not particularly concentrated, as were some immigrant groups, in a few occupations. Table 1, drawn from our 20 percent sample, shows that blacks were distributed more widely than the sample of Poles.

The failure of blacks to establish occupational networks in the steel industry was apparent. Only 10.8 percent of southern-born blacks were in the metal industries while nearly 40 percent were scattered through general labor occupations such as hod carrier or day laborer. Blacks were also found in substantial numbers in transportation (teamster, drayman), public service (barber, waiter), and domestic service (porter, janitor, servant). Poles, in contrast, were almost completely unrepresented in service and transportation jobs. Austrian and German Poles clearly funneled their incoming migrants into metal production. Not surprisingly, a federal survey several years after

Table 1
Industrial Employment of Adult Males by Ethnicity, Pittsburgh, 1900

Industry	Southern-born Black	Russian Pole	Austrian Pole	German Pole
Labor	39.9%	54.8%	42.4%	34.8%
Metal	10.8%	19.1%	47.5%	43.7%
Commerce	1.4%	11.0%	1.0%	4.1%
Construction	2.6%	1.6%	2.0%	2.6%
Transportation	12.3%	3.6%	4.0%	2.6%
Public Service	7.2%	0.6%	1.0%	1.5%
Domestic Service	11.0%	0.5%	0.0%	0.7%
Other	14.8%	8.8%	2.1%	10.0%
N	1165	651	99	292

Source: U.S. Bureau of the Census, Manuscript Schedules of Population, 1900, Pittsburgh, RG 29 (National Archives). Sample data. All employed males age sixteen and over are included. The classification "labor" is taken from the manuscript census schedules. Some of these individuals probably worked in the metal industries. Other sources, however, indicate that few of them were black.

1900 noticed that blacks in Pittsburgh had established themselves in a variety of occupational enclaves. The report noted "quite a hundred" blacks in business as printers, grocers, hairdressers, and restaurant owners. About one-half of the "drivers" in the city were black.[20]

By 1910 blacks remained scattered throughout the occupational spectrum and had still not permeated the steel industry. Only 507 blacks were found among 19,686 men working in Pittsburgh's blast furnaces and rolling mills. Of nearly 10,000 "clerks" in the city only 87 were black. Immigrants remained clustered in one specific category—laborers in blast furnaces and rolling mills. Blacks were widely distributed in occupations such as janitors, draymen, teamsters, and domestic servants.[21] One contemporary observer even thought such variety was encouraging and a sign of advancement.[22]

The hiring practices that closed blacks out of the large and highly organized industries meant that kin and friends were unreliable in aiding blacks in securing work once in the city. Being widely scattered through the work force, especially among numerous small-scale firms, meant blacks in Pittsburgh had little influence in procuring positions for kin back home. More than other groups, blacks were on their own in finding work. This is confirmed by the oral data.

Interviews revealed that Afro-American migrants to Pittsburgh usually had to procure work on their own and were only occasionally able to rely on kin or friends for employment. Ben E. followed his father to a coal mine, worked there for six months, and then decided to leave for Pittsburgh. Although he had friends in the city, he was forced to find work on his own as a limestone loader at the American Steel and Wire Company. When work was slack, he obtained employment himself in a Kentucky coal mine and, after returning to the city, at the Jones and Laughlin Steel plant's boiler department. His experience was not unique. Jean B. simply persisted in talking a foreman into hiring him on a labor gang. Some started businesses of their own. Gertrude D. testified that her husband began by contracting his own work as a plasterer. Another migrant hired himself out to contractors as a cement finisher, wallpaper hanger, and plasterer. Floyd T. started a small trucking and hauling concern with his brother. Hezikiah M. told of his brother who opened a small print shop.[23]

Without other means of assistance, black migrants developed strategies for dealing with white foremen, which frequently included boastful claims of work abilities. The fact that blacks were forced to resort to such practices is further evidence that foremen were reluctant to hire them and of the underlying racism they were forced to overcome. Harrison G. left Georgia for Pittsburgh and encountered a long line of potential employees at the Jones and Laughlin Steel plant. When his turn arrived, he told the foreman he could perform better than anyone else. Harrison explained that such boasting was part of his "strategy" for getting a job. Other blacks promised potential employers that they would "play it straight and go home when the job was done," "stay out of mischief," and remain on the job for a long time. Forced to project himself as an individual, a black such as James N. approached prospective employers and asserted he was "a good man whom the company could use." Ernest F. received no assistance at all in obtaining a job in a brick plant and simply approached the foremen on his own. Harrison G. secured a position at a South Side steel plant by showing a foreman he could load scrap even faster than a "bunch of hunkies."[24] Certainly this analysis casts doubt upon contemporary views that claimed black migrants were "idlers and loafers" who sought "easy money."[25]

Arriving at the same time as blacks, Polish immigrants also sought work in the industrial city. Most treatments of Polish immigration to America are not only fragmentary but blind to the various origins of Polish newcomers. Generally speaking, Poles entered Pittsburgh in successive waves from provinces under the control of Germany, Russia, and Austria. Beginning in the early 1870s, German Poles began settling in the "strip district" along Penn Avenue and further north in Lawrenceville. German Poles predominated in Herron Hill (Polish Hill) and the South Side before 1900. After the late 1890s, Austrian Poles from Galicia joined German Poles on the South Side and Russian Poles in the Lawrenceville section.[26]

Poles moving to Pittsburgh could be grouped into two categories. Those from Prussia moved to America almost entirely in family units and had little intention of returning to a country where German policies made it increasingly difficult for Poles to own land. Poles from the Austrian and the Russian sectors were more likely to arrive in Pittsburgh as single males and either return to Europe or reconstruct families in America. Like blacks, Poles were mobile before moving to Pittsburgh. Industrial Silesia and cities such as Poznan and Warsaw were attracting temporary wage earners as early as 1870. John S. and his father temporarily left their farm in Russian Poland to earn wages. While the children were growing up in Poland, Valerian D. recalled, his father had mined coal in Germany. Joseph B. was sent to Pittsburgh to earn wages for his family and eventually returned to Poland, only to see his own son leave for America.[27]

Characteristically, kinship was also crucial for Poles moving to the city. The mother of Joseph D. was brought from Gdańsk (Prussia) to "Polish Hill" by an uncle who ran a grocery store. Valerian D. was brought to McKeesport, Pennsylvania, by his father in 1906. Peter L. avoided service in the Russian army by following a brother to the Steel City. The parents of Joseph B. were brought from Russian Poland by relatives. With two sisters and a brother already working in the city, the father of Stephanie L. left German Poland in 1899 with his wife and daughter. Joseph B. sent passage for two brothers and a sister to join him on the South Side. Joseph Z. attracted two brothers to the Oliver Iron and Steel plant.[28]

Although blacks and Poles may have similarly relied on relatives during the migration process, there was a critical difference in the role of kin behavior of the two groups. Poles were clearly more effective in obtaining work for family and friends. They were particularly successful in establishing occupational beachheads at the steel mills of Jones and Laughlin and Oliver on the South Side, at Heppenstall's and the Pennsylvania Railroad yards in Lawrenceville, and at Armstrong Cork Company, the H. J. Heinz plant, and other large industrial plants. Thus, Poles were clustered in a few industries when compared to the more widely dispersed blacks. Valentine B. gained his first job in America on the railroad through his brother. Brothers also assisted

Peter H. in obtaining employment in a foundry making castings for mines. Ignacy M. left Russian Poland in 1912 and relied on his brother to get him a position piling steel beams at the Jones and Laughlin plant. Joseph D. left Prussia for a job in a mill that was procured by his wife's uncle. A cousin found Edward R. work at a machine shop. John S. followed friends from Galicia in 1909 but needed relatives to acquire machinists work for him. Charles W. relied on relatives to gain him access to domestic work for Americans and boarding house tasks among the Poles.[29] The impact of these practices had implications for the families of newly arrived blacks and Poles. Partly because black families had difficulty in securing jobs for kin, their children were raised in a framework of self-sufficiency. An examination of the socialization process in migrant families revealed that blacks had clearly decided how children could secure their goals. Given the nature of class and racial subordination, young blacks emerged from their formative years with a sense of individualism, a realization that survival would ultimately depend upon their own personal resourcefulness.[30]

Strong individualism usually surfaced in black adolescents. Rather than emerging as adults fixed to the responsibilities of their families of origin, migrants prior to 1918 and their children looked toward a future that they alone would shape. Sally S. recalled that her brother left the family farm in Mississippi for a Florida sawmill "when he was big enough to work on his own." After several years her brother left Florida for Washington, DC. Roy M. "had the urge to leave home" at age sixteen. He reasoned that if he could work in the fields of Arkansas he could surely work for his own wages. His move north, not uncharacteristically, was preceded by a period in an Arkansas sawmill. Before he was twenty, Grant W. had moved to Pittsburgh, obtained a job in a glass factory, worked at a steel foundry, and launched a semi-professional baseball career. Several female respondents left home on their own at age twenty to attend school, perform domestic service, or hire out for "day work" in Pittsburgh. The father of William H. told his son at his twenty-first birthday, "you are your own man and you can go on your own." Ernest F. did not even tell his father when he left school to procure a job, although his father generally allowed him to make his own decisions.[31]

Often rising individual aspirations clashed with parental authority—a fact that suggested a certain tension between parents' emotional ties and their pragmatic conclusion about what was needed for adult survival. The resulting strain pushed some young blacks into a search for their own means of sustenance. Jasper A. left his family farm not only because he was tired of farming but because his father worked him "pretty hard." Roy M. expressed similar displeasure with "strict parents who would not allow him to pursue his own interests." Characteristically, both the brother and father of Olive W. had run away from home at age fourteen to work in Florida sawmills. One Pittsburgh respondent had the feeling that his father was "too repressive" and showed insufficient "trust" in his son. Grant W. argued with a stepmother over keeping his own wages and, although he felt "close" to his father, left home twice before age seventeen to work on his own.[32] A striking example of black individualism and self-reliance was Gertrude D., who, at age sixteen, lived alone in Nashville after her mother died. She acquired a job scrubbing laundry and became completely self-supporting. After several years she married and accompanied her husband to Pittsburgh.[33]

Early employment among children in working-class families was certainly not unique. A recent study in Philadelphia concluded that "most urban American families were able to operate with a margin of comfort to the degree that they could count on a steady contribution from their laboring children of both sexes."[34] Such a pattern was not as evident among Pittsburgh's black migrant families. This is not to say that black children never contributed their wages to their parents. They sometimes did, although often for a specific purpose such as the education of a brother or sister. But black progeny were considerably more likely than immigrant children to retain their own wages rather than relinquish them to parents. Grant W., to cite a case in point, contributed part of his wages until he was sixteen so that his sister could finish high school. As soon as she graduated, he kept his earnings for himself. Floyd T. unloaded box cars as a teenager but discussed the matter of his wages with his parents and was allowed to "manage for himself." Jasper A. described his relationship with his parents as intimate but seldom sent money to them in the South. Queen W. kept her own wages at age fifteen when she went to Norfolk to do domestic work. A young worker, whose family moved from Virginia, did give some of his wages to his family but kept most for himself. James N. kept a similar portion of his early wages. Olive W. gave her parents occasional support but kept most of her wages for her own use. She did not recall her brothers and sisters turning anything over to her parents. Similarly, a survey of unmarried black migrants in Pittsburgh in 1917 found that less than 45 percent sent money to relatives.[35]

Unlike black youth who tended to launch careers of their own and retain wages, young Polish workers remained attached to their families of origin and contributed most of their earnings to their parents. Socialization in Polish families functioned in a manner which insured both the inevitability of child labor and the relinquishing of earnings for family use at least until marriage. Before 1930, young Poles learned their lessons well. Ray C. expressed his reason for remaining in Lawrenceville as a young man: "I felt down deep I had an obligation to take care of my mother." Joseph D. never had to be told to assist his family. "I always thought dad had hard luck so I would stick with them [parents] until the other kids got old enough to work," he explained. The tendency of young Poles to consider family obligations was stated clearly by Edward R.: "We looked forward to the time when we got to the legal age. When we got to that point we quit school and got a job because we knew the parents needed money. . . . That's just the way we were raised."[36]

Carrying out the dictates of their upbringing, Polish youth nearly always gave their earnings to their mothers, the usual manager of Polish family finances.[37] Stanley N. "hustled newspapers" at mill gates and gave his three-dollar-per-week profit to his mother. Joseph B. and his brothers sold enough newspapers on Polish Hill to nearly equal his father's weekly salary of $12.50. After the father of John K. had his leg crushed at Carnegie Steel, John began working in a grocery store and giving his wages to his mother. Peter L. helped his parents by working in a butcher shop at age sixteen. In order to assist their families of origin, hundreds of young Poles found employment with glass manufacturers on the South Side by the age of fourteen, including many who worked at night.[38]

Young Polish girls were also expected to assist parents until marriage. In fact, it was not uncommon for Polish children to live in the same house with their parents for several years after marriage, something that was rarely found among blacks.[39] On the South Side Polish girls packed and inspected nuts and bolts at Oliver Iron and Steel. Stephanie W. recalled that all her sisters worked at either H. J. Heinz or the South Side Hospital and contributed their wages to their mother. At age sixteen Stephanie worked in a store that needed a "Polish girl" for its Polish clientele. Josephine B. left school after the eighth grade and did "day work" in Mount Lebanon, an upper-middle-class suburb. She and her brother who worked in a nearby coal mine relinquished all their earnings to their parents. Joseph D. recalled that all of his sisters left school at age thirteen and worked in a cigar factory.[40]

Another way to evaluate the impact of the greater ability of Poles to provide jobs for kin is to examine family structure. In the 20 percent sample from the 1900 census, we can divide sample families into three groups according to family composition—nuclear, extended, and augmented—and into four groups according to stage in life cycle—newlyweds, young families, midstage, and mature. A nuclear family consisted of one or both parents and their children; an extended family included other relatives living in the home; an augmented family included nonrelative lodgers and boarders whose presence was intended to supplement the family income. Newlywed families were defined as childless couples; young families were those in which there were no working children and the wife was under age forty-five. Midstage families had employed children and/or a wife over age forty-five; mature families had children living outside the home (Table 2).[41]

The data reveal that, during the critical middle years when children attained working age, black families became less nuclear while Polish families

Table 2
Family Structure by Family Stage and Ethnicity, Pittsburgh, 1900

Family Structure	Southern-born Black	Russian Pole	German Pole
Young-Family Stage			
Nuclear	63.4%	72.6%	80.4%
Extended	13.4%	10.3%	9.8%
Augmented	23.3%	17.1%	9.8%
N	172	146	92
Mid-Stage			
Nuclear	52.2%	90.2%	93.2%
Extended	17.4%	0.0%	0.0%
Augmented	30.4%	9.8%	6.8%
N	46	41	44

Source: U.S. Bureau of the Census, Manuscript Schedules of Population, 1900, Pittsburgh, RG 29 (National Archives).

became more nuclear. This suggests that growing children in Polish families were contributing to family income so that paying boarders or relatives were displaced. On the other hand, the increase in boarders and lodgers among blacks at the same time as the children reached working age suggests that those children were not contributing to the household economy.

The pattern is further substantiated by looking at the number of unrelated boarders living with families in different stages (Table 3). Black families increased the number of unrelated boarders in their households from the young-family to the middle-family stages. Polish families did just the opposite. The average number of unrelated boarders among young southern-born black families was 4.5. This figure grew to 6.4 by the midstage. Between these two periods in the family cycle Russian Poles lowered the mean number of unrelated boarders from 4.9 to 3.5. German Poles reduced their average from 4 to 1. While the number of boarders in most households seemed high, it should not be forgotten that these figures were drawn from a period of widespread migration, when boarders were not only commonplace but important sources of family revenue.

The post-1900 occupational mobility patterns of blacks and Poles revealed the effects of their dissimilar responses to employment opportunities and racial discrimination. Unable to ensure jobs for kin and forced to rely on individual resourcefulness, blacks experienced both greater upward and greater downward occupational mobility between 1900 and 1915 (Table 4). Between 1900 and 1910, for instance, black upward movement was 32.7 percent while that of German Poles was only 21.2 percent. In the same period, however, blacks were almost twice as likely to slip downward. The high rates of mobility out of the city have resulted in dismayingly small sample cells. Admittedly the full extent of upward and downward mobility does not appear in the table. More detailed analysis of the career patterns of each group, however, revealed almost no movement from blue-collar to white-collar worker or vice versa. In fact, nearly all movement occurred between unskilled and semiskilled cohorts. Thus, while blacks experienced more upward and downward mobility than Poles, the differences were generally insignificant. Black workers most often moved from unskilled to semiskilled and back to unskilled occupations. This greater movement of blacks, however, represents considerable movement from job to job—horizontal mobility—and reflects the lack of occupational

Table 3
Mean Number of Unrelated Boarders in Household by Ethnicity and Family Stage, Pittsburgh, 1900

	Young-Family	Mid-Stage
Southern-born Black	4.5	6.4
Russian Pole	4.9	3.5
German Pole	4.0	1.0

Source: U.S. Bureau of the Census, Manuscript Schedules of Population, 1900, Pittsburgh, RG 29 (National Archives).

Table 4
Occupational Mobility for Selected Male Ethnic Groups
at Five-Year Intervals, Pittsburgh, 1900–1915

Group	N 1900	% Upward			% Downward			% Same		
		1905	1910	1915	1905	1910	1915	1905	1910	1915
Southern-born Blacks	1165	24.3	32.7	30.2	14.9	16.8	21.3	60.9	50.5	47.7
Russian Poles	651	21.7	25.0	39.0	1.3	2.7	8.6	76.9	72.2	52.2
German Poles	292	14.1	21.2	21.4	6.4	9.0	14.3	79.5	69.7	64.3

Source: U.S. Bureau of the Census, Manuscript Schedules of the Population, 1900, Pittsburgh, RG 29 (National Archives); *R. L. Polk Pittsburgh Directory*, 1905, 1910, 1915.

security afforded to black workers. Poles, following kin into the workplace, failed to match either the upward or downward levels of black mobility. Rather, they moved routinely into blue-collar jobs, probably without actively pursuing alternatives, generally remained at the same occupational levels, and established clusters in various industries.

Clearly, not all newcomers to the city functioned the same way. The encounters of Poles and blacks with Pittsburgh effected dissimilar models of accommodation. These differences, however, were not simply the result of premigration cultures or the assumed disintegrating effects of the urban milieu. Both groups evidenced strong kinship attachments before and during the migration process. That they operated in somewhat different ways does not necessarily suggest that one was more dysfunctional than the other. In actuality both Polish and black families remained intact, and parents worked effectively to socialize their children in a manner which would facilitate their survival. What caused their adaptive courses to differ was the preference of employers for immigrants rather than blacks, which frustrated the implementation of black kinship in the procurement of work. In the face of urban conditions both blacks and Poles resorted to premigration traditions—blacks because they had to, Poles because they were able to. But neither premigration culture nor urban racism functioned independently. Adjustment was ultimately a product of the interaction of one with the other. Poles were objects of discrimination, but they actually benefited in a perverse way from their image as dull but steady workers by being allowed to rely on their traditional kinship ties. Neither Poles nor blacks moved rapidly up any ladder of succession. Poles, however, avoided intense racial hostility and planted their feet firmly on the lower rungs of the occupational hierarchy.

Explanations such as Gutman's analysis of the black family or Kessner's view of immigrants, which posit a basic continuity in the way kinship functioned in premigration and urban settings, must be modified to account for this interactional process which occurred between newcomers and the city. In reacting to the model of the city as a destroyer of social values and networks, historians too readily identified various ethnic values and behavior as residues of premigration cultures. But adaptation often involved strategic reactions to specific conditions. Black parents could not insist upon support from their progeny as frequently because they could not offer meaningful economic contacts in return. This was true in the rural South and urban North. Able to bring their sons into the workplace, however, Poles possessed greater leverage in demanding support from children and determining their occupational careers. When the transfer of land could no longer be used as a basis for family solidarity in peasant Poland, Poles found a surrogate in industrial America—jobs. The degree to which newcomers could rely on kinship, of course, could not entirely account for divergent patterns of adaptation, but it was certainly an important ingredient.

When European immigration declined and black migration from the South increased after 1917, racial hostility between immigrants and blacks became intense as blacks encountered emerging patterns of ethnic solidarity, especially in steel plants and among railroad workers.[42] At the Jones and Laughlin plant, for instance, Germans predominated in the carpenter shop, Poles in the hammer shop, and Serbs in the blooming mill. This was unfortunate since limited oral data suggested that the initial relations between Poles and blacks were considerably better before 1920, with visitations in each other's homes not uncommon. After being allowed to implement kinship ties in gaining jobs, however, immigrants were unwilling to welcome later arrivals into their established enclaves.

NOTES

[1]The classic statement of this view is Paul Frederick Cressey, "Population Succession in Chicago: 1898–1930," *American Journal of Sociology*, LXIV (July 1938), 61. Cressey's view is modified by Thomas Kessner, *The Golden Door: Italian and Jewish Immigrant Mobility in New York City, 1880–1915* (New York, 1977), 156–60. Believing that Cressey's view of ethnic settlement was too static, Kessner stressed continual turnover within immigrant communities. See also Humbert Nelli, *The Italians in Chicago, 1880–1930: A Study in Ethnic Mobility* (New York, 1970), 45–48; W. Lloyd Warner and Leo Srole, *The Social Systems of American Ethnic Groups* (New Haven, 1945), 2; Stephan Thernstrom, *The Other Bostonians: Poverty and Progress in the American Metropolis, 1880–1970* (Cambridge, 1973), 176–77; Thomas Sowell, *Race and Economics* (New York, 1975), 149–50.

[2]See Thernstrom, *Other Bostonians*, 177–78, 186–87.

[3]Frank Furstenberg, Jr., Theodore Hershberg, and John Modell, "The Origins of the Female-Headed Black Family: The Impact of the Urban Experience," *Journal of Interdisciplinary History*, VI (Autumn 1975), 232; Theodore Hershberg, "Free Blacks in Antebellum Philadelphia: A Study of Ex-Slaves, Freeborn, and Socioeconomic Decline," *Journal of Social History*, 5 (Winter 1971–1972), 192–204.

[4]Josef J. Barton, *Peasants and Strangers: Italians, Rumanians, and Slovaks in an American City, 1890–1950* (Cambridge, 1975), 54, 89–90; Victor Greene, *For God and Country: The Rise of Polish and Lithuanian Ethnic Consciousness in America, 1860–1910* (Madison, Wisc., 1975), 28–29, 35–36; Herbert G. Gutman, *The Black Family in Slavery and Freedom, 1750–1925* (New York, 1976), 450–52; Elizabeth Pleck, "The Two-Parent Household: Black Family Structure in Late Nineteenth-Century Boston," *Journal of Social History*, 6 (Fall 1972), 3–31; Sowell, *Race and Economics*, 144–45. See also Helena Znaniecki Lopata, *Polish Americans: Status Competition in an Ethnic Community* (Englewood Cliffs, N.J., 1976), 4; Kessner, *Golden Door*, 24–43; Virginia Yans-McLaughlin, *Family and Community: Italian Immigrants in Buffalo, 1880–1930* (Ithaca, N.Y., 1977), 55–81.

[5]Robert L. Crain and Carol Sachs Weisman, *Discrimination, Personality, and Achievement: A Survey of Northern Blacks* (New York, 1972), 10–18, 103–08, 120–23; Kessner, *Golden Door*, 111; Barton, *Peasants and Strangers*, 48–63, 125; Yans-McLaughlin, *Family and Community*, 203–10; Thernstrom, *Other Bostonians*, 176–77; John Bodnar, *Immigration and Industrialization: Ethnicity in an American Mill Town, 1870–1940* (Pittsburgh, 1977), 73, 136–37. For other comparisons of the black and immigrant experience, see Joseph S. Roucek

and Francis J. Brown, "The Problem of the Negro and European Immigrant Minorities: Some Comparisons and Contrasts," *Journal of Negro Education*, 8 (July 1939), 299–312. Roucek and Brown argued that immigrants were more optimistic than blacks. See also John J. Appel, "American Negro and Immigrant Experience: Similarities and Differences," *American Quarterly*, XVIII (Spring 1966), 95–103; Charles H. Wesley, *Negro Labor in the United States, 1850–1925: A Study in American Economic History* (New York, 1927), 75–78, 199; Timothy L. Smith, "Native Blacks and Foreign Whites: Varying Responses to Educational Opportunity in America, 1880–1950," *Perspectives in American History*, VI (1972), 309–35; John R. Commons, *Races and Immigrants in America* (New York, 1907), 147–52. Comparisons of Irish and blacks can be found in Oscar Handlin, *Boston's Immigrants, 1790–1865: A Study in Acculturation* (Cambridge, 1941), 137, 213, 221; Niles Carpenter, *Nationality, Color, and Economic Opportunity in the City of Buffalo* (Buffalo, 1927), 190–91; J. Iverne Dowie, "The American Negro: An Old Immigrant on a New Frontier," in *In the Trek of the Immigrants: Essays Presented to Carl Wittke*, ed. O. Fritiof Ander (Rock Island, Ill., 1964), 241–60; Gilbert Osofsky, *Harlem, the Making of a Ghetto: Negro New York, 1890–1930* (New York, 1966), 34–40.

[6]Kessner, *Golden Door*, 179–80.

[7]Carter G. Woodson, *A Century of Negro Migration* (Washington, 1918), 36, 147–66; David M. Katzman, *Before the Ghetto: Black Detroit in the Nineteenth Century* (Urbana, Ill., 1973), 64; Florette Henri, *Black Migration: Movement North, 1900–1920* (Garden City, 1975), 152–53, 352; Gunnar Myrdal, Richard Sterner, and Arnold Rose, *An American Dilemma: The Negro Problem and Modern Democracy* (New York, 1944), 191–97; U.S. Dept. of Labor, *Negro Migrations in 1916–1917* (Washington, 1919).

[8]Clyde Vernon Kiser, *Sea Island to City: A Study of St. Helena Islanders in Harlem and Other Urban Centers* (New York, 1932), 149–52.

[9]Carrie J. interview by Peter Gottlieb, July 23, 1976, tape recording, Pittsburgh Oral History Project (Pennsylvania Historical and Museum Commission, Harrisburg). The oral histories used in this study are drawn from a larger oral project on Poles, Italians, and Afro-Americans in the Pittsburgh area conducted between 1974 and 1978. A questionnaire developed by the project director, John Bodnar, was used in all interviews to insure the comparability of data. A copy of the questionnaire and all tapes are available at the Pennsylvania Historical and Museum Commission.

[10]Olive W. interview by Gottlieb, July 23, 1976, tape recording, Pittsburgh Oral History Project; William H. interview by Gottlieb, June 17, 1976, *ibid.*; Floyd T. interview by Gottlieb, May 11, 1976, *ibid.*; Ben E. interview by Gottlieb, July 31, 1974, *ibid.* A small stream of Pittsburgh blacks left Texas and Arkansas, moved to Gary and Chicago, and eventually secured work in Pittsburgh. See Florence W. interview by John Bodnar, July 27, 1976, *ibid.*; Walter M. interview by Bodnar, July 28, 1977, *ibid.*

[11]Hezikiah M. interview by Gottlieb, Oct. 8, 1976, tape recording, Pittsburgh Oral History Project.

[12]Gutman, *Black Family*, 455.

[13]Jean B. interview by Gottlieb, June 29, 1976, tape recording, Pittsburgh Oral History Project.

[14]William H. interview. See also Edgar P. interview by Bodnar, August 14, 1977, tape recording, Pittsburgh Oral History Project.

[15]James N. interview by Gottlieb, June 28, 1976, tape recording, Pittsburgh Oral History Project; Queen W. interview by Gottlieb, Oct. 8, 1976, *ibid.*; Anonymous interview by John Bodnar, Aug. 11, 1977, *ibid.* Some black women found "day work" from Jewish families in the city.

[16]Olive W. interview; Walter M. interview. The importance of kinship in the urban migration process is discussed more fully in Charles Tilly and C. Harold Brown, "On Uprooting, Kinship, and the Auspices of Migration," *International Journal of Comparative Sociology*, 8 (Sept. 1967), 139–64. See also Arthur F. Raper, *Preface to Peasantry: A Tale of Two Black Belt Counties* (Chapel Hill, 1936), 71, for a discussion of black migration from Georgia in the 1930s. Although covering a later period than this study, Raper noticed the continuing relationship between kinship and migration.

[17]R. R. Wright, Jr., "One Hundred Negro Steel Workers," in *Wage Earning Pittsburgh*, ed. Paul Underwood Kellogg (New York, 1914), 97–104.

[18]Abraham Epstein, *The Negro Migrant in Pittsburgh* (Pittsburgh, 1918), 30–34; Emmett J. Scott, *Negro Migration during the War* (New York, 1920), 125.

[19]Peter Roberts, "Immigrant Wage-Earners," in *Wage Earning Pittsburgh*, ed. Kellogg, 37–41.

[20]U.S. Congress, 62 Cong., 1 sess., Serial 6082, *Cost of Living in American Towns* (Washington, 1911), 338–39.

[21]U.S. Department of Commerce, Bureau of the Census, *Thirteenth Census of the United States Taken in the Year 1910*, Vol. IV: *Population 1910: Occupation Statistics* (Washington, 1914), 590–91. Although blacks had not made large incursions into the steel industry, their average wages in 1910 exceeded those of Polish and Italian workers in the mills. See U.S. Congress, Senate, *Reports of the Immigration Commission, Immigrants in Industry*, Part 2: *Iron and Steel Manufacturing* (2 vols., Washington, 1911) I, 63. Actually blacks had made greater inroads into manufacturing plants in Pittsburgh than in other northern cities such as Cleveland and New York. See Kenneth Kusmer, *A Ghetto Takes Shape: Black Cleveland, 1870–1930* (Urbana, Ill., 1976), 66–67. Thomas Sowell has called the period before 1910 a "promising" period for urban blacks because they established many small businesses. Sowell, *Race and Economics*, 120. For a discussion of Negro experience with iron manufacturing in the South, see Wesley, *Negro Labor in the United States*, 242–44.

[22]Helen A. Tucker, "The Negroes of Pittsburgh," *Charities and the Commons*, 21 (Jan. 2, 1909), 602.

[23]Ben E. interview; Olive W. interview; Jean B. interview; Gertrude D. interview by Gottlieb, tape recording, Pittsburgh Oral History Project; Anonymous interview; Floyd T. interview; Hezikiah M. interview.

[24]Harrison G. interview by Gottlieb, Aug. 23, 1974, tape recording; Pittsburgh Oral History Project; Ben E. interview; James N. interview; William J. interview by Bodnar, Aug. 11, 1977, *ibid.*

[25]Louise Venable Kennedy, *The Negro Peasant Turns Cityward: Effects of Recent Migrations to Northern Centers* (New York, 1930), 122. Of course, discrimination kept blacks out of some jobs. In one glass plant "white workers 'ran them out'" and the company abandoned further attempts at hiring blacks. Epstein, *Negro Migrant in Pittsburgh*, 30–32. On the other hand, by 1910 hundreds of blacks were found as laborers, furnacemen, heaters, and pourers. Carnegie Steel employed about 1,500 blacks before 1916. *Wage Earning Pittsburgh*, ed. Kellogg, 112. In nineteenth-century Philadelphia blacks complained about their inability to get skilled jobs for their sons, a suggestion that black kinship ties were undermined. Hershberg, "Free Blacks in Antebellum Philadelphia," 192.

[26]*Historja Parafji SW. Wojciecha B.M.* (Pittsburgh, 1933); *Pamietnik of St. Adalbert's Parish* (Pittsburgh, 1915). Waclaw Kurszka, *Historya Polska w. Ameryce* (13 vols., Milwaukee, 1905–1913), II, 6–7. "Audit of International Institutes Material on Pittsburgh's Nationality Communities," American Council for Nationalities Services Papers, Shipment 4, Box 2, Archives of Industrial Society (University of Pittsburgh, Pittsburgh). Stanley E. interview by Bodnar, Sept. 9, 1976, tape recording, Pittsburgh Oral History Project.

[27]See Stefan Kieniewicz, *The Emancipation of the Polish Peasantry* (Chicago, 1969), 58–63, 190–94; Celina Bobinska and Andrzej Pilch, eds., *Employment-Seeking Emigration of the Poles World Wide, XIX and XX C.*, (Krakow, 1975), 17–65; Witold Kula, Nina Assorodobraj-Kula, and Marcin Kula, *Listy Emigrantow z Brazylii I Stanow Zjednoczonych, 1880–1891* (Warsaw, 1973), 240–41, 251–52, 273–74; John S. interview by Bodnar, Sept. 30, 1976, tape recording, Pittsburgh Oral History Project; John B. interview by Bodnar, March 3, 1976, *ibid.*, Valerian D. interview by Gottlieb, July 8, 1974, *ibid.*; Stanley P. interview by Gregory Mihalik, Nov. 11, 1976, *ibid.*; Stanley E. interview; Walter K. interview by Gottlieb, July 2, 1974, *ibid.*

[28]Joseph D. interview by Mihalik, Sept. 17, 1976, tape recording, Pittsburgh Oral History Project; Valerian D. interview; Peter L. interview by Mihalik, Sept. 17, 1976, *ibid.*; Joseph B. interview by Mihalik, May 13 and 20, 1976, *ibid.*; Stephanie L. interview by Bodnar, March 24, 1976, *ibid.*; John B. interview; Francis P. interview by Bodnar, Jan. 10, 1976, *ibid.*

[29]Valentine B. interview by Bodnar, Sept. 22, 1976, tape recording, Pittsburgh Oral History Project; Stanley N. interview by Bodnar, Sept. 22, 1976, *ibid*; Joseph B. interview; John B. interview; Helen M. interview by Bodnar, Jan. 17, 1976, *ibid.*; Peter H. interview by Gottlieb, June 26, 1974, *ibid.*; Ignacy M. interview by Gottlieb, July 2, 1974, *ibid.*; Joseph D. interview; Edward R. interview by Mihalik, Sept. 10, 1976, *ibid.*; John S. interview; Michael S. interview by Bodnar, Jan. 16, 1976, *ibid.*; Francis P. interview; Charles W. interview by Mahalik, Dec. 10, 1976, *ibid.*

[30]Eugene D. Genovese, *Roll, Jordan, Roll: The World the Slaves Made* (New York, 1974), 505–05. Genovese found a similar strong individualism in slave families. He argued that the relatively happy childhood of slave children resulted in "independent spirited adults."

[31]Sally S. interview by Clarence Turner, June 18, 1976, tape recording, Pittsburgh Oral History Project; Roy M. interview by Gottlieb, July 9, 1974, *ibid.*; William H. interview; Ernest F. interview by Gottlieb, April 20, 1976, *ibid.*; Anonymous interview; Grant W. interview by Gottlieb, July 12, 1976, *ibid.*

[32]Walter W. interview by Turner, Feb. 14, 1973, tape recording, Pittsburgh Oral History Project; Jasper A. interview by Gottlieb, July 12, 1976, *ibid.*; Roy M. interview; Olive W. interview; Ross P. interview by Bodnar, Aug. 10, 1977, *ibid.*; Grant W. interview. For the argument that during periods of rapid social change children achieved an increasing degree of independence, see Kenneth Soddy and Mary C. Kidson, eds., *Men in Middle Life* (London, 1967), 293. This movement toward independence may emanate from parents as well as children.

[33]Gertrude D. interview.

[34]John Modell, Frank F. Furstenberg, Jr., and Theodore Hershberg, "Social Change and Transitions to Adulthood in Historical Perspective," *Journal of Family History*, 1 (Autumn 1976), 29.

[35]Grant W. interview; Floyd T. interview; Jasper A. interview; Ernest F. interview; Queen W. interview; Anonymous interview; James N. interview; Olive W. interview; Epstein, *Negro Migrant in Pittsburgh*, 24. Recent studies have offered additional evidence that blacks were choosing an individual rather than a collective approach to survival. This does not imply an absence of emotional attachments or kinship assistance among blacks. But out of a deep concern for their children, black parents were nurturing attitudes of self-sufficiency. They were unable to offer material resources or social connections to assist their survival in adult life. Historian Crandall A. Shifflett, in a study of rural black families in 1880 Virginia, found that they reduced the number of nonworking consumers in their household during the early years of marriage so that there would be fewer mouths to feed. As families progressed to middle years and children became old enough to work, Shifflett discovered the ratio of consumers (nonworkers) to workers gradually diminished. One explanation for Shifflett's declining consumer population in middle-aged black families was the possible departure of young black workers to pursue their own individual quests. See Crandall A. Shifflett, "The Household Composition of Rural Black Families: Louisa County, Virginia, 1880," *Journal of Interdisciplinary History*, VI (Autumn 1975), 244–45.

[36]Joseph D. interview; John K. interview by Bodnar, Sept. 12, 1977, tape recording, Pittsburgh Oral History Project; Ray C. interview by Mihalik, July 1, 1976, *ibid.*; Edward R. interview.

[37]Polish women, in contrast to black women, seldom worked after marriage unless their husbands were killed or incapacitated. In addition to managing finances they usually paid all bills and insurance. See interview with Francis P.

[38]Stanley N. interview; Joseph B. interview; John K. interview; Peter L. interview. Elizabeth Voltz, "The Child Labor Question," clipping in Civic Club of Allegheny County Records, 1846–1849, Box 3, Archives of Industrial Society.

[39]A contradiction in the data may seem evident when this statement is compared with Table 2 which shows that 0 percent of midstage Polish families were extended. The reason for the difference is that the census data was generated from a period in time—1900—when most Polish families had been in America for only about a decade and still had relatively few married children. The oral data revealed the dynamics of the Polish family in the three decades after 1900 when the second generation began to initiate families of their own.

[40]The employment of young girls at Oliver Iron and Steel was detailed in the *Pittsburgh Leader*, April 5, 1912, pp. 1, 16. See also John B. interview; Stephanie W. interview by Bodnar, March 21, 1976, tape recording, Pittsburgh Oral History Project; Francis P. interview; Stanley E. interview; Joseph D. interview; Peter L. interview; Josephine B. interview by Bodnar, March 3, 1976, *ibid.* Similar employment of young girls for family reasons in the early industrial revolution is discussed in Louise A. Tilly, Joan W. Scott, and Miriam Cohen, "Women's Work and European Fertility Patterns," *Journal of Interdisciplinary History*, VI (Winter 1976), 447–76; Tamara K. Hareven, "Laborers of Manchester, New Hampshire, 1912–1922: The Role of Family and Ethnicity in Adjustment to Industrial Life," *Labor History*, 16 (Spring 1975), 249–65.

[41]The life-cycle model is more accurate when tied to the age of the mother and more likely to reflect the childbearing and childrearing years. For further explanation of the model used in this essay, see Shifflett, "Household Composition of Rural Black Families," 242; Thomas K. Burch, "Comparative Family Structure: A Demographic Approach," *Estadistica*, XXVI (June 1968), 291–93; and Thomas K. Burch, "The Size and Structure of Families: A Comparative Analysis of Census Data," *American Sociological Review*, 32 (June 1967), 347–63.

[42]See Kusmer, *A Ghetto Takes Shape*, 157, 175; Allan H. Spear, *Black Chicago: The Making of a Negro Ghetto, 1890–1920* (Chicago, 1967), 34, 111, 150, 201; Osofsky, *Harlem*, 45–81; Emmett J. Scott, "Additional Letters of Negro Migrants of 1916–1918," *Journal of Negro History*, IV (Oct. 1919), 460–61; St. Clair Drake and Horace R. Cayton, *Black Metropolis: A Study of Negro Life in a Northern City* (New York, 1945), 91–93; Thaddeus Radzialowski, "The Competition for Jobs and Racial Stereotypes: Poles and Blacks in Chicago," *Polish American Studies*, XXXIII (Autumn 1976), 5–18.

Part Three

The Twentieth-Century City

Introduction

The United States emerged as a dynamic urban society during the industrial era. The patterns of urbanization and urban living shifted, often dramatically so, in the years after 1920, but growth remained a constant feature of the urban landscape. By the end of the twentieth century, suburbia had come to dominate the American residential pattern. More than 100 million Americans, or over 40 percent of the nation's population, resided in the suburbs by the 1980s, a larger proportion than for those who lived in central cities or rural areas. However, in many ways, municipal boundaries had become blurred, as city and suburban populations pushed out the residential periphery far beyond anything imagined in the nineteenth century. By the early 1980s some twenty-nine urban centers in the United States each had more than 1 million residents; many of these "supercities" were created by the filling in of empty space between existing cities and metropolitan areas.

Vast, sprawling metropolitan areas thus came to characterize urban America by the 1980s. The New York City metropolitan region, for instance, contained more than 16 million people spread over 3,600 square miles, while the Los Angeles urbanized area of about 2,200 square miles was home to almost 12 million. According to one study, the urbanized northeastern seaboard of the United States will contain about 80 million people, or one-fourth of the nation's population, by the year 2000. These statistics barely begin to suggest the consequences of several decades of volatile demographic, economic, social, and political change.

Huge population shifts within metropolitan regions have become commonplace in the United States since about 1940. The older cities of the Northeast and Midwest—cities that experienced the industrial revolution of the late nineteenth century—have been losing substantial numbers of residents to suburban regions. The classic example is St. Louis, which suffered a 50 percent population loss between 1950 and 1980, leaving the city with roughly the same population it had in 1890. Similarly, by 1980 Detroit had lost about one-third of its 1950 population of about 1.8 million. Both Pittsburgh and Detroit lost 37 percent of their population base between 1950 and 1980. Most of the "rustbelt" or "snowbelt" cities experienced similar population declines (Table 1). Boston lost about 30 percent of its population between 1950 and 1980, while Baltimore dropped by about 20 percent, Philadelphia by 18.5 percent, and New York by 10.3 percent. For smaller cities the trend of central city population decline was much the same: Buffalo, Providence,

Table 1
Representative Snowbelt Cities

City and Year	Central City Population	Metropolitan Area Population	Percentage Metropolitan Population in Central City	Percentage City Black	Percentage City Hispanic	Percentage City Foreign-Born
Baltimore						
1950	949,708	1,337,373	71.0	23.7	N/A	5.4
1980	786,775	2,174,023	36.2	54.8	1.0	3.1
Boston						
1950	801,444	2,369,986	33.8	5.0	N/A	18.0
1980	562,994	2,763,357	20.4	22.5	6.5	15.5
Chicago						
1950	3,620,962	5,495,364	65.9	13.6	N/A	14.5
1980	3,005,078	7,103,624	42.3	39.8	14.1	14.5
Cleveland						
1950	914,808	1,465,511	62.4	16.2	N/A	14.5
1980	573,822	1,898,825	30.2	43.8	3.1	5.8
Detroit						
1950	1,849,568	3,016,197	61.2	16.3	N/A	14.9
1980	1,203,339	4,353,413	27.6	63.0	2.4	5.7
New York						
1950	7,891,957	12,911,994	61.1	9.5	N/A	22.6
1980	7,071,639	16,121,278	43.9	25.3	19.9	23.6
Philadelphia						
1950	2,071,605	3,671,048	56.4	18.2	N/A	11.2
1980	1,688,210	4,716,818	35.8	37.8	3.8	6.4
Pittsburgh						
1950	676,806	2,213,236	30.6	12.2	N/A	9.6
1980	423,938	2,263,894	18.7	24.0	.8	5.2
St. Louis						
1950	856,796	1,681,281	51.0	18.0	N/A	4.9
1980	453,085	2,356,460	19.2	45.4	1.2	2.6

Sources: U.S. Census, 1950 and 1980. All metropolitan area population statistics for 1950 are for Standard Metropolitan Area. Except for New York, all metropolitan area population statistics for 1980 are for Standard Metropolitan Statistical Area; New York statistics are for Standard Consolidated Statistical Area.

Youngstown, Minneapolis, Rochester, Newark, and Jersey City all lost between 25 percent and 37 percent of their 1950 population.

Several consequences flowed from these central city population shifts. Most of those fleeing the cities were middle-class and working-class whites who found in the suburbs a more pleasant life-style and an opportunity to demonstrate their upward economic mobility. Thus, while the central cities suffered the consequences of a declining population base, the suburban rings surrounding the cities were expanding at an enormous rate, even as early as midcentury. Central city populations were on the downswing, but virtually

every major industrial city witnessed large population increases in its metropolitan area between 1950 and 1970. The trend began reversing slightly in
a few northeastern and midwestern metropolitan areas between 1970 and
1980. During that decade, seven of the thirty-nine largest metropolitan areas
contracted in population: New York, Philadelphia, St. Louis, Pittsburgh,
Cleveland, Milwaukee, and Buffalo. But generally the metropolitan population trend was upward for the industrial cities during the entire 1950–80
period, with increases ranging from 16.7 percent in Boston to 44.3 percent
in Detroit and 62.6 percent in Baltimore (Table 1).

As the urban whites fled for the suburban frontier, the shrinking central
cities came to be more heavily populated by poor and low-income people, by
blacks, Hispanics, and other new immigrant groups. Clearly, the rapid turnover of urban population left the central cities with a declining population
base characterized by precarious economic circumstances. A 1979 study by
investigative journalist Ken Auletta demonstrated, for example, that almost
2 million middle-income people abandoned New York City between 1945 and
the late 1970s, while at least that many low-income people moved in. As a
result, Auletta has suggested, New York City "has developed a permanent
underclass." As the population turned over and the cities aged, housing stock
and infrastructure deteriorated, social problems and conflicts intensified, and
deindustrialization occurred. The combination of a declining tax base and
higher welfare and service costs pushed some cities like New York and Cleveland to the brink of bankruptcy in the 1970s.

At the same time, the central cities have become home to heavy concentrations of black Americans. A great black migration from the rural and
urban South to the urban North began during and after World War I. The
human flow from the South slowed during the depression era of the 1930s
but surged forward again after 1940. About 1.5 million blacks migrated from
the South to the North and West each decade between 1940 and 1970. As
the whites moved to the expanding suburbs after World War II, aided by
favorable federal housing, mortgage, and highway programs, the newly arrived
blacks moved into the aging inner-city neighborhoods. This process of population displacement has dramatically altered the demographic character of
the modern American city. Black population majorities or near majorities
now prevail in such northern cities as Detroit, Baltimore, Washington, Chicago, Cleveland, St. Louis, Philadelphia, Newark, and Gary. Blacks also
became numerically dominant in many southern cities, including Atlanta,
Birmingham, Richmond, and New Orleans. In 1890 about 90 percent of black
Americans lived in the South, but by 1970 less than one-half of the black
population remained in the region. Similarly, early in the twentieth century,
blacks were heavily rural, but by the 1980s they had become the most urbanized of all racial and ethnic groups in the United States.

The twentieth-century American city has other newcomers, too. An enormous Hispanic migration to the urban Southwest and to selected other cities
has added to the ethnic, linguistic, and political complexity of urban America.
By the late 1980s about 800,000 Hispanics lived in the Miami metropolitan
area, about 45 percent of the entire population. The arrival of massive waves

of Cubans after the success of Fidel Castro's Cuban Revolution in 1959 caused a virtual demographic revolution in south Florida. Hispanics made up about 20 percent of New York City's population in the 1980s. Puerto Ricans began coming to New York in sizable numbers by midcentury, and in more recent years they have been joined by hundreds of thousands of Colombians, Dominicans, and other Latin newcomers. In Los Angeles, the Hispanics—largely Mexican and Mexican-American—totaled 27.5 percent of the city's entire population in 1980. In Houston, San Antonio, Albuquerque, El Paso, and other southwestern cities, the proportion of Hispanic residents is rising rapidly. Even in Chicago, in the center of the industrial snowbelt, Mexican, Cuban, and Puerto Rican newcomers have pushed the Hispanic population to about 14 percent in 1980 (Tables 1 and 2). Most demographers agree that Hispanics will surpass blacks as the nation's largest minority group by the end of this century.

The modern American city, like its industrial era counterpart, also has exercised a magnetic attraction for millions of new immigrants. European immigrants provided the manpower to propel the industrial revolution in nineteenth-century America, but now the newcomers are arriving from all over the globe, especially from Third World nations. From Central America, South America, Asia and the Pacific region, the Caribbean, and the Middle East, immigrants have been pouring into the United States, driven by revolution, oppression, famine, or economic aspiration. As in the past, the city has provided the widest range of opportunities for social adjustment and economic advancement. Typically, the largest ethnic/immigrant groups in Los Angeles, in addition to Mexicans, are Iranians, Salvadorans, Japanese, Chinese, Filipinos, Koreans, Vietnamese, Arabs, Israelis, Colombians, Hondurans, Guatemalans, Cubans, East Indians, Pakistanis, and Samoans and other Pacific Islanders. As one writer has suggested, Los Angeles is "a racial and cultural borderland" standing "on a frontier between Europe and Asia and between Anglo and Hispanic cultures." Much of urban America now shares some of the ethnic and cultural complexity of Los Angeles.

The central cities have become new melting pots, and even some older, inner suburbs have received an infusion of black, Hispanic, and new immigrant population. But most of the suburban periphery continues to be overwhelmingly white and mostly middle class. The suburban phenomenon dates back to the middle years of the nineteenth century, when new transit technology permitted a more widespread spatial distribution of urban population. Simultaneously, changing conceptions of the role of family and home emphasized the salutary effect of domesticity and private residential space, while romanticized views of nature encouraged Americans to distance themselves from the congestion, commercialism, and other problems of the rapidly growing cities. Also, the introduction in the mid-nineteenth century of a cheap, new building technology—the "balloon-frame" house—transformed home building into a profitable industry for land speculators and suburban developers.

The suburban pattern intensified in the twentieth century. The automobile displaced city mass transit systems and opened up distant fringe areas for suburban development, such as Levittown twenty-five miles east of New

Table 2
Representative Sunbelt Cities

City and Year	Central City Population	Metropolitan Area Population	Percentage Metropolitan Population in Central City	Percentage City Black	Percentage City Hispanic	Percentage City Foreign-Born
Albuquerque						
1950	98,815	145,673	67.8	1.2	N/A	2.6
1980	331,767	454,499	73.0	2.3	33.8	4.5
Atlanta						
1950	331,314	671,797	49.3	36.6	N/A	1.3
1980	425,022	2,029,710	20.9	66.6	1.4	2.3
Dallas						
1950	434,462	614,799	70.7	13.1	N/A	1.9
1980	904,074	2,974,805	30.4	29.3	12.2	6.1
Houston						
1950	596,163	806,701	73.9	20.9	N/A	2.9
1980	1,595,167	2,905,353	54.9	27.6	17.6	9.8
Los Angeles						
1950	1,970,358	4,367,911	45.1	8.7	N/A	12.5
1980	2,966,850	11,497,568	25.8	17.0	27.5	27.1
Miami						
1950	249,276	495,084	50.4	16.2	N/A	10.8
1980	346,865	1,625,781	21.3	25.1	56.0	53.7
Phoenix						
1950	106,818	331,770	32.2	4.9	N/A	6.7
1980	789,704	1,509,052	52.3	4.8	14.8	5.7
San Antonio						
1950	408,442	500,460	81.6	7.0	N/A	8.0
1980	785,809	1,071,954	73.3	7.3	53.7	8.3
San Diego						
1950	334,387	556,808	60.1	4.5	N/A	7.0
1980	875,538	1,861,846	47.0	8.9	14.8	15.0

Sources: U.S. Census, 1950 and 1980. All metropolitan area population statistics for 1950 are for Standard Metropolitan Area. Except for Los Angeles, all metropolitan area population statistics for 1980 are for Standard Metropolitan Statistical Area; Los Angeles statistics are for Standard Consolidated Statistical Area.

York City on Long Island. Most important in the twentieth-century development of suburbia, however, was the shaping role of the federal government after the mid-1930s. Federal highway, housing, mortgage, and tax policies helped promote the dispersal of the urban population, particularly the white population, in the years after World War II. The poor, the blacks, and other minorities remained behind in the deteriorating central cities.

Suburbia has grown tremendously since midcentury, but demographers also have noted the more recent growth of rural or nonmetropolitan areas. In fact, during the 1970s, rural and small-town America grew more rapidly than the urban and suburban regions of the nation. As a 1983 demographic analysis in *Scientific American* has suggested, the level of urbanization had slowed for the first time during that decade. While urban populations were still growing, "the fraction of the nation's population in urbanized areas is no longer increasing." Much of this nonmetropolitan growth stemmed from industrial relocation. In the thirty years after 1947, for instance, New York and Chicago alone lost some 900,000 manufacturing jobs as a result of shifting American economic and business patterns. By contrast, between 1970 and 1978, about 700,000 new manufacturing jobs were created in nonmetropolitan areas. Population follows jobs, which explains why people have moved to these regions distant from the big central cities. But in many ways, some demographers have suggested, these new population clusters "represent small centers of urban culture transplanted to the countryside and enabled to survive by recent advances in communications, transportation, and methods of industrial production."

The rise of nonmetropolitan America reflected the shifting character of the American urban and industrial economy. The manufacturing economies of the cities of the industrial heartland have experienced dramatic transformation, even significant decline in many cases. Not only has production been shifted to nonmetropolitan areas but to less developed nations as well. Multinational corporations have shut down factories in the old industrial belt and transferred production to South Korea, Taiwan, Mexico, and Third World nations. High labor costs in the United States, stiff foreign competition, higher energy costs in the 1970s and early 1980s, and numerous corporate mergers all resulted in a massive reorganization of the American economy. A renewed drive for productivity and profit prompted corporate decision making that led to factory closings, heavy blue-collar unemployment, and troubled times in such basic industries as textiles, automobiles, and steel. Large cities with diverse economies have adjusted to change, but single-industry cities, such as steel-producing Gary and Youngstown, have withered economically. Some observers have postulated the obsolescence of the nation's aging industrial cities.

As more traditional forms of manufacturing and production declined, a postindustrial and service-oriented economy rose to take its place. This process of economic transformation was well under way in the aftermath of World War II. In fact, as early as 1955 blue-collar manufacturing laborers were outnumbered by service and professional workers. The industrial sector employed fewer than half as many workers as the growing service economy by the 1980s. Over the past thirty to forty years the American economy has experienced a sort of "deindustrialization" in which basic industry has suffered a dramatic reversal.

During that same period, however, the economy has been powered by tremendous expansion in the "postindustrial" service sector. Since the late 1960s over 38 million new service jobs have been created in the United States, many of which are now held by women who entered the labor force in large numbers in the postwar era. The service economy now employs over 75 million American workers, about 70 percent of the work force. Central to the rapidly growing service economy has been expansion in governmental services, education, medical care, computer technology, information processing, business services, recreational activities, shopping malls, fast-food and motel chains, and airline travel. Such new service industries have become essential ingredients in the new American economy.

The fortunes of the modern American city have been bound up in the structural transformation of the nation's economy. One consequence of this economic change can be seen in the declining populations of the older, heavily industrial cities of the Northeast and Midwest. Central city employment has suffered, too, because the low-skill newcomers—the blacks, Hispanics, and other new immigrants—often lack the training or skills required for most "high-tech" jobs in the information-processing sector. The low-skill service jobs that are available are also low-pay jobs, leaving the aging central cities with chronic problems of underemployment, unemployment, poverty, and social welfare. The city, in short, has been unable to avoid the human and social consequences of the postindustrial economic transformation.

Also linked to the shifting American economy is the dramatic rise of the "sunbelt" cities of the South and Southwest. In 1920 nine of the ten largest U.S. cities were located in the Northeast and Midwest. The same was true in 1950. Only Los Angeles was able to break into the top ten cities in population during that period. With a little over 600,000 people in 1950, Minneapolis was larger than Atlanta, Dallas, Houston, Phoenix, San Antonio, or San Diego. But thirty years of shifting economic and demographic activity have made a big difference. By 1980 five of the ten largest American cities were located in the Southwest: Los Angeles, Houston, Dallas, Phoenix, and San Diego (Table 2).

These sunbelt cities never experienced the nineteenth-century industrial revolution; they are twentieth-century automobile cities, less densely settled and more widely spread over the urban and suburban landscape. Aided by mid-twentieth-century highway building and widespread automobile ownership in the postwar era, sunbelt city population pushed out the urban and metropolitan periphery to an extent unimagined in the industrial era. Annexation of surrounding territory, which had virtually ceased for older cities by the early twentieth century, became a way of life in the urban Southwest. Between 1950 and 1980, for instance, Houston grew from 160 to 556 square miles, Oklahoma City from 51 to 603 square miles, and Phoenix from 17 to 324 square miles. By contrast, Philadelphia has remained stable at 130 square miles since the 1850s, St. Louis has not added to its 62 square miles since 1876, and New York City's 299 square miles of territory have remained unchanged since 1898. In one way, however, the newer southwestern cities are similar to the older northern cities: despite massive annexations, the peripheral suburban regions of the metropolitan sunbelt are growing more rapidly than the central city areas (Table 2).

The explosive urban development of the sunbelt South and Southwest stemmed largely from the deep structural changes in the American economy. With little inherited from the industrial era, the sunbelt cities have grown along with the new service economy. Actually, urban growth in the sunshine regions began in earnest during World War II, when the federal government built dozens of new air bases, naval bases, and military training facilities in the southern and western states. This vast federal investment persisted into the Cold War era, and heavy military and defense spending has continued to sustain prosperity and urban growth in the region. From San Francisco, Los Angeles, and San Diego on the West Coast to Pensacola, Tampa, Miami, and Jacksonville in Florida, the sunbelt cities have profited from the federal military connection. Military airfields surrounded San Antonio, aircraft production boosted Seattle and Los Angeles, the aerospace industry propelled Houston's post-1950 expansion, and big U.S. Navy facilities fueled growth and prosperity in San Diego and Jacksonville.

At the same time, the emerging sunbelt cities were benefiting from the vast structural changes taking place in the American economy. High-tech industries such as electronics and computers, along with energy development in the southwestern "oil patch," provided important stimulus to urbanization. As postwar prosperity roared ahead after 1950, the amenities factor came into play. Americans with more leisure time and higher disposable incomes avidly began to pursue recreational interests. Every American child wanted a trip to Disneyland in California or Disney World in Florida. The completion of the federal highway system permitted even working-class Americans to become winter vacationers in the sunshine regions of the country. And, as Americans lived longer and retired earlier, the elderly began a migration of their own to Florida, Arizona, southern California, and other retirement havens in the urban sunbelt. For whatever reason, 5.5 million Americans migrated from the Northeast and Midwest to the sunbelt regions during the 1970s.

Clearly, a major impetus for sunbelt city growth has been the shifting pattern of the American economy. In the postindustrial era, the looming skyscrapers of Atlanta, Miami, Houston, Dallas, and Los Angeles suggest the power and the persistence of the information age. There have been some setbacks, as reflected in the impact of recent oil-price declines on the economic vitality of the Houston area. Generally, however, the new urban America of the South and Southwest has benefited enormously from the growth of the service economy. Some of the older northern cities with diverse economies have adjusted to economic change; Chicago and New York remain booming business centers, even as their peripheral areas—now known as the "outer city"—surge ahead as well. But the sunbelt migrants have been pursuing new avenues of economic opportunity. As urban historian James F. Richardson has observed, "Now, and for the foreseeable future, it looks as if those cities that people want to live in will be those that generate the greatest employment opportunities." The shifting urban pattern, in short, reflects some long-term migration tendencies.

Urban demographic and economic changes have been paralleled by important transformations in the political life of urban America. Beginning in the New Deal era of the 1930s, the federal government initiated for the first time a political partnership with the cities. President Franklin D. Roosevelt built a new Democratic party coalition, relying heavily on the urban electorate for his political success. As federal intervention, initiative, and activism became the order of the day, social legislation and public works programs flowed out of New Deal Washington, much of it aimed at city people and urban problems. From the age of Roosevelt to the beginning of the Reagan era, the cities sought out and became reliant on the federal connection. Public housing, urban renewal, mass transit, highway and public works construction, and public welfare were all funded with massive infusions of federal dollars. When President Lyndon B. Johnson revived the New Deal spirit with his Great Society initiatives, the war on poverty, community development efforts, the model cities program, and the civil rights crusade had their roots in the cities. At about the same time, an "urban crisis" was discovered by the media in the 1960s, especially when explosions of racial violence rocked cities across the nation, from Harlem to Watts, from Chicago and Detroit to Newark and Washington, DC.

The burned-out ghettos of the late 1960s suggested to many the failure of federal urban policy. In fact, the federal programs that shaped urban America after the mid-1930s did not always have positive effects. A national transportation policy emphasizing highways and the automobile ultimately siphoned population and economic activities away from the central city and toward the urban periphery. Urban expressways tore through existing neighborhoods, destroyed still good housing, and left huge empty spaces in the urban cores. Federal mortgage policies, especially FHA and VA, made it possible for working-class urbanites to obtain their dream house in the suburbs. Federal public housing programs promoted residential segregation of the races and encouraged the image of suburbia as a haven from the problems of the city. A residential appraisal system initiated by the Home Owners Loan Corporation, another New Deal agency, resulted in the redlining and ultimate physical decay of many inner-city urban neighborhoods. Thus, a new era of federal-city cooperation emerged by mid-twentieth century, but unanticipated consequences flowed from the implementation of the new federal programs.

The frustrations of urban policymaking, along with a changing national political climate, have brought a dramatic reversal of public policy and federal activism in the urban arena. The Reagan era has witnessed massive federal cutbacks in the public works and social programs that moved the cities forward in the 1960s. Turning back the governmental intervention that marked the New Deal, President Ronald Reagan has sought to restore social policy to the marketplace. With fewer financial resources and greater responsibilities, the cities are once more approaching a crisis stage, especially in the provision of human and social services.

These changes have come at a time when the urban political pattern is experiencing major transformation. The shifting demography of the cities has now been reflected in the political structure. As the black population of the central cities has surged, so also have blacks come to dominate urban politics in many cities, large and small. Beginning in 1967, when black mayors were first elected in Cleveland and Gary, blacks have succeeded to the mayoralty in Detroit, Philadelphia, Chicago, Newark, New Orleans, Los Angeles, Atlanta, Richmond, Birmingham, and Washington, DC, to name only a few major cities. The old political machines that dominated such cities as Chicago and Detroit are in disarray, as black political leaders have built new coalitions with Hispanic voters and white liberals. The old Chicago Democratic machine that kept Mayor Richard J. Daley in office for twenty years is now moribund, internally divided, and bitterly racist in its political outlook. Meanwhile, former Congressman Harold Washington, who first defeated the Chicago machine in 1983, seems stronger than ever.

Sweeping political transformations have affected the sunbelt cities, too. Lacking powerful ethnic voting blocs and a machine tradition, these cities most often were controlled politically by local business and professional elites. Motivated by the booster mentality, the urban elites sought to govern in the interests of the central city business community, at least until the 1950s. The rapid growth of suburbia, however, resulted in newer forms of urban political conflict in which city and suburb struggled for dominance and control. Many of the issues were spatial, or territorial, such as where highways or public housing would be located, or what areas would be annexed, or which schools integrated by busing. Some places resolved these conflicts with experiments in new governmental structures, as in the creation of a metropolitan government for Miami-Dade County in 1957 and city-county consolidations in Nashville in 1962 and Jacksonville in 1967.

The vast demographic transformations of the cities since the 1960s pushed urban politics into a new and more participatory phase, one in which city-suburban battles have been supplanted by issues revolving around race, ethnicity, and neighborhood. Neighborhoods and local communities, urban historian Carl Abbott has written, have now "become focal points for political action." In Miami, for instance, with its "tri-ethnic" population of whites, blacks, and Hispanics, virtually every local political issue is perceived in terms of race and ethnicity. As the newcomers to the cities—the peoples from Asia and Latin America, from the Caribbean and the Pacific Basin—become citizens and voters, this new pattern of pluralistic urban politics will certainly intensify.

As in the industrial era, the twentieth-century American city has served as a center of growth, diversity, and dynamic change. Despite evidence of decline in some areas, the city has demonstrated a capacity for adaptation to new circumstances. While many central cities are troubled, a new urban vitality can be found in the outer city on the fringes of the metropolitan areas. Although fragmented socially, the city seemed to be periodically regenerated as new population groups came to make their home there. As the traditional industrial economy faded, newer forms of economic activity appropriate to the service economy took the place of older patterns of production. The changing urban political structure has reflected the dramatic demographic and economic shifts of recent decades, and new issues emerged as new political players came to center stage. The progressives of the early twentieth century thought of the American city as "the hope of the future." As the history of the twentieth-century city suggests, tension existed between the utopian vision and the urban reality. It is quite likely that, although the details will surely be different, the twenty-first century American city will continue to offer the nation a threshold for change, growth, and renewal.

In the following essays, urban historians pursue some of the diverse strands of twentieth-century urban life in the United States. In his article, ROGER W. LOTCHIN develops a number of suggestive arguments about the emerging links between urbanization and militarism. A considerable literature has illus-trated the role of federal military and defense spending in promoting urban development during and after World War II. Lotchin now pushes this con-vergence of urban and military interests back at least to the 1920s. He also shifts the focus of study to the West Coast, particularly California, which was relatively undeveloped in the early twentieth century but urbanizing rapidly. The transfer of the main U.S. naval fleet to the Pacific Ocean in 1919 had important consequences. Political and business leaders in San Francisco, Los Angeles, and San Diego leaped at the opportunity to attract naval and other military facilities to their cities, often competing with one another for federal largesse. Military expenditures boosted local economies and spurred urban development. Military and naval needs dictated waterfront uses, city planning efforts, and patterns of urban spatial expansion. In the two decades before World War II, California's largest cities developed important symbiotic alli-ances with the military establishment. As Lotchin demonstrates, federal policy had a shaping role in the development of the urban West in the twentieth century.

My own article develops further the links between federal policy and the twentieth-century American city, exploring some of the consequences of fed-eral activism in Miami during the 1930s. Miami was a typical southern city when it came to race relations during that period. Its white civic elite sought to eliminate the large, blighted black neighborhood close to the central busi-ness district. The public housing programs of Franklin D. Roosevelt's New Deal provided an opportunity to achieve that goal, while simultaneously planting the nucleus of a new and distant black community five miles away. Another federal program, the Home Owners Loan Corporation (HOLC), also was turned to the interests of the Miami civic leadership. Using a property appraisal system initiated by the Federal Housing Administration, the HOLC redlined the entire Miami metropolitan area, strengthening the process of residential segregation and hastening the city's physical decay. New Deal activism has often been portrayed as beneficial to urban America, but this Miami case study suggested an alternative interpretation.

Government policy has shaped the twentieth-century city, but so has technology. This was especially true of the automobile. We have come a long way since 1899, when the *Literary Digest* noted of this newfangled device: "The ordinary 'horseless carriage' is at present a luxury for the wealthy; and altho its price will probably fall in the future, it will never, of course, come into as common use as the bicycle." KENNETH T. JACKSON demonstrates how the automobile has restructured the pattern of everyday life and altered the character of the urban landscape. Widespread car ownership after World War II, along with a massive highway building program, promoted a cen-terless suburban sprawl typified by the Los Angeles metropolitan area. In the freeway-centered civilization, a new roadside architecture sprang up to accommodate people on the move. Motels, drive-in theaters, gas stations, shopping centers, fast-food restaurants, even drive-in churches and mortuaries have become integral parts of the suburban, automobile culture. Similarly, corporate America discovered the joys and profits of a suburban business location, resulting in a substantial decentralization of economic activity. The negative side of this postwar urban transformation can be found in the environmental costs of automobility, the visual blight of the typical roadside landscape, and a growing energy dependence to support the car culture.

The twentieth century also has witnessed an urban transformation in the American Southwest. Some historians have argued that towns and cities "spearheaded" westward expansion since the early nineteenth century. As BRADFORD LUCKINGHAM points out, despite the popular mythology about cowboys and Indians, the West had a high level of urbanization as early as 1880. One hundred years later the West was more urbanized than any other section of the nation. Luckingham traces the pattern of city growth in four cities neglected by most urban historians: El Paso, Albuquerque, Tucson, and Phoenix. The completion of the transcontinental railroads facilitated the early growth of the urban Southwest. Rapid expansion since World War II, however, has resulted from federal military spending, the concentration of air bases in the region, and the "amenities factor" attracting business and population to the sunbelt cities. The southwestern cities, Luckingham concludes, have served as "spearheads of desert development."

RICHARD C. WADE begins his essay with the urban troubles of the 1960s, then pushes back to the urban crisis of 1900. Despite our current problems, he argues, present-day urbanites have better housing, better schools, and better government than their counterparts in 1900. Cities today are safer, healthier, and less crowded; contemporary city people are better off financially, enjoy more creature comforts, and have more leisure time than in the past. However, two unresolved problems continue to plague the contemporary city: the division between central city and suburb, and the tension between blacks and whites. In one sense, the two problems are related, since blacks are concentrated residentially in the central cities and the suburbs are mostly white. Only an effective public policy, Wade contends, can resolve these two urgent issues, a public policy that supersedes the disparate governmental units of the metropolis and that addresses the racism that keeps blacks confined to the inner-city ghetto.

The final essay reviews, from the perspective of the urban geographer, the dramatic spatial changes taking place in the contemporary city. MICHAEL P. CONZEN argues that "a new epoch in urban development" has arrived. It is characterized by slower rates of urban growth, even declines in the big cities of the manufacturing belt, along with a sort of "counterurbanization" reflected in rural and nonmetropolitan growth. The new urban pattern also has been marked by the diffusion of technology, the emergence of a powerful service economy, and the urbanization of the sunbelt regions. Old central city cores have declined, as redlining, racial segregation, and suburban decentralization have taken their toll. Large-scale federal urban redevelopment has ended, but some revitalization has occurred. The private sector has financed construction of new office building skyscrapers in the central business districts of most big cities, thereby bringing a new and striking skyline to urban America. Gentrification of older housing, revitalization of commercial structures, and historic restoration projects hold out some hope for the future. But many problems remain, in the central urban areas and in the outer city as well. Conzen stresses the need for more effective regional planning to address the metropolitan problem.

The essays gathered in Part Three exemplify the historical scholarship on the twentieth-century American city. They touch upon important interpretive issues and identify some of the powerful forces and shaping influences that have brought urban America to its present condition. They also suggest directions for the reader who seeks a more detailed exploration of twentieth-century urban development and change.

The Metropolitan-Military Complex in Comparative Perspective: San Francisco, Los Angeles, and San Diego, 1919–41

*Roger W. Lotchin**

For most of the interwar period, urban California upheld the claims of peace while pursuing the instruments of war. The explanation for this seeming inconsistency lies less in the fear of external aggression than in the efforts of city builders and Navy men to mate two monumental forces in modern America: militarization and urbanization. By analyzing their convergence in California, where both urbanization and militarization have appeared in an extreme form, this essay seeks to explore their relationship and to assess its significance for American and urban history. Due to its West Coast pre-eminence, the Navy provides an excellent test case with which to begin.

Although historians of earlier eras and other countries have noted the frequent convergence of the city and the sword, historians of twentieth-century American cities have neglected the topic. Given the enhanced importance of both militarization and urbanization, it would seem appropriate to bring the connection between urban and military history back into focus. In the process, this essay will consider the importance of this connection to a number of subtopics: the rise and timing of the military-industrial complex; federal urban policy affecting cities, or the "New Federalism"; metropolitanism; the influence of cities upon national defense policy; some little-noticed outcomes of city politics; the integration of the military with civilian society; and the rise of the alliance between Sunbelt cities and the military establishment.

The story goes back at least to 1919, to metropolitanism among California cities, to the decline of the "Cool Grey Lady" [San Francisco], and to what might be called the "second coming" of the Great White Fleet. The second

*Roger W. Lotchin is professor of history at the University of North Carolina, Chapel Hill. Reprinted from Journal of the West 18 (July 1979): 19–30, with permission. Copyright 1979 Journal of the West Inc. No additional copies may be made without the express permission of the author and of the editor of Journal of the West.

decade of the century found the main components of urban California unsure of their status and competing furiously for pre-eminence. In 1920 the census would show that Los Angeles had forged ahead in population, but that city remained relatively unindustrialized compared to similar or even smaller Eastern cities.[1] San Francisco and San Diego had grown impressively between 1910 and 1920, but both had lost ground to the explosive Southland metropolis of Los Angeles. Thus, despite their vigor, each of these Sunbelt cities had to cope with its own version of relative decline—or status anxiety.

The transfer of the fleet to the Pacific in 1919 seemed at least a partial answer to these problems. Although strategic factors have not generally been considered important to the process of urbanization, they were crucial to the development of urban California—and long before World War II.[2] The sinking of the German fleet after World War I, the increase of the Navy during that conflict, the United States' rivalry with Japan, and the scrapping of Admiral Mahan's One-Fleet Theory all allowed the relocation of the major portion of the American fleet to Pacific waters between 1919 and 1921. Even before the ships had cleared the locks at Panama and steamed north, every city on the West Coast scrambled to get a share of the naval booty.[3]

Although the competing cities always deferred publicly to the opinions of the Navy's experts and the imperatives of "national defense," other considerations were paramount in civilian minds. It is well known that international insecurity and Depression-born unemployment provided a powerful stimulus to martial expenditure in the 1930s, but military spending had an earlier, more diverse, and more specifically urban rationale in metropolitan California. San Francisco saw this military money as a general economic multiplier which would restore its predominance; and that city as well as San Diego and Los Angeles hoped that militarily stimulated manufacturing would help overcome the Sunbelt's industrial lag.[4] San Diego wanted economic stabilization from its military payrolls, and, in addition, saw defense dollars as the means to redress its chronic balance of payments deficit.[5] Finally, all three regarded Navy dollars and development as a means to commercial aggrandizement.

The Navy's imperatives were different, being military instead of economic; but until well into the Roosevelt Administration, its dilemma was similar. Its decline was both relative and absolute. Congressional economizers assaulted the Navy's budget from 1919 on; air-power advocates questioned its role; the Washington Naval Limitation Treaty froze its strength; and government neglect and hostile public opinion kept this service below treaty strength for years thereafter.[6] Thus, the Navy needed civilian allies to protect itself from further slippage just as urban California needed military resources to realize its schemes of development and defense. This mutual problem brought the civilian and military sectors into a close association that lasted for twenty years.

Even before the Navy steamed to the West, that service had worked out plans for the allocation of its resources on the Pacific Coast. Secretary of the Navy Josephus Daniels announced in 1919 that the Mahan One-Fleet Theory was dead and that, after a decent burial, half of the Navy would be stationed in Pacific waters.[7] To accommodate the fleet, the Navy had planned a series of shore installations. These were distributed both strategically and politically. The Navy had learned in World War I that an emergency would require many shore facilities not always needed in time of peace, and they made sure that these would be placed in or, in the case of Portland, near the major West Coast metropolitan areas. The two most desirable plums were to be given to Puget Sound and San Francisco Bay respectively, and the Bay Area was to have the main West Coast operating base of the fleet.[8] This facility would cost $60,000,000 to $100,000,000, would bring with it as many as 45,000 naval personnel, and was grandiosely referred to in Northern California as the "American Singapore."[9]

These allocations had been made by the naval experts, and the various urban spokesmen never tired of commending an arrangement so obviously in the interest of national defense. Such an argument appealed to a generation of businessmen and politicians undergoing Taylorization in the economic world and experiencing the more specifically urban version of this idea in the realm of government—the "Goo Goo doctrine of expertise" frequently employed in American cities on behalf of charter and structural reform. In fact, the Goo Goo doctrine of expertise formed the basis of the political strategies worked out by coast cities to get and hold the fleet and to distribute naval resources among the Pacific cities. For instance, all the cities united in demanding the fleet for Pacific waters, citing the naval experts and their various strategic theories to back up this claim. Once the sailors had been secured, the cities again publicly deferred to the experts' judgment in placing their facilities around the coast and even within specific parts of the various metropolitan areas. In the San Francisco Bay Area, for example, the two leading contenders for the operating base site, Alameda and Hunter's Point in San Francisco, each fought vigorously for that prize but agreed to let the naval experts decide ultimately.[10]

This logical formula should have contained the political in-fighting for naval personnel and material, but in practice various influences undermined the doctrine of expertise. For one thing, the successive fleet commanders had considerable discretion as to where they would station the Pacific Navy; and each time they moved it around, they whetted local appetites for permanent possession. At the same time, technological development rendered obsolete the decisions of earlier experts. The dawning importance of air power called into question the choice of San Francisco Bay as a main base, and the use of carriers and larger battleships made certain Bay Area sites, such as Mare Island, obsolete or at least obsolescent. Simultaneously, the multiplying urban advantages of the Southland increased that area's ability to handle the entire fleet, and military improvements to the installations there strengthened southern claims even more. Moreover, the naval experts frequently disagreed. The future role of the Mare Island Navy Yard, the location of the main operating base, the site of the West Coast dirigible base, the strategic defense perimeter of the fleet, and even the supposedly dead issue of the One-Fleet Theory aroused enormous controversy within the Navy itself.[11] These discords, in turn, sabotaged the Navy's claim to expertise and encouraged the civilian defense boosters to take sides based on metropolitan interests rather than on national defense grounds. This recrudescence of metropolitanism further undermined the doctrine of expertise and encouraged the Navy in self-defense to play off one city against another.[12]

These problems surfaced very quickly and just as quickly centered on the issue of the main West Coast operating base. Some of the Navy's placements were readily accepted, and shore installations grew up from them. Between 1920 and 1923, for example, Congress confirmed San Diego's possession of its marine base and naval field, moved the Bay Area's naval training station at Treasure Island to San Diego, and approved the creation of an operating base, a new naval district, a supply depot, a destroyer base, and a major naval hospital at that southern city.[13] Its Southland neighbor, Los Angeles, got a submarine base; the two shared the fleet anchorage; and Southern California remained the fleet training ground.[14] San Francisco Bay representatives agreed to most of these decisions, thinking their own share was forthcoming soon. And according to naval plans, it should have been.

In 1920, Secretary of the Navy Josephus Daniels had accorded the Bay Area operating base at Alameda a high priority, but metropolitan politics revised the Navy's shopping list.[15] This political opposition was led by Vallejo, located at the northern end of San Pablo Bay. That city depended upon the adjacent Mare Island Navy Yard to an extraordinary degree, and Vallejo feared that a main West Coast operating base at either Alameda or Hunter's Point would mean the dismantling of its own Navy facility, since the new base supposedly had to be centralized. In addition, Vallejo wanted the new base for itself. From 1920 to 1925, Congress listened to the representatives of Vallejo rather than to the Navy and San Francisco and annually refused the appropriations to initiate the American Singapore.[16]

Despite allegations that the Washington arms limitation agreements and Republican budget cutting caused these rejections, these matters were not important. The Navy did not have shore installations to accommodate even the tonnage allowed under the limitations treaty, and the amount needed to initiate the San Francisco base was a trifling amount of the naval appropriations, much less of the national budget. Instead, the extremely decentralized patterns of urbanization in metropolitan San Francisco proved decisive. Geography and history had left the Bay Area even more fragmented than Los Angeles. In particular, San Francisco and Vallejo lacked the physical contiguity and the obvious identity of interests of Long Beach and Los Angeles in the south. As a result, Vallejo's Congressman Charles Curry, possibly with outside help from the south, masterminded San Francisco's defeat.[17]

This failure left the Navy with its battle fleet stationed on the Pacific Coast without a main operating base. The construction of the main base at San Francisco Bay, considered indispensable by the Navy, was stalled, while the minor installations went on building. The fleet was stationed in the south, but the main West Coast supply depot remained in Vallejo; and Mare Island and Bremerton, Washington, held on to their dry docks. This forced the sailors to steam hundreds of miles for supplies or repairs.[18] Although the Navy designated San Francisco an operating base in 1923, for the entire 1920s the strategic disposition of naval resources on the West Coast continued to reflect this pattern of Bay Area and West Coast urbanization rather than the designs of the Navy's strategic operations planners.

In the meantime, with the base issue stalemated, each of the cities forged ahead in lesser ways, improving their physical facilities and building a close interface with the military. As these ties matured, the militarization of urban California insinuated itself into many other phases of urbanization, urbanism, and local history: city planning, metropolitan decentralization, the search for community, police-community relations, the media, city politics, government, society, urban renewal, metropolitan cooperation, and the development of urban welfarism. Perhaps city politics reflected the growing entente between the city and the sword most clearly. In each of the major California cities, new political alliances grew up to attract major military investment, Army as well as Navy, to protect naval investment in the Pacific, and to back the Navy on key matters of national military policy.

Since large urban areas, or metropolitan "families," as the *San Francisco Examiner* put it, supplied the bases for these alliances, the term "metropolitan-military complex" would seem more appropriate than "military-industrial complex."[19] Industries singly or in groups provided only one element in these local coalitions, and not necessarily the most important one. In fact, as was noted earlier, the militarization of urban California was a means to overcome the industrial lag of the area. Probably the most important leadership element in each coalition was the city government, particularly the mayors. James Rolph and Angelo Rossi of San Francisco and the appropriately named John Forward of San Diego stand out among these executive leaders of urban navalism, but many others played similar roles.[20] Besides government, the metropolitan-military coalitions included Down Town clubs, chambers of commerce, labor councils, the media, local Congressmen, shipping groups, veterans' organizations, Propeller clubs, harbor commissions, diverse businesses, and dozens of other organizations.[21] In addition, Hollywood, of course, provided other bona fide defense experts to the Los Angeles grouping. Although the literature on metropolitan cooperation has focused on the consolidation of governments, military metropolitanism was also crucial to the growth of area-wide cooperation in urban California.

Everywhere these political ties were institutionalized. In the Bay Area, the San Francisco and other urban-military pressure groups came under the umbrella of the Bay Cities Naval Affairs Committee, which was part of the Bay Area Industrial Development Committee. Los Angeles had both a military affairs committee of the Board of Alderman and a mayor's committee on naval base development. San Diego had an Army and Navy committee of the Chamber of Commerce, and other organizations featured the same kind of institutional relationships.[22] The Navy, perhaps unwittingly, facilitated this institutionalization in 1920 by a reorganization which added local districts to the bureau system already in existence. This geographic decentralization produced naval districts at San Diego, San Francisco, and Seattle, with the same population bases and many of the same empire-building interests as their urban navalist counterparts.

These ties were supplemented by others to the federal government in Washington. Each of the cities tried to secure representation on the U.S. Shipping Board, to get a member on the House Naval Affairs or Rivers and Harbors committees, and to woo the U.S. Army Corps of Engineers. Each cultivated members of the naval officer corps politically, and each secured valuable service allies, both within the Eleventh and Twelfth Naval Districts at San Diego and San Francisco and within the central offices of the Navy as well.[23] The service members of the metropolitan-military complexes were less stable due to their frequent moves. However, ex-servicemen, especially in San Diego where many retired, were more stable and often played a significant role, holding important civilian posts after their military careers had ended.[24] These local alliances constituted relatively long-term political coalitions of government, service, and business personnel, comparable to what today is called the military-industrial complex.

All these groups represented the elites of urban California, but they accurately expressed the wishes of the mass of city dwellers as well. Every major California metropolitan area donated large and immensely valuable tracts of land to the Navy, and the voters usually ratified these gifts at special referenda, frequently by stunning majorities.[25] Whether we ultimately judge the growing partnership of the city and the sword as an encouragement to militarism or as a prudent development of national defense in a dangerous world, it is clear that the elite and the electorate agreed upon it.

Other more subtle, yet nonetheless political, links supplemented these overt ones. Just as the ties of the metropolitan-military complexes stretched upward to Washington, they also descended into everyday urban politics. City politicians found themselves constantly faced with the necessity of raising a new subsidy, providing another piece of land, finding a new anchorage, winning yet another referendum, or supplying some new benefit. This, in turn, led the civilian-military partners into considerable city planning efforts. From 1920 on, the Navy participated in Bay Area harbor and transportation planning that eventuated in the bridging of San Francisco Bay. Los Angeles shared this experience, and San Diego improved upon it. San Diego was known to the Navy as the city that tried harder. Unlike San Francisco, San Diego vetoed its own bridge scheme at the behest of the Navy. Moreover, that city also planned well in advance of naval demands to improve its harbor in order to secure ever greater military patronage. It set up a harbor trust fund, reminiscent of the contemporary highway trust fund, to finance port development—administered by the harbor commission and insulated from the ordinary pressure of "politics." This arrangement guaranteed the Navy a continuing commitment to its interests.[26] The Los Angeles Harbor Commission claimed $30,000,000 worth of improvements devoted to the same end. Even before the New Deal, federal funds aided these efforts. Although such long-range, comprehensive planning was unusual for its time, it reinforced rather than altered the decentralizing dynamics of urban spatial development. Despite the fact that urban historians have almost completely ignored the military origins of city planning, these were certainly important in the California military cities.[27]

Throughout the 1920s and 1930s, the civilian-military interface grew steadily closer in other spheres. The Navy continually courted the media, and the press repaid the compliment with interest. The newspapers publicized military activities fully, opened their columns to service spokesmen advocating defense measures, and frequently denounced those opposing them, particularly pacifists, whose activities the Navy and Army feared.[28] Rotary, veteran, commercial, and other clubs supplemented the media communications pipeline by frequent invitations to Navy speakers to present service views. Social events added to the growing entente. The Southland Navy Ball held in Los Angeles annually was *the* event of the early Southland "society" calendar.[29] Harbor Day in San Francisco went even farther, working both the classes and the masses into the social interface. This was a massive civic-military festival which featured a "society" Navy Ball as well as one for the sailors and something for almost everyone else—sham battles, inspection tours, concerts, water shows, aerial shows, and so forth.[30] The Navy took these exercises seriously. On Memorial Day, the ships would be spread out from one end of the Coast to the other to participate in commemorative services; while at other times all or part of the Pacific squadron would appear at such "national defense" events as the Portland Rose Festival, the San Diego Exposition, and the Golden Gate Bridge Fiesta. The latter two claimed the entire fleet in 1935 and 1937.[31] Urban California used these occasions to encourage a sense of community, both because many thought that the process of urbanization had fragmented it and because these celebrations were a way to mobilize the entire populace behind further demands for naval largesse.[32] The Navy linked itself to this sense of community wherever possible—naming a cruiser for San Francisco and a dirigible for Los Angeles and fulsomely praising pliant San Diego.

These efforts paid off for both sides. The naval investment grew steadily over the years, and, in turn, urban California moved progressively toward a kind of military welfarism. Reversing the contemporary practice that allocates extra federal funds for areas impacted by the military, urban California subsidized the Navy instead. Besides dredging its harbors, either through local, rivers and harbors, or its PWA and RFC funds, urban California gave away massive portions of its enormously valuable waterfront. By 1929, San Diego had already allocated one-third of its waterfront to the Navy and by 1955, had donated nearly 3,000 acres. Alameda twice gave 5,340 acres; and Los Angeles, San Mateo County, Oakland, Vallejo, and others followed suit.[33] Special piers, docks, and other facilities added to the sailors' convenience. In San Francisco, special public works relief programs, municipal civil service exemptions, city employment preference, paid vacations for civilian military trainees, free use of the Civic Auditorium, a war memorial building built on urban renewal land, and free rides for thousands of sailors on the Municipal Railway benefited veterans and servicemen. San Diego rented dancehalls, established special servicemen's relief committees upon the advent of the Depression, supplied cut-rate water to its bases, leased municipal airport land, and constructed spur tracks, seaplane landings, made land, and many recreation facilities for the sailors. As usual, San Diego went all out. In 1933, when a storm literally washed the fleet out of its poorly protected anchorage at San Pedro, one cruiser division was relocated at San Diego. Its commander called the Harbor Commission about additional recreation facilities for the new arrivals, and the next day the bulldozers began building ball fields and tennis courts on made land that the city had created in 1928—just in case.[34] The Navy pushed especially hard to get the harbor improvements and land donations, almost ritually threatening to decamp if it were turned down. San Diego in particular was bombarded with these threats, although it is difficult to see how that city could have been more cooperative short of electing an admiral to the mayoralty.[35]

The city and the sword were drawn together by a host of other mutual interests that were both local and strategic in nature and which, in turn, produced valuable support for the Navy's position on national defense. A prosperous American merchant marine ("the second line of defense") in the Pacific, a thriving aircraft industry, a revival of West Coast shipbuilding, drydocks to repair both merchant and military vessels, airport construction, pilot training, and, especially after 1929, rearmament would benefit both parties.[36] The regional character of such issues often overcame metropolitan jealousies and produced regional political coalitions that helped realize these goals. These positions were not without their delicious ironies. Until well into the 1930s, civilian defense boosters rated the menace of their Japanese trading partners below that of Hitler and Mussolini. Simultaneously, they supported the placement of most of the fleet ("the first line of defense") in Pacific waters and the creation of a vast urban-military infrastructure to accommodate it.[37]

As these institutional relationships matured in the 1920s and early 1930s, the urban installations of the Navy continued to grow. What Robert Caro called "stake driving" in his biography of Robert Moses holds true of urban-military affairs as well. Once a stake had been driven or a project started, it would grow to completion and sometimes beyond. Unfortunately, the main operating base at Alameda had not yet received its first stake by 1920 and remained stalled the rest of the decade. That jeopardized the naval interest in the entire San Francisco region. Both the political infighting of the Bay Area and the growing importance of the southern metropolitan areas led the Navy to cast longing glances southward. As the harbors in the Southland improved, as its metropolitan infrastructure supplied more of what the Navy needed, and as its cooperation increased, the Navy wavered in its commitment to San Francisco Bay.[38]

While Los Angeles drove stakes and San Diego burrowed ever deeper into its harbor floor, San Francisco and its Bay allies waited for the base to appear. Then in 1929 the House Naval Affairs Committee's investigation of a West Coast dirigible base site revealed that the Navy was split several ways over the operating base question as well as over that of the dirigible station. An almost comic parade of expert military witnesses, backed by their metropolitan-civilian allies and armed with strategic theories tailor-made for each city, marched before the committee, asserting the superiority of their own West Coast localities. Carl Vinson joined in the spirit of things and asserted the claims of the historic South; and Congressman McClintic of Oklahoma even put forward the name of Oklahoma City as a compromise dirigible station site, though he did have the self-restraint not to ask for a naval base.[39]

Sunnyvale in the Bay Area finally got the nod, but not before the Bay Area metropolitan-military complex had been badly shaken. After 1929 it organized for sustained action.[40] Sunnyvale also initiated the reconciliation with Vallejo, since that city eventually came to support the claims of the south-bay dirigible site and joined the Bay Area base coalition. And although it amounted to only a $5,000,000 commitment, the establishment of a base at Sunnyvale broke the long dry spell for the San Francisco Bay Area. As many from the Southland recognized, that minor airship station was really the entering wedge for the operating base, since dirigibles were supposed to operate with the fleet.[41]

By 1933, an ever more threatening world situation, plus the elevation of a President and Congress more anxious to end unemployment and rebuild the Navy, brought fresh naval resources into the West Coast contest. However, money had never really been the problem. Politics had; and, fortunately for the Bay Area, its own stalemate broke in these same years. Congressman Curry died in 1930, and in 1933 the metropolitan-military complex at Los Angeles moved openly to secure the coveted main West Coast operating base. Admiral Thomas J. Senn, commandant of the Eleventh Naval District, backed this move, and the Navy Department allowed him to investigate the idea.[42] A main operating base would have duplicated the dry-dock and supply facilities of Mare Island, and this threat solidified the adherence of Vallejo to the San Francisco coalition while galvanizing that group into redoubling its efforts.

By this time, however, the Navy had already lurched back into San Francisco's camp. In fact, Admiral C. C. Cole, commandant of the Twelfth Naval District at San Francisco, had by 1930 conceived the strategy that, together with the ominous threats from the south, would finally break the deadlock amongst Bay Area cities. Cole noted that the Navy could no longer hope for a centralized base at Alameda because the process of urbanization had claimed much of the land and threatened other potential Bay Area base sites as well.[43] To salvage the situation, the Navy hit upon a base strategy that matched military decentralization to the urban decentralization and the urban rivalry of the Bay Area.

The Navy conceived a secret plan for the new operating base. It would be decentralized around the bay; it would be built up one step at a time instead of in one dramatic burst; and it would contain something for each of the cities competing for naval riches.[44] This plan was finished by 1932, and the Navy then devised an ingenious maneuver to implement it. To quiet the suspicions of Los Angeles and San Diego, the Navy played down the immediate need for new shore facilities and asked Congress to concentrate its spending on the "floating Navy" and the existing installations instead.[45] Congress did, and then the Navy began pointing to the overtaxed shore facilities which needed more money to handle the expanded fleet. This strategy of overload worked to the distinct advantage of San Francisco; it had been denied so much for so long that its overloading was more dramatic when the ships and planes finally came.[46] In the meantime, Twelfth Naval District Commandant G. W. Laws brought the warring Bay Area factions together to negotiate a peace treaty, which coincided with a media blitz, reinvigorated pressure group activity, and renewed Congressional activity by civilian Bay Area service boosters.[47] The Navy went farther. What the newspapers called the "most significant" war games in naval history—an attack on coastal cities to test their air defenses—occurred just before the advent of the Roosevelt Administration in 1933. The new administration, from which the Navy expected great things, came to power just as the West Coast newspapers broadcasted the news that the mock attack had proven the coastal cities defenseless.[48]

From that point onward, Bay Area fortunes brightened. A new supply depot, a major naval air station, a new shipyard, a training station, improvements to Mare Island, an aeronautical research laboratory, and, in 1938, shipbuilding subsidies rapidly overcame the Bay Area naval lag.[49] San Francisco missed out on a West Coast naval academy, and, fortunately, the Navy and other bay cities rejected "the City's" clamorous suggestion to obliterate a large portion of San Pablo and San Francisco bays with a massive military-industrial landfill.[50] However, by 1941 the Bay Area had finally gained the position that the Navy had assigned it over twenty years earlier. It had secured the main operating base and a total naval investment of one billion dollars.[51] Interestingly enough, Los Angeles, which still claimed the main fleet anchorage, apparently did not learn of the secret base buildup in the Bay Area until mid-1937.[52]

The Southland metropolitan-military complexes likewise claimed further resources during these years, but they were usually additions to existing installations rather than new ones. San Diego, for example, added the Army half of North Island to its naval air station, gained a minor dry dock in 1935, and extensively dredged its harbor in 1931 and 1936.[53] Los Angeles likewise crept ahead, acquiring Reeves Field, expanding its artificial harbor, and claiming a growing proportion of the burgeoning fleet until war claimed the sailors.

This brief consideration of the comparative dimension of the city and the sword suggests several conclusions. Western civilian-service ties that have been called the military-industrial complex obviously came before, rather than during or after, World War II, as has been generally supposed.[54] In this part of the Sunbelt, these ties had an urban rather than an industrial base.[55] They were also significant to both national defense policy and Western economic development. Quite possibly, they were as, or more, important than those civilian-military ties since discovered at the national level in this period.[56] Most certainly, the metropolitan-military complexes provide us with new insights into the topic of twentieth-century metropolitanism, city politics in general, and city planning in particular. Also, urban navalism allows us to reopen the discussion of the historic relationship between the city and the sword and to do it in such a way as to speak to national history as well as to urban. Not only do the metropolitan-military complexes reveal something about national defense and economic development, they also tell something about federal policy affecting cities that we have long overlooked in favor of things like housing, FHA, relief, and public works, which may not have been any more important.[57] And finally, the study of the city and the sword casts new light on the historic role of urbanism and urbanization as an integrative force—not, in this case, for blacks, women, or immigrants—but for the military. The comparative view of urban California certainly would not support the conclusions of Samuel P. Huntington that the military in the 1920s returned to their prewar isolation from society, that they were harassed by "business pacifism," or that civilians did not try to take advantage of them.[58] Although the experience of urban California would not support the speculation of Lewis Mumford that cities *generate* the forces of war, urban California certainly stood ready to use these forces for *civilian* purposes. If they were not "Merchants of Death," the urban navalists surely qualified as "Merchants of Defense."

NOTES

[1]Robert M. Fogelson, *The Fragmented Metropolis: Los Angeles, 1850–1930* (Cambridge, Massachusetts, 1967), 132.

[2]For the impact of military matters on urban affairs after World War II, see Gerald Nash, *The American West in the Twentieth Century: A Short History of an Urban Oasis* (Englewood Cliffs, N.J., 1973).

[3]See Committee on Naval Affairs, *Hearings Before the Committee on Naval Affairs: Appropriation Bill Subjects, 1919*, U.S. Congress, House of Representatives, 66th Cong., 1st sess., 1919, pt. 2 (Washington, D.C., 1919).

[4]*San Francisco Journal of Commerce*, April 7, 1920, p. 1. Cited hereafter as *Journal of Commerce*. *Los Angeles Examiner*, October 4, 1933, p. 16, ed.

[5]*San Diego Union*, Feb. 26, 1933, I, 1; Jan. 29, 1933, I, 12.

[6]Donald W. Mitchell, *History of the Modern American Navy* (New York, 1946), p. 250ff; Vincent Davis, *The Admirals' Lobby* (Chapel Hill, N.C., 1967), pp. 3–157.

[7]*Hearings . . . on Naval Affairs . . . 1919, op cit.*, pp. 60–61.

[8]*Ibid.* Naval allocations of West Coast resources appear throughout this hearing.

[9]U.S. Congress, *Congressional Record*, 66th Cong., 3rd. sess., 1921, LX, p. 4126–140.

[10]Naval Affairs Committee, *Hearings . . . on Estimates Submitted by the Secretary of the Navy, 1920*, U.S. Congress, 66th Cong., 2nd sess., pp. 1096–1103 (Washington, D.C., 1920).

[11]Committee on Naval Affairs, *Hearings on Sundry Legislation Affecting the Naval Establishment, 1929–30*, U.S. Congress, 71st sess., 1930, throughout (Washington, D.C., 1930).

[12]"In unmistakable terms, naval officials assert San Diego must meet this competition [of rival Pacific Coast ports] by accentuating its own harbor program." *San Diego Union*, Jan. 15, 1933, II, 1.

[13]Edward J. P. Davis, *The United States Navy and U.S. Marine Corps at San Diego* (San Diego, 1955), pp. 29–73.

[14]*Hearings . . . on Estimates . . . 1920, op. cit.*, pp. 2334–335.

[15]*Ibid.*, p. 2227.

[16]Lt. Commander Arnold S. Lott, *A Long Line of Ships: Mare Island's Century of Naval Activity in California* (Annapolis, Md., 1954), pp. 183–206.

[17]Robert G. Albion, "The Naval Affairs Committees, 1816–1947," *United States Naval Institute Proceedings*, 78 (Nov. 1952), 1234; U.S. Congress, *Congressional Record*, 71st Cong., 3rd sess., 1931, LXXIV, pt. 5:5408–410.

[18]Adm. Wm. D. Leahy, Chief of Naval Operations, to Congressman Byron N. Scott, Dec. 29, 1937, General Correspondence, 1926–1940, General Records of the Department of the Navy, RG 80 (National Archives).

[19]*San Francisco Examiner*, July 1, 1922, I, 16, ed.

[20]*San Diego Union*, Feb. 26, 1933, I, 1.

[21]San Francisco Board of Supervisors, *Journal of the Proceedings*, Vol. 36, No. 1 (April 7, 1941), p. 607. Cited hereafter as *Journal*.

[22]*San Diego Union*, April 12, 1933, II, 8.

[23]*San Francisco Examiner*, April 4, 1933, p. 19.

[24]*San Diego Union*, Feb. 17, 1935, I, 5.

[25]*San Francisco Daily Commercial News*, Jan. 26, 1921, p. 1. Cited hereafter as *Daily Commercial News*.

[26]*San Diego Union*, June 25, 1933, I, 1, 10, and II, 1 give the historical background of the San Diego interlock.

[27]*Los Angeles Times*, May 15, 1937, II 4, ed.; Jan. 8, 1938, I, 9.

[28]*Ibid.*, Jan. 24, 1937, II, 4; *Daily Commercial News*, March, 1935, p. 8.

[29]*Los Angeles Times,* Jan. 3, 1937, IV, 1.

[30]*San Francisco Examiner,* August 1, 1933, p. 5.

[31]San Francisco Board of Supervisors, *Journal* . . . , Vol. 32, No. 1 (March 29, 1937), pp. 499–500; *San Diego Union,* August 8, 1935, I, 2.

[32]*San Diego Union,* June 18, 1933, II, 1; *San Francisco Call and Post,* Jan. 3, 1925, p. 7.

[33]Davis, p. 72; *Daily Commercial News,* Jan. 26, 1921, p. 1.

[34]*San Diego Union,* Feb. 23, 1933, II, 5.

[35]*Ibid.,* Jan. 15, 1933, II, 1; Oct. 18, 1935, I, 4.

[36]*Los Angeles Times,* March 27, 1933, II, 4; *San Francisco Examiner,* July 8, 1922, I, 22, ed; Jan. 2, 1923, I, 26; Jan. 31, 1933, ed. pg.; *Down Town* (San Francisco), Jan. 25, 1939, p. 1; *Daily Commercial News,* April 10, 1940, p. 8; U.S. Congress, *Congressional Record,* 69th Cong., 2nd sess., 1927, LXVIII, pt. 2; 990–97, 1735–736.

[37]*Los Angeles Times,* March 27, 1933, II, 4, ed.; *San Diego Union,* March 10, 1935, I, 6; U.S. Congress, *Congressional Record,* 75th Cong., 3rd sess., 1938, LXXXIII, pt. 4:3767.

[38]Memo from Director of Material Division to Chief of Naval Operations, June 3, 1928, General Correspondence, 1926–1940, RG 80 (National Archives).

[39]*Hearings on Sundry Legislation . . . 1929–30, op. cit.,* pp. 2633, 2696, 2774, 2826, 2700–701, 2713.

[40]*San Francisco Chronicle,* May 14, 1929, ed. pg.; May 22, 1929, ed. pg.; June 15, 1929, ed. pg.

[41]Memo from Director of Material Division to Chief of Naval Operations, *op. cit.*

[42]*Biographical Directory of the American Congress 1774–1971* (Washington, D.C., 1971), p. 813; *San Diego Union,* Jan. 30, 1933, I, 1; *Los Angeles Examiner,* Sept. 30, 1933, I, 5.

[43]W. C. Cole to Chief of Naval Operations, Nov. 14, 1930, Confidential Correspondence, 1927–1939, General Records of the Department of the Navy, RG 80 (National Archives).

[44]*Ibid.*

[45]Statements by Secretary of the Navy Claude Swanson in *San Francisco Examiner,* Sept. 25, 1933, p. 17 and Oct. 21, 1933, p. 5.

[46]Subcommittee of the Committee on Appropriations, House of Representatives, *Hearings on the Navy Department Appropriations Bill for 1939* (Washington, D.C., 1938), pp. 820–25.

[47]*Daily Commercial News,* Sept. 12, 1933, p. 4; Sept. 14, 1933, p. 4.

[48]*San Diego Union,* Jan. 23, 1933, I, 1; Feb. 18, 1933, I, 5.

[49]*San Francisco Chronicle,* June 25, 1938, p. 11; E. P. Hartman, *Adventures in Research: A History of Ames Research Center, 1940–1965* (Washington, D.C., 1970), pp. 1–42.

[50]San Francisco Board of Supervisors, *Journal* . . . , Vol. 36, No. 2 (Nov. 13, 1941), pp. 2161–163, 2167.

[51]*San Francisco Downtowner,* May 29, 1941, pp. 1–2.

[52]*Los Angeles Times,* May 9, 1937, I, 11.

[53]Davis, pp. 29–73; *San Diego Union,* June 27, 1934, I, 4; Jan. 6, 1935, I, 17; *Los Angeles Times,* Jan. 2, 1937, Annual Midwinter Number, p. 11.

[54]The usual interpretation of the military-industrial complex stresses the importance of World War II or the Cold War. See, for example, Richard Polenberg, *War and Society: The United States, 1941–1945* (Philadelphia, 1972).

[55]Benjamin F. Cooling, ed., *War, Business, and American Society: Historical Perspectives on the Military-Industrial Complex* (Port Washington, New York, 1977) and Paul Koistinen, "The 'Industrial-Military Complex' in Historical Perspective: The Interwar Years," *Journal of American History, 56* (March, 1970), 819–39 stress the importance of industrial ties to the military, but correctly emphasize the importance of earlier periods in civil-military relations.

[56]For these latter, see the works of Cooling and Koistinen.

[57]For a recent historical work on federal urban policy, see Mark I. Gelfand, *A Nation of Cities: The Federal Government and Urban America, 1933–1965* (New York, 1975).

[58]Samuel P. Huntington, *The Soldier and the State: The Theory and Politics of Civil-Military Relations* (Cambridge, Mass., 1964), pp. 282, 312.

Trouble in Paradise:
Race and Housing in Miami
during the New Deal Era

*Raymond A. Mohl**

It is one of the axioms of twentieth-century urban history that the New Deal forged a new relationship between the federal government and the cities. Before the 1930s, city governments generally had been limited in their powers and functions by state legislative control over city charters. The lack of sufficient home rule often prevented municipal governments from embarking on necessary programs of physical development or social reform. The New Deal, however, created myriad new federal agencies and provided vast sums for relief, recovery, and reform. Although the Roosevelt administration had little in the way of a systematic urban policy, much of the new federal activism was directed to the cities and their problems. One study in 1936 noted some "500 points of contact between the federal bureaucracy and the cities in the fields of planning, zoning, education, health, internal improvements, relief, and housing." Another study pointed out that the Roosevelt administration was the first to become "intimately concerned with urban life and city problems."[1]

Traditional interpretations of the New Deal era generally asserted the salutary effect of the new programs on urban America. Recent historical research, however, has begun to sketch out a somewhat different analysis, one that suggests that New Deal urban programs had negative as well as positive consequences. Some urban historians have demonstrated that New Deal work and welfare programs actually strengthened rather than dismantled the old political machines.[2] Others have concluded that New Deal city planners relentlessly promoted the automobile culture, while simultaneously undermining mass transit systems.[3] Still other historians have noted the New Deal's mixed record in the area of housing. Slum clearance and public housing projects were promoted only in lukewarm fashion so as not to offend powerful advocates of the free-market economy. At the same time, federal mortgage

*Raymond A. Mohl is professor of history at Florida Atlantic University. Reprinted from Prologue: The Journal of the National Archives 19 (Spring 1987): 7–21. Copyright by Raymond A. Mohl.

programs and highway construction encouraged middle-class and working-class whites to flee the central cities for the lily-white suburbs, leaving urban blacks and the poor behind.[4] Thus, while it is clear that the New Deal initiated a new era of federal-municipal cooperation and activism, it is also evident that this new relationship entailed unanticipated costs.

This was clearly the case in Miami during the New Deal era, particularly with respect to housing. New Dealers, with help from local political and business leaders, implemented federal public housing and mortgage programs in Miami by the mid-1930s. A succession of federal housing agencies financed several public housing projects, first for blacks and then for whites. The Home Owners Loan Corporation (HOLC), another new federal agency, conducted an extensive real estate appraisal of the Miami housing market in order to systematize the HOLC mortgage program. Both efforts stemmed from the liberal reformist impulse of the New Deal, but both had long-term and not altogether positive consequences in shaping Miami's future growth and development.

New Deal housing reform began in 1933, when Franklin D. Roosevelt's new Public Works Administration (PWA) launched a slum clearance and public housing program. The PWA's Housing Division first supported limited-dividend housing corporations in a number of cities, but it soon went on to direct federal housing construction. Both methods, generally, were slow in producing results. By 1937 the PWA had initiated only seven limited-dividend projects and forty-nine public housing projects. In 1937 the United States Housing Authority (later reorganized as the Public Housing Administration) replaced the PWA as a provider of public housing, working through state and local housing agencies.[5]

Public Housing in Miami

Action on public housing in Miami began in late 1933, when the limited-dividend Southern Housing Corporation submitted an application to the PWA Housing Division. Organized by several leading members of the city's downtown white business elite, the Southern Housing Corporation wanted both slum clearance and low-cost housing for Miami's blacks. The project soon foundered for lack of private investment, but in 1934 the PWA decided to go ahead with a federally financed housing project.[6]

The need for such action on housing for blacks was compelling. By the early 1930s most of Miami's black population of over twenty-five thousand were crowded into a 350-acre section just northwest of the central business district known at the time as "Colored Town." Today it is called Overtown. The area was covered over with tiny, dilapidated shacks, sometimes as many as fifteen on a single 50 × 100-foot lot. Most buildings lacked electricity, toilets, bathing facilities, and hot water. Municipal services were noticeable by their absence, streets were unpaved and unlit, and contagious diseases were rampant. This "deplorable slum district," the *Miami Herald* editorialized in 1934, had become the "plague spot" of Miami.[7] In its application to the

PWA, the Southern Housing Corporation contended that "the sanitary conditions are a menace to the whole city . . . and a shame and disgrace to the
respectable citizens of Miami." But obviously the situation was worse for the
blacks who lived there.[8]

Blacks were heavily concentrated in this shack town because there were
few other places for them to live in Miami at the time. A small black community had been established in Coconut Grove, mainly by Bahamian blacks
who came to Miami early in the twentieth century. Farther north, two small
black subdivisions emerged in the 1920s. At first a sparsely settled but integrated area, Brownsville was located between Northwest 41st Street and
Northwest 53d Street and west of 27th Avenue. Developed by a white real
estate man named Floyd W. Davis, the Liberty City subdivision was home
to a few hundred blacks in the neighborhood of Northwest 62d Street and
17th Avenue (see Map 1). The New Deal housing program provided Miami's
civic elite with an opportunity to do something about black housing conditions
in the central Negro district, but it also had important implications for the
future development of Liberty City.[9]

Support for the PWA housing program was widespread among Miami's
business and political leaders. If the correspondence in the PWA records in
the National Archives is any guide, Miami attorney John C. Gramling served
as the point man for the civic elite in securing federal housing in Miami.
Arriving in Miami from Alabama as a young man in 1898, Gramling became
active in public affairs, serving first as a justice of the peace, then as city
judge, county judge, and state's attorney. By the 1920s, Gramling had emerged
as an important city booster. He had established his own law firm and had
become involved in local Democratic politics, real estate development, and
extensive sugar cane production near Lake Okeechobee. As one writer put it
in 1921, Gramling was "deeply interested in everything that tends to build
up the city and community."[10] When the limited-dividend Southern Housing
Corporation was organized in 1933, Gramling provided the chief motivating
energy. That project failed, but Gramling remained undeterred. In a barrage
of correspondence with federal officials in 1934 and 1935, Gramling argued
the case for the black public housing project and, once it was approved,
guided federal officials through the thickets of state and local politics.[11]

Gramling was not the only supporter of public housing for blacks in
Miami. By early 1934 the PWA project had been endorsed by the *Miami
Herald* and by the *Miami Daily News*, as well as by the Miami City Commission
and a long list of civic and business leaders, some of whom were appointed
to the Miami Advisory Committee on Housing.[12] The black community was
supportive, too. The *Miami Times*, the city's black newspaper, editorialized
in favor of the project. Through such groups as the Miami Colored Chamber
of Commerce and the Negro Civic League, Miami's black leaders endorsed
the housing plan.[13] As Gramling put it in a letter to Eugene H. Klaber of the
PWA Housing Division, "all of our papers and best citizens are in favor of
the project."[14]

The story laid out here in its essential outlines conforms to a traditional
view of the federal-local relationship during the New Deal era. The New
Dealers wanted to help with urban problems, and Miami's local leaders took

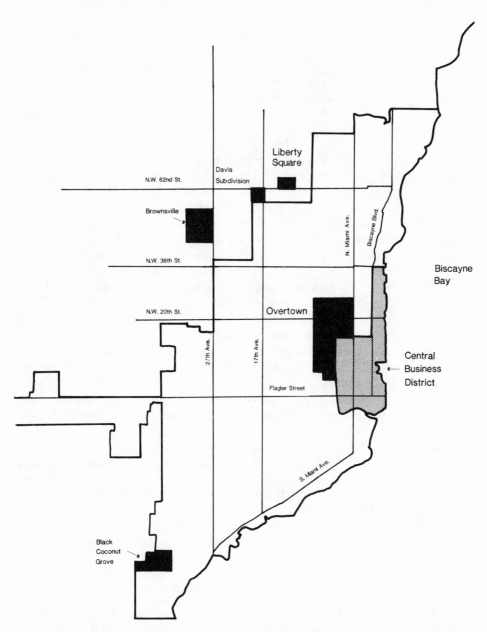

Map 1. Miami's black neighborhoods in the 1930s, showing the location of the proposed Liberty Square federal housing project.

advantage of federal largesse to bring housing reform to their town. But there are other and better explanations for what happened. One aspect of the story is partially hidden in the PWA records and other sources in Washington. These materials address the crucial question of motivation. The evidence clearly suggests that the Miami civic elite sought to eliminate the downtown black community entirely to make way for further expansion of the business district. Liberty Square, the proposed black public housing project, was to be located on Northwest 62d Street between 12th and 14th Avenues and was envisioned as the nucleus of a new and distant black community five to six miles from the city core (see Map 1).

Another part of the story lies in the hidden links among some members of the Miami business leadership. In particular, John Gramling served as the personal attorney of Floyd W. Davis, the developer of the small black subdivision near the proposed PWA housing project. Gramling and Davis had worked together in organizing the limited-dividend Southern Housing Corporation. Davis owned much of the unoccupied land surrounding his Liberty City subdivision, including the land ultimately purchased by the federal government for the black housing project. Davis stood to profit enormously if the PWA project stimulated the private housing market for blacks in the neighborhood. The connection between Gramling and Davis was not widely known at the time, but it helps to explain Gramling's active role in promoting the federal housing project, and especially his support for the 62d Avenue location. Gramling appeared to federal housing officials to be a disinterested local leader, but it is obvious that he had a personal stake in housing decisions for Miami blacks.[15] Thus, questions of land, profit, business expansion, and white racism appear more significant than any publicly stated interest in housing reform in the development of public housing for blacks in New Deal Miami.

The Miami civic elite was not noticeably altruistic when it came to the black community. John Gramling's hostile attitude toward blacks, for instance, was well known. While serving as a city judge, Gramling often praised the police for clamping down on Bahamian blacks who preached or practiced racial equality.[16] Similarly, A. B. Small, a county judge, civic leader, and active promoter of the black housing project, expressed a fairly typical kind of paternalism toward blacks. In a 1935 letter to PWA Housing Director A. R. Clas, Small wrote:

> I am one of those, being a true-bred Southern man and a descendant of slave owners, who feel that the negroes are the wards of the white people and that we ought to be very scrupulous in trying to see to it that they are given proper living conditions, and I am one of those who would do anything I can to bring this about.

It was in "the best interests of the city," Small argued in his benevolent way, to build the PWA project not downtown where most of the blacks lived, but at the 62d Street location.[17]

Gramling and other white promoters of federal housing for blacks in Miami consistently used a public health argument as the primary justification

for the black project more than five miles north of the city. In their correspondence with federal officials, Gramling and others repeatedly depicted the
black shack town near the business district as "a constant and deadly menace
to the health of the community." Syphilis, tuberculosis, and influenza were
widespread in the area, Gramling noted on numerous occasions, but it was
the whites, not the blacks, that he was worried about. "From this cess-pool
of disease the white people of Greater Miami draw their servants," Gramling
wrote to Klaber of the PWA in February 1934. Again in October, Gramling
used a similar argument: "This project will be one of the greatest blessings
that Miami ever had. It will not only eliminate the possibility of fatal epidemics here, but fix it so that we can get a servant freed from disease."[18]

Miami's white leaders worried about the oft-stated health "menace" in
the black community, but they also used this argument to mask another
motive. Indeed, PWA and other records clearly reveal this underlying purpose
of the Miami business and political leadership, that of completely displacing
the downtown black neighborhood. Writing to Klaber in February 1934,
Gramling tipped his hand about the true purpose of the new project: "The
people of Miami realize that something must be done and the newspapers
agree with me that it ought to be done in the manner so that we could
eventually remove the entire colored population from the dump in which they
are now living."[19] Opponents of the Liberty Square project—including white
"Colored Town" slum lords and whites who lived near the 62d Street location—
also recognized the hidden agenda of the downtown civic elite. For example,
a newly organized citizens' group called the Nor'west League deluged Washington with protests over the location of the new black housing project.
According to the league, the housing program was "a secret project instigated
by self-interested businessmen, real estate developers or officials . . . anxious
to shove its negroes anywhere to get rid of them." As Isabelle Sanderson,
secretary of the Nor'west League bluntly put it in a letter to the PWA,
"Everybody thinks this model negro settlement idea is lovely—for somebody
else's neighborhood."[20]

The removal of blacks from "Colored Town" would pave the way for
slum clearance and the expansion of the Miami business district. Despite the
depression, the city was growing rapidly in the 1930s. Miami, the *Herald*
asserted in 1934, was "enjoying a boom that is greater in many respects than
the dizzy, swaggering days of 1925." The city's population rose by 64 percent,
from 110,637 in 1930 to 172,172 in 1940. Dade County population increased
by over 87 percent during the decade. The bust was over, and Miami tourism,
real estate, business, and building construction all were looking good. Clearly,
the business community perceived the arrival of federal slum clearance and
housing programs as an opportunity to eliminate the eyesore of "Colored
Town" and to push out the boundaries of the central business area.[21]

Other Miami civic leaders were thinking along the same lines as Gramling.
George E. Merrick, for instance, the Coral Gables developer who had lost his
fortune in the collapse of the 1920s boom, was back in the thick of Miami
real estate activities by the mid-1930s. In a speech to the Miami Realty Board
in May 1937, Merrick proposed "a complete slum clearance . . . effectively

removing every negro family from the present city limits." This black removal, Merrick asserted, was "a most essential fundamental" for the achievement of Miami's ambitious planning goals.[22]

About the same time, the Dade County Planning Council, of which Merrick was chairman, announced its "negro resettlement plan." This plan, the council asserted, was "based upon very intensive research through the best national authorities and experience, as well as upon the consensus of the best thought on the subject here in South Florida." The idea was to cooperate with the city of Miami "in removing [the] entire Central Negro town to three Negro Park locations, and establishment there of three model negro towns." One of the planned communities was to be located on distant agricultural land on the Tamiami Trail west of the city limits. The plan envisioned other black communities west of Perrine to the south and west of Opa-locka to the north. Distance was not a problem, the planning report noted, since "an exclusive negro bus line service directly from these negro areas to the heart of Miami" would be established. The Dade County Commission unanimously adopted the planning report, and it was enthusiastically endorsed by the *Miami Herald*.[23]

Thus the forces unleashed by the New Deal housing program had a dramatic and shaping impact on Miami. The availability of federal housing funds mobilized the civic elite, who saw in slum clearance a golden opportunity to push the blacks out of the downtown area. The Liberty Square project drew upon an undisguised racism among the city's decision makers. It also generated several decades of racial tension in the northwest area where the 243-unit project ultimately was completed in 1937.[24]

The seemingly simple decision to provide housing for blacks had other consequences, too. As Floyd Davis and John Gramling had anticipated, the Liberty Square housing project became the nucleus of a new and rapidly growing black ghetto, the enormous fifteen-square mile area now known as Liberty City. A tacit agreement among city officials, black leaders, and real estate developers designated the northwest area of Miami for future black settlement. Previously confined to the limited territory of Overtown, blacks rapidly pushed out the boundaries of Liberty City, sweeping into undeveloped land as well as white working-class neighborhoods on the northern fringes of Miami. As in such cities as Chicago and Detroit, the racial turnover of existing neighborhoods in Miami was a process filled with tension, conflict, and violence.[25]

Although smaller in population, the black central district remained, obviously frustrating the ambitious segregation plans of Gramling, Merrick, and others. But the black-removal goals of the downtown business leaders have never completely disappeared from the scene. The highway building mania of the late 1950s and early 1960s accomplished some of the black removal program. The construction of interstate highways 95 and 395 gouged wide swaths through the center of Overtown. A single interchange on the North-South Expressway (I-95), for instance, destroyed the housing of 2,500 Overtown families in the early 1960s. Urban renewal programs in the 1960s provided new opportunities to achieve the same end. In a 1964 study, geographer Harold M. Rose noted that "a recently proposed urban renewal project, if instituted, would result in the elimination of this historic center of Negro settlement, which has been blamed for stifling the economic growth of the central business district."[26] More recently, Metro-Dade County and City of Miami office buildings and parking lots have gobbled up most of southeast Overtown. The so-called Park West Project will bring upscale townhouses, trendy retail shops, and perhaps a sports arena to the eastern fringes of Overtown. Close observers of the Miami political scene know that the idea of pushing the business district into what remains of Overtown is fully alive in the mid-1980s.[27]

It would, moreover, be difficult to describe Miami's early experience with public housing as a roaring success. From 1937, when Liberty Square was completed, until 1949, only three public housing projects with 1,515 units had been completed, one for blacks and two for whites. An aggressive antislum campaign in 1949 and 1950 led to a successful referendum permitting the Miami Housing Authority to construct an additional 1,500 public housing units, but ten years later only half that number had been completed. Not until the 1960s and the creation of the Metro-Dade County Department of Housing and Urban Development—"Little HUD," as it was called—did public housing in the area get serious attention. But despite the relatively meager results in terms of housing units actually completed, it should be clear that federal intervention beginning in the New Deal years shaped Miami's urban physical and spatial development.[28]

The Home Owners Loan Corporation

Another New Deal federal agency—the Home Owners Loan Corporation (HOLC)—had an equally pernicious influence on the development of segregated housing patterns in Miami, as well as in other cities. Established in 1933 the HOLC was designed to grant long-term, low-interest mortages to homeowners who were unable to secure regular mortgages, who were in danger of losing their homes through default or foreclosure, or who sought to recover homes already lost by foreclosure. The HOLC developed an elaborate appraisal and rating system by which to evaluate neighborhoods in every city. HOLC appraisers, usually local bankers and real estate men, assigned each neighborhood to one of four categories, beginning with the most desirable or "A" sections through the least desirable or "D" areas. These appraisal decisions were plotted on "residential security maps," on which the four categories were color-coded: green for those areas designated "A," blue for the "B," yellow for the "C," and red for the "D." These maps, the HOLC noted, "graphically reflect the trend of desirability in neighborhoods from a residential viewpoint." As urban historian Kenneth T. Jackson has suggested, the HOLC appraisal system actually initiated "redlining," the practice by banks and other lending institutions of refusing to grant mortgages or other loans in older, poorer, and black neighborhoods.[29]

How did redlining work in actual practice? The HOLC "residential security maps" were accompanied by detailed area descriptions compiled by the local appraisers. The area descriptions listed the characteristics of Miami

neighborhoods; the economic and occupational status of residents; positive
and detrimental influences in the neighborhood; and the type, age, and price
of buildings. In addition, the appraisers noted any "restrictions set up to
protect the neighborhood," an obvious reference to discriminatory deed
restrictions.[30] The HOLC made two such residential surveys in Miami during
the 1930s, one in 1936 and another in 1938.

In the surveys of Miami, as well as of other cities, the HOLC began with
a general statement describing the four different neighborhood categories.
The "A" areas were new and well planned, with a homogeneous population
and well-built, high-priced homes; these sections of Miami, HOLC appraisers
wrote in 1938, were "synonymous with the area where good mortgage lenders
with available funds are willing to make their maximum loans." The "B"
neighborhoods were slightly less good, although "still desirable." The houses
were older, the residents less wealthy, the areas less uniform in architecture
and building style, and the availability of mortgage money "slightly limited."[31]
The "C" category was assigned to sparsely developed sections on the metropolitan fringe and to areas of transition characterized by age, obsolescence,
poor building or maintenance, inadequate transportation and utilities, lack
of zoning or building restrictions, and closeness to black neighborhoods. They
were, HOLC appraisers said in 1936, "definitely declining." The least desirable "D" rating went to so-called hazardous areas, "neighborhoods in which
the things that are now taking place in the C neighborhoods have already
happened." Specifically, the "D" sections were inhabited by blacks and "low
grade white population" and characterized by such "detrimental influences"
as a low percentage of home ownership, dilapidated housing, poor sanitation,
industrial land uses, and nearness to trash dumps, incinerators, and railroads.[32]

Although the HOLC was a federal agency, its appraisal decisions were
made by local mortgage brokers and real estate men. The 1936 survey, for
instance, was prepared by a HOLC official and four Miami realtors. The
1938 survey was made by a HOLC man and seven local realtors and mortgage
bankers. The participation of Miami realtor and savings and loan president
Lon Worth Crow on both surveys typified the involvement of the city's civic
elite in the local workings of the HOLC. Arriving in Miami in 1913 from
west Florida, where he had operated a lumber and sawmill business, Crow
quickly became an inveterate city booster. He served for twenty-seven years
as a director of the Miami Realty Board and for several years in the 1920s
as president of the Miami Chamber of Commerce. As one admirer put it,
Crow "concerned himself with practically every kind of vital problem connected with his city and its life. He had a keen sense of civic pride and loyalty
to Miami and worked tirelessly for its welfare and growth." Similarly, a 1936
biographical sketch of Crow noted that he "has always been alert in fostering
any project beneficial to the Greater Miami area." Like John Gramling, Lon
Worth Crow found in the new federal housing programs an opportunity to
shape Miami to his own liking.[33]

As might be suspected, the HOLC appraisals of Miami neighborhoods
reflected the bias of the local appraisers. The 1936 survey assigned the "A"
designation to only a few small sections of the metropolitan area. These
included a portion of Miami Beach north of Lincoln Road, sections of Coral

Gables and Miami Shores, a few bayfront neighborhoods north and south of the business district, and the Biscayne Bay islands between Miami and Miami Beach. These were neighborhoods of larger and more expensive homes on sizable lots; their residents were "native-born whites" who ranged from "the extremely wealthy" to professionals, "salaried executives," and retired businessmen. It is not surprising to learn that the HOLC appraisers themselves lived in these same neighborhoods. Of the Miami Beach section, the appraisers noted with approval that "the northward movement of Jews from the southern part of the island . . . is limited in most cases by deed restrictions." The 1938 survey was even more parsimonious with the "A" rating, some of the north bayshore neighborhoods being downgraded to the "B" category.[34]

The appraisers were relatively generous in the assignment of the "B" rating in 1936. A few Miami Beach, Coral Gables, and Miami bayfront areas received this second-grade rating, as did a few older Miami neighborhoods (Riverside, Lawrence, Shenandoah, Shadowlawn, and Biltmore). However, the 1938 appraisal downgraded some of these areas to the "C" category because of the encroachment of businesses, tourist homes, and boarding houses, as well as the "infiltration of Cubans." (There is a sense of déjà vu here in this reference to exiles from the Cuban revolution of 1933).[35]

There were no "C" designations in 1936, but virtually the entire remainder of the metropolitan area received the lowest "D" rating. As might be expected, the downtown black section near the central business district was assigned to the "D" category. So also were "some of the outlying southwest sections of Miami and practically all of the northwest sections, including Hialeah." The brand new Liberty Square housing project of the PWA was also assigned the lowest rating, even though it was not yet completed.[36] The 1938 appraisers were even tougher in their real estate evaluations. Many "A" and "B" neighborhoods were downgraded, and a large number of new "C" and "D" areas were designated. The 1938 HOLC map reveals a smattering of green and blue, and a vast expanse of yellow and red covering the entire metropolitan area.[37] By 1938, Miami for all practical purposes had been redlined by the local real estate and banking community (see Map 2).

The Miami appraisers of the HOLC noted the hesitancy of banks and mortgage lenders to invest in the "C" and "D" neighborhoods. Mortgage money for home purchase or home building generally was described as "ample" in "A" and even some "B" areas. But in the "C" areas mortgage money was "limited." In the white, working-class Shadowlawn section, for instance, mortgage money was "limited," even though the area was "close to good transportation and schools and shopping centers" and despite the fact that portions of the area were "being improved with houses too good for the area." In the judgment of the HOLC appraisers, the "trend of desirability" of Shadowlawn over the next ten to fifteen years was "down."[38] Banks and other lending institutions were reluctant to invest in these "C" neighborhoods, even though their populations were entirely white. According to the HOLC these areas were in the process of "transition," a code word which meant that they were near black neighborhoods and that they might soon be less white and more black. For the "D" neighborhoods, a single word described the availability of mortgage money from local institutions—"None."[39]

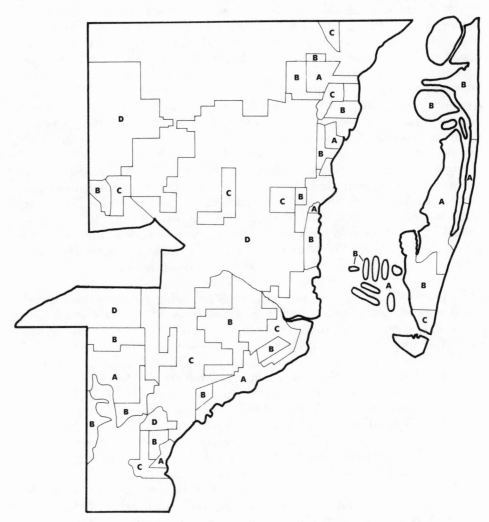

Map 2. 1938 Home Owners Loan Corporation map of Miami, showing allocation of neighborhoods to one of four appraisal categories.

The impact of the HOLC in Miami, it should be clear, was to consign the city's black sections, as well as adjacent white areas, to a future of physical decay and intensified racial segregation. Some HOLC mortgage loans were made in "C" and "D" neighborhoods, but local financial institutions strengthened their earlier discriminatory loan practices. As Jackson has written, "the damage caused by the HOLC came not through its own actions, but through the influence of its appraisal system on the financial decisions of other institutions."[40] HOLC "residential security maps" were available to local bankers (after all, they had an important role in drawing them up), and the HOLC appraisal categories were used in evaluating mortgage and loan applicants.

The Federal Housing Administration (FHA), which insured private mortages for home construction, also used the HOLC appraisal categories and probably the HOLC residential security maps. In fact, housing scholar Charles Abrams has written, the FHA "set itself up as the protector of the all-white neighborhood" and "became the vanguard of white supremacy and racial purity—in the North as well as the South." It is also clear that the FHA had a discriminatory loan record in Miami. According to Elizabeth Virrick, author of a 1960 study of Miami housing, it was "well-known locally that Negroes in Dade County were refused FHA commitments until recently."[41] Thus, the Home Owners Loan Corporation, a federal agency originally designed to help poor homeowners combat the Depression, was effectively turned against the people who most needed it.

The effect of federal redlining was to hasten the physical decay of the city and strengthen the process of residential segregation. Several studies have demonstrated that of more than one hundred large American cities, Miami had the highest degree of residential segregation by race in 1940, 1950, and 1960.[42] This was not a racial pattern that happened by accident. Residential segregation and the rapid physical deterioration of the black inner city, moreover, has had devastating human and social consequences in Miami. Race riots in 1968, 1980, and 1982 revealed the extent of black anger and frustration. A succession of studies has singled out housing as one of the most pervasive and serious grievances of Miami's blacks.[43] The redlining of urban America, initiated in the New Deal era by the Home Owners Loan Corporation and carried through by the Federal Housing Administration, has had devastating and long-term consequences for Miami.

This Miami research conforms to several recent studies elaborating the shaping impact of federal intervention on urban development and change since the 1930s.[44] The New Dealers put together a new Democratic coalition—one largely held together by a vast federal investment in urban employment programs and new urban construction. But although the funding came from Washington, the implementation and direction of these various urban programs were left to local governments and local leaders. The much-vaunted liberalism of the New Deal was often tempered in cities like Miami by segregation and the opportunism of local entrepreneurs.

NOTES

[1] Zane L. Miller, *The Urbanization of Modern America: A Brief History* (New York, 1973), 161; George E. Mowry and Blaine A. Brownell, *The Urban Nation, 1920–1980* (New York, 1981), 79. For a general overview of the subject, see William H. Wilson, "A Great Impact, A Gingerly Investigation: Historians and the Federal Effect on Urban Development," in Jerome Finster, ed., *The National Archives and Urban Research* (Athens, OH, 1974), 113–23.

[2] Bruce M. Stave, *The New Deal and the Last Hurrah: Pittsburgh Machine Politics* (Pittsburgh, 1970); Lyle W. Dorsett, *The Pendergast Machine* (New York, 1968); Lyle W. Dorsett, *Franklin D. Roosevelt and the City Bosses* (Port Washington, NY, 1977); Charles H. Trout, *Boston, The Great Depression, and the New Deal* (New York, 1977). See also the essays by Stave and Dorsett in John Braeman et al., eds., *The New Deal: The State and Local Levels* (Columbus, OH, 1975), 376–419.

[3] Mark S. Foster, *From Streetcar to Superhighway: American City Planners and Urban Transportation, 1900–1940* (Philadelphia, 1981).

[4]Charles Abrams, *Forbidden Neighbors: A Study of Prejudice in Housing* (New York, 1955), 229–30; Stephen J. Diner and Helen Young, eds., *Housing Washington's People: Public Policy in Retrospect* (Washington, DC, 1983), 169–75; Kenneth T. Jackson, *Crabgrass Frontier: The Suburbanization of the United States* (New York, 1985), 190–230; Joseph L. Arnold, *The New Deal in the Suburbs: A History of the Greenbelt Town Program, 1935–1954* (Columbus, OH, 1971).

[5]Public Works Administration, *America Builds: The Record of the PWA* (Washington, DC, 1939), 207–17; Timothy L. McDonnell, *The Wagner Housing Act: A Case Study of the Legislative Process* (Chicago, 1957), 29–50; Mark I. Gelfand, *A Nation of Cities: The Federal Government and Urban America, 1933–1965* (New York, 1975), 59–65.

[6]"Application of the Southern Housing Corporation, Miami, Florida, to the Administration of Public Works, Division of Housing, Washington, DC, for Financing Low Cost Housing Project at Miami, Florida," December 19, 1933, Records of the Public Housing Administration (hereafter cited as PHA Records), Record Group 196, Box 299, National Archives, Washington, DC; Horatio B. Hackett to Harold L. Ickes, October 18, 1934, ibid., Box 297; A. R. Clas to M. J. Orr, July 15, 1935, ibid., Box 299.

[7]*Miami Herald*, January 28, August 29, 1934; Chas. S. Thompson, "The Growth of Colored Miami," *The Crisis* 49 (March 1942): 83–84; Paul S. George, "Colored Town: Miami's Black Community, 1896–1930," *Florida Historical Quarterly* 56 (April 1978): 432–47.

[8]"Application of the Southern Housing Corporation," PHA Records, Box 299.

[9]Raymond A. Mohl, "Black Immigrants: Bahamians in Early Twentieth-Century Miami," *Florida Historical Quarterly* 65 (January 1987): 271–97; Reinhold P. Wolff and David K. Gillogly, *Negro Housing in the Miami Area: Effects of the Postwar Building Boom* (Coral Gables, FL, 1951); Elizabeth L. Virrick, "New Housing for Negroes in Dade County, Florida," in Nathan Glazer and Davis McEntire, eds., *Studies in Housing and Minority Groups* (Berkeley, CA, 1960), 135–43; Harold M. Rose, "Metropolitan Miami's Changing Negro Population, 1950–1960," *Economic Geography* 40 (July 1964): 221–38. On blacks in Miami, see Warren M. Banner, *An Appraisal of Progress, 1943–1953* (New York, 1953); and James W. Morrison, *The Negro in Greater Miami* (Miami, 1962). For an interpretation of the thought and activities of the "civic elite" in the urban South, see Blaine A. Brownell, *The Urban Ethos in the South, 1920–1930* (Baton Rouge, 1975).

[10]E. V. Blackman, *Miami and Dade County, Florida: Its Settlement, Progress and Achievement* (Washington, DC, 1921), 104–5; Tracy Hollingsworth, *History of Dade County, Florida* (Miami, 1936), 146.

[11]Dozens of Gramling letters to federal housing officials can be found in PHA Records, Boxes 297–301.

[12]*Miami Herald*, August 9, 1934; John L. Gramling to Eugene H. Klaber, January 22, 1934, PHA Records, Box 301; Clas to Orr, July 15, 1935, ibid., Box 299.

[13]*Miami Times*, January 20, 1934, clipping, PHA Records, Box 301; R. E. S. Toomey to Robert D. Kohn, January 15, 1934, ibid., Box 299; Miami Colored Chamber of Commerce, "To Whom It May Concern," May 17, 1935, PHA Records, Box. 301.

[14]Gramling to Klaber, January 24, 1934, PHA Records, Box 301.

[15]Floyd W. Davis to Clas, July 28, August 13, 1935, PHA Records, Box 301; Tom Petersen, "Reaching for Utopia: The Origins of the Liberty Square Housing Project," unpublished manuscript, 12.

[16]Paul S. George, "Criminal Justice in Miami, 1896–1930" (Ph.D. diss., Florida State University, 1975), 158–59.

[17]A. B. Small to Clas, May 31, 1935, PHA Records, Box 298.

[18][Miami] *Friday Night*, January 12, 1934, clipping, PHA Records, Box 301; Gramling to Klaber, February 19, 1934, ibid., Box 299; Gramling to Hackett, October 17, 1934, ibid., Box 301.

[19]Gramling to Klaber, February 19, 1934, PHA Records, Box 299.

[20]Isabelle Sanderson to Hackett, April 19, 1935, PHA Records, Box 297; Sanderson to Clas, May 17, 1935, ibid., Box 297.

[21]*Miami Herald*, February 21, 1934. On Miami's growth during this period, see Raymond A. Mohl, "Miami: The Ethnic Cauldron," in Richard M. Bernard and Bradley R. Rice, eds., *Sunbelt Cities: Politics and Growth since World War II* (Austin, 1983), 58–99.

[22]George E. Merrick, *Planning the Greater Miami for Tomorrow* (Miami, 1937), 11.

[23]Dade County Planning Board, Minutes, August 27, 1936, typescript in George E. Merrick Papers, Box 2, Historical Association of Southern Florida, Miami; Dade County Planning Council, "Negro Resettlement Plan," 1937, mimeo in National Urban League Papers, pt. 1, ser. 6, Box 56, Library of Congress.

[24]Abrams, *Forbidden Neighbors*, 120–36; Stetson Kennedy, "Miami: Anteroom to Fascism," *The Nation* 173 (December 1951): 546–47.

[25]Recent studies confirming this pattern for other cities include Arnold R. Hirsch, *Making the Second Ghetto: Race and Housing in Chicago, 1940–1960* (Cambridge, 1983); and Dominic J. Capeci, Jr., *Race Relations in Wartime Detroit: The Sojourner Truth Housing Controversy, 1937–1942* (Philadelphia, 1984).

[26]*Miami Negroes: A Study in Depth* (Miami, 1968), 23; Rose, "Metropolitan Miami's Changing Negro Population," 224. For the negative consequences of highway urban renewal programs generally, consult Martin Anderson, *The Federal Bulldozer: A Critical Analysis of Urban Renewal, 1949–1962* (Cambridge, 1964); Scott Greer, *Urban Renewal and American Cities: The Dilemma of Democratic Intervention* (Indianapolis, 1965); and Sam Bass Warner, Jr., *The Urban Wilderness: A History of the American City* (New York, 1972), 37–52.

[27]Robert M. Press, "Miami's Overtown: Blacks Fight Inequality to Revive Community," *Christian Science Monitor*, March 20, 1984; *Miami Herald*, November 30, December 28, 1981, January 5, 1982, December 2, 1983, May 19, June 26, August 12, 1984, August 10, September 7, 1986; *Miami Times*, December 16, 1982, June 5, 1986; *Miami News*, October 6, 1983, May 1, 1984.

[28]*Better Housing: [First] Report of the Housing Authority of the City of Miami* (Miami, 1940); Haley Sofge, "Public Housing in Miami," *Florida Planning and Development* 19 (March 1968): 1–4; Aileen Lotz, "The Birth of 'Little Hud,'" ibid. 19 (January 1968): 1–3, 6; and (February 1968): 1–3, 12. See also Richard O. Davies, "One-third of a Nation: The Dilemmas of America's Housing, 1607–1970," in Finster, *The National Archives and Urban Research*, 41–55.

[29]"Security Area Map, Miami, Florida," and "Analysis of Realty Area Map of Miami, Florida," both 1936, Records of the Home Owners Loan Corporation (hereafter cited as HOLC Records), Record Group 195, National Archives, Washington, DC; "Security Area Descriptions: Metropolitan Miami, Florida," September 24, 1938, ibid. See also Jackson, *Crabgrass Frontier*, 190–218; Lowell C. Harriss, *History and Policies of the Home Owners' Loan Corporation* (New York, 1951).

[30]"Security Area Descriptions: Metropolitan Miami," 1938, HOLC Records.

[31]Ibid.

[32]"Security Area Map" and "Analysis of Realty Area Map of Miami," 1936, HOLC Records.

[33]Hollingsworth, *History of Dade County*, 118–20; *The East Coast of Florida*, 3 vols. (Delray Beach, FL, 1962), 3:532.

[34]"Analysis of Realty Area Map of Miami," 1936, HOLC Records; "Security Area Descriptions: Metropolitan Miami," 1938, ibid.

[35]Ibid.

[36]"Analysis of Realty Area Map of Miami," 1936, ibid.

[37]"Security Area Map, Miami, Florida," 1938, ibid.

[38]"Security Area Descriptions: Metropolitan Miami," 1938, ibid.

[39]Ibid.

[40]Jackson, *Crabgrass Frontier*, 203.

[41]Ibid., 203, 213–15; Abrams, *Forbidden Neighbors*, 229–30; Virrick, "New Housing for Negroes in Dade County," 140.

[42]Donald O. Cowgill, "Trends in Residential Segregation of Non-Whites in American Cities, 1940–1950," *American Sociological Review* 21 (February 1956): 43–47; Karl E. Taeuber and Alma F. Taeuber, *Negroes in Cities: Residential Segregation and Neighborhood Change* (Chicago, 1965), 40–41; Annemette Sorenson et al., "Indexes of Racial Residential Segregation for 109 Cities in the United States, 1940–1970," *Sociological Focus* 8 (1975): 125–42.

[43]National Commission on the Causes and Prevention of Violence, *Miami Report: The Report of the Miami Study Team on Civil Disturbances in Miami, Florida, during the Week of August 5, 1968* (Washington, DC, 1969); U.S. Commission on Civil Rights, *Confronting Racial Isolation in Miami* (Washington, DC, 1982); Bruce Porter and Marvin Dunn, *The Miami Riot of 1980: Crossing the Bounds* (Lexington, MA, 1984).

[44]John H. Mollenkopf, *The Contested City* (Princeton, NJ: 1983); Roger W. Lotchin, ed., *The Martial Metropolis: U.S. Cities in War and Peace* (New York, 1984).

The Drive-in Culture of Contemporary America

*Kenneth T. Jackson**

The postwar years brought unprecedented prosperity to the United States, as color televisions, stereo systems, frost-free freezers, electric blenders, and automatic garbage disposals became basic equipment in the middle-class American home. But the best symbol of individual success and identity was a sleek, air-conditioned, high-powered, personal statement on wheels. Between 1950 and 1980, when the American population increased by 50 percent, the number of their automobiles increased by 200 percent. In high school the most important rite of passage came to be the earning of a driver's license and the freedom to press an accelerator to the floor. Educational administrators across the country had to make parking space for hundreds of student vehicles. A car became one's identity, and the important question was: "What does he drive?" Not only teenagers, but also millions of older persons literally defined themselves in terms of the number, cost, style, and horse-power of their vehicles. "Escape," thinks a character in a novel by Joyce Carol Oates. "As long as he had his own car he was an American and could not die."

Unfortunately, Americans did die, often behind the wheel. On September 9, 1899, as he was stepping off a streetcar at 74th Street and Central Park West in New York, Henry H. Bliss was struck and killed by a motor vehicle, thus becoming the first fatality in the long war between flesh and steel. Thereafter, the carnage increased almost annually until Americans were sustaining about 50,000 traffic deaths and about 2 million nonfatal injuries per year. Automobility proved to be far more deadly than war for the United States. It was as if a Pearl Harbor attack took place on the highways every two weeks, with crashes becoming so commonplace that an entire industry sprang up to provide medical, legal, and insurance services for the victims.

The environmental cost was almost as high as the human toll. In 1984 the 159 million cars, trucks, and buses on the nation's roads were guzzling millions of barrels of oil every day, causing traffic jams that shattered nerves and clogged the cities they were supposed to open up and turning much of

*Kenneth T. Jackson is professor of history at Columbia University. Reprinted from Crabgrass Frontier: The Suburbanization of the United States by Kenneth T. Jackson. Copyright 1985 by Oxford University Press. Reprinted by permission.

228

the countryside to pavement. Not surprisingly, when gasoline shortages created long lines at the pumps in 1974 and 1979, behavioral scientists noted that many people experienced anger, depression, frustration, and insecurity, as well as a formidable sense of loss.[1]

Such reactions were possible because the automobile and the suburb have combined to create a drive-in culture that is part of the daily experience of most Americans. Because of unemployment and war, per capita motor vehicle ownership was stable (at about 30 million vehicles) between 1930 and 1948, and as late as 1950 (when registrations had jumped to 49 million) an astonishing 41 percent of all American families and a majority of working-class families still did not own a car. Postwar prosperity and rising real wages, however, made possible vastly higher market penetration, and by 1984 there were about seventy motor vehicles for every one hundred citizens, and more cars than either households or workers. Schaeffer and Sclar have argued that high auto ownership is the result of real economic needs rather than some "love affair" with private transportation. Moreover, the American people have proven to be no more prone to motor vehicle purchases than the citizens of other lands. After World War II, the Europeans and the Japanese began to catch up, and by 1980 both had achieved the same level of automobile ownership that the United States had reached in 1950. In automotive technology, American dominance slipped away in the postwar years as German, Swedish, and Japanese engineers pioneered the development of diesel engines, front-wheel drives, disc brakes, fuel-injection, and rotary engines.[2]

Although it is not accurate to speak of a uniquely American love affair with the automobile, and although John B. Rae claimed too much when he wrote in 1971 that "modern suburbia is a creature of the automobile and could not exist without it," the motor vehicle has fundamentally restructured the pattern of everyday life in the United States. As a young man, Lewis Mumford advised his countrymen to "forget the damned motor car and build cities for lovers and friends." As it was, of course, the nation followed a different pattern. Writing in the *American Builder* in 1929, the critic Willard Morgan noted that the building of drive-in structures to serve a motor-driven population had ushered in "a completely new architectural form."[3]

The Interstate Highway

The most popular exhibit at the New York World's Fair in 1939 was General Motors' "Futurama." Looking twenty-five years ahead, it offered a "magic Aladdin-like flight through time and space." Fair-goers stood in hour-long lines, waiting to travel on a moving sidewalk above a huge model created by designer Norman Bel Geddes. Miniature superhighways with 50,000 automated cars wove past model farms en route to model cities. Five million persons peered eventually at such novelties as elevated freeways, expressway traffic moving at 100 miles per hour, and "modern and efficient city planning—breath-taking architecture—each city block a complete unit in itself (with) broad, one-way thoroughfares—space, sunshine, light, and air." The message of "Futurama" was as impressive as its millions of model parts: "The job of building the future is one which will demand our best energies, our most fruitful imagination; and that with it will come greater opportunities for all."[4]

The promise of a national system of impressive roadways attracted a diverse group of lobbyists, including the Automobile Manufacturers Association, state-highway administrators, motor-bus operators, the American Trucking Association, and even the American Parking Association—for the more cars on the road, the more cars would be parked at the end of the journey. Truck companies, for example, promoted legislation to spend state gasoline taxes on highways, rather than on schools, hospitals, welfare, or public transit. In 1943 these groups came together as the American Road Builders Association, with General Motors as the largest contributor, to form a lobbying enterprise second only to that of the munitions industry. By the mid-1950s, it had become one of the most broad-based of all pressure groups, consisting of the oil, rubber, asphalt, and construction industries; the car dealers and renters; the trucking and bus concerns; the banks and advertising agencies that depended upon the companies involved; and the labor unions. On the local level, professional real estate groups and home-builders associations joined the movement in the hope that highways would cause a spurt in housing turnover and a jump in prices. They envisaged no mere widening of existing roads, but the creation of an entirely new superhighway system and the initiation of the largest peacetime construction project in history.[5]

The highway lobby inaugurated a comprehensive public relations program in 1953 by sponsoring a national essay contest on the need for better roads. The winner of the $25,000 grand prize was Robert Moses, the greatest builder the world has yet known and a passionate advocate of the urban expressway. The title of his work was "How to Plan and Pay for Better Highways." As his biographer Robert A. Caro has noted, Moses was "the world's most vocal, effective and prestigious apologist for the automobile," and he did more than any other single urban official to encourage more hesitant officials to launch major road-building efforts in their cities.[6]

The Cold War provided an additional stimulus to the campaign for more elaborate expressways. In 1951 the *Bulletin of the Atomic Scientists* devoted an entire issue to "Defense through Decentralization." Their argument was simple. To avoid national destruction in a nuclear attack, the United States should disperse existing large cities into smaller settlements. The ideal model was a depopulated urban core surrounded by satellite cities and low-density suburbs.

Sensitive to mounting political pressure, President Dwight Eisenhower appointed a committee in 1954 to "study" the nation's highway requirements. Its conclusions were foregone, in part because the chairman was Lucius D. Clay, a member of the board of directors of General Motors. The committee considered no alternative to a massive highway system, and it suggested a major redirection of national policy to benefit the car and the truck. The Interstate Highway Act became law in 1956, when the Congress provided for a 41,000-mile (eventually expanded to a 42,500-mile) system, with the federal government paying 90 percent of the cost. President Eisenhower gave four reasons for signing the measure: current highways were unsafe; cars too often became snarled in traffic jams; poor roads saddled business with high costs for transportation; and modern highways were needed because "in case of atomic attack on our key cities, the road net must permit quick evacuation of target areas." Not a single word was said about the impact of highways on cities and suburbs, although the concrete thoroughfares and the thirty-five-ton tractor-trailers which used them encouraged the continued outward movement of industries toward the beltways and interchanges. Moreover, the interstate system helped continue the downward spiral of public transportation and virtually guaranteed that future urban growth would perpetuate a centerless sprawl. Soon after the bill was passed by the Senate, Lewis Mumford wrote sadly: "When the American people, through their Congress, voted a little while ago for a $26 billion highway program, the most charitable thing to assume is that they hadn't the faintest notion of what they were doing."

Once begun, the Interstate Highway System of the United States became a concrete colossus that grew bigger with every passing year. The secret of its success lay in the principle of nondivertibility of highway revenues collected from gasoline taxes. The Highway Trust Fund, as it was called, was to be held separately from general taxes. Although no less a personage than Winston Churchill called the idea of a nondivertible road fund "nonsense," "absurd," and "an outrage upon . . . common sense," the trust fund had powerful friends in the United States, and it easily swept all opposition before it. Unlike European governments, Washington used taxes to support the highway infrastructure while refusing assistance to railroads. According to Senator Gaylord Nelson of Wisconsin, 75 percent of government expenditures for transportation in the United States in the postwar generation went for highways as opposed to 1 percent for urban mass transit.[7]

The inevitable result of the bias in American transport funding, a bias that existed for a generation before the Interstate Highway program was initiated, is that the United States now has the world's best road system and very nearly its worst public transit offerings. Los Angeles, in particular, provides the nation's most dramatic example of urban sprawl tailored to the mobility of the automobile. Its vast, amorphous conglomeration of housing tracts, shopping centers, industrial parks, freeways, and independent towns blend into each other in a seamless fabric of concrete and asphalt, and nothing over the years has succeeded in gluing this automobile-oriented civilization into any kind of cohesion—save that of individual routine. Los Angeles's basic shape comes from three factors, all of which long preceded the freeway system. The first was cheap land (in the 1920s rather than 1970s) and the desire for single-family houses. In 1950, for example, nearly two-thirds of all the dwelling units in the Los Angeles area were fully detached, a much higher percentage than in Chicago (28 percent), New York City (20 percent), or Philadelphia (15 percent), and its residential density was the lowest of major cities. The second was the dispersed location of its oil fields and refineries, which led to the creation of industrial suburbs like Whittier and Fullerton and of residential suburbs like La Habra, which housed oil workers and their families. The third was its once excellent mass transit system, which at its peak included more than 1,100 miles of track and constituted the largest electric interurban railway in the world.[8]

The Pacific Electric Company collapsed in the 1920s, however, and since that time Los Angeles has been more dependent upon the private automobile than other large American cities. Beginning in 1942, the Los Angeles Chamber of Commerce, the automobile club, and elected officials met regularly to plan for a region-wide expressway network. They succeeded, and southern California's fabled 715 miles of freeways now constitute a grid that channels virtually all traffic and sets many communal boundaries. They are the primary form of transportation for most residents, who seem to regard time spent in their cars as more pleasurable than time walking to, waiting for, or riding on the bus. More than a third of the Los Angeles area is consumed by highways, parking lots, and interchanges, and in the downtown section this proportion rises to two-thirds. Not surprisingly, efforts to restore the region's public transportation to excellence have thus far failed. In 1976, for example, the state of California attempted to discourage single-passenger automobiles by reserving one lane in each direction on the Santa Monica Freeway for express buses and car pools. An emotional explosion ensued that dominated radio talk shows and television news, and Los Angeles's so-called "diamond lanes" were soon abolished.[9]

More recently, southern California has followed the growing national enthusiasm for rail transit, and Los Angeles broke ground in 1984 for an eighteen-mile, $3.3 billion subway that will cut underneath the densely built, heavily trafficked Wilshire Boulevard corridor, cut through Hollywood, and end up in the residential San Fernando Valley. The underground will hopefully be the centerpiece of an eventual 160-mile network, second in size in the United States only to New York City's.

The Garage

The drive-in structure that is closest to the hearts, bodies, and cars of the American family is the garage. It is the link between the home and the outside world. The word is French, meaning storage space, but its transformation into a multipurpose enclosure internally integrated with the dwelling is distinctively American.

In the streetcar era, curbs had been unbroken and driveways were almost unknown. A family wealthy enough to have a horse and carriage would have stored such possessions either in a public livery stable or in a private structure at the rear of the property. The owners of the first automobiles were usually sufficiently affluent to maintain a private stable. The first cars, therefore, which were open to the elements, often found lodging in a corner of the stable, side by side with the carriages they were soon to replace. These early accommodations for the automobile were often provided with gasoline tanks, for filling stations at the time were few and far between. This and the fact that cars often caught fire were good and sufficient reasons to keep the motor vehicles away from the family.[10]

After World War I, house plans of the expensive variety began to include garages, and by the mid-1920s driveways were commonplace and garages had become important selling points. The popular 1928 *Home Builders* pattern book offered designs for fifty garages in wood, Tudor, and brick varieties. In affluent sections, such large and efficiently planned structures included housing above for the family chauffeur. In less pretentious neighborhoods, the small, single-purpose garages were scarcely larger than the vehicles themselves, and they were simply portable and prefabricated structures, similar to those in Quebec today, that were camouflaged with greenery and trellises. As one architect complained in 1924: "The majority of owners are really ashamed of their garages and really endeavor to keep them from view," and he implored his readers to build a garage "that may be worthy of standing alongside your house." Although there was a tendency to move garages closer to the house, they typically remained at the rear of the property before 1925, often with access via an alley which ran parallel to the street. The car was still thought of as something similar to a horse—dependable and important, but not something that one needed to be close to in the evening.[11]

By 1935, however, the garage was beginning to merge into the house itself, and in 1937 the *Architectural Record* noted that "the garage has become a very essential part of the residence." The tendency accelerated after World War II, as alleys went the way of the horse-drawn wagon, as property widths more often exceeded fifty feet, and as the car became not only a status symbol, but almost a member of the family, to be cared for and sheltered. The introduction of a canopied and unenclosed structure called a "car port" represented an inexpensive solution to the problem, particularly in mild climates, but in the 1950s the enclosed garage was back in favor and a necessity even in a tract house. Easy access to the automobile became a key aspect of residential design, and not only for the well-to-do. By the 1960s garages often occupied about 400 square feet (about one-third that of the house itself) and usually contained space for two automobiles and a variety of lawn and woodworking tools. Offering direct access to the house (a conveniently placed door usually led directly into the kitchen), the garage had become an integrated part of the dwelling, and it dominated the front facades of new houses. In California garages and driveways were often so prominent that the house could almost be described as accessory to the garage. Few people, however, went to the extremes common in England, where the automobile was often so precious that living rooms were often converted to garages.[12]

The Motel

As the United States became a rubber-tire civilization, a new kind of roadside architecture was created to convey an instantly recognizable image to the fast-moving traveler. Criticized as tasteless, cheap, forgettable, and flimsy by most commentators, drive-in structures did attract the attention of some talented architects, most notably Los Angeles's Richard Neutra. For him, the automobile symbolized modernity, and its design paralleled his own ideals of precision and efficiency. This correlation between the structure and the car began to be celebrated in the late 1960s and 1970s when architects Robert Venturi, Denise Scott Brown, and Steven Izenour developed such concepts as "architecture as symbol" and the "architecture of communication." Their book, *Learning From Las Vegas*, was instrumental in encouraging a shift in taste from general condemnation to appreciation of the commercial strip and especially of the huge and garish signs which were easily recognized by passing motorists.[13]

A ubiquitous example of the drive-in culture is the motel. In the middle of the nineteenth century, every city, every county seat, every aspiring mining town, every wide place in the road with aspirations to larger size, had to have a hotel. Whether such structures were grand palaces on the order of Boston's Tremont House or New York's Fifth Avenue Hotel, or whether they were jerry-built shacks, they were typically located at the center of the business district, at the focal point of community activities. To a considerable extent, the hotel was the place for informal social interaction and business, and the very heart and soul of the city.[14]

Between 1910 and 1920, however, increasing numbers of traveling motorists created a market for overnight accommodation along the highways. The first tourists simply camped wherever they chose along the road. By 1924, several thousand municipal campgrounds were opened which offered cold water spigots and outdoor privies. Next came the "cabin camps," which consisted of tiny, white clapboard cottages arranged in a semicircle and often set in a grove of trees. Initially called "tourist courts," these establishments were cheap, convenient, and informal, and by 1926 there were an estimated two thousand of them, mostly in the West and in Florida.

Soon after clean linens and comfortable rooms became available along the nation's highways, it became apparent that overnight travelers were not the only, or even the largest, pool of customers. Convenience and privacy were especially appealing to couples seeking a romantic retreat. A well-publicized Southern Methodist University study in 1935 reported that 75 percent of Dallas area motel business consisted of one man and one woman remaining for only a short stay. Whatever the motivation of patrons, the success of the new-style hotels prompted Sinclair Lewis to predict in 1920:

> Somewhere in these states there is a young man who is going to become
> rich. He is going to start a chain of small, clean, pleasant hotels, standardized
> and nationally advertised, along every important motor route in the country.
> He is not going to waste money on gilt and onyx, but he is going to have
> agreeable clerks, good coffee, endurable mattresses and good lighting.[15]

It was not until 1952 that Kemmons Wilson and Wallace E. Johnson opened their first "Holiday Inn" on Summer Avenue in Memphis. But long before that, in 1926, a San Luis Obispo, California, proprietor had coined a new word, "motel," to describe an establishment that allowed a guest to park his car just outside his room. New terminology did not immediately erase the unsavory image of the roadside establishments, however. In 1940 FBI Director J. Edgar Hoover declared that most motels were assignation camps and hideouts for criminals. Perhaps he was thinking of Bonnie and Clyde, who had a brief encounter with the law at the Red Crown Cabin Camp near Platte City, Missouri, one evening in July of 1933. Many of Hoover's "dens of vice" were once decent places that, unable to keep up, turned to the "hot pillow trade." Some Texas cabins, said the FBI director, were rented as many as sixteen times a night, while establishments elsewhere did business by the hour, with "a knock on the door when the hour was up."[16]

Motels began to thrive after World War II, when the typical establishment was larger and more expensive than the earlier cabins. Major chains set standards for prices, services, and respectability that the traveling public could depend on. As early as 1948, there were 26,000 self-styled motels in the United States. Hard-won respectability attracted more middle-class families, and by 1960 there were 60,000 such places, a figure that doubled again by 1972. By that time an old hotel was closing somewhere in downtown America every thirty hours. And somewhere in suburban America, a plastic and glass Shangri-La was rising to take its place.[17]

Typical of the inner-city hotels was the Heritage in Detroit. The big bands once played on its roof, and aspiring socialites enjoyed crepe-thin pancakes. In 1975 a disillusioned former employee gestured futilely, "It's dying; the whole place is dying," as the famed hotel closed its doors. By 1984 about fifty historic establishments in downtown areas, such as the Peabody in Memphis, the Mayflower in Washington, the Galvez in Houston, the Menger in San Antonio, and the Biltmore in Providence were reopening with antique-filled rooms and oak-paneled bars. But the trend remained with the standard, two-story motel.[18]

The Drive-in Theater

The downtown movie theaters and old vaudeville houses faced a similar challenge from the automobile. In 1933 Richard M. Hollinshead set up a 16-mm projector in front of his garage in Riverton, New Jersey, and then settled down to watch a movie. Recognizing a nation addicted to the motorcar when he saw one, Hollinshead and Willis Smith opened the world's first drive-in movie in a forty-car parking lot in Camden on June 6, 1933. Hollinshead profited only slightly from his brainchild, however, because in 1938 the United States Supreme Court refused to hear his appeal against Loew's Theaters, thus accepting the argument that the drive-in movie was not a patentable item. The idea never caught on in Europe, but by 1958 more than four thousand outdoor screens dotted the American landscape. Because drive-ins offered bargain-basement prices and double or triple bills, the theaters tended to favor movies that were either second-run or second-rate. Horror films and teenage romance were the order of the night, as *Beach Blanket Bingo* or *Invasion of the Body Snatchers* typified the offerings. Pundits often commented that there was a better show in the cars than on the screen.[19]

In the 1960s and 1970s the drive-in movie began to slip in popularity. Rising fuel costs and a season that lasted only six months contributed to the problem, but skyrocketing land values were the main factor. When drive-ins were originally opened, they were typically out in the hinterlands. When subdivisions and shopping malls came closer, the drive-ins could not match the potential returns from other forms of investments. According to the National Association of Theater Owners, only 2,935 open-air theaters still operated in the United States in 1983, even though the total number of commercial movie screens in the nation, 18,772, was at a thirty-five-year high. The increase was picked up not by the downtown and the neighborhood theaters, but by new multiscreen cinemas in shopping centers. Realizing that the large parking lots of indoor malls were relatively empty in the evening, shopping center moguls came to regard theaters as an important part of a successful retailing mix.[20]

The Gasoline Service Station

The purchase of gasoline in the United States has thus far passed through five distinct epochs. The first stage was clearly the worst for the motorist, who had to buy fuel by the bucketful at a livery stable, repair shop, or dry goods store. Occasionally, vendors sold gasoline from small tank cars which they pushed up and down the streets. In any event, the automobile owner had to pour gasoline from a bucket through a funnel into his tank. The entire procedure was inefficient, smelly, wasteful, and occasionally dangerous.[21]

The second stage began about 1905, when C. H. Laessig of St. Louis equipped a hot-water heater with a glass gauge and a garden hose and turned the whole thing on its end. With this simple maneuver, he invented an easy way to transfer gasoline from a storage tank to an automobile without using a bucket. Later in the same year, Sylvanus F. Bowser invented a gasoline pump which automatically measured the outflow. The entire assembly was labeled a "filling station." At this stage, which lasted until about 1920, such an apparatus consisted of a single pump outside a retail store which was primarily engaged in other businesses and which provided precious few services for the motorist. Many were located on the edge of town for safety and to be near the bulk stations; those few stations in the heart of the city did not even afford the luxury of off-street parking.

Between 1920 and 1950, service stations entered into a third phase and became, as a group, one of the most widespread kinds of commercial buildings in the United States. Providing under one roof all the functions of gasoline distribution and normal automotive maintenance, these full-service structures were often built in the form of little colonial houses, Greek temples, Chinese pagodas, and Art Deco palaces. Many were local landmarks and a source of community pride. One cartoonist in the 1920s mocked such structures with a drawing in which a newcomer to town confused the gas station with the state capitol. Grandiose at the time, many of them molder today—deserted, forlorn structures with weeds growing in the concrete where gasoline pumps once stood. Their bays stand empty and silent, rendered that way by changing economics, changing styles, and changing consumer preferences.

After 1935 the gasoline station evolved again, this time into a more homogeneous entity that was standardized across the entire country and that reflected the mass-marketing techniques of billion-dollar oil companies. Some of the more familiar designs were innovative or memorable, such as the drumlike Mobile station by New York architect Frederick Frost, which featured a dramatically curving facade while conveying the corporate identity. Another popular service station style was the Texaco design of Walter Dorwin Teague— a smooth white exterior with elegant trim and the familiar red star and bold red lettering. Whatever the product or design, the stations tended to be operated by a single entrepreneur and represented an important part of small business in American life.

The fifth stage of gasoline-station development began in the 1970s, with the slow demise of the traditional service-station businessman. New gasoline outlets were of two types. The first was the super station, often owned and operated by the oil companies themselves. Most featured a combination of self-service and full-service pumping consoles, as well as fully equipped "car care centers." Service areas were separated from the pumping sections so that the two functions would not interfere with each other. Mechanics never broke off work to sell gas.

The more pervasive second type might be termed the "mini-mart station." The operators of such establishments have now gone full circle since the early twentieth century. Typically, they know nothing about automobiles and expect the customers themselves to pump the gasoline. Thus, "the man who wears the star" has given way to the teenager who sells six-packs, bags of ice, and preprepared sandwiches.[22]

The Shopping Center

Large-scale retailing, long associated with central business districts, began moving away from the urban cores between the world wars. The first experiments to capture the growing suburban retail markets were made by major department stores in New York and Chicago in the 1920s, with Robert E. Wood, Sears's vice president in charge of factories and retail stores, as the leader of the movement. A student of population trends, Wood decided in 1925 that motor-vehicle registrations had outstripped the parking space available in metropolitan cores, and he insisted that Sears's new "A" stores (their other retail outlets were much smaller) be located in low-density areas which would offer the advantages of lower rentals and yet, because of the automobile, be within reach of potential customers. With the exception of Sears's flagship store on State Street in Chicago (which was itself closed in 1983), Woods's dictum of ample free parking was rigorously followed throughout the United States. Early examples of the formula were the Pico Boulevard store in Los Angeles and the Crosstown store in Memphis. A revolution in retailing followed. Writing in the *American Builder* in 1929, the critic Willard Morgan found it natural that traffic congestion at the center would drive thousands of prospective customers to turn instead to suburban marketing centers.[23]

Another threat to the primacy of the central business district was the "string street" or "shopping strip," which emerged in the 1920s and which was designed to serve vehicular rather than pedestrian traffic. These bypass roads encouraged city dwellers with cars to patronize businesses on the outskirts of town. Short parades of shops could already have been found near the streetcar and rapid transit stops, but, as has been noted, these new retailing thoroughfares generally radiated out from the city business district toward low-density, residential areas, functionally dominating the urban street system. They were the prototypes for the familiar highway strips of the 1980s which stretch far into the countryside.[24]

Sears's big stores were initially isolated from other stores, while the retail establishments of highway strips were rarely unified into a coordinated whole. The multiple-store shopping center with free, off-street parking represented the ultimate retail adaptation to the requirements of automobility. Although the *Guinness Book of World Records* lists the Roland Park Shopping Center (1896) as the world's first shopping center, the first of the modern variety was Country Club Plaza in Kansas City. It was the effort of a single entrepreneur, Jesse Clyde Nichols, who put together a concentration of retail stores, and used leasing policy to determine the composition of stores in the concentration. By doing that, Nichols created the idea of the planned regional shopping center.

Begun in 1923 in a Spanish-Moorish style with red tile roofs and little towers—its Giralda Tower is actually a replica of the original in Seville— Country Club Plaza featured waterfalls, fountains, flowers, tree-lined walks, and expensive landscaping. As the first automobile-oriented shopping center, it offered extensive parking lots behind ornamented brick walls. Most buildings were two stories high, with the second-floor offices typically occupied by physicians, dentists, and attorneys, whose presence would help stimulate a constant flow of well-heeled visitors. An enormous commercial success, Country Club Plaza stood in organic harmony with the prairie surroundings, and it soon became the hub of Kansas City's business and cultural activities.[25]

Nichols's Country Club Plaza generated considerable favorable publicity after it became fully operational in 1925, and by the mid-1930s the concept of the planned shopping center, as a concentration of a number of businesses under one management and with convenient parking facilities, was well known and was recognized as the best method of serving the growing market of drive-in customers. But the Great Depression and World War II had a chilling effect on private construction, and as late as 1946 there were only eight shopping centers in the entire United States. They included Upper Darby Center in West Philadelphia (1927); Suburban Square in Ardmore, Pennsylvania (1928); Highland Park Shopping Village outside Dallas (1931); River Oaks in Houston (1937); Hampton Village in St. Louis (1941); Colony in Toledo (1944); Shirlington in Arlington, Virginia (1944); and Belleview Square in Seattle (1946). Importantly, however, they provided many of the amenities that shoppers would take for granted half a century later. In 1931, for example, Highland Park Village outside Dallas offered department, drug, and food stores, as well as banks, a theater, beauty and barber shops, offices, studios, and parking for seven hundred cars. The Spanish architecture was uniform throughout, and the rental charge included a maintenance fee to ensure that the property was adequately cared for during the term of the lease.[26]

The first major planned retail shopping center in the world went up in Raleigh, North Carolina in 1949, the brainchild of Homer Hoyt, a well-known author and demographer best known for his sector model of urban growth.

Thereafter, the shopping-center idea caught on rapidly in the United States and less rapidly in Canada, where the first shopping center—Dixie Plaza near Toronto—did not open until 1954. The most successful early examples, such as Poplar Plaza in Memphis, offered at least thirty small retailers, one large department store, and parking for five hundred or more cars. By 1984 the nation's 20,000 large shopping centers accounted for almost two-thirds of all retail trade, and even in relatively centralized cities like New York, Boston, and San Francisco downtown merchants adapted to the suburban shift. Easy facilities for parking gave such collections of stores decisive advantages over central city establishments.[27]

The concept of the enclosed, climate-controlled mall, first introduced at the Southdale Shopping Center near Minneapolis in 1956, added to the suburban advantage. A few of the indoor malls, such as the mammoth Midtown Plaza in Rochester, New York, were located downtown, but more typical were Paramus Park and Bergen Mall in New Jersey; Woodfield Mall in Schaumburg outside Chicago; King's Plaza and Cross Country outside Gotham; and Raleigh Mall in Memphis—all of which were located on outlying highways and all of which attracted shoppers from trading areas of a hundred square miles and more. Edward J. Bartolo, Sr., a self-made millionaire and workaholic, operated from a base in Youngstown, Ohio, to become the most prominent mall developer in the United States, but large insurance companies, especially the Equitable Life Assurance Society, increasingly sought high yields as shopping-center landlords.

During the 1970s, a new phenomenon—the super regional mall—added a more elaborate twist to suburban shopping. Prototypical of the new breed was Tyson's Corner, on the Washington Beltway in Fairfax County, Virginia. Anchored by Bloomingdale's, it did over $165 million in business in 1983 and provided employment to more than 14,000 persons. Even larger was Long Island's Roosevelt Field, a 180-store, 2.2 million square foot megamall that attracted 275,000 visitors a week and did $230 million in business in 1980. Most elaborate of all was Houston's Galleria, a world-famed setting for 240 prestigious boutiques, a quartet of cinemas, 26 restaurants, an Olympic-sized ice-skating pavilion, and two luxury hotels. There were few windows in these mausoleums of merchandising, and clocks were rarely seen—just as in gambling casinos.[28]

Boosters of such megamalls argue that they are taking the place of the old central business districts and becoming the identifiable collecting points for the rootless families of the newer areas. As weekend and afternoon attractions, they have a special lure for teenagers, who often go there on shopping dates or to see the opposite sex. As one official noted in 1971: "These malls are now their street corners. The new shopping centers have killed the little merchant, closed most movies, and are now supplanting the older shopping centers in the suburbs." They are also especially attractive to mothers with young children and to the elderly, many of whom visit regularly to get out of the house without having to worry about crime or inclement weather.[29]

In reality, even the largest malls are almost the opposite of downtown areas because they are self-contained and because they impose a uniformity of tastes and interests. They cater exclusively to middle-class tastes and contain no unsavory bars or pornography shops, no threatening-looking characters, no litter, no rain, and no excessive heat or cold. As Anthony Zube-Jackson has noted, their emphasis on cleanliness and safety is symptomatic of a very lopsided view of urban culture.

Despite their blandness, the shopping malls and the drive-in culture of which they are a part have clearly eclipsed the traditional central business districts, and in many medium-sized cities the last of the downtown department stores has already closed. The drive-in blight that killed them, like the Dutch elm disease that ravaged Eastern towns in years past, has played hopscotch from one town to another, bringing down institutions that had once appeared invincible. The targets of this scourge, however, were not trees, but businesses, specifically the once-mighty department stores that anchored many a Main Street.

The most famous retailing victim of the drive-in culture thus far has been the stately J. L. Hudson Company of Detroit. It was a simple fact that all roads in the Motor City led to Hudson's. Featuring tall chandeliers, wood-paneled corridors, and brass-buttoned doormen, the twenty-five story, full-square-block emporium at its height ranked with Macy's in New York and Marshall Field in Chicago as one of the country's three largest stores. After 1950, however, the once-proud store was choked by its own branches, all of them in outlying shopping centers. As soon as Hudson's opened Northland, its biggest suburban outlet and one of the earliest in the nation, sales downtown began to fall. They declined from a peak in 1953 of $153 million to $45 million in 1981. Finally, in 1981, the downtown landmark closed its doors for good.[30] Hudson's was a victim of the product that made Detroit: the car.

In a Christmastime obituary for Detroit's most famous retailer, a WWJ radio commentator maintained that white flight to the suburbs, hastened by the Motor City's 1967 race riot, helped deal Hudson's a mortal blow. Actually, the ninety-one-year-old store was killed by the free parking, easy accessibility, and controlled environment of the megamalls.

By the 1960s, the primary rival to the shopping center as the locus of brief, informal communication and interaction had become the highway strip, with its flashing neon signs and tacky automobile showrooms. Especially in medium-sized cities, the vitality after dark is concentrated in the shopping malls or along the highway, not along Main Street.

The House Trailer and Mobile Home

The phenomenon of a nation on wheels is perhaps best symbolized by the uniquely American development of the mobile home. "Trailers are here to stay," predicted the writer Howard O'Brien in 1936. Although in its infancy at that time, the mobile-home industry has flourished in the United States. The house trailer itself came into existence in the teens of this century as an individually designed variation on a truck or a car, and it began to be produced commercially in the 1920s. Originally, trailers were designed to travel, and they were used primarily for vacation purposes. During the Great Depression of the 1930s, however, many people, especially salesmen, entertainers, construction workers, and farm laborers, were forced into a nomadic way of life as they searched for work, any work. They found that these temporary trailers on rubber tires provided the necessary shelter while also meeting their economic and migratory requirements. Meanwhile, Wally Byam and other designers were streamlining the mobile home into the classic tear-drop form made famous by Airstream.[31]

During World War II, the United States government got into the act by purchasing tens of thousands of trailers for war workers and by forbidding their sale to the general public. By 1943 the National Housing Agency alone owned 35,000 of the aluminum boxes, and more than 60 percent of the nation's 200,000 mobile homes were in defense areas. The government also built prefabricated homes without wheels near weapons factories. The ticky-tacky quality of these prefabricated shanty towns gave prefabs a lingering bad image, which remained after the war, when trailers found a growing market among migratory farm workers and military personnel, both of whom had to move frequently.

Not until the mid-1950s did the term "mobile home" begin to refer to a place where respectable people could marry, mature, and die. By then it was less a "mobile" than a "manufactured" home. No longer a trailer, it became a modern industrialized residence with almost all the accoutrements of a normal house. By the late 1950s, widths were increased to ten feet, the Federal Housing Administration (FHA) began to recognize the mobile home as a type of housing suitable for mortgage insurance, and the maturities on sales contracts were increased from three to five years.

In the 1960s, twelve-foot widths were introduced, and then fourteen, and manufacturers began to add fireplaces, skylights, and cathedral ceilings. In 1967 two trailers were attached side by side to form the first "double wide." These new dimensions allowed for a greater variety of room arrangement and became particularly attractive to retired persons with fixed incomes. They also made the homes less mobile. By 1979 even the single-width "trailer" could be seventeen feet wide (by about sixty feet long), and according to the Manufactured Housing Institute, fewer than 2 percent were ever being moved from their original site. Partly as a result of this increasing permanence, individual communities and the courts began to define the structures as real property and thus subject to real estate taxes rather than as motor vehicles subject only to license fees.[32]

Although it continued to be popularly perceived as a shabby substitute for "stick" housing (a derogatory word used to describe the ordinary American balloon-frame dwelling), the residence on wheels reflected American values and industrial practices. Built with easily machined and processed materials, such as sheet metal and plastic, it represented a total consumer package, complete with interior furnishings, carpets, and appliances. More importantly, it provided a suburban type alternative to the inner-city housing that would otherwise have been available to blue-collar workers, newly married couples, and retired persons. After 1965 the production of factory-made housing (the term preferred by the industry) rarely fell below 200,000 per year, and in Florida, Wyoming, and Montana they typically accounted for more than a quarter of all new housing units. By 1979 manufactured housing was a $3.1 billion industry, and the nation counted more than ten million mobile-home dwellers. These figures exclude the "motor homes" made popular by Winnebago in the 1970s, the modular homes that are built on a floor system like a conventional house, and the prefabricated houses for which parts are built in a factory and shipped in sections to be assembled on the site.[33]

A Drive-in Society

Drive-in motels, drive-in movies, and drive-in shopping facilities were only a few of the many new institutions that followed in the exhaust of the internal-combustion engine. By 1984 mom-and-pop grocery stores had given way almost everywhere to supermarkets, most banks had drive-in windows, and a few funeral homes were making it possible for mourners to view the deceased, sign the register, and pay their respects without emerging from their cars. Odessa Community College in Texas even opened a drive-through registration window.

Particularly pervasive were fast-food franchises, which not only decimated the family-style restaurants but cut deeply into grocery store sales. In 1915, James G. Huneker, a raconteur whose tales of early twentieth-century American life were compiled as *New Cosmopolis*, complained of the infusion of cheap, quick-fire "food hells," and of the replacement of relaxed dining with "canned music and automatic lunch taverns." With the automobile came the notion of "grabbing" something to eat. The first drive-in restaurant, Royce Hailey's Pig Stand, opened in Dallas in 1921, and later in the decade, the first fast-food franchise, "White Tower," decided that families touring in motorcars needed convenient meals along the way. The places had to look clean, so they were painted white. They had to be familiar, so a minimal menu was standardized at every outlet. To catch the eye, they were built like little castles, replete with fake ramparts and turrets. And to forestall any problem with a land lease, the little white castles were built to be moveable.

The biggest restaurant operation of all began in 1954, when Ray A. Kroc, a Chicago area milkshake-machine salesman, joined forces with Richard and Maurice McDonald, the owners of a fast-food emporium in San Bernardino, California. In 1955 the first of Mr. Kroc's "McDonald's" outlets was opened in Des Plaines, a Chicago suburb long famous as the site of an annual Methodist encampment. The second and third, both in California, opened later in 1955. Within five years, there were 228 golden arches drive-ins selling hamburgers for 15 cents, french fries for 10 cents, and milkshakes for 20 cents. In 1961 Kroc bought out the McDonald brothers, and in the next twenty years this son of an unsuccessful realtor whose family came from Bohemia built an empire of 7,500 outlets and amassed a family fortune in excess of $500 million. Appropriately headquartered in suburban Oak Brook, Illinois, the McDonald's enterprise is based on free parking and drive-in access, and its methods have been copied by dozens of imitators. Late in 1984, on an interstate highway north of Minneapolis, McDonald's began construction of the most complete drive-in complex in the world. To be called McStop, it will feature a motel, gas station, convenience store, and, of course, a McDonald's restaurant.[34]

Even church pews occasionally were replaced by the automobile. In early 1955, in suburban Garden Grove, California, the Reverend Robert Schuller, a member of the Reformed Church in America, began his ministry on a shoestring. With no sanctuary and virtually no money, he rented the Orange Drive-In movie theater on Sunday mornings and delivered his sermons while standing on top of the concession stand. The parishioners listened through speakers available at each parking space. What began as a necessity became a virtue when Schuller began attracting communicants who were more comfortable and receptive in their vehicles than in a pew. Word of the experiment— "Worship as you are . . . In the family car"—spread, the congregation grew, and in 1956 Schuller constructed a modest edifice for indoor services and administrative needs. But the Drive-in Church, as it was then called, continued to offer religious inspiration for automobile-bound parishoners, and in succeeding sanctuaries facilities were always included for those who did not want a "walk-in" church. By 1969 he had six thousand members in his church, and architect Richard Neutra had designed a huge, star-shaped "Tower of Power," situated appropriately on twenty-two acres just past Disneyland on the Santa Ana Freeway. It looked like and was called "a shopping center for Jesus Christ."[35]

In 1980 a "Crystal Cathedral" was dedicated on the grounds. Designed by Philip Johnson, the $26 million structure is one of the most impressive and gargantuan religious buildings on earth. More than 125 feet high and 415 feet wide, its interior is a stunning cavern without columns, clad in over 10,000 panes of transparent glass. Yet the drive-in feature remains. Instead of separate services for his indoor and outdoor followers, Schuller broadcasts his message over the radio from an indoor/outdoor pulpit. At the beginning of each session, two 90-foot glass walls swing open so that the minister can be seen by drive-in worshippers. Traditionalists come inside the 3,000-seat "Crystal Cathedral," while those who remain in the "pews from Detroit" are directed to the announcement: "If you have a car radio, please turn to 540 on your dial for this service. If you do not have a radio, please park by the amplifiers in the back row." The appeal has been enormously successful. By 1984, Schuller's Garden Grove Community Church claimed to be the largest walk-in, drive-in church in the world. Its Sunday broadcasts were viewed by an estimated one million Californians and commanded the nation's highest ratings for religious programming.

The Centerless City

More than anyplace else, California became the symbol of the postwar suburban culture. It pioneered the booms in sports cars, foreign cars, vans, and motor homes, and by 1984 its 26 million citizens owned almost 19 million motor vehicles and had access to the world's most extensive freeway system. The result has been a new type of centerless city, best exemplified by once sleepy and out-of-the-way Orange County, just south and east of Los Angeles.

After Walt Disney came down from Hollywood, bought out the ranchers, and opened Disneyland in 1955, Orange County began to evolve from a rural backwater into a suburb and then into a collection of medium and small towns. It had never had a true urban focus, in large part because its oil-producing sections each spawned independent suburban centers, none of which was particularly dominant over the others. The tradition continued when the area became a subdivider's dream in the 1960s and 1970s. By 1980 there were twenty-six Orange County cities, none with more than 225,000 residents. Like the begats of the Book of Genesis, they merged and multiplied into a huge agglomeration of two million people with its own Census Bureau metropolitan area designation—Anaheim, Santa Ana, Garden Grove. Unlike the traditional American metropolitan region, however, Orange County lacked a commutation focus, a place that could obviously be accepted as the center of local life. Instead, the experience of a local resident was typical: "I live in Garden Grove, work in Irvine, shop in Santa Ana, go to the dentist in Ana-heim, my husband works in Long Beach, and I used to be the president of the League of Women Voters in Fullerton."[36]

A centerless city also developed in Santa Clara County, which lies forty-five miles south of San Francisco and which is best known as the home of "Silicon Valley." Stretching from Palo Alto on the north to the garlic and lettuce fields of Gilroy to the south, Santa Clara County has the world's most extensive concentration of electronics concerns. In 1940, however, it was best known for prunes and apricots, and it was not until after World War II that its largest city, San Jose, also became the nation's largest suburb. With fewer than 70,000 residents in 1940, San Jose exploded to 636,000 by 1980, supersed-ing San Francisco as the region's largest municipality. As the automobile-based circulation system matured, the county's spacious orchards were easily developed, and bulldozers uprooted fruit trees for shopping centers and streets. Home builders, encouraged by a San Jose city government that annexed new territory at a rapid pace and borrowed heavily to build new utilities and schools on the fringes of town, moved farther and farther into the rural outskirts. Dozens of semiconductor and aerospace companies expanded and built plants there. In time, this brought twice-daily ordeals of bumper-to-bumper traffic on congested freeways. The driving time of some six-mile commutes lengthened to forty-five minutes, and the hills grew hazy behind the smog. As Santa Clara County became a national symbol of the excesses of uncontrolled growth, its residents began to fear that the high-technology superstars were generating jobs and taxes, but that the jobs attracted more people, and the taxes failed to cover the costs of new roads, schools, sewers, and expanded police and fire departments.[37]

The numbers were larger in California, but the pattern was the same on the edges of every American city, from Buffalo Grove and Schaumburg near Chicago, to Germantown and Collierville near Memphis, to Creve Coeur and Ladue near St. Louis. And perhaps more important than the growing number of people living outside of city boundaries was the sheer physical sprawl of metropolitan areas. Between 1950 and 1970, the urbanized area of Wash-ington, DC, grew from 181 to 523 square miles, of Miami from 116 to 429, while in the larger megalopolises of New York, Chicago, and Los Angeles, the region of settlement was measured in the thousands of square miles.

The Decentralization of Factories and Offices

The deconcentration of post-World War II American cities was not simply a matter of split-level homes and neighborhood schools. It involved almost every facet of national life, from manufacturing to shopping to professional services. Most importantly, it involved the location of the workplace, and the erosion of the concept of suburb as a place from which wage-earners commuted daily to jobs in the center. So far had the trend progressed by 1970 that in nine of the fifteen largest metropolitan areas suburbs were the principal sources of employment, and in some cities, like San Francisco, almost three-fourths of all work trips were by people who neither lived nor worked in the core city. In Wilmington, Delaware, 66 percent of area jobs in 1940 were in the core city; by 1970, the figure had fallen below one quarter. And despite the fact that Manhattan contained the world's highest concentration of office space and business activity, in 1970, about 78 percent of the residents in the New York suburbs also worked in the suburbs. Many outlying communities thus achieved a kind of autonomy from the older downtown areas. A new "Americanism" even entered the language—"beltway"—to describe the broad expressways that encircled every important city by 1975 and that attracted employers of every description.[38]

Manufacturing is now among the most dispersed of nonresidential activities. As the proportion of industrial jobs in the United States work force fell from 29 percent to 23 percent of the total in the 1970s, those manufacturing enterprises that survived often relocated either to the suburbs or to the lower-cost South and West. Even tertiary industries, which do not utilize assembly-line processes and which require less flat space than larger factories, have adapted to the internal-combustion engine with peripheral sites. As early as 1963, industrial employment in the United States was more than half suburban based, and by 1981, about two-thirds of all manufacturing activity took place in the "industrial parks" and new physical plants of the suburbs. The transition has been especially hard on older workshop cities, where venerable factories are abandoned as employers are lured outward by the promise of open land, easy access to interstate highways, and federal investment tax credits. Between 1970 and 1980, for example, Philadelphia lost 140,000 jobs, many of them with the closing down or moving away of such Quaker City mainstays as Philco-Ford, Cuneo Eastern Press, Midvale Heppenstall Steel, Bayuk Cigar, Eaton and Cooper Industries' Plumb Tool Division, and the Container Corporation.[39]

Office functions, once thought to be securely anchored to the streets of big cities, have followed the suburban trend. In the nineteenth century, businesses tried to keep all their operations under one centralized roof. It was the most efficient way to run a company when the mails were slow and uncertain and communication among employees was limited to the distance that a human voice could carry. More recently, the economics of real estate and a revolution in communications have changed these circumstances, and many companies are now balkanizing their accounting departments, data processing divisions, and billing departments. Just as insurance companies, branch banks, regional sales staffs, and doctors' offices have reduced their costs and presumably increased their accessibility by moving to suburban locations, so also have back-office functions been splitting away from front offices and moving away from central business districts.

Corporate headquarters relocations have been particularly well-publicized. Although the publishing firm of Doubleday and Company moved to quiet Garden City on Long Island in 1910 and Reader's Digest shifted to Pleasantville, New York, in Westchester County in 1936, the overall trend of corporate movement was toward central business districts until about 1950. The outward trend began in earnest in 1954, when the General Foods Corporation moved its home office from midtown Manhattan to a spacious, low-slung campus surrounded by acres of trees and free parking in suburban White Plains. The exodus reached a peak between 1955 and 1980, when, arguing, "It's an altogether more pleasant way of life for all," more than fifty corporations, including such giants as International Business Machines, Gulf Oil, Texaco, Union Carbide, General Telephone, American Cyanamid, Xerox, Pepsico, U.S. Tobacco, Chesebrough-Pond's, Nestlé, American Can, Singer, Champion International, and Olin, abandoned their headquarters in New York City.[40]

Because Manhattan remained the dominant center of the nation's corporate and financial life, most companies simply moved within the region to more bucolic surroundings, principally in one of three small areas: a strip of central Westchester County from the Hudson River past White Plains to the Connecticut border, the downtown of Stamford and adjacent Greenwich in Fairfield County, Connecticut, and a narrow slice through the heartland of Morris and Somerset Counties in New Jersey. All three areas built more than 16 million square feet of office space between 1972 and 1985, or more than exists in all but a handful of American cities.

The trend was particularly strong toward Connecticut, where executives could have the benefit of Gotham's business and cultural advantages without the bother of New York State's income taxes. In 1960 when the first urban renewal plans were drawn up for downtown Stamford, no consideration was given to building any commercial office space there. In the next three decades, however, while the original proposals were delayed by community resistance, Stamford's urban renewal plans were redrawn to reflect changes in corporate attitudes toward relocating out of Gotham and into more comfortable suburban locations. For Stamford the delay was beneficial. When companies began their Manhattan exodus, Stamford had available space downtown. By 1984, Fairfield County was the third leading corporate headquarters site in the United States, after only New York City and Chicago.

Several studies have pointed out that the most important variable in determining the direction of a corporate shift was the location of the home and country club of the chief executive officer of the particular company. In fact, top officers were often the only ones to benefit from the suburban shifts. When A & W Beverages made the move from Manhattan to White Plains early in 1984, the company lost its entire support staff in the transition and had to spend a small fortune on severance costs. "Some of these people had been with us for many years, so we had to ask ourselves what we should do with loyal and good workers who will no longer have a job," said Craig Honeycutt, director of personnel for A & W, about the employees who quit rather than commute from Manhattan, Brooklyn, or New Jersey to White Plains.[41]

Because the construction of suburban office headquarters tends to be expensive, the purpose of most such moves is to improve employee morale and productivity as much as to reduce costs. To this end, a company typically hires a well-known architect to design a rustic complex on the model of a college campus or a self-contained village. Free parking and easy access to interstate highways presumably make possible a longer work day, while stone piazzas, landscaped gardens, impressive sculpture, and splashing water fountains, as well as gymnasiums, showers, and saunas presumably make possible a more relaxed one. Company-owned cafeterias replace the downtown restaurants, shopping districts, and even noontime concerts of the city centers. To some employees the result is "close to perfect." Others find the campus environment boring and bemoan that "the main thing of interest out here is what's new in the gift shop."

Corporate relocation in the postwar period has been overwhelmingly a city-to-suburb phenomenon rather than a regional shift. The move of Gulf Oil to Houston and of American Airlines to Dallas, both from New York, were exceptions to this general rule. Only occasionally have large firms shifted both from a city to a suburb and from one region to another. The Johns-Manville Company, which transferred in the 1970s from a Manhattan office tower to a sleek and gleaming spaceship-style structure in the midst of a 10,000-acre ranch in the foothills of the Rocky Mountains, is a clear exception. Perhaps coincidentally the Johns-Manville Corporation was saved from bankruptcy in 1982 only by the intervention of a court.

Since World War II, the American people have experienced a transformation of the manmade environment around them. Commercial, residential, and industrial structures have been redesigned to fit the needs of the motorist rather than the pedestrian. Garish signs, large parking lots, one-way streets, drive-in windows, and throw-away fast-food buildings—all associated with the world of suburbia—have replaced the slower-paced, neighborhood-oriented institutions of an earlier generation. Some observers of the automobile revolution have argued that the car has created a new and better urban environment and that the change in spatial scale, based upon swift transportation, has formed a new kind of organic entity, speeding up personal communication and rendering obsolete the older urban settings. Lewis Mumford, writing from his small-town retreat in Amenia, New York, has emphatically disagreed. His prize-winning book, *The City in History*, was a celebration of the medieval community and an excoriation of "the formless urban exudation" that he saw American cities becoming. He noted that the automobile megalopolis was not a final stage in city development but an anticity which "annihilates the city whenever it collides with it."[42]

The most damning indictment of private transportation remains, however, the 1958 work of the acid-tongued John Keats, *The Insolent Chariots*. He forcefully argued, as have others since that time, that highway engineers were wrong in constantly calling for more lanes of concrete to accommodate yet more lines of automobiles. Instead, Keats's position was that motorcars actually created the demand for more highways, which in turn increased the need for more vehicles, and so on ad infinitum. More ominously, he surmised, public expenditures for the automobile culture diverted funds from mass transit and needed social services.[43]

The automobile lobby swept everything and everybody before it, however, and it was not until the first oil boycott of 1973 that Americans would seriously ponder the full implications of their drive-in culture. Especially in the 1950s, expressways represented progress and modernity, and mayors and public officials stumbled over themselves in seeking federal largesse for more and wider roads. Only a few people realized that high-speed roads accelerated deconcentration, displaced inner-city residents, contributed to the decay of central business districts, and hastened the deterioration of existing transportation systems. As Raymond Tucker, mayor of St. Louis and former president of the American Municipal Association, put it, "The plain fact of the matter is that we just cannot build enough lanes of highways to move all of our people by private automobile and create enough parking space to store the cars without completely paving over our cities and removing all of the . . . economic, social, and cultural establishments that the people were trying to reach in the first place."

Because structures built to accommodate the demands of the automobile are likely to have an ephemeral life, it is a mistake for cities to duplicate suburban conditions. In 1973 a RAND study of St. Louis suggested as an alternative strategy that the city become "one of many large suburban centers of economic and residential life" rather than try to revive traditional central city functions. Such advice is for those who study statistics rather than cities. Too late, municipal leaders will realize that a slavish duplication of suburbia destroys the urban fabric that makes cities interesting. Memphis's Union Avenue, once a grand boulevard lined with the homes of the well-to-do, has recently fallen victim to the drive-in culture. In 1979 one of the last surviving landmarks, an elegant stone mansion, was leveled to make room for yet another fast-food outlet. Within three years, the plastic-and-glass hamburger emporium was bankrupt, but the scar on Union Avenue remained.

There are some signs that the halcyon days of the drive-in culture and automobile are behind us. More than one hundred thousand gasoline stations, or about one-third of the American total, have been eliminated in the last decade. Empty tourist courts and boarded-up motels are reminders that the fast pace of change can make commercial structures obsolete within a quarter-century of their erection. Even that suburban bellwether, the shopping center, which revolutionized merchandising after World War II, has come to seem small and out-of-date as newer covered malls attract both the trendy and the family trade. Some older centers have been recycled as bowling alleys or industrial buildings, and some have been remodeled to appeal to larger tenants and better-heeled customers. But others stand forlorn and boarded up. Similarly, the characteristic fast-food emporiums of the 1950s, with uniformed "car hops" who took orders at the automobile window, are now relics of the past. One of the survivors, Delores Drive-in, which opened in Beverly Hills in 1946, was recently proposed as an historic landmark, a sure sign that the species is in danger.[44]

Notes

[1]The thesis that road-watching is a delight and that the highway might be a work of art is expressed in Donald Appleyard, Kevin Lynch, and John R. Myer, *The View From the Road* (Cambridge, 1964). See also, Paul W. Gikas, "Crashworthiness as a Cultural Ideal," *Michigan Historical Quarterly*, XIX (Fall 1980), 704. An unconvincing strident defense of the automobile and the expressway system is David Brodsly, *L.A. Freeway: An Appreciative Essay* (Berkeley, 1982).

[2]Schaeffer and Sclar, *Access for All: Transportation and Urban Growth* (London, 1975), 39–41. See also, Jean-Pierre Bardou, Jean-Jacques Chanaron, Patrick Fridenson, and James M. Laux, *The Automobile Revolution: The Impact of an Industry* (Chapel Hill, trans., 1982); Joel A. Tarr, *Transportation Innovation and Changing Spatial Patterns: Pittsburgh, 1850–1934* (Pittsburgh: Transportation Research Institute, Carnegie-Mellon University, 1977); James J. Flink, *The Car Culture* (Cambridge, 1975); and James R. Dunn, Jr., *Miles to Go; European and American Transportation Policies* (Cambridge, 1981). The leading authority on the "car culture," James J. Flink, is now working on an ambitious international history of the automobile age.

[3]Willard Morgan, "At Last—A Place to Park," *American Builder*, July 1929, 58–60; and *New York Times*, May 22, 1979.

[4]Ed Cray, *Chrome Colossus: General Motors and Its Times* (New York, 1980), 326.

[5]Cray, *Chrome Colossus*, 356–58. The best study of the origins of the Interstate Highway system is Mark H. Rose, *Interstate: Express Highway Politics, 1941–1956* (Lawrence, Ks., 1979).

[6]Robert A. Caro, *The Power Broker: Robert Moses and the Fall of New York* (New York, 1974), passim.

[7]James J. Flink, "The Automobile Revolution in Worldwide Comparative Perspective" (Paper presented at the Detroit Historical Society Conference on the Automobile and American Culture, Wayne State University, Detroit, October 1, 1982). Kenneth T. Jackson, "The Crabgrass Frontier: 150 Years of Suburban Growth in America," in Raymond A. Mohl and James F. Richardson, eds., *The Urban Experience: Themes in American History* (Belmont, Ca., 1973), 196–221. See also, Rose, *Interstate*, 75–79.

[8]An excellent recent study of Los Angeles suburbanization is Fred W. Viehe, "Black Gold Suburbs: The Influence of the Extractive Industry on the Suburbanization of Los Angeles, 1890–1930," *Journal of Urban History*, VIII (November 1981), 3–26.

[9]United States Bureau of the Census, *Census of Housing, 1950*, Volume I, chapter 1, table 32. Since 1975 downtown Los Angeles has begun to revive, especially as large corporations like Atlantic Richfield, the Bank of America, and Wells Fargo Bank have built major skyscrapers there. More importantly, recent residential complexes have added a 24-hour atmosphere to the once-desolate nighttime scene. The lively Mexican quarter along Broadway also gives diversity to the central business district. In terms of residential density, Los Angeles suburbs are typically more closely packed than the post-World War II automobile suburbs of Eastern cities like Philadelphia, New York, Washington, and Boston. Partly because of extraordinarily high land prices, partly because of the absence of rainfall, partly because of the large amount of undevelopable land, and partly because of a Spanish tradition that emphasizes enclosed space rather than open lawns, average lot sizes even in exclusive L.A. suburbs like Palos Verdes were less than one-fifth of an acre in 1980. By contrast, equivalently located and priced homes in the eastern cities just mentioned were typically located on at least one-half of an acre and often much more.

[10]The best work on the garage is Folke T. Kihlstedt, "The Automobile and the Transformation of the American Home, 1910–1935," *Michigan Historical Quarterly*, XIX (Fall 1980), 555–70. See also, Charles Moore, Gerald Allen, and Donlyn Lyndon, *The Face of Houses* (New York, 1974), 183–87; and J. B. Jackson, "The Domestication of the Garage," *Landscape*, XX (Winter 1976), 10–19.

[11]The first book exclusively devoted to the problem of sheltering automobiles was Dorothy and Julian Olney, *The American Home Book of Garages* (Garden City, N.Y., 1931). See also, *New York Times*, October 11, 1984.

[12]A 1922 *New York Times* advertisement for the Kindred-McAvoy homes in Long Island City in Queens promised "two 7-room apartments, with 20 windows each and a 4-car garage."

[13]Robert Venturi, Denise Scott Brown, and Steven Izenour, *Learning From Las Vegas* (Cambridge, 1972).

[14]Paul Lancaster, "The Great American Motel," *American Heritage*, XXXIII (June-July 1982), 100–8. In 1925 Florida alone registered 178 tourist courts.

[15]An outstanding study of automotive tourism is Warren James Belasco, *Americans on the Road: From Autocamp to Motel, 1910–1945* (Cambridge, 1979). See also, David L. Lewis, "Sex and the Automobile: From Rumble Seats to Rockin' Vans." *Michigan Historical Quarterly*, XIX (Fall 1980), 518–28; and *This Fabulous Century*, 272–73.

[16]Lewis, "Sex and the Automobile," passim.

[17]By 1972, when there were approximately 43,500 motels in the United States, there were approximately twice as many motels as hotels in the country. *New York Times*, February 23, 1972.

[18]*New York Times*, October 19, 1975; and *New York Times*, July 19, 1981.

[19]According to a *New York Times* article on May 30, 1982, Hollinshead opened the drive-in in 1934 on the back wall of his machine-parts shop in Camden, New Jersey. The number of drive-in theaters

peaked at 4,063 in 1958 and was down to 3,484 in 1976, when Texas led all states with 264 and Alaska was last with only one.

[20]*New York Times*, November 7, 1983.

[21]The best-illustrated and most thorough study of the service station is Daniel I. Vieyra, *Fill'er Up: An Architectural History of America's Gas Stations* (New York, 1979), especially 1–14.

[22]Two excellent short essays on the gas station appeared by William K. Stevens and Paul Goldberger in *New York Times*, February 7, 1982. See also, Gary Herbert Wolf, "The Gasoline Station and the Evolution of a Building Type as Illustrated Through a History of the Sun Oil Company Gasoline Stations" (Thesis, University of Virginia, 1974); K. Lonberg-Holm, "The Gasoline Filling and Service Station," *Architectural Record*, LXVII (June 1930), 561–68; *Louisville Courier-Journal*, December 11, 1983; Alexander Guth, "The Automobile Service Station," *The Architectural Forum*, XLV (July 1926), 33–56; Bruce Lohof, "The Service Station in America: The Evolution of a Vernacular Building Type," *Industrial Archeology*, XI (Spring 1974), 1–13; and Henry Ozane, "The Service Station," *Architectural Record*, XCV (February 1944), 70–82.

[23]Willard Morgan, "At Last—A Place to Park," 58–60. On the deconcentration policies of Sears, Roebuck and Company, see Arthur Rubloff, "Shopping Center Development and Operation," *The Appraisal Journal*, XXX (1962), 75–77; Boris Emmet and John E. Jeuck, *Catalogues and Counters: A History of Sears, Roebuck and Company* (Chicago, 1950); and Leonard Z. Breen, "A Study of the Decentralization of Retail Trade Relative to Population in the Chicago Area, 1929–1948" (Ph.D. dissertation, University of Chicago, 1956).

[24]Blaine A. Brownell, "The Automobile and Urban Structure" (Paper presented at the annual meeting of the American Studies Association, San Antonio, Tx., November 6, 1975); and Brownell, "A Symbol of Modernity: Attitudes Toward the Automobile in Southern Cities in the 1920's," *American Quarterly*, XXIV (March 1972), 20–44. See also, Howard L. Preston, *Automobile Age Atlanta: The Making of a Southern Metropolis, 1900–1935* (Athens, Ga., 1979).

[25]J. C. Nichols, "The Planning and Control of Outlying Shopping Centers," *The Journal of Land and Public Utility Economics*, II (January 1926), 17–22.

[26]My list of early shopping centers is partly borrowed from John B. Rae, *The Road and the Car in American Life* (Cambridge, 1971), 230. For a quantitative analysis of the spread of this merchandising concept, see Yehoshua S. Cohen, *Diffusion of an Innovation in an Urban System* (Chicago: The University of Chicago Department of Geography Research Paper No. 140, 1972). See also, James Simmons, *The Changing Pattern of Retail Location* (Chicago: The University of Chicago Department of Geography Research Paper No. 92, 1964).

[27]For example, in 1979, the percentage of metropolitan retail trade taking place outside the city was 70 percent in Boston, 67 percent in St. Louis, and 68 percent in Hartford. John C. Van Nostrand, "The Queen Elizabeth Way: Public Utility Versus Public Space," *Urban History Review*, XII (October 1983), 1–23.

[28]During the 1979 gasoline shortage, the customer bases of the largest regional malls shrunk from a thirty-mile radius to a ten-mile radius, and weekend and social trips to the malls were also curtailed. On the changing image and size of Tyson's Corner, see Megan Rosenfeld, "Tyson's Corner: An Example of Suburbia's Future," *Washington Post*, February 20, 1977. See also, *New York Times*, November 10, 1981.

[29]Quoted in the *New York Times*, February 5, 1971. Although the main shopping and business districts in European areas tend to be in the center of the cities, American-style malls are gaining popularity. Skarholmen Center, southwest of Stockholm, is surrounded by the largest parking lot in Scandinavia and is similar to the regional shopping centers of the United States.

[30]Anthony Zube-Jackson, 104–5. See also, *New York Times*, November 10, 1981; Ross J. McKeever, *Shopping Centers: Principles and Policies* (Washington: Urban Land Institute Technical Bulletin No. 20, 1953); Homer Hoyt, "The Current Trends in New Shopping Centers: Four Different Types," *Urban Land*, XII (1953), No. 4; and *New York Times*, December 31, 1982.

[31]The published material on the history of mobile homes is very spare. The social aspects of the subject are covered in Donald Olen Cowell, *Mobile Homes: A Study of Trailer Life* (Philadelphia, 1941). The most comprehensive treatment is Carleton M. Edwards, *Homes for Travel and Living: The History and Development of the Recreational Vehicle and Mobile Home Industry* (East Lansing, privately printed, 1977). On the conversion of trucks into residence, see Jane Lidz, *Rolling Homes: Handmade Houses on Wheels* (New York, 1979). See also, *New York Times*, June 27, 1982.

[32]Although the practice was already a decade old, beginning in 1969, Congress officially authorized the Federal Housing Administration (FHA) to issue government-insured mortgages for mobile home park sites. In April 1979, the New Jersey Supreme Court ruled that mobile homes were real property and could be taxed as such. An examination of late 1970s attitudes toward trailering and mobile homes is Michael Aaron Rockland, *Homes on Wheels* (New Brunswick, N.J., 1980).

[33]A mobile home, unlike a modular structure, has a metal undercarriage that remains even when the house is in place on blocks. A modular home can be set up on a site in a few days; a prefab home may take several weeks of on-site labor to put together. Partly for reasons of prejudice and partly for reasons of preference, black Americans occupy only a disproportionately small percentage (2 percent in 1960, for example) of mobile home units.

[34]A campaign is presently under way to give landmark status to the earliest existing McDonald's hamburger stand, which is located in Downey, California. The Pointe Coupee Funeral Home in New Roads, Louisiana, began the drive-in funeral practice in 1976 with rather substantial fanfare. James G. Huneker, *New Cosmopolis: Book of Images* (New York, 1915), 76–77, 82; Lewis, "Sex and the Automobile," 524; and Paul Hirshorn and Steven Izenour, *White Towers* (Cambridge, 1979); *New York Times,* January 15, 1984.

[35]The most complete information about Schuller's Drive-in Church comes from *The Story of a Dream,* a 28-page booklet available at the church bookstore for one dollar. Free walking tours of the grounds are provided free of charge every half hour. See also, *Decision,* XII (March 1971), 6; Thomas Hines, "Designing for the Motor Age: Richard Neutra and the Automobile," *Oppositions: A Journal for Ideas and Criticism in Architecture,* XXI (Summer 1980), 35–51; and Judith and Neil Morgan, "Orange, a Most California County," *National Geographic,* December 1981, pp. 750–79.

[36]Quoted in the *New York Times,* May 30, 1971.

[37]Although Santa Clara County was the envy of civic boosters around the United States, in 1979 it instituted measures to curtail industrial development. Susan Benner, "Storm Clouds Over Silicon Valley," *Inc.,* September 1982, pp. 84–89.

[38]Both the 1970 and the 1980 federal censuses contain detailed information on the journey-to-work of a selected sample of Americans. See also, Marion Clawson, *Suburban Land Conversion in the United States: An Economic and Governmental Process* (Baltimore, 1971), 232–34.

[39]Leon Moses and Harold F. Williamson, "The Location of Economic Activities in Cities," *American Economic Review,* LVII (May 1967), 214–15; Kenneth T. Jackson, "The Effect of Suburbanization on the Cities," in Philip C. Dolce, ed., *Suburbia: The American Dream and Dilemma* (Garden City, 1976), 89–110; *New York Times,* August 15, 1981.

[40]The most sensible voice on this topic is that of the Regional Plan Association, and especially its vice president for research, Boris Pushkarev. See, for example, Pushkarev, "Transportation Crawling Towards Consolidation," *New York Affairs,* V (1978), 75–90. Two fine scholarly analyses are Peter O. Muller, *The Suburbanization of Corporate Headquarters* (Washington, Conn., 1978); and Barry Bluestone et al., *Corporate Flight* (Washington, 1981).

[41]*Intercorp,* February 7, 1984, p. 26; *New York Times,* February 20, 1984. A British study in 1976 found that 800 businesses had moved from London to new and expanded towns between 1966 and 1974. *New York Times,* June 30, 1977.

[42]Lewis Mumford, *The City in History: Its Origins, Its Transformations, and Its Prospects* (New York, 1961), 505.

[43]John Keats, *The Insolent Chariots* (New York, 1958).

[44]Lewis, "Sex and the Automobile," 518–28. The argument that the automobile will continue to dominate urban transportation for the foreseeable future is forcefully made by Mark S. Foster, "The Automobile in the Urban Environment: Planning for an Energy Short Future," *The Pacific Historian,* II (Fall 1981), 23–31.

The American Southwest:
An Urban View

*Bradford Luckingham**

In the past four decades scholars have created an important body of knowledge in the field of western American urban history. Articles and books have called attention to the urban dimension of the western experience, and urban dwellers have been given as much credit for developing the American West as other pioneers and promoters.[1]

From the beginning, western cities served as "spearheads of the American frontier." Urban developers worked to reproduce familiar city patterns in the new country, and by 1830 Pittsburgh, Cincinnati, Louisville, and St. Louis represented the paramount influence in the Ohio Valley. A similar process occurred in the Great Lakes area. The builders of Cleveland, Detroit, Chicago, and Milwaukee, like earlier urban pioneers and promoters, were a conspicuous part of the westward movement. By 1870 the lake cities exhibited the same dominant influence over their region that older urban centers exerted over their respective hinterlands, and this rapid city growth in the West was viewed as fundamental to the development of the expanding nation.[2]

In Texas, too, patterns of urbanization were established during the middle years of the nineteenth century. During the period from 1836 to 1865, Houston, Galveston, Austin, and San Antonio came of age as major centers of cultural, social, economic, and political influence in the state. Texans looked to the cities not only for culture but for vital services. As one urban historian has put it, "They read urban newspapers, sought out urban society, borrowed money, traded raw materials and purchased goods from urban merchants."[3]

Even the Rocky Mountain mining camps and the Kansas cattle towns served as agents of urban civilization, despite the myth of the "Wild West" popularized in the media. The rough and violent times were by comparison a relatively short interval in the lifespan of a typical mining camp or cattle town. Illustrating the urban impulse on the frontier, the maturing communities, led by businessmen and editors, quickly established urban institutions and sought to attain the coveted "prize of city status."[4]

*Bradford Luckingham is professor of history at Arizona State University. Reprinted from Western Historical Quarterly 15 (July 1984): 261–80. Reprinted by permission of Western Historical Quarterly and Bradford Luckingham.

The quest for urban status was also evident in the frontier regions of the Far West. As Earl Pomeroy has observed, "From the time of the first American settlements, the Pacific slope was significantly urban. Even those Far Westerners who did not live in cities looked to them to an unusual degree; even in states and areas where population was sparse, society was remarkably urbanized." San Francisco, Los Angeles, Salt Lake City, Portland, Seattle, and other leading cities of the region played a crucial role in the development of the Far West, as had their counterparts in the East and Midwest. Indeed, this area did not evolve from rural beginnings to city endings but saw its cities develop at the same time as did its ranches, farms, and mines.[5]

According to observers, a significant urban consciousness or urban pride existed in the West by 1890, and by that year, in virtually every aspect of life, as John W. Reps has noted, urban residents and institutions "dominated western culture and civilization." The lure of the city in the region continued into the twentieth century, and as it evolved, the West, led by its urban centers, became more prominent in the life of the nation. During the Great Depression and World War II, the federal government became increasingly involved in the growth of the Far West, and that relationship, along with new as well as traditional technological and social factors, gave impetus to the unprecedented economic boom and population explosion of the 1950s. During that decade and beyond, as Gerald D. Nash has detailed, the metropolitan Far West, notably in California, led the way in establishing the region as "a pacesetter for the nation."[6]

That the cities led the way in making the Far West "a pacesetter for the nation" in the post-World War II years emphasized the persistent role of urban centers in the westward movement. Some 25 million people moved across the Mississippi River from 1945 to 1965, and the vast majority of them settled in the urban West. By 1965 more than two-thirds of the inhabitants of the American West were urban dwellers. In 1967, Wallace Stegner, new editor of *The American West*, urged contributors to be more aware of the urban dimension. As he put it, "The American West, whatever its frontier past, is in the twentieth century increasingly urban. The western American is, by the millions, a city dweller, even if he wears boots and a Stetson and grows whiskers for Frontier Days. Seven out of eight readers of this magazine are city dwellers." Moreover, according to Carl Abbott, the "level of urbanization" in the American West surpassed that of the rest of the country by 1880. During the next sixty years, the region maintained a slight edge, but following World War II it rapidly extended its lead. By 1980, 83 percent of the population of the American West lived in urban areas compared to 73 percent for the country as a whole. "To a greater extent than many of us realize," Abbott has declared, "the history of the West is the history of its cities."[7]

A pattern of urban dominance may also be seen in the history of the Southwest—a region defined as including Arizona, New Mexico, and the western promontory of Texas. El Paso, Albuquerque, Tucson, and Phoenix have been the most important urban centers in the Southwest since the nineteenth century, and they are among the fastest growing cities in the nation today. In fact, since the beginnings of Spanish settlement in the seventeenth century, what Walter Prescott Webb called an "oasis civilization" existed in the Southwest. While the English established towns on the East Coast and in the interior, Spanish pioneers were creating Santa Fe (1610), Paso del Norte (1659), Albuquerque (1706), and Tucson (1776) on the northern frontiers of New Spain. These oasis towns served not only as centers of life in the region but also as outposts of civilization and spearheads of desert development. Urban growth accompanied or preceded the opening of the surrounding country, and the towns acted as links between vast, unpopulated areas and the outside world.[8]

In 1821, Mexico won its independence from Spain, and more Anglos (white people of non-Hispanic descent) began to enter the towns to do business. In 1846 war broke out between the United States and Mexico, and following that conflict Anglos increasingly found their way to the oases—now the urban centers of the American Southwest. They joined with local Hispanics in the further development of El Paso, Albuquerque, and Tucson; in 1867, Anglo pioneers created Phoenix. By 1880 promoters of all four of these river communities were involved in the coming of the railroads, which were the key to their emergence as the four principal cities of the Southwest.[9]

The importance of the coming of the railroads to the Southwest cannot be overestimated. As on other frontiers, railroads encouraged urbanization. Leaders in the four towns, aware of the close relationship between transportation innovations and urban growth, promoted the presence of railroads. They knew that the "natural wealth" of the area could never attain "proper development" until a railroad system evolved. Railroad routes, an Albuquerque editor declared in 1872, would place developers "in communication with the outside world and offer inducements to population and capital."[10]

Albuquerque leaders boosted their town and "cooperated" with company officials in order to attract the main line of the Atchison, Topeka and Santa Fe Railroad, and when it bypassed the towns of Santa Fe and Bernalillo and went to Albuquerque, the future of that town as "the metropolis of New Mexico" was assured. When the town celebrated the arrival of the railroad on April 22, 1880, William C. Hazeldine said it all when he declared it to be "the day of all days in Albuquerque, a day long expected and anxiously looked forward to by the friends of progress and advancement."[11]

Hazeldine's declaration reflected the sentiment of leaders of all four of the communities regarding the significance of proper railroad connections. "We have sprung into a city," asserted Judge Allan Blacker when the Southern Pacific first arrived in El Paso on May 26, 1881. The railroads "will bring within our grasp great probabilities and grand possibilities." By late 1880 not one, but four, railroads were constructing tracks toward the Texas border town from four different directions, and this development promised to make it the future railroad hub of the Southwest.[12]

When the railroads arrived in the four towns in the 1880s, they all gained considerably in population. Railroad contact with the outside world, including transcontinental routes operated by the Southern Pacific and the Atchison, Topeka and Santa Fe railroads, provided links to the national economy and helped the towns to expand as trade and distribution centers for productive hinterlands. Their emergence as vital hubs facilitated the economic exploitation of the Southwest, and they played a large role in civilizing the region.

They became the centers of business districts, military posts, and universities. Stores and factories, schools and churches, banks and hotels, hospitals and courthouses, theaters and saloons, all served the people of the four cities and their surrounding areas.

As in other western towns, the four desert centers experienced the "business of sin" during their "Wild West" days, but by the turn of the century all four cities had creditably survived their youth and had achieved recognition as the centers of civility in the region. All four served as county seats, and Phoenix was the capital of Arizona Territory. Santa Fe had managed to retain the capital of New Mexico Territory, but in every other respect it lost out to Albuquerque, which by 1900 exceeded Santa Fe in population. Promoters worked diligently to develop the cities into desirable places for those looking for amenities as well as opportunities. The amenities included the climate, and the sun culture was boosted endlessly. Each of the towns became havens for health seekers as well as prime locations for tourist resorts; they became famous for their hospitals as well as their hotels.[13]

The towns, in fact, stand as excellent examples of the impact of amenities on regional urban growth. Following the arrival of the railroad in the Southwest, doctors around the country started sending patients to the four oases for the winter. "The climate of El Paso is the finest in the Union," declared local boosters, "and the dry refined air of the region is a luxury to breathe." At the same time, Albuquerque promoters called their town "an ideal spot for the health seeker." In Tucson and Phoenix, observers noted the benefits of "perpetual sunshine." Many of those who came to the desert centers for their health did recover sufficiently to lead productive lives, and some made outstanding contributions to the development of the region. Affluent, healthy tourists also were given every encouragement to visit the cities, and they were provided with the services of several large, modern hotels equipped to meet their needs. For example, the Santa Rita Hotel in Tucson, the Hotel Adams in Phoenix, the Alvarado Hotel in Albuquerque, and the Hotel Paso del Norte in El Paso all enjoyed reputations as centers of luxury in the Southwest.[14]

Opportunities in the Southwest included mining, farming, and ranching, but many people came to the region to share in the progress of growing communities. As a newcomer to El Paso in the 1880s declared, "I wanted to be in the coming metropolis; I was anxious to grow up with the frontier town." Many of these success seekers became effective leaders and boosters of the desert hubs. As members of the local business and civic elite who were willing to combine private interests with community interests, they often directed, with growth and development in mind, the economic, political, and cultural lives of their respective cities.[15]

Among the outstanding leaders of the Phoenix elite, for example, was Dwight Heard. A successful businessman in Chicago, Heard moved to Phoenix in 1897 hoping the climate would help him recover his health. Heard and his wife Maie were both impressed with the Arizona capital, and he along with some of his friends in Chicago began investing in the economic growth of the city and the Salt River Valley, while Maie became involved in raising the cultural tone of the city. Heard opened his home, the finest in Phoenix, to potential investors from the East and Midwest and did everything he could to encourage their interest in the Phoenix area. His investment company, specializing in real estate, became a leading force in the development of the city and the valley. His newspaper, the *Arizona Republican*, exerted a strong influence on politics and other aspects of life in Phoenix and the rest of the state. Heard was an active civic promoter and an ardent booster; he and his wife were instrumental in securing many benefits for the city, including the Heard Museum. When Dwight Heard died in 1929, he was eulogized as "Arizona's greatest citizen."[16]

While visionary leaders in the Southwest worked hard to make their cities transportation hubs, trade and distribution centers, health meccas, tourist attractions, gateways to Mexico, and the site of government agencies, military installations, and industrial firms, they also promoted the resource development of the hinterlands. They helped establish transportation and communication networks throughout the region that brought the countryside and the population centers into closer contact. The cities served as bases for the occupation of the territory; and as both the rural and urban sectors grew, they made demands on each other. By providing local markets and national and international transportation outlets, the desert communities stimulated farming, mining, and livestock-raising pursuits in the region. The cities as points of attachment operated as economic conduits between the Southwest and the outside world, as collectors of exports from the surrounding area, and as distributors of imports from around and beyond the nation. Urban promoters often acted as middlemen and mediators between the Southwest communities and the world beyond. Cotton, copper, cattle, and other regional interests were encouraged to look to the four hubs of the Southwest for vital services and facilities. A rural-urban interdependence developed, and cooperation was usually valued more than conflict. For the most part, mutual interest in growth and prosperity helped the cities and their surrounding areas to maintain a satisfactory association.[17]

Local leaders often led the way in the struggle to gain advantages useful to regional as well as urban development. For example, following a severe drought in the late 1890s, Phoenix leaders and central Arizona farming interests decided that a water storage system was the answer to the area's problem. Joining together, they formed the Salt River Valley Water Users' Association, and that organization, taking advantage of the National Reclamation Act of 1902, supported the federal government in the construction of nearby Roosevelt Dam, completed in 1911. This and similar endeavors brought vital stability to the water supply, allowed irrigation control, assured agricultural growth in the valley, and as it prospered, so did Phoenix. The area became the leading agricultural producer in the Southwest. Urban promoters were behind other water conservation projects in the region as well; El Paso promoters, for instance, were instrumental in securing federal government support for the construction of Elephant Butte Dam on the Rio Grande River in 1916.

The success of the reclamation projects illustrated the importance of water to the development of the urban Southwest. Since the beginning, the oases towns had depended on adjacent river flows and deep underground wells for local sustenance, but the rivers were unreliable, and underground sources were limited. The "water management" systems created by Roosevelt and Elephant Butte Dams benefited the Phoenix and El Paso areas the most. Albuquerque suffered from floods caused by the erratic behavior of the uncontrolled Rio Grande River north of Elephant Butte Dam, and Tucson reaped the consequences of possessing the most limited water supply of the four major cities in the region.

The reclamation projects also demonstrated the vital contribution of the federal government to the growth of the urban Southwest. In each case, federal money and federal expertise proved indispensable in seeing the projects through to completion, and once in place they delivered a considerable advantage to the oases involved. But it took more than the cooperation of Washington to realize the successful urbanization of the desert. As on other frontiers, the progress of the towns often depended on the quality of the people who lived in and promoted them. In Phoenix and El Paso, local leaders spent considerable time both at home and in Washington lobbying in behalf of their goals. Urban developers realized "you cannot dream your town into a city; you must build and boost it into one." This attitude could make the difference between urban success and failure. To neglect to boost growth and development for the city and the surrounding area was to risk decline and defeat in the urban sweepstakes.[18]

While Albuquerque and Tucson lagged behind El Paso and Phoenix as centers of business and agricultural life, they competed as climate and cultural centers. Health seekers and tourists continued to flock to the sunshine cities, while physical facilities and social amenities multiplied. New modes of transportation, including the automobile and the airplane, made it easier to travel to the desert centers, "where winter never comes." Some boosters were especially proud of local educational institutions. Because of the University of Arizona, for example, the *Arizona Star* called Tucson the "Athens of Arizona." The four oases, in addition to providing economic functions, served as transmitters of civilization, and urban promoters benefited the region by instituting social and cultural services in their respective cities. They encouraged and supported schools, colleges, churches, libraries, museums, theaters, and other agents of civilization. Exhibiting an urban consciousness, they helped to refine the Southwest by making the cities the social and cultural enrichment centers of the region.[19]

The urban centers also influenced the social structure of the region. As the oases developed, they became increasingly attractive to Anglo elements, and as they assumed power in the regional centers of the Southwest, they utilized Mexicans as an underclass to help them realize their goals, including economic growth. Having achieved a dominant position in each community, the Anglos acquired more wealth, influence, and prestige, and from these positions of strength, dictated the terms of the ethnic arrangement, which invariably found the majority of the Mexicans and Mexican Americans living on the "wrong side of the tracks." For the majority of Hispanics, as well as the less numerous blacks and Indians, upward mobility proved elusive and poverty remained a problem.[20]

By the 1920s developers had promoted into adoption a host of characteristics common to cities elsewhere, from street and park development to health, fire, and police protection. In this respect, the cities of the Southwest were not unique; they were more imitative than innovative, and they reflected the national culture. As on other urban frontiers, the maturing cities of the desert region were in many ways similar to those throughout the rest of the nation.

In some instances, however, urban leaders in the Southwest had secured advantages especially useful to desert development, such as water storage projects, and at times regional urbanites set the pace for their counterparts elsewhere in the country. For example, they were quick to accept the motor vehicle as a primary mode of transportation. In each of the centers the use of the auto and the bus sent streetcar systems into a decline from which they never recovered. Reliance on the automobile, the bus, and the truck contributed to residential and business dispersal, and as a result, the concept of decentralization gained impetus in the 1920s.

The motor age transformed the urban Southwest as much as the railroads had in the nineteenth century. Suburbs were seen as extensions of the urban cores, and despite their costs in extended services, the "wide open spaces" seemed to offer an escape from the problems of high-density city life. The automobile era enabled the desert cities and suburbs to expand in a low-density pattern of settlement, and this variety of spatial growth afforded a high degree of freedom and a pleasant atmosphere in which to live. The automobile was among the amenities that provided the "good life" promoted by boosters of the four oases.

Also in the 1920s each of the historic transportation crossroads embraced the airplane and its potential and thus they became regional aviation centers by the end of the decade. In 1930, as in 1900, the four cities continued to serve as the principal junction points in the transportation structure of the Southwest, acting as vital links connecting the cities, not only with each other but also with national and international rail, highway, and air service networks. With the increasing importance of these cities as transportation hubs over the years, they became more dominant over their surrounding areas and more attractive to potential residents and business investors.

By 1930 these four cities, led by El Paso—called by some observers the "Chicago of the Southwest" because of its superior railroad and industrial facilities, including the largest copper smelter in the world—were well established as the leading urban centers in the region. Phoenix retained its position as the second largest city in the Southwest, enabling its leaders to laud it as "truly the capital of Arizona, the hub of new developments. As Phoenix goes, so goes Arizona." Tucson, the "second city of Arizona" since being surpassed by Phoenix in the 1920 census, edged out for third place in the regional urban hierarchy Albuquerque, which was "the metropolis of New Mexico" since it had surpassed Santa Fe in population in the 1900 census. The four cities had spearheaded the growth of civilization in the region, and they had exerted an important influence on the development of west Texas, Arizona, and New Mexico.[21] (Table 1.)

Each of the four cities suffered less from the Great Depression than many of their counterparts elsewhere, and except for El Paso, a border city that witnessed a large exodus of Mexicans, they all increased their populations in the 1930s. As in the past, people from not only outside the region but from

Table 1
Population Growth by Decades

City	1880	1890	1900	1910	1920	1930
El Paso	736	10,338	15,906	32,279	77,560	102,421
Phoenix	1,708	3,152	5,544	11,134	29,053	48,118
Tucson	7,007	5,150	7,531	13,193	20,292	32,506
Albuquerque	2,315	3,785	6,238	11,020	15,157	26,570

Source: U.S. Census of Population, 1880–1930.

within it migrated to the cities of the Southwest in search of a future. The urban centers seemed to offer more help to individuals, if not always in jobs, at least in services. New Deal programs especially provided welcome relief and gave impetus to recovery. During the decade a strong relationship developed between the federal government and the urban Southwest as the people of the cities turned to Washington for aid and received it.[22]

After 1940 all four cities continued to benefit greatly from close relations with the nation's capital as the federal government poured large sums of money into the communities, helping to make them major military and high-technology centers. During World War II each of them became the home of important military bases and defense plants. Local organizations such as chambers of commerce worked closely with regional representatives in Washington to secure these valuable assets. Inducements, including building sites, materialized, as every form of cooperation was extended. Fine flying weather and the government's program to locate military bases and defense plants inland to protect them from possible air attacks also helped. As in the past, federal funds and projects stimulated the local economy, and a significant amount of growth and development in the region was due to government or public investment; in short, the crucial role played by "Uncle Sam" in creating the boom in the urban Southwest during and after World War II can hardly be overestimated.

During the cold war, military installations in the urban Southwest continued to serve as part of the national defense effort, and former war plants looked not only to the military but to civilian markets as well. A multiplier effect took hold, and as more industries moved to the urban centers of the region, they attracted others. Predominant were light and clean industries, especially electronics firms, and they flourished in the low-humidity climate so necessary to their success. Electronics plants used little water, and they produced high-value, low-weight products that could be easily shipped overland. The relatively isolated location of the cities was no problem in electronics production because, as one observer declared, "A truckload is worth a million dollars." The region's modern transportation network included everything from trucking lines and major highways to transcontinental railroads and international airlines.

It was important to tourist businesses in the "clean cities" of the Southwest that pollution-free industries settle in the region. City developers encouraged smokeless plants in order to preserve "the sunshine and pure atmosphere" of the oases. In Phoenix, for example, the sun shone 85 percent of the time, a statistic that pleased manufacturers. Business could meet production schedules without being interrupted by adverse weather.

Amenities, including the climate, continued to influence migration to the desert centers. The mass production of air conditioners in the 1950s and the consequent "age of refrigeration" not only attracted manufacturers and brought an extended tourist season to the cities but also made them more comfortable for those permanent residents unable to leave for the coast or the mountains during the hot summer months. Executives and workers also appreciated the nearby mountains and manmade lakes and the active, but casual, year-round life-style that emphasized informal outdoor leisure living. A Douglas Aircraft official in Tucson in the early 1950s revealed that "we came here for the flying conditions and the airport facilities but we've been pleasantly surprised by other advantages. The labor supply, for instance. We can recruit engineers, electronics people, machinists—anything we need. Workers like it here and don't want to move away." Suitable conditions for both work and play seemed to meet in the urban Southwest, and the opportunities and the amenities appealed to many technical and professional people and their families.

During the 1950s the air-conditioned regional hubs offered unprecedented opportunities and amenities, and led by Phoenix, the largest city in the Southwest by 1960, they were making strides toward metropolis status. In Phoenix, manufacturing had become the city's principal source of income by 1955. Between 1948 and 1960 nearly three hundred manufacturing enterprises opened their doors as manufacturing employment in the metropolitan area tripled. The annual income from manufacturing rose from under $5 million in 1940 to over $435 million in 1963. As a result, Phoenix achieved economic diversification, and the Valley of the Sun emerged as the metropolitan center of commerce and industry in the Southwest.[23]

A major reason the Arizona capital moved ahead of the Texas city in the 1950s was the attitude and ambition of its leaders. Southwest urban promoters frequently noted the aggressive tactics of Phoenicians. As one El Pasoan declared, in the Arizona capital "industrial scouts are met at the plane, entertained, offered free land, tax deals, and an electorate willing to approve millions in business-backed bond issues." By comparison, he lamented, "El Paso does nothing," and as a result it "has lost its spot as the number-one city in the Southwest." And, he concluded, "Unless we start hustling after new industry, we're going to wind up in serious trouble."[24]

Phoenix moved to the top of the urban hierarchy in the Southwest in the 1950s and remained there during the next two decades, with manufacturing holding its lead as the most dynamic growth sector. By the end of 1977, the Arizona capital had 74.4 percent of the total manufacturing employment in the state, and the annual income from manufacturing in the Phoenix area had increased to $2.5 billion, up from $4.8 million in 1940. Electronics and aerospace plants dominated the industrial landscape in the Valley of the Sun, and in 1980 the area ranked third in the nation behind metropolitan San Francisco and metropolitan Boston as a high-technology center. Other cities in the Southwest could not keep up with the promoters of the Arizona metropolis. As a bank president in El Paso put it in December 1978, "I hate to express it publicly, but it's true our leadership has been sort of mediocre. We didn't have the influx of well-educated people in the industrial and commercial world. Phoenix did. Some of these kinds of people are coming here now." At the same time, another El Paso businessman remarked that "we haven't always done a selling job of what we've got. Phoenix has done a better job."

In the 1970s the Texas city broadened its outlook. Early in the decade, the newly formed El Paso Development Corporation announced that "the western tip of Texas has always depended upon copper, cotton, cattle, and climate and more recently on the clothing industry as the basis of livelihood for the people living here." The city's "phenomenal growth during the past three decades has been reflected by a similar growth in the five C's as well as a steady expansion at Ft. Bliss." However, for the city to reach its true potential, it "must seek and acquire new industry." By the late 1970s, with the support of public officials and private interests on both sides of the border, major electronics firms such as RCA, General Electric, Sylvania, and West-inghouse had located in El Paso and Juarez. At the same time, Tucson and Albuquerque also attracted industry, including high-technology firms of the caliber of IBM, Gates-Learjet, National Semiconductor, and Digital Equipment.[25]

As the population rose, the urban centers not only continued to serve more tourists as well as their increasing resident populations but also remained the trading and distribution hubs for vast regions of towns, farms, ranches, and mines. They functioned as the service stations of the Southwest. Employment increases within the services and trade sectors accounted for a sizable percentage of the total increase in employment registered in the thirty years before 1980. In fact, by that year the services sector provided the most jobs in each of the metropolitan areas, and the importance of that sector to the regional economy was clear.

The growth of government programs and institutions, ranging from military bases to state universities, provided more jobs and also contributed to the population explosion and economic boom. Fort Bliss in El Paso became known as the air defense center of the world, and Kirtland Air Force Base in Albuquerque served as one of the major national defense installations in the Southwest. Others were Davis-Monthan Air Force Base in Tucson and Luke Air Force Base in Phoenix. Phoenix remained the capital of Arizona, and each of the cities continued to function as centers of government employment and government activity at all levels. Public institutions of higher learning in each of the urban areas served not only as economic generators but also as cultural and intellectual leaders in the Southwest. They offered excellent undergraduate and graduate programs and provided increasing instruction in business and engineering to satisfy the demands of the new high-technology society they and the cities of the region wished to represent. Arizona State University in Tempe (part of the Phoenix metropolitan complex) recorded 39,431 students in 1980, up from 11,128 in 1960. Record-breaking enrollments also occurred at the University of Arizona at Tucson, the University of New Mexico in Albuquerque, and the University of Texas at El Paso.[26]

The growth of the universities reflected the magnitude of the great migration to the Southwest since World War II. The economy of the regional hubs, based largely on government spending, remained strong. Opportunities and amenities continued to increase in the Southwest urban centers, while cities elsewhere became increasingly less inviting. To continue to attract high-technology companies to the region, urban leaders promoted support for local institutions of higher learning. As each of the metropolitan hubs joined the competition to become another "Silicon Valley" of the West, pressure mounted to give massive amounts of dollars to local universities, especially their business and engineering schools. For example, an Arizona State University official recently noted that "a $38 million Engineering Excellence Program, designed to establish ASU as a major research center nationally, is on target." Prompted by a "burgeoning growth of high-tech industries," the "goal is to propel ASU into the ranks of the foremost engineering programs in the United States." The "school will be working closely with industry to turn the Valley of the Sun into a 'silicon oasis.'" The high-tech-oriented urban universities of the Southwest, with their new research facilities, boosters declared, were needed not only to encourage more private and public investment in the urban areas but also to help make the region a vital part of the new computer world. Quality institutions were necessary to educate the population to meet the scientific and social demands of business and society in the new Southwest.[27]

Agriculture, despite urban encroachment, also continued to be important to the welfare of the metropolitan Southwest, but it is declining because of the heavy demands it makes on water supplies. For example, in Arizona in 1980, agriculture was using 89 percent of the water consumed, as opposed to 7 percent being used by the cities and 4 percent being utilized by industry. In 1979 in the Tucson area, farmers were using 75 percent of the water, although they accounted for only 2 percent of the work force. The city of Tucson, being totally dependent on groundwater, had already purchased and retired from cultivation some 11,000 acres of irrigated agricultural land in order to meet increasing urban needs. The fate of farming, therefore, in the Tucson area may well be doomed to extinction if metropolitan area growth continued to prevail.

Experts have declared that water shortages will not stem from the population influx because more of the water supply can be diverted from agricultural to nonagricultural users. Moreover, the conservation of water has become a planning priority on both the state and municipal levels. For example, the 1980 Groundwater Management Act in Arizona, which regulates the use of water by irrigators and requires better water management in the urban centers, will force groundwater conservation in the metropolitan areas, and that action could very well serve as a model for the region. Voluntary water conservation programs also have been encouraged in the cities, with Tucson leading the way. Higher water-use rate structures and public education programs implemented in the cities in recent years have resulted in voluntary reductions in water consumption. The goal is to cut waste by making water conservation a way of life in the desert cities. In addition, local leaders have continued to work with representatives and officials in Washington to secure support for water projects in the Southwest that will supply more of that precious commodity to the urban centers; for example, the completion of the federally funded Central Arizona Project by the late 1980s, which will bring Colorado River water to Phoenix and Tucson, is being vigorously promoted by a variety of metropolitan interests. As in the past, boosters aware that serious water problems could lead to limited growth have called for action.[28]

Urban leadership has exerted a strong influence over the entire region. In practically every field of endeavor, urban leaders have stood out. An *Arizona Republic* survey in December 1981 declared that the twenty most powerful people in the state of Arizona were Anglos from Phoenix. Anglos were in control of each of the oases as well as the region. The *Albuquerque Journal* in February 1980 noted in a local power study that out of fifty-five "wielders of clout" in the city, only five were Hispanic. In December 1978 the *El Paso Times* reported that not a single Hispanic was among the twenty-five most influential men in the economic life of the city. At the same time, more members of minority groups, many of them business and professional people, moved into the middle class. The positive effect of such dynamic forces as the G.I. Bill, the civil rights movement, and the growth of the economy made it possible for individual Hispanics to benefit from new educational and employment opportunities, but progress for Hispanics as a group (the largest minority group in the urban Southwest) proved to be slow. In El Paso, for example, as Oscar J. Martinez put it in 1980, Hispanics "as a community have traveled only a short distance in their quest to achieve parity with the Anglo population. Economically and socially, a gulf still separates the two groups."[29]

Meanwhile, newcomers of all ages from within and without the region continued to flock to the air-conditioned capitals of the Southwest where opportunities and amenities seemed to blend so well. Most of the newcomers were young, the median age of the population being below the national average. In Tucson in 1980, the average age was 28.2; in Albuquerque it was 24.7. For many newcomers, it was a chance to work America's newest boom frontier. As one observer put it regarding Phoenix, "The mood is here; the word is out; this is the place. The city is going somewhere, and it is attracting more than an average share of people who want to go somewhere with it." As a result of this dynamic appeal, the four oases experienced phenomenal growth, and Phoenix set the pace. By 1980 it ranked as the ninth largest city in the nation, up from twentieth in 1970. (Table 2.)

The four major metropolitan areas of the Southwest were dominated by the central cities. In 1980, 78 percent of the population of El Paso County lived in El Paso, while 73 percent of the people of Bernalillo County lived in

Table 2
Population Growth by Decades

City	1940	1950	1960	1970	1980
Phoenix	65,414	106,818	439,170	584,303	789,704
El Paso	98,810	130,485	276,687	322,261	425,259
Tucson	35,752	45,454	212,892	262,933	330,537
Albuquerque	35,449	95,815	201,189	244,501	331,767

Source: U.S. Census of Population, 1940–1980.

Albuquerque. In Arizona, 52 percent of Maricopa County's population resided in Phoenix, while 65 percent of the population in Pima County made Tucson their home. Only in Maricopa County did sizable incorporated centers develop outside the central city. As Phoenix experienced more growth following World War II, nearby settlements, including Tempe, Scottsdale, and Mesa to the east and Glendale to the west, became larger satellites of Phoenix. Although they were small communities in 1940, they thrived along with Phoenix during the next forty years, and as a result, there emerged one vast, auto-connected metropolitan complex, with the capital city in the middle.[30] (Table 3.)

As time passed, the metropolitan hubs of the Southwest came to dominate the region more than ever. In 1980, Phoenix was the fastest growing among the top thirty metropolitan areas in the nation, and by that year, the four urban complexes accounted for 67 percent of the regional population. An oasis civilization had prevailed in the Southwest; it was part of that larger "oasis civilization" in the American West, first noted by Walter Prescott Webb in 1957 and later developed by Gerald D. Nash in 1973, that has dominated much of the history of the trans-Mississippi country since the nineteenth century. The Southwest seemed less urban than other parts of the nation because of the vast stretches of land that remained unoccupied by people between the four oases, but it was an urban region, too, with urban dwellers comprising almost two-thirds of its inhabitants. The popularity of the cities was clear; in Arizona, for instance, nearly 80 percent of the entire state's population lived in metropolitan Phoenix and Tucson by 1980. The region contained four of the leading metropolitan centers in the burgeoning Sun Belt—a "new" American section that lay south of the 37th parallel and extended across the country from North Carolina to southern California. Since World War II, the ongoing decline of the old Snow Belt urban centers in the Northeast and Midwest had caused a shift in demographic and economic power toward the rising urban centers of the Sun Belt in the South, Southwest, and in southern California.[31]

Currently, the four hubs are part of the "new" urban America, and it is part of the "big change" in the nation. In 1980 the census for the first time in American history indicated that the West and the South had more people than the North and the East. Among the fastest-growing states were those

Table 3
Population of Phoenix and Neighboring Communities

City	1940	1950	1960	1970	1980
Phoenix	65,414	106,818	439,170	584,303	789,704
Mesa	7,224	16,670	33,772	63,049	152,453
Tempe	2,906	7,684	24,897	63,550	106,742
Glendale	4,855	8,179	15,696	36,228	97,172
Scottsdale	1,000	2,032	10,026	67,823	88,412
Chandler	1,239	3,799	9,531	13,763	29,673

Source: U.S. Census of Population, 1940–1980.

located in the Sun Belt Southwest. The census of 1980 also uncovered a massive shift in economic activity that had encouraged the population change. The Sun Belt Southwest gained new jobs as well as new people, while the Snow Belt lost both jobs and people. The shift appears to be irreversible, and experts have predicted that the four regional metropolitan complexes will be among the top ten employment centers in the country during the remainder of the century. The lure of the cities cannot be denied. Opportunities and amenities, despite the problems of growth, will continue to draw people to them as long as the new restructuring of America persists. The Phoenix metropolitan area, for example, contained a population of 1.5 million in 1980; demographers expect it to exceed 2.3 million by 1990. (See Table 4.)[32]

From the beginning, the urban dimension has been a major factor in the history of the American Southwest. Without an appreciation of its crucial role in the growth and development of the region, the story is incomplete. The four metropolitan areas represent the centers of life in a land of wide open spaces. Although these areas are the focal points of an oasis civilization, in the past many historians either dismissed their role in the region entirely or accorded it an insignificant place. Until recently, there were no biographies of any of the cities, hor were there any comparative studies; but the urban Southwest can no longer be ignored or slighted. The urban pioneers of the Southwest deserve as much credit for developing the region as the trappers, miners, farmers, ranchers, and cowboys most often dwelled upon by historians. Living in the modern Southwest—an urban region—and searching for a "usable past," some scholars have found more meaning in an urban Southwest with an urban past; to them the urban dimension of the past deserves at least as much attention as other vital elements. From their perspective, it is clearly time to redress the imbalance in southwestern historiography. As it has for other regions, an urban view should provide a fuller understanding of the history of the American Southwest.

Table 4
Population of the Four Southwest Standard Metropolitan Statistical Areas

City	1940	1950	1960	1970	1980
Phoenix (Maricopa County)	186,193	331,770	663,510	971,225	1,509,052
Tucson (Pima County)	72,838	141,216	265,660	351,667	531,443
El Paso (El Paso County)	131,067	194,968	314,070	359,291	479,899
Albuquerque	69,391	145,673	276,400	333,266	454,499
(Bernalillo County with parts of Sandoval County added in 1960, 1970, 1980)					

Source: U.S. Census of Population, 1940–1980.

NOTES

[1]For the current state of western American urban history see Bradford Luckingham, "The Urban Dimension of Western History," in Michael P. Malone, ed., *Historians and the American West* (Lincoln, 1983), 323–43.

[2]Richard C. Wade, *The Urban Frontier: The Rise of Western Cities, 1790–1830* (Cambridge, 1959); Bayrd Still, "Patterns of Mid-Nineteenth Century Urbanization in the Middle West," *Mississippi Valley Historical Review*, XXVIII (September 1941), 187–206.

[3]Kenneth W. Wheeler, *To Wear a City's Crown: The Beginnings of Urban Growth in Texas, 1836–1865* (Cambridge, 1968), 165–66.

[4]Duane A. Smith, *Rocky Mountain Mining Camps: The Urban Frontier* (Bloomington, 1967); Robert R. Dykstra, *The Cattle Towns* (New York, 1971).

[5]Earl Pomeroy, *The Pacific Slope: A History of California, Oregon, Washington, Idaho, Utah, and Nevada* (New York, 1966), 120.

[6]Lawrence H. Larsen, *The Urban West at the End of the Frontier* (Lawrence, 1978); John W. Reps, *Cities of the American West: A History of Frontier Urban Planning* (Princeton, 1979), 694; Gerald D. Nash, *The American West in the Twentieth Century: A Short History of an Urban Oasis* (Englewood Cliffs, 1973), 6.

[7]Wallace Stegner, editorial, *American West*, IV (February 1967), 5; Carl Abbott, "Building Western Cities: A Review Essay," *Colorado Heritage* (January 1984), 39–46.

[8]Walter Prescott Webb, "The American West: Perpetual Mirage," *Harper's Magazine*, 214 (May 1957), 25–31. For the Spanish period see Oakah L. Jones, Jr., *Los Paisanos: Spanish Settlers on the Northern Frontier of New Spain* (Norman, 1979); Henry F. Dobyns, *Spanish Colonial Tucson: A Demographic History* (Tucson, 1976); C. L. Sonnichsen, *Pass of the North: Four Centuries on the Rio Grande* (El Paso, 1968); Marc Simmons, *Albuquerque: A Narrative History* (Albuquerque, 1982); Joseph D. Lippert, "Plaza to Main Street: Urbanization in Arizona and New Mexico, 1610–1860" (doctoral dissertation, Northern Arizona University, 1983). My definition of the Southwest follows that of the eminent geographer, D. W. Meinig, in his *Southwest: Three Peoples in Geographical Change, 1600–1970* (New York, 1971).

[9]For the Mexican and prerailroad eras see Lippert, "Plaza to Main Street"; Sonnichsen, *Pass of the North*; Oscar J. Martinez, *Border Boom Town: Ciudad Júarez since 1848* (Austin, 1978); Simmons, *Albuquerque*; Terry Lehman, "Santa Fe and Albuquerque, 1870–1900: Conflict in the Development of Two Southwestern Towns" (doctoral dissertation, Indiana University, 1974); C. L. Sonnichsen, *Tucson: The Life and Times of an American City* (Norman, 1982); Bradford Luckingham, *The Urban Southwest: A Profile History of Albuquerque, El Paso, Phoenix, and Tucson* (El Paso, 1982).

[10]*Albuquerque Review*, April 24, 1880. For the importance of railroad promotion on other urban frontiers see Charles N. Glaab, "Historical Perspective on Urban Development Schemes," in Leo F. Schnore, ed., *Social Science and the City: A Survey of Urban Research* (New York, 1968), 197–219; also William Silag, "Gateway to the Grasslands: Sioux City and the Missouri River Frontier," *Western Historical Quarterly*, XIV (October 1983), 396–414.

[11]*Albuquerque Review*, April 29, 1880; Victor Westphall, "Albuquerque in the 1870's," *New Mexico Historical Review*, XXIII (October 1948), 253–68; Simmons, *Albuquerque*.

[12]*El Paso Herald*, June 1, 1881; Edward A. Leonard, *Rails at the Pass of the North* (El Paso, 1981).

[13]Geoffrey P. Mawn, "Phoenix, Arizona: Central City of the Southwest, 1870–1920" (doctoral dissertation, Arizona State University, 1979); Karen Lynn Smith, "From Town to City: A History of Phoenix, 1870–1912" (master's thesis, University of California, Santa Barbara, 1978); Simmons, *Albuquerque*; Sonnichsen, *Tucson*.

[14]*El Paso Times*, January 2, 1890; *Albuquerque Morning Journal*, February 12, 1912; Luckingham, *The Urban Southwest*, 26.

[15]Luckingham, *The Urban Southwest*, 26; Sonnichsen, *Pass of the North*, 215.

[16]G. Wesley Johnson, Jr., "Dwight Heard in Phoenix: The Early Years," *Journal of Arizona History*, 18 (Autumn 1977), 259–78. For the importance of urban promoters on other frontiers of the American West see Bradford Luckingham, "The City in the Westward Movement: A Bibliographical Note," *Western Historical Quarterly*, V (July 1974), 295–306.

[17]Sonnichsen, *Pass of the North*; Martinez, *Border Boom Town*; Simmons, *Albuquerque*; Sonnichsen, *Tucson*; Luckingham, *The Urban Southwest*.

[18]Luckingham, *The Urban Southwest*; Mawn, "Phoenix, Arizona"; Karen Smith, "The Magnificent Experiment: Building the Salt River Reclamation Project, 1890–1917" (doctoral dissertation, University of California, Santa Barbara, 1982).

[19]Erna Fergusson, *Our Southwest* (New York, 1941); Douglas D. Martin, *The Lamp in the Desert: The Story of the University of Arizona* (Tucson, 1960); Sonnichsen, *Tucson*; Simmons, *Albuquerque*; Luckingham, *The Urban Southwest*.

[20]Luckingham, *The Urban Southwest*; Mario T. García, *Desert Immigrants: The Mexicans of El Paso, 1880–1920* (New Haven, 1981); Martinez, *Border Boom Town*; Ray B. West, Jr., ed., *Rocky Mountain Cities* (New York, 1949); Shirley J. Roberts, "Minority-Group Poverty in Phoenix: A Socio-Economic Survey," *Journal*

of Arizona History, 14 (Winter 1973), 348–54; James E. Officer, "Sodalities and Systemic Linkage: The Joining Habits of Urban Mexican-Americans" (doctoral dissertation, University of Arizona, 1964).

[21]Bradford Luckingham, "The Southwestern Urban Frontier, 1880–1930," *Journal of the West*, XVIII (July 1979), 40–50. For a good study of the similarities in western urban development see Larsen, *The Urban West*. For the impact of water, climate, and the motor vehicle on a desert city of the far western urban frontier see Robert M. Fogelson, *The Fragmented Metropolis: Los Angeles, 1850–1930* (Cambridge, 1967).

[22]Sonnichsen, *Pass of the North*; Simmons, *Albuquerque*; Sonnichsen, *Tucson*; Michael Kotlanger, "Phoenix, Arizona: 1920–1940" (doctoral dissertation, Arizona State University, 1983); Luckingham, *The Urban Southwest*.

[23]Luckingham, *The Urban Southwest*; Michael Konig, "Phoenix in the 1950s: Urban Growth in the 'Sunbelt,'" *Arizona and the West*, 24 (Spring 1982); Michael Konig, "Toward Metropolis Status: Phoenix, 1945–1960" (doctoral dissertation, Arizona State University, 1983); Sonnichsen, *Pass of the North*; Simmons, *Albuquerque*; Sonnichsen, *Tucson*.

[24]Luckingham, *The Urban Southwest*, especially 75–82.

[25]Ibid., 84.

[26]Ibid., 96–97; Sonnichsen, *Pass of the North*; Simmons, *Albuquerque*; Robert Turner Wood, "The Transformation of Albuquerque, 1945–1972" (doctoral dissertation, University of New Mexico, 1980); Sonnichsen, *Tucson*.

[27]*Phoenix Gazette*, March 15, 1984; Luckingham, *The Urban Southwest*.

[28]Luckingham, *The Urban Southwest*.

[29]Ibid.; Oscar J. Martinez, *The Chicanos of El Paso: An Assessment of Progress* (El Paso, 1980), 39; Joseph V. Metzgar, "Guns and Butter: Albuquerque Hispanics, 1940–1975," *New Mexico Historical Review*, 56 (April 1981), 117–39. For the power studies see (Phoenix) *Arizona Republic*, December 13, 1981; *Albuquerque Journal*, February 26, 1980; *El Paso Times*, December 17–28, 1978. See also (Tucson) *Arizona Daily Star*, July 16, 1978.

[30]Luckingham, *The Urban Southwest*; Bradford Luckingham, "Phoenix: The Desert Metropolis," in Richard M. Bernard and Bradley R. Rice, eds., *Sunbelt Cities: Politics and Growth since World War II* (Austin, 1983), 309–27.

[31]Luckingham, "Phoenix"; Luckingham, *The Urban Southwest*; Howard N. Rabinowitz, "Growth Trends in the Albuquerque SMSA, 1940–1978," *Journal of the West*, XVIII (July 1979), 62–74; Howard N. Rabinowitz, "Albuquerque: City at a Crossroads," in Bernard and Rice, eds., *Sunbelt Cities*, 255–67; Don Bufkin, "From Mud Village to Modern Metropolis: The Urbanization of Tucson," *Journal of Arizona History*, 22 (Spring 1981), 63–98; Webb, "The American West"; Nash, *The American West in the Twentieth Century*; Carl Abbott, "The American Sunbelt: Idea and Region," *Journal of the West*, XVIII (July 1979), 5–18. Recent popular accounts of the four cities, each of which contains hundreds of illustrations, include George Fitzpatrick and Harvey Caplin, *Albuquerque—100 Years in Pictures, 1875–1975* (Albuquerque, 1975); John Bret Harte, *Tucson: Portrait of a Desert Pueblo* (Woodland Hills, California, 1980); G. Wesley Johnson, *Phoenix: Valley of the Sun* (Tulsa, 1982); Leon Metz, *City at the Pass: An Illustrated History of El Paso* (Woodland Hills, California, 1980).

[32]Abbott, "The American Sunbelt"; Carl Abbott, *The New Urban America: Growth and Politics in Sunbelt Cities* (Chapel Hill, 1981); John Naisbitt, *Megatrends: Ten New Directions Transforming Our Lives* (New York, 1982).

America's Cities Are (Mostly) Better than Ever

*Richard C. Wade**

More than a decade ago the phrase "urban crisis" crept into our public conversation. Since then it has become a cliché, connoting a wide range of persistent and dangerous problems confronting our cities. Moreover, the phrase, like "missile crisis" or "energy crisis," suggests both newness and immediate danger. The rioting, arson, and looting that erupted in the 1960s fortified this general impression. Presumably something unprecedented had happened. Urban life had become unmanageable; in the professional and popular view, cities were "ungovernable."

Something new, indeed, had happened. It was not that American cities had not known violence and race conflict before. They ran like thick red lines through the history of many cities. But the scale and ubiquity of the modern outbreaks had no earlier analogue. Large and small cities, both north and south, witnessed almost simultaneous explosions; the number of dead and injured and the amount of property damage easily exceeded those of anything previous. Few people predicted the rioting, hence most sought for an explanation in very recent developments—black migrations, the slow pace of desegregation, unemployment, broken families, and the Vietnam War.

Yet the fires of the 1960s were not the arson of a single decade or generation. Urban society had been accumulating combustibles for well over a century. The seventies have simply tamped down the flames while the ashes still smolder and, unless the historical sources of the present crisis are better understood and public policy changed, a recurrence, next time probably worse, is almost inevitable. New York City's experience during the 1977 blackout ought to have served as the first alarm for the nation.

What baffled most commentators in the sixties was that the convulsions came at a time when urban experts confidently had asserted that the nation's cities were overcoming their afflictions. There had been, for example, a marked decline in the percentage of substandard housing; there were relatively fewer urban poor than ever before; hospital beds had caught up with need; federal

*Richard C. Wade is Distinguished Professor of History at the City University of New York. Reprinted by permission from American Heritage 30 (February–March 1979): 6–13. Copyright 1979 by American Heritage Publishing Company.

programs were bringing health care to an unprecedented number of people; schools had reduced class size; new skylines attested to renewed downtown vitality; municipal government, though scarred by occasional scandals, was demonstrably more competent than it once had been.

To the historian the argument had a superficial validity. One only had to compare the city of 1970 with the city of 1900 to measure municipal progress. At the turn of the century every city had its concentrations of wretched neighborhoods where poor people huddled in rundown or jerry-built houses and in tenements lacking even toilets or running water. Primitive coal stoves provided the heat; kerosene lamps the light. Family cohesiveness, always fragile, often cracked under the weight of these oppressive circumstances. Nor were these conditions exceptional. Jacob Riis's *How the Other Half Lives* described the festering slums on New York's Lower East Side in 1890; but as the title suggests, he was also discussing the predicament of over 50 percent of the city's population. Indeed, a congressional inquiry into urban housing at about the same time demonstrated that every metropolis matched New York's dilapidated, unsanitary, and dangerous dwellings.

Nor was there much in the neighborhood to compensate for the miseries of home life. The droppings of thousands of horses made even crossing the street hazardous. Garbage clogged thoroughfares; sanitation carts picked their way through congested avenues and alleys once a week at best. Cheap shops and uninspected markets lined the sidewalks. No traffic regulations prevented horse-drawn trucks and carts, electric trolleys, and private hacks from creating a continual cacophony, day and night. And dense smoke from coal-burning factories and office buildings rolled darkly through downtown. Worse still, crime and violence were constant companions of slum dwellers.

Three institutions attenuated the misery of the slum—the church, the school, and the saloon. And they were attractive precisely because they provided what the tenement and neighborhood lacked. The church was clean and uncongested; its friendly priest, minister, or rabbi cared about the parishioners and their families. Even the most primitive schools took the children out of the tenement and into rooms that were at least heated in the winter. The saloon was bright and congenial, and the husband could meet with friends and neighbors away from the oppressive crowding of the apartment. Yet these oases could not conceal—indeed they only magnified—the grinding deprivation of the lives of these people. Later commentators would invest the "good old neighborhood" with charm, conviviality, and livability; but to most of its residents, life was a losing struggle against filth, noise, and disorder.

The whole family was drawn into the contest. Jobs for anyone were scarce and irregular. Good, steady work that permitted the father to feed, clothe, and shelter his family on his own was very rare. The wife and children usually had to enter the already overcrowded job market. Mothers and daughters sewed, packaged nuts, made artificial flowers. Young boys sold newspapers, picked coal, collected rags, ran errands. Frequent depressions did away with even these menial tasks.

Schooling was brief. Children dropped out, not at fourteen or fifteen, but at eight or nine. Even so, education was often inadequate: classrooms were crowded, teachers poorly trained and politically selected. No audiovisual aids or paraprofessional help assisted the beleaguered instructor; the truant officer became a familiar figure in the neighborhood. Reformers sought vainly to get class sizes down to fifty and replace patronage appointments with professionals.

Conditions in the area were tolerable only because those who lived there considered them temporary. Residential turnover was high; one of every five families had a different address each year. Most, of course, moved only a short distance and often because they could not pay the rent. But a significant number found housing in more pleasant communities away from the old slum. Scholars later argued over the percentage who "made it" out; yet every resident knew someone who did; a relative, perhaps, or someone on the block or in the parish. But the possibility of escape was as much a part of the experience as confinement.

The change over the subsequent three-quarters of a century was dramatic. In 1902, Robert Hunter estimated that over half the urban population lived beneath the poverty line. By 1970 that figure had fallen to less than 20 percent, even though the definition of poverty had been raised substantially. Density in the inner city dropped drastically; Jacob Riis found over 300,000 people per square mile living in New York's tenth ward; today, any concentration over 75,000 a square mile is considered intolerable. Public policy and private development removed the most visible downtown slums, though cancerous nodes remained behind. Public housing, with all its problems, replaced the most depressed and dilapidated areas. New building in the outer city and suburbs provided modern accommodations for an exploding urban population. In the sixties, experts argued over whether "substandard" housing composed 15 or 18 percent of the total stock; judged by the same standards seventy years earlier, it would have composed more than half.

Even the crime rate was probably higher in 1900, though there is no way to prove it. Police organization was primitive, and systematic reporting of crime was still decades away. Politicians hired and fired the force; collusion between criminals and police was common. Constant gang warfare jeopardized the peace of nearly every downtown area. Political reformers always promised the "restoration of law and order."

Municipal governments were too weak to control matters. State governments granted cities only modest powers, and then only grudgingly. Corruption riddled most city halls and municipalities. Political bosses and special interests united to plunder the public till. Lincoln Steffens made a national reputation with the book entitled *The Shame of the Cities*, which chronicled the boodle, bribery, and chicanery that he contended characterized nearly every American city. Good government forces occasionally broke the unseemly ring, but usually not for long.

In short, the present city, for all its problems, is cleaner, less crowded, safer, and more livable than its turn-of-the-century counterpart. Its people are more prosperous, better educated, and healthier than they were seventy years ago.

The slow but steady improvement in municipal affairs was the result of both particular historical conditions of the twentieth century and the

efforts of many generations of urban dwellers. American cities enjoyed continued growth and expansion for most of the period. They were also the vital
centers of a surging national economy. As the country became increasingly
urban, the best talent and greatest wealth gravitated to the metropolis, where
a huge pool of skilled and unskilled labor could be easily tapped. This combination made it possible for the United States to become the most powerful
industrial nation in the world.

Technological changes, themselves largely products of the urban explosion, permitted new advances in municipal management. Subways, elevateds,
and automobiles facilitated the movement of people throughout the expanding
metropolis, retiring horses to the country. Modern medicine increased the
effectiveness of public health measures. Electricity and central heating
improved the comfort of new housing, and the long-term mortgage made
home ownership easier to manage. Movies, radio, and television democratized
entertainment, if they did not always elevate it. New laws forced more children
into schools and kept them there longer.

Though progress was often sporadic, city government widened its competence and improved its performance. Tensions between reformers and urban
machines resulted in permanent gains, for after each revolt was beaten back,
some improvements were always retained. Civil service slowly produced a
bureaucracy that, for all its clumsiness, was distinctly superior to the earlier
rampant patronage system. Zoning put a measure of predictability, if not
control, into land use. And nearly everywhere the quality of urban leadership
was noticeably better than before. A few old-time bosses persisted, but they
were viewed as quaint anachronisms rather than as the logical expressions
of city politics.

This considerable achievement rested on two historical conditions—the
general prosperity of the period and the ample municipal limits which permitted expanding economic activity to take place within a single political
jurisdiction. Except for the Great Depression and occasional sharp dips in
the business index, American cities generally witnessed sustained growth.
Even wartime did not interrupt the expansion; indeed, immense military
spending acted as a swift stimulus to urban economies. Municipal progress
cost money—a lot of it—and American cities generally had it to spend. And
when they did not, they borrowed, confident that the future would be even
more prosperous.

This was, moreover, the age of the self-sufficient city. Municipal bound-
aries were wide and continually enlarging. In 1876 St. Louis reached out into
neighboring farm land and incorporated all the area now within its city limits.
In one swift move in 1889, Chicago added over 125 square miles to its territory.
And in 1898, New York absorbed the four surrounding counties—including
Brooklyn, the nation's fourth largest city—making it the world's Empire City.

In 1900 municipal boundaries were generous, almost always including
unsettled and undeveloped land. As populations grew, there were always
fresh areas to build up. This meant that all the wealth, all the commerce, all
the industry, and all the talent lay within the city. When serious problems
arose, all the resources of the metropolis could be brought to bear to solve

them. More prosperous than either the state or federal governments, the cities needed no outside help; indeed they met any interference with the demand for home rule.

For as long as these historical conditions prevailed, American cities could make incremental progress in attacking even the most vexing problems. But after the Second World War, two divisive elements entered the metropolis, destroying its economic and governmental unity and profoundly altering its social structure. The first division was between suburb and city; the second between black and white. Actually, these fissures always had been present, but not on the same scale or with the same intensity, and certainly not with the same significance.

Suburbanization is almost as old as urbanization. American cities always have grown from the inside out; as population increased, it spilled outside municipal limits. Initially these suburbs were not the exclusive resort of the wealthy; many poor lived there to avoid city taxes and regulations. But railroad development in the mid-nineteenth century produced modern commuting suburbs: Chicago had fifty-two of them by 1874. Though suburbs grew rapidly, their numbers were always relatively small and their locations governed by rail lines. By the 1920s the automobile spawned a second generation of suburbs, filling in the areas between the older ones and setting off an unprecedented building boom beyond the municipal limits.

The crash of 1929 put an end to suburban expansion for fifteen years. During the Depression, people could not afford new housing, and when war came, the military consumed all available construction material. But the pent-up demand broke loose with the coming of peace. By 1970 the census reported that more people in the metropolitan regions lived outside the municipal boundaries than within. All cities, even smaller ones, were surrounded by numerous small jurisdictions, self-governing, self-taxing—and growing.

The historical remedy to this problem—annexation of surrounding areas— was no longer available. In most states the process required a majority of the voters in both the cities and the suburbs to support consolidation, and after 1920 the outlying areas were increasingly against incorporation. The cities, now with fixed boundaries, gradually lost population, while the suburbs experienced steady growth.

Moreover, this demographic change profoundly altered the social structure of the metropolis. The middle class rapidly evacuated the old city in favor of the suburbs. In turn, they were replaced by migrants from the South and from Latin America. The newcomers were mostly poor and racially distinct. With little education or skills, they were tax consumers rather than tax producers. They needed help on a large scale. Most of all they needed jobs. But industry and commerce had followed the outward movement of people. At just the time municipal government faced additional responsibilities, it saw its revenue base shrinking. Inevitably, various groups fell to quarreling over these limited resources, producing new tensions and anxieties.

The rioting of the 1960s revealed another fissure in the metropolis—the division between black and white. Some blacks always had lived in cities, even under slavery. But the "peculiar institution" had confined most to the Southern countryside. After the Civil War, former slaves without land or urban skills drifted into Southern cities, where they quickly composed a large portion of the population. The urban South accommodated the newcomers within an elaborate system of segregation. The separation of the races was accomplished both by custom and, after 1896, under Jim Crow statutes.

The massive Northern migration of rural Southern blacks in this century, however, slowly altered the racial composition of nearly every city across the country. Municipal governments adopted no new policies to deal with the influx. Indeed, they assumed that the same process that had incorporated millions of immigrants into the metropolitan mainstream would also be available to blacks. That is, the newcomers initially would congregate at the heart of town, increase their numbers, get an economic foothold, and then gradually disperse into more pleasant residential neighborhoods away from the congested center. This process, though often cruel and painful, had served the immigrants, the city, and the country well.

But the blacks' experience was fundamentally different. They did, indeed, gather at the center, and there they found what immigrants always had found: wretched housing, overcrowded neighborhoods, high unemployment, inadequate schools, littered streets, garbage-strewn alleys, rampant crime, and endemic disorder. However, the new ghetto, unlike the old, did not loosen and disperse. Rather, it simply spread block by block, oozing out over adjacent communities. White residents retreated while blacks moved into new areas beyond downtown. Later, a generation would grow up that knew only the ghetto and its debilitating life.

The immigrant ghetto had been tolerable because it was thought to be temporary, a rough staging ground for upward and outward mobility. Blacks increasingly perceived the ghetto to be their permanent home. And each federal census fortified this apprehension as the index of racial segregation moved steadily upward. There was, of course, some modest leakage here and there, but the barriers to escape remained formidable.

This confinement had two consequences that were different from those of the old ghetto. The first was the alienation of its black middle class. They, after all, had done what they were supposed to do: stayed in school, kept out of serious trouble, got higher education, and made good money. But they were still denied, by the color of their skin alone, that most important symbol of success in America—the right to live in a neighborhood of their own choosing with schools appropriate to their ambitions for their children.

The size of this black middle class is large; indeed, no other group has had a success story quite equal to it. In 1950 the federal census listed about 10 percent of American blacks as "middle class"; by 1960 that figure had climbed to nearly 18 percent; by 1970 it had jumped above one-third. To be sure, it often required two breadwinners in the family to achieve this status; that, plus ambition and hard work. For these people, continued *de facto* residential segregation was especially cruel. Even in fashionable black neighborhoods, hope turned into resentful bitterness.

For the less successful, the situation was much worse. The black ghetto contained the city's worst housing, schools, and community institutions. It generated few jobs and experienced soaring unemployment. Crime rates were high, gang warfare common, and vice rampant. All this contributed to the breakdown of family life and the encouragement of dependency. Newcomers always had found it difficult to adjust to the ghetto; race compounded the problem. In the sixties, daily frustrations spilled over into violence. The young struck out against the symbols of their oppression that were closest at hand, reducing large ghetto areas to ashes.

Race, then, greatly widened the already yawning gap between city and suburb. Every important issue that arose within the metropolis reflected this division. School busing became the symbolic question: without residential segregation, no busing would be necessary. "Affirmative action" became a euphemism for introducing minorities into employment areas previously monopolized by whites. The collapse of mass transit left blacks riding in the front of the bus but with diminishing numbers of white companions. While crime rates rose in the suburbs, popular stereotypes still associated violence with inner-city minorities. In short, uniting the metropolis would have been difficult enough; the addition of race introduced an enormously complicating factor.

In the seventies the inner cities quieted down. But the new tranquillity came from black resignation rather than from a larger measure of justice. The unemployment figures contained the warning: 10 percent in older cities; 20 percent in the ghettos; 40 percent among minority youth. In addition, middle-class blacks ran into all kinds of obstacles when trying to escape to the suburbs. The courts were ambivalent about legal restrictions, especially zoning, which had the effect of exclusion. And social pressures in the suburbs were often not very subtle. As a result, the ghetto still festered; indeed, its boundaries expanded each week.

Yet certain factors hold out some hope for the future. For example, suburbs are finding that they are no more self-sufficient than the cities. The same forces that led to urban decay earlier are now spreading into the surrounding communities. This is particularly true of those suburbs adjacent to the city limits. Indeed, the phrase "inner suburbs" surely will join "inner city" as shorthand for the long list of urban ills in the eighties. And for much the same reasons. They are the oldest part of suburban America. In order to keep taxes down, they allowed most of their land to be developed. Now there is no room for expansion. The new suburbanites go farther out; new industrial and commercial installations also bypass the closer-in suburbs. Large numbers of older residents, their children now gone, head for retirement areas or back to the city. Newer shopping centers in outlying suburbs skim off dollars from local merchants. Worse still, crime rates grow faster in these communities than in any other part of the metropolis.

In addition, suburban government is the weakest link in our governmental system. Until recently, residential participation in local affairs was low; most communities hired professional managers to make budgets and administer day-to-day affairs. Voting was light for local offices, and though suburbanites vote heavily Republican in national elections, suburban politics remain consciously nonpartisan. Hence, when the crisis moved in, most suburbs lacked

the tradition or tools to grapple with it. By the 1970s new suburban newspapers began to reveal the often scandalous relations between some developers
and many town halls. Voters increasingly turned down bond issues, even for
schools. The inner suburbs' one trump card is that they still control the
suburban lobby in most states. They played that card to get some relief for
all local governments, hence they became the major beneficiaries. Yet neither
this nor federal revenue-sharing programs could do more than postpone the
inevitable fiscal impasse. When New York City slid toward bankruptcy, Yon-
kers, located in one of the nation's richest suburban counties, was placed in
receivership.

The extension of city problems into the suburbs poked large holes in the
crabgrass curtain that previously had separated the two parts of the metropolis. Now their common predicament created the possibility of a new cooperation to replace the hostility that historically had divided city and suburb.
The inner suburbs were reluctant to recognize their own decline, but by the
seventies they recognized that they had to trade part of their independence
for outside help.

For the first time, a substantial suburban population has a stake in a
united metropolis. The inner ring is no longer self-sufficient. It relies increasingly on state and federal aid rather than on its indigenous tax base. Hence,
its most serious problems cannot be solved without cooperation with the city
as well as with neighboring suburbs. In the 1950s the movement for metropolitan government was essentially a big-city strategy; now that concept has
natural allies. To be sure, the notion of a single governmental jurisdiction is
politically impossible except in a few places.

A consolidation of effort by function, however, is already imperative. In
housing, education, transportation, water, pollution, and police, control
depends on devising programs that employ a concentrated, cooperative regional
approach. Even this requires a change in state and federal policies, which
presently funnel funds into old governmental units rather than into intergov-
ernmental ones. But the crisis of the inner suburbs has produced the necessary
condition for a fundamental shift in public policy based on metropolitan
realities rather than on anachronistic political jurisdictions.

New demographic changes also brought some easing of racial tensions.
The massive movement of blacks from the South to Northern cities virtually
has stopped; indeed, some experts detect a slight reverse of the flow. The
breaking of segregation and the availability of jobs in Southern cities made
them at least as attractive as Northern ones. Moreover, urban black birth
rates dropped rapidly. This reduced ghetto tensions somewhat but not ghetto
conditions. In addition, the election of black mayors in many parts of the
country lessened the feeling of isolation and powerlessness of urban blacks.
The relative quiet of the ghetto in the seventies was somewhat deceptive but
did provide some breathing space for the nation if the nation had the ingenuity
and will to seize it.

But time is running out and we have not used it wisely to heal racial
divisions or reduce urban-suburban tensions. Federal policy has neglected
cities in favor of surrounding communities. Revenue-sharing formulas were
based largely on population rather than on need; government installations

usually were placed in outlying areas; special programs for the inner cities were either reduced or dismantled. Worse still, urban economies, historically the nation's most resilient, recovered more slowly from recurring recessions than the suburbs with their newer facilities. And the outward flow of jobs and middle-class city dwellers continued unabated. The problem is more severe in the older areas of the Northeast and Midwest. Yet the "Sunbelt" cities show the same symptoms. The acids of urban decay do not recognize the Mason-Dixon line.

The persistence of the urban crisis has led many Americans to look else-where for solutions. But a look outward indicates that what some thought was a peculiarly American question is, in fact, an international urban crisis. Rome's fiscal management makes New York's look frugal; the inadequacy of London's inner-city schools is more than a match for their American counterparts; Frankfurt's pollution experts travel to Pittsburgh for advice; few American housing commissioners would trade jobs with their opposite numbers in Sydney. Russian urban experts see their limited growth policies overwhelmed by illegal migration; the smog in Sarajevo would frighten even an Angelino; Rumania's ambitious satellite city plan has not inhibited the growth of Bucharest or produced any "new towns"; more than three decades after World War II, no major city in Eastern Europe has dented its housing shortage.

The record of foreign cities on race is no more instructive. British urban centers are producing their own "New Commonwealth" ghettos; not a single black sits in Parliament. Amsterdam cannot handle its old colonists of different color. Paris and Marseilles have been unable to assimilate their French Algerians. Moscow couldn't manage even a small number of African students; in Bucharest, urban renewal is gypsy removal. In Sydney and Auckland, the aborigines, though small in number, face the usual range of discrimination. Indeed, the immigration policies of Canada and Australia are designed to avoid the issue.

The fact is that no society has learned to manage a large metropolis, nor has any society succeeded in solving the question of race. If these problems are to be solved, it will be done here in the United States. Perhaps that is the way it should be. Our national history has been almost conterminous with the rise of the modern city; racial diversity always has been a part of the American experience. We have managed in the past to take millions of people with different backgrounds, languages, and religions and incorporate them into the metropolitan mainstream.

In facing the present urban crisis, we only need draw upon our best traditions. But if we do not begin to unite the metropolis and to disperse the ghetto in the next four years, the eighties will be a decade of renewed tension and turmoil and will bear out Wendell Phillips's grim prophecy of a hundred years ago: "The time will come when our cities will strain our institutions as slavery never did."

American Cities in Profound Transition: The New City Geography of the 1980s

*Michael P. Conzen**

A merican cities have crossed a watershed in the last few years and appear
to be evolving a new growth pattern, functional composition, and spatial
structure. The period since the Second World War, during which general
urban growth was strong, suburbanization rapid, and central city decline
precipitous, has now given way to a phase of markedly slower growth, the
redistribution of growth within the size classes and regional systems of cities,
and major shifts in the structure of urban economies. Not all trends and
processes have been reversed or seriously modified, but sufficient changes
have occurred in tandem to warrant the notion that a new epoch in American
urban development has arrived.

These changes have implications for the geographical restructuring of the
nation's urban system as a whole, for the employment structure and social
patterns of metropolitan areas, for the planning and financing of the built
environment, for the political relations between cities and suburbs, and for
the general quality of life for urban Americans. This review considers each
of these issues as they relate to the changing geography of America's metropolitan areas.

Slow Growth and "Counterurbanization"

For the first time since the Great Depression the population of metropolitan
areas is growing more slowly than the national total (10.2 and 11.4 percent,
respectively, between 1970 and 1980), and after decades of annual increases
over 2 percent it is now growing at half that rate. The greatest slowdown has
occurred in the largest metropolitan regions, which actually registered -0.5
percent decline in population over the decade, and the healthiest growth has

*Michael P. Conzen is professor of geography at the University of Chicago. Reprinted
from Journal of Geography 82 (May–June 1983): 94–102. Reprinted by permission
of Journal of Geography and the National Council for Geographic Education.

been in metropolises with under 500,000 people (U.S. Bureau of the Census 1981a). These shifts have stabilized the proportion of Americans living in cities at just under 75 percent.

The causes of this historic deceleration in growth are a mixture of socio-demographic trends and technological change. Death rates have been mostly constant, but birth rates have fallen significantly since the postwar baby boom, from 18.2 to 15.8 per thousand during the 1970s. High costs and reduced availability of energy have directly threatened urban living standards. Meanwhile, a "rural renaissance" has occurred in the form of increased migration to small towns, whether for retirement, second homes, or as a response to the mystique of rural living in "safe" places removed from big-city ills. Such movements have been aided by the broad diffusion of new technology for both domestic comfort (telephone and television) and business decentralization (computers and coaxial cable).

There are both positive and negative implications in sharply reduced rates of general urban growth. On the negative side, many areas are losing existing and anticipated employment as industries reorganize and relocate in an era of heavy foreign imports and internal disparities in regional costs of business. Competition for growth among cities is intensifying, leading in some cases to lowered wages, polluting industries, and greater external control of local resources. Weak places are seeking aid from central government, and the urge to place regional stability before efficiency is encouraging a conservative welfare economy. Finally, slow growth promotes tighter job mobility and consequent social status rigidity, and a dwindling tax base to cope with aging housing and urban infrastructure. Benefits, on the other hand, accrue in lower house prices, crime rates, urban stress, and reduced demand for new capital projects because there are fewer newcomers to accommodate (Phillips and Brunn 1980).

The new phenomenon of small towns and nonmetropolitan growth in the face of large-city stagnation and decline has been called "counterurbanization" (Berry 1980a). It reflects an outright reversal of patterns prevailing up to the 1960s, and larger numbers of people are now leaving metropolitan areas for nonmetropolitan places than moving in the other direction. To imply that urbanization has ceased altogether would be misleading, however, for numerous rural regions continue to suffer significant population losses, towns grow into metropolises, and many large cities are still gaining in population, if less vigorously than before. Nonetheless, the move to small towns and rural areas from large cities is significant and represents more than a response to sentimental preferences. Light manufacturing and high-technology businesses relocate or are newly established in nonmetropolitan regions because low-cost inputs are more critical than market proximity. The resulting employment has spurred a new round of growth for existing smaller urban places and encouraged the proliferation of "exurbia"—scattered residential developments set in agricultural districts without urban amenities, and thus dependent for economic and social services on local but often distant villages and towns. Exurban developments are potentially vulnerable to changes in employment patterns and rises in fuel costs, and have few governmental mechanisms to deal with urban-related problems.

Sunbelt Urbanization and the National Shift
to a Service Economy

If slow growth and counterurbanization describe major facets of urban change in America, they are not without a striking geographical dimension. Growth has been so regionally selective over the last decade as to suggest a dichotomy between "sunbelt" growth and "snowbelt" (or "frostbelt") decline (Perry and Watkins 1977). Every major metropolitan region in the south and west grew at least 10 percent between 1970 and 1980. Phoenix grew by 55 percent to a size of 1.5 million inhabitants, and Fort Myers, Florida, grew by 95 percent to over 200,000 people. Meanwhile, no major metropolitan area in the historic Manufacturing Belt grew more than 10 percent, and thirteen urban regions actually declined in total population, Buffalo by as much as 8 percent. The healthy growth of southern and western cities has been apparent for several decades, but the uniform arrest of northeastern cities on this scale was unforeseen (Fisher and Mitchelson 1981).

The reasons for sunbelt growth are many, but lower labor costs, lower rates of labor union membership, cheaper land, local government inducements, and fewer public regulations are among the chief reasons. To earlier industrial shifts, such as those of textiles and furniture from the northeast to the Piedmont south, have been added more recent examples such as scientific instruments and machinery, and lower-skill clothing factories, some taking advantage of Mexican immigrant concentrations near the border. Military installations and procurement activities have disproportionately benefited southern cities, thanks to their long-lasting government representatives in Washington. Southern and western cities have also capitalized on their warm regional climates and offered avoidance of, or escape from, the inefficiencies and burdens of high corporate taxes and aging urban infrastructure of northern cities, particularly their crowded environments and clogged transport facilities.

What, then, has been the effect of this remarkable shift in urban growth on the hierarchy and functional structure of the national urban system? The primary result has been the opportunity for the sunbelt to "catch up" with the northeast in general levels of urbanization. There are almost as many large metropolitan areas in the south and west as in the northeast and central regions, a striking change from the pattern in 1910 or even in 1960 (Conzen 1981; Borchert 1972). The actual functional structure of the urban system, however, has not been so radically altered in space as this partial equalization might suggest. Much of the recent southern urban growth has reinforced the roles of regional-level nodal centers and added some specialized residential and military-industrial centers with limited national roles in the system. What has not changed has been the location of national metropolitan nodes, the major concentration of heavy industrial capacity in the northeast, and the similar regional clustering of specialized, large corporate-industrial complexes, linked to heavy investments in research and development and close to advanced corporate services such as finance, insurance, and real estate intermediaries (Malecki 1982; Stephens and Holly 1981).

The sunbelt has succeeded in gaining an increased share of national production and growth in service industries, but the fundamental shift toward a service-based urban systems economy has deeper ramifications. In 1948 manufacturing employed one-third of the American workforce, and service functions accounted for just over one-half; by 1977 the proportions were one-quarter and two-thirds, respectively (Stanbach et al. 1981, pp. 12–13). The strongest growth in services occurred in health, corporate financial services, and government.

The consequence of this secular shift in the economy was to set cities of comparable size on divergent paths, some to thrive on a wide range of services and others to prosper on a narrow range of specialized activities. Three locational tendencies resulted from the intensification of the service economy. First, services of a "residentiary" nature, serving the local population and business complex, continued to be uniformly distributed with population. Second, "export" services which catered to nationally operating corporations and distributors concentrated in larger metropolises because of scale economies and market concentration, often the cities in the medium-to-large category benefiting the most. This concentration occurred because corporate growth linked headquarters offices increasingly to the essential producer-service firms in the large cities rather than to their own plants. Third, manufacturing followed the reverse pattern of the export services, moving to smaller cities. Buffeted by setbacks in basic industries, such as automobiles and steel, and the trend to internationalization of production in these industries, manufacturing passed through three overlapping phases: suburbanization (mostly within the manufacturing belt); regionalization (move to the sunbelt, especially military, electronics, and aerospace industries); and decentralization (move to small towns and nonmetropolitan areas, especially the electrical machinery industry) (Stanbach et al. 1981).

The result has been that growth has disproportionately favored the sunbelt, but the general service transformation has affected sunbelt and frostbelt sections of the country. With regard to the latter, the northeast has been able to reinforce its comparative advantage in key intermediary services, especially finance, stimulated in part by southern growth (Cohen 1977). Furthermore, the northeast has retained growth in high-technology skilled industries whereas much of the sunbelt's gain, with the exception of aerospace activity, particularly in California, has been in cheaper, routine production. Nonetheless, strong growth of regional nodal centers in the sunbelt has been helped by corporate mergers, maturing regional markets, and the high costs of the traditional metropolitan centers. These same factors acted differently on the snowbelt nodal centers, with some succeeding in repositioning themselves to offer the best mixture of advanced corporate services, such as Boston, Philadelphia, Cincinnati, and Columbus, and others like Detroit, Pittsburgh, and Cleveland were notably less successful (Stanbach et al. 1981, pp. 102–6).

High general costs in metropolitan centers reflect social commitments to a considerable degree, and strong economic development does not always produce a quality environment. A recent study graded American cities on their "quality of life," based on 120 variables reflecting economic, political, environmental, health, educational, and social conditions (Liu 1975). Many growth cities in the sunbelt offer the least attractive living environments, probably an historical legacy which it will be interesting to see if the new growth will or will not eradicate. In addition to the climatically blessed Pacific-coast cities (Terjung 1967), many northern snowbelt cities score well on "quality of life," a characteristic that many skill-based industries and companies offering advanced services take seriously and are willing to contribute towards sustaining.

Major Agents of Change within Metropolitan Areas

National trends in the urban economy and system of cities are affecting the historical patterns of intrametropolitan spatial structure by altering the variable speed of several fundamental processes of redistribution. On the economic side, the general growth impulses that have centralized activity increasingly in American cities since early industrialization continue to operate, but at a slightly reduced level and much more selectively, thanks to improvements in communications. Progressive specialization of productive and service roles continues at ever-higher levels, promoting the expansion of facilities. These two forces are accommodated physically through higher central densities and geographical deconcentration, resulting in the further development of the economic core of the metropolis ("downtown") and the multiplication of suburban developments. Socially, stratification by race, status, and life-style continues to be expressed in spatial segregation, enhanced by political fragmentation at the metropolitan scale. Social mobility is related to economic expansiveness, and slower growth appears to be restricting geographical mobility as a corollary of status change, thereby interrupting the relatively smooth operation of the filtering process in the residential housing market (Holleb 1981). The combination of these economic and social forces has produced a profound imbalance in metropolitan geography between rapacious suburban growth and central city decline. In addition, however, an emerging countersymmetry can now be seen in various elements of core revitalization on the one hand and the emergence of some serious suburban problems on the other.

Decentralization and Fringe Development

In 1960 the American population lived in almost exactly equal proportions in central cities, suburbs, and nonmetropolitan areas. By 1975 the suburban component had risen to 39.1 percent, but the central city portion had fallen to 29.6 percent. If one considers only population residing within official metropolitan areas, by 1980 six out of every ten inhabitants lived in the suburbs. This average masked strong variations between generally northeastern metropolises (Newark, 83.2 percent suburban; Pittsburgh, 81.3; and St. Louis, 80.8) and southern and western places (San Antonio, 26.6; Houston, 45.1; and Phoenix, 47.7). Nonetheless, by 1980 all but five metropolitan regions in the nation over 1 million in population housed more residents in their suburbs than in their central cities.

The decentralization of metropolitan patterns affected not only population and housing but also, more significantly, jobs. St. Louis provides a representative example of a large, highly suburbanized metropolis. By 1980 more than two-thirds of its entire labor force worked in the suburbs, which also accounted for 79.7 percent of the total retail employment (U.S. Bureau of the Census 1981b). The suburbs also contained 62.7 percent of the jobs in finance, insurance, and real estate activities, generally the least decentralized sector of the metropolitan economy. In contrast, New Orleans remains one of the most centralized major metropolises (43.9 percent of total employment in suburbs), but even here there are now more jobs in manufacturing, wholesaling, and retailing in the suburbs than in the central city. Retailing historically has been the first and the fastest sector to suburbanize, following its market, and not surprisingly the national aggregate of suburban sales now heavily outweighs that of the traditional CBD, as illustrated in the case of Chicago. Sales in Chicago's Loop (CBD) totaled $933 million in 1977, but sales at Woodfield Mall alone—the world's largest planned shopping center—had reached $273 million. In fact, twelve of the leading thirty shopping areas in the nation were not CBDs but suburban shopping malls, and in Atlanta two such centers, Lennox Square and Cumberland, did more business than the city's CBD ($315, $276, compared with $271 million respectively) (Morrill 1982). The great wave of suburban mall construction has now ended, thanks to the economic downturn, and attention has turned to medium-sized infill developments. Some ambitious ventures, such as the "Old Chicago" mall and amusement complex built in a Bolingbrook cornfield in suburban Chicago, have miscalculated demand and even been forced to close.

Decentralization of industry and retailing has been long established. More recent has been the movement of offices and corporate headquarters to the suburbs. Already in 1970, New York City and Minneapolis-St. Paul counted one-half or more of their office space outside the central city (Manners 1974), a trend which has intensified. The proliferation of so many jobs in the "outer city" (Muller 1981) has changed commuting flows to the extent that movement from suburbs to the core CBD in New England represents only 3.4 percent of the volume, whereas 61.4 percent involves "lateral" movement between different suburbs (Plane 1981). This has produced a situation in which many suburbanites have little need and less desire to visit the traditional "downtown" any more. In a well-to-do Philadelphia suburb, only one-quarter of the residents visits downtown more than once a month, and nearly one-fifth travels there less than twice a year (Zikmund 1971). The reason is that, in general, many suburban rings are approaching a kind of institutional completeness that spells local autonomy for day-to-day living. Indeed, geographers have observed the rise of multifunctional foci in the suburbs to rival the original downtown, both traditional style nodes such as Clayton in metropolitan St. Louis and the more recent "suburban freeway corridors" (SFCs)—vast linear, car-oriented commercial/institutional strips stretching for several kilometers—such as the I-494 Bloomington strip in metropolitan Minneapolis-St. Paul (Kersten and Ross 1968; Baerwald 1978). Although the great era of freeway building, when the federal government subsidized 90 percent of the construction costs, is now over and most metropolitan freeway networks are basically complete, SFC development is concentrating enough traffic to encourage local governments to embroider the freeway system with "neighborhood" additions.

Central City Decline and Core Revitalization

The legacy of decentralization might have been less depressing had the nineteenth-century process of urban annexation not run out of steam and halted in the face of suburban political separatism. With only a few notable exceptions, Houston and Indianapolis for different reasons being the most celebrated, metropolitan growth has left the modern central city locked in the grip of a vast suburban "noose," and decentralization has displaced new growth to the periphery at the expense of the core. Nearly all the suburban trends just discussed can be inverted to describe the worsening condition of the central cities. The litany of decline is well known: enormous losses in employment, middle-class tax-paying families, and tax-paying corporations (especially industrial producers). Left behind is an aging housing stock, an increasing proportion of poor and minorities, particularly blacks and Hispanics, and a deteriorating infrastructure of utilities and urban services, particularly public schools. The result is a heavier burden of support for a shrinking tax base, leading to an overall decline in the quality of life and increased competition for scarce funds.

As the middle classes removed to the suburbs, they have withdrawn tax support and consumer spending power. Between 1970 and 1977, central cities lost an estimated $65 billion in residents' income because of migration (Sternlieb and Hughes 1979). As a result, federal revenue-sharing has become a vital component of central city fiscal survival. By 1978 one-half of all revenues taken in by cities with over 500,000 inhabitants was provided by the federal government, and for Detroit, Buffalo, and Cleveland the proportion reached nearly 70 percent, compared with levels of 13.1, 8.3, and 2.1 percent, respectively, as recently as 1967 (Christian 1982, p. 434). Even so, some cities have come dangerously close to bankruptcy, such as New York City and Cleveland, and others, like Chicago, are not helped by political power structures that divert lean resources to the advantage of patronage machines (Brune 1981). Furthermore, financial institutions have long practiced "redlining," a form of urban disinvestment in which mortgages are denied in certain zones, usually dilapidated districts that are coincidentally occupied by poor residents (Darden 1980). National legislation and community pressure have begun to reduce the incidence of "redlining."

Even where "redlining" did not automatically follow the block-busting techniques of the 1950s and 1960s that helped intensify ghetto areas, racial segregation has remained a fixture in American central cities. Slight declines in measurable segregation have been noted in the last decade (Van Valey et al. 1976), and black suburbanization is not insignificant (Nelson 1980), but the large black ghettos seem a long-term element of inner-city social space.

One problem is that the departure of the mainly white middle class no longer opens up large quantities of available housing. The changing demography of the central city is reflected in rising numbers of nonfamily households and female-headed households that are exerting considerable pressure on the available housing stock (Sternlieb and Hughes 1979, pp. 629–30; DeVise 1979). Thus, poor blacks and Hispanics face the squeeze between the slumlord-propelled cycle of neighborhood decay and abandonment (with "torching" of buildings producing piecemeal urban deserts like those produced wholesale earlier by urban renewal) and the possibility of displacement through "gentrification" in selected localities with suitable remaining housing (Henig 1980).

Gentrification is one aspect of a broad urban revitalization that has been acclaimed as the new urban trend of the 1970s (Lipton 1977; Winters 1979; Cybriwsky 1980). Enthusiasts have even trumpeted the emergence of a major "back-to-the-city" movement. Recent studies have shown, however, that gentrifiers and new downtown dwellers have overwhelmingly central city origins, and exceptionally few suburbanites are actually being lured to live in the urban core (Kern 1981). Furthermore, those developments contributing to the revitalization of the core are fairly specialized in nature and quite restricted in their geography.

The era of large-scale, federally funded "urban renewal" is now over, thanks to complex community reaction and fiscal austerity. But in its heyday urban renewal brought some spectacular changes, both good and bad (for the example of Boston, see Vollmar 1981). It succeeded in rebuilding and redefining the social character and land use of significant zones of the inner city, some within or on the edge of downtown, some in more obviously residential areas. Characteristic of the process were heavy government involvement in all phases, a certain planning rigidity, and often a failure to complete the task. Today, developments contributing to revitalization fall in several categories, with considerable overlap, and display a much wider range of participation.

Historical trends have drained the CBD and its environs of much manufacturing, wholesaling, and retailing activity. Together with the decline of railroad commutation and the pressure for car storage, these trends have rendered much of the built environment of the urban core empty, underused, and derelict (St. Louis, perhaps, suffered too much central "renewal," see Ford 1979). But decentralization has not robbed the CBD of its centrality for a wide array of business functions, and as a result, the office industry and its associated functional complexes have boomed in the cores of most of the largest cities. The decade of the 1970s has seen many places acquire new downtown skylines, and in New York, notwithstanding the city's recent flirtation with fiscal disaster and a history of losing corporate headquarters (Quandt 1976), new skyscraper construction is proceeding with vigor. Sustained office developments today engross huge tracts of land, deprive the streetscape of its human scale and pedestrian traffic (except during rush hours), and transfer increasing amounts of the downtown to corporate control (Burns and Kay 1981). They also generate development of related facilities for visitors and employees such as convention halls, hotels, restaurants, and specialty retailing, increasingly "packaged" in giant multibuilding, but unified, development complexes, such as the World Trade Center (Ruchelman

1978), the World Financial Center in New York, and the Illinois Center in Chicago.

This corporate nexus generates much local and out-of-town traffic to the downtown, and coupled with substantial tourist activity, provides an increasing rationale for commercial revitalization involving restoration and conversion of special historic buildings. Quincy Market offers such a focus in Boston (Vollmar 1981), and the Rouse Company has made a career out of similar ventures in other cities (for example, Harbor Place in Baltimore; Fulton Market in New York; and Grand Avenue in Milwaukee). Such projects have generally won the support and admiration of historic preservation groups (Ford 1979). They provide an antidote to the anonymous world of office towers by inviting visitor and resident alike to experience the city center together in large crowds as "theatre," anchored by the pitifully few remnants of historical fabric. Most substantial cities with suitable buildings now contain both new and old examples of preservation and commercial revival, notably New Orleans (French Quarter), San Antonio (River Walk), Seattle (Pioneer Square), Albuquerque (Old Town), and Washington (Georgetown).

Increasing white-collar employment of the office-CBD and attractions of near-central living have stimulated heavy demand for housing. This demand has produced much new construction, generally high-rise in type, in such centers as Chicago's Gold Coast, Sandburg Village, and newer sites such as Dearborn Village (the redeveloped site of a former railroad terminal). In addition, a substantial wave of renovation and remodeling of old central housing has occurred. This extends not only to Philadelphia's Society Hill, Boston's South End, and Chicago's Old Town, but also to former commercial premises such as factories and warehouses. The "loft" has made a hit with more than just artists, and in New York special districts have been zoned to allow loft conversions for residential use (Zukin 1982); and in Chicago, Hubbard Street and Printers Row form the nuclei of similar activity.

Developments of these types are certainly changing the appearance of the urban core in many large American cities, but they represent often extremely small portions of the land use, building stock, and population of the central city. Detroit's Renaissance Center, trolley mall, and Greektown (complete with its Rouse-type Trapper's Alley commercial rehabilitation project) barely make a dent in the prevailing condition of the deteriorated downtown, now having lost its historic "flagship" department store (Hudson's). Beyond the American downtown, many neighborhoods possess sufficient architectural character for reclamation—and many pockets are being rehabilitated—but they do not begin to balance the vast districts of mediocre, decayed, or blasted housing. It is an open question whether enough private gentrifiers will materialize to reverse the decades of disinvestment, and "save" the inner city (Berry 1980b).

Suburban Problems and Metropolitan Solutions

Despite significant changes in the urban core, the long-term future of the central city is still clouded. At the same time, however, it should not be assumed that the "outer city" is free of difficulties. Suburbs age, and problems arise from that fact alone. Others derive from the locational and physical circumstances of particular suburbs, and yet others diffuse from the central city.

Metropolitan Chicago has well over two hundred incorporated suburban municipalities, only about fifteen of which have roots reaching back into the nineteenth century. Others are foundations of the early and middle twentieth century, some like Skokie growing on the basis of industrial relocation. Now firms are leaving Skokie because expansion is impossible, and the "village" is experiencing the problems of aging roads, sewers, and a declining tax base. In all, metropolitan Chicago contains 1,214 distinct local government bodies (including school and special district authorities), by far the highest in the nation. Many have jurisdiction over extraordinarily shaped territories, reflecting lax, inefficient, and uncoordinated annexation practices. There are forty-three cities in the metropolitan area besides Chicago—cities in name, legal standing, and with some of the expected bureaucratic appurtenances. The smallest, the City of Oak Brook Terrace, had 2,285 inhabitants in 1980. All remaining municipalities are "villages," the largest of which is Arlington Heights Village, with 66,116 inhabitants. Some problems migrate with residents beyond the central city. Suburban crime is becoming significant (property crime naturally follows the wealth), and fourteen suburbs now boast higher rates for serious crime than the City of Chicago. In view of this unwelcome trend, the Village of Morton Grove has become the first municipality in the country to prohibit private gun ownership—a radical sociological event.

Many suburbs have few problems because their residents are wealthy enough to require few public services and to amply line municipal treasuries with their taxes. Others are less fortunate and suffer the costs of fragmentation, small scale, and virtual lack of planning. The extreme reaction to undisciplined suburban sprawl is the totally planned new community, and a currently interesting example is that of Woodlands, Texas, located thirty miles (forty-eight kilometers) north of downtown Houston (and, perhaps more revealingly), fifteen miles (twenty-four kilometers) north of Houston International Airport). This 17,000-acre "packaged" development is so controlled that prospective residents are vetted, and camper-vans cannot be parked in private driveways (Reynolds 1980). But most suburbs have not developed in a programmed fashion, and their myriad service needs require coordination, including cooperation with the central cities they depend on for their economic and social externalities.

Closing Observations

Regional planning has become a reluctant necessity for American metropolitan areas, and yet municipalities are loathe to surrender local control, because it has been a means by which suburbanities could abandon the problems of the central city and still benefit from big-city economic as well as cultural facilities. The most workable solutions so far have involved some city-county consolidations, allowing Nashville, Indianapolis, Minneapolis-St. Paul, and

Atlanta, for example, a measure of control over their fringe expansion. More broadly, however, increased federal support of municipal financial affairs has brought concomitant pressure for greater planning coordination at the metropolitan scale.

Certain dimensions of the urban experience in the United States persist: continued functional specialization, geographical decentralization, and social segregation. Some former constants have changed: growth is more subdued and regionally biased, and administrative barriers are being overcome even as they proliferate. More significantly, the increasing scale of urban development and complexity of organization have brought not only more government but also more pervasive and powerful influence and control by private corporations, not easily counterbalanced by communities and individuals, and not easily convinced of their broader social responsibilities. But, above all, America's cities are now so numerous, large, and many so mature that the erstwhile cheapness and allure of the "new" is being increasingly supplemented with an appreciation of the value of the "old." The long era in American history of the urban build-and-demolish cycle based on unlimited resources, unlimited fringe expansion, and widely sanctioned social separation may be giving way to one based more on finite resources, commitment to adequate social overhead costs, and the already capitalized environment.

REFERENCES

Baerwald, T. 1978. "The emergence of a new 'Downtown.'" *Geographical Review* 68:308–18.

Berry, B. J. L. 1980a. "Urbanization and counterurbanization in the United States." *Annals of the American Academy of Political and Social Science* 451:13–20.

———. 1980b. "Inner city futures: an American dilemma revisited." *Transactions*, Institute of British Geographers NS 5:1–28.

Borchert, J. R. 1972. "America's changing metropolitan regions." *Annals*, Association of American Geographers 62:352–73.

Brune, T., ed. 1981. *Neglected Neighborhoods: Patterns of Discrimination in Chicago City Services*. Chicago: Community Renewal Society.

Burns, E. K., and Kay, J. 1981. "Land ownership trends in Salt Lake City's central business district." *Yearbook of the Association of Pacific Coast Geographers* 43:23–35.

Christian, C. M. 1982. "The impact of federal and state policies upon local governments' fiscal conditions." In *Modern Metropolitan Systems*, eds. C. M. Christian and R. A. Harper, pp. 417–53. Columbus: Charles Merrill.

Cohen, R. B. 1977. "Multinational corporations, international finance, and the sunbelt." In *The Rise of the Sunbelt Cities*, eds. D. C. Perry and A. J. Watkins, pp. 211–26. Beverly Hills: Sage.

Conzen, M. P. 1981. "The American urban system in the nineteenth century." In *Geography and the Urban Environment: Progress and Applications*, Vol. 4, pp. 295–347. London: John Wiley.

Cybriwsky, R. A. 1980. "Revitalization trends in downtown-area neighborhoods." In *The American Metropolitan System: Present and Future*, eds. S. D.
   Brunn and J. O. Wheeler, pp. 21–36. New York: V. H. Winston/Wiley.

Darden, J. T. 1980. "Lending practices and policies affecting the American
   metropolitan system." In *The American Metropolitan System: Present and
   Future*, eds. S. D. Brunn and J. O. Wheeler, pp. 93–110. New York: V. H.
   Winston/Wiley.

DeVise, P. 1979–80. "The expanding singles housing market in Chicago:
   implications for reviving city neighborhoods." *Urbanism Past and Present*
   9:30–9.

Fisher, J. S., and Mitchelson, R. L. 1981. "Forces of change in the American
   settlement pattern." *Geographical Review* 71:298–310.

Ford, L. R. 1979. "Urban preservation and the geography of the city in the
   USA." *Progress in Human Geography* 3:211–38.

Henig, J. R. 1980. "Gentrification and displacement within cities: a comparative approach." *Social Science Quarterly* 61:638–52.

Holleb, D. B. 1981. "Housing and the environment: shooting at moving
   targets." *Annals of the American Academy of Political and Social Science* 453:180–
   221.

Kern, C. R. 1981. "Upper income renaissance in the city: its sources and
   implications for the city's future." *Journal of Urban Economics* 9:106–24.

Kersten, E. W., and Ross, D. R. 1968. "Clayton: a new metropolitan focus
   in the St. Louis area." *Annals*, Association of American Geographers
   58:637–49.

Lipton, S. G. 1977. "Evidence of central city revival." *Journal of the American
   Planning Association* 43:136–47.

Liu, B. 1975. *Quality of Life: Indicators in the U.S. Metropolitan Areas, 1970: A
   Comprehensive Assessment*. Washington, D.C.: U.S. Environmental Protection Agency.

Malecki, E. J. 1982. "Federal R and D spending in the United States of
   America: some impacts on metropolitan economies." *Regional Studies*
   16:19–35.

Manners, G. 1974. "The office in the metropolis: an opportunity for shaping
   metropolitan America." *Economic Geography* 50:93–110.

Morrill, R. L. 1982. "Continuing deconcentration trends in trade." *Growth
   and Change* 13:46–8.

Muller, P. O. 1981. *Contemporary Suburban America*. Englewood Cliffs, New
   Jersey: Prentice-Hall.

Nelson, K. P. 1980. "Recent suburbanization of blacks: how much, who, and
   where." *Journal of the American Planning Association* 46:287–300.

Perry, D. C., and Watkins, A. J., eds. 1977. *The Rise of the Sunbelt Cities*.
   Beverly Hills: Sage.

Phillips, P. D., and Brunn, S. D. 1980. "New dynamics of growth in the
   American metropolitan system." In *The American Metropolitan System: Pres-
   ent and Future*, eds., S. D. Brunn and J. O. Wheeler, pp. 1–20. New York:
   V. H. Winston/Wiley.

Plane, D. A. 1981. "The geography of urban commuting fields: some empirical
   evidence from New England." *Professional Geographer* 33:182–8.

Quandt, W. 1976. *The Exodus of Corporate Headquarters from New York City*. New York: Praeger.

Reynolds, J. P. 1980. "A new town in the sunbelt." *Town and Country Planning* 49:356–8.

Ruchelman, L. I. 1978. "The New York Trade Center in perspective." *Urbanism Past and Present* 6:29–38.

Stanbach, T. M., Bearse, P. J., Noyelle, T. J., and Karasek, R. A. 1981. *Services: The New Economy*. Cambridge, Massachusetts: Allanheld, Osmun.

Stephens, J. D., and Holly, B. P. 1981. "City system behaviour and corporate influence: the headquarters location of US industrial firms, 1955–1975." *Urban Studies* 18:285–300.

Sternlieb, G., and Hughes, J. W. 1979. "Back to the city: myths and realities." *Traffic Quarterly* 33:617–36.

Terjung, W. H. 1967. "Annual physioclimatic stresses and regimes in the United States." *Geographical Review* 57:225–40.

U.S. Bureau of the Census. 1981a. *Statistical Abstract of the United States, 1981*. Washington, D.C.

————. 1981b. *County Business Patterns, 1980*. Washington, D.C.

Van Valey, T., Roof, W. C., and Wilcox, J. E. 1976. "Trends in residential segregation: 1960–1970." *American Journal of Sociology* 82:831–4.

Vollmar, R. 1981. "'Urban renewal' in Boston/USA." *Geographische Rundschau* 33:2–11.

Winters, C. 1979. "The social identity of evolving neighborhoods." *Landscape* 23:8–14.

Zikmund, J. 1971. "Do suburbanites use the central city?" *Journal of the American Planning Association* 37:192–5.

Zukin, S. 1982. *Loft Living: Culture and Capital in Urban Change*. Baltimore: Johns Hopkins University Press.

Part Four

The Historiography of
Urban America

New Perspectives on American Urban History

*Raymond A. Mohl**

The writing of American history has been transformed dramatically over the past two decades. In particular, a new interest in social history has energized the field and substantially altered the way historians research, understand, and interpret the past. In the field of urban history, a subdivision of the larger province of social history, scholars have brought exciting new perspectives to the study of the American city. New methods, new approaches, and new interpretations have enlightened dim corners of the urban past and pushed back the frontiers of historical understanding.

The rise of the American industrial city came to be one of the dominant characteristics of the late nineteenth century. Since the turn of the twentieth century, the city in its various permutations has continued to reflect or to shape modern American social, economic, and political life. Yet American historians, Richard C. Wade has suggested, "arrived at the study of the city by slow freight."[1] The historians lagged far behind scholars in other disciplines, who by 1900 had begun to apply the tools of the social sciences to the examination of urban America and its problems. Indeed, American urban history as a distinctive field of scholarly inquiry does not date much earlier than 1940, when Arthur M. Schlesinger published his landmark article, "The City in American History."[2] But interest in the field grew rather slowly, and by the mid-1950s only a few universities offered courses on the subject. Progress in urban history research was also less than dynamic, the chief accomplishments being several fine urban biographies and a handful of monographs. Among the best were the works of Carl Bridenbaugh on the colonial seaport towns, Oscar Handlin's study of Boston's immigrants, and Richard C. Wade's *The Urban Frontier.*[3]

The decade of the 1960s, however, brought powerful changes to the historical profession, changes that affected research and writing in urban history in significant ways. The mainstream consensus history that grew out of the conditions of the Great Depression, the Second World War, and the Cold

Raymond A. Mohl is professor of history at Florida Atlantic University. Reprinted with revisions from International Journal of Social Education 1 (Spring 1986): 69–97. Reprinted by permission.

293

War peaked in the Eisenhower era of the 1950s but began to crack amidst the social strains and political conflicts of the 1960s. The ghetto riots of the 1960s and the social-crusading spirit of the Kennedy-Johnson years riveted attention on the American city and its discontents. The writing of history generally reflects the climate of opinion at any particular moment in time, and certainly this was the case in the 1960s. Traditional interest in political and diplomatic history—a sort of elitist history concerned with the ideas and activities of decision makers, opinion-shapers, and power-wielders—gave way to a new and invigorated commitment to social history broadly considered. American historians began to examine with new interest such subjects as race, ethnicity, and class, and the ways in which people ordered their lives in the family, at work, and in various group and community settings; they began to look into the social values, behaviors, and processes that shaped the lives of people; and they began to pay attention to the local level as well as the national, and to the people at the bottom of the social hierarchy as well as at the top. As social historian Olivier Zunz has suggested, the appearance of this newer form of social history "generated great excitement in the progressive and eclectic intellectual atmosphere of the sixties."[4]

These shifts in historiographical tradition coincided with two other powerful changes in the America of the 1960s. First, the computer revolution made possible a more careful and exact social science history based on analysis of massive amounts of information collected, stored, and manipulated by computer. Second, the arrival of the baby boom generation at the college gate spurred an explosion of graduate education, generating in turn a substantial amount of new research as young historians wrote dissertations, articles, and books. By the end of the 1960s the historiographical landscape had been altered considerably from the mid-1950s, the heyday of the consensus historians.[5]

Urban history, in particular, was energized by the convergence of these changing social patterns and historiographical trends. The ferment of scholarly innovation and shifting interests pushed urban history in at least two new directions in the early 1960s. Each new path was illuminated by an important and innovative book—one path by Sam Bass Warner's *Streetcar Suburbs: The Process of Growth in Boston, 1870–1900* (1962), and the other by Stephan Thernstrom's *Poverty and Progress: Social Mobility in a Nineteenth-Century City* (1964).

Warner's work had an ecological slant, focusing on the spatial redistribution of population in the Boston metropolitan area in response both to technological innovation in urban transit and to the rural appeal of suburbia. He also used an inventive methodology. The examination of some 23,000 building permits for three Boston suburbs enabled him to make certain judgments about construction patterns, architectural and building styles, and the class structure underlying neighborhood formation. The result was a book that leaped beyond the established parameters of urban history and provided powerful insights into the growth of the American industrial city.[6]

In *Streetcar Suburbs* and in some of his other work, Warner essentially dealt with the process of urbanization. In rejecting more traditional approaches to urban history, such as urban biography or the study of social problems or political movements within an urban context, he demonstrated the ways in which fresh thinking can be historiographically liberating. Warner was not entirely alone in this emphasis on urbanization in the early 1960s. Eric Lampard, who has published a number of suggestive articles over thirty years, was also an early advocate of the study of urbanization as a "societal process." Studying urbanization from this perspective, Lampard argued, required urban historians to examine such "interacting elements" as population, topography, economy, social organization, political process, civic leadership, and urban imagery.[7] In a similar vein, Roy Lubove suggested the utility of the "city-building process" as a conceptual framework for analyzing decision making, social organization, and urban change. Lubove illustrated this methodology in a little-heralded but nevertheless important book, *Twentieth-Century Pittsburgh: Government, Business, and Environmental Change* (1969).[8]

The work of Stephan Thernstrom staked out a second new path in American urban history in the 1960s. In *Poverty and Progress*, he tested the widely asserted conception of nineteenth-century America as a land of opportunity for the urban working class. Drawing samples from manuscript census schedules for Newburyport, Massachusetts, between 1850 and 1880, Thernstrom pioneered in the use of new kinds of sources and in quantitative analysis, although he did not ignore more traditional literary sources. His chief concern was the relatively narrow question of social mobility rather than the larger process of urbanization or city building. Nevertheless, Thernstrom's approach was widely imitated and came to be associated with a "new urban history."[9]

Younger historians began pumping out a stream of books and articles replicating Thernstrom's work for other cities. By the early 1970s the new urban history had been taken over by the quantifiers in the Thernstrom tradition who were mostly studying mobility and related issues.[10] Indeed, when Thernstrom catalogued the achievements of the new urban history in a 1971 article, he wrote primarily of findings about mobility. These included tremendously high rates of urban population turnover, positive correlations between economic failure and spatial mobility, and a general fluidity in rates of occupational and social mobility, although rates varied for different economic classes and ethnic groups, and blacks had considerably fewer opportunities.[11]

Thernstrom's approach rather than Warner's came to dominate among practitioners of the new urban history by the early 1970s. Michael Frisch has suggested that the popularity and influence of Thernstrom's *Poverty and Progress* "stemmed less from the book's substance than from the way it brought together a number of diverse concerns central to the historiographical moment." These included a methodology conducive to quantification at the beginning of the computer age, a model that could be applied easily to other communities, and, finally, a concern for nonelitist history, or history from the bottom up, at the height of the political radicalism of the 1960s. As Frisch put it, "Quantification, as applied by Thernstrom, . . . came to be invested with an aura of social and political relevance," making this particular approach appealing to a younger generation of urban historians.[12]

Thus, the new urban history came to be perceived as a special sort of quantitative history. Yet, ironically, at about the same time that he was carrying his quantitative methodology to a new level of sophistication in his prize-winning book, *The Other Bostonians* (1973), Thernstrom had begun having second thoughts about the term "new" urban history. Indeed, as he confessed in an interview in the *Journal of Urban History* in 1975, he had not only given up the term, but he also had even stopped labeling himself as an urban historian at all. Rather, Thernstrom contended that urban historians were really engaged in social history, and that "the modern city [was] so intimately linked to the society around it, and [was] so important a part of the entire social order that few of its aspects [could] safely be examined in isolation."[13]

Always difficult to categorize, Warner, too, rejected the emerging notion of a new urban history. In a 1977 article he labeled the narrow mobility studies "a bare-boned empiricism" and "a quantitative antiquarianism," the purpose behind such studies "lost in technique." Nothing, he suggested, was "more likely to put a researcher on a false track than the advertisement: new urban history." Building on his earlier emphasis on the process of urbanization, Warner asserted that the central focus of urban history should be the spatial distribution of population, institutions, activities, and artifacts—the basic elements in all human communities that are continuously evolving in relation to each other over time.[14] By the mid-1970s, therefore, the two chief pioneers of new ways of doing urban history had abandoned or rejected the notion altogether.

The new urban history made one last gasp, however. Theodore Hershberg and others associated with the Philadelphia Social History Project promoted the continued viability of a new, quantified urban history. In an important article in 1978 and in the introduction to a collection of essays on Philadelphia, Hershberg provided yet another prescriptive statement about urban history. For him, the essential distinction between the old and the new urban history was one between the city as site and the city as process. By site, he meant "the conceptual treatment of the city as a passive backdrop to whatever else [was] the subject of central concern." By contrast, he wrote, "urban as process should be thought of as the dynamic modelling of the interrelationships among environment, behavior, and group experience—three basic components in the larger urban system." Such an approach, Hershberg contended, would explain what was distinctively different about life and change in the city. By Hershberg's account, neither Warner nor Thernstrom had been pursuing a new urban history; they were simply working within the older tradition of urban as site rather than urban as process.[15] Interestingly, at about the same time that Warner and Thernstrom were abandoning the idea of a new urban history as unsatisfying and incomplete, a new band of purists was tossing the pioneers off the team, consigning their work to the historiographical scrap heap.

Through the 1970s, then, debates over the new urban history held center stage within the discipline. This apparent absorbing interest, however, tended to mask the fact that an extensive urban history literature was pouring from the university presses and filling the scholarly journals—a literature that often paid little attention to the new urban history controversy.[16] Indeed, for some areas of urban history the new quantitative or social science approaches has little relevance or application. The sort of microlevel analysis of work, residence, family, and group experience typical of the Hershberg school is important and informative, but many dimensions of the urban experience cannot be addressed in exactly that way. The new urban history has been particularly unhelpful in suggesting alternative ways of approaching the twentieth-century American city. In his book, for instance, Hershberg concentrates almost exclusively on the years 1850 to 1880, and only one of its fourteen chapters even ventures into the twentieth century. This concentration on the nineteenth century clearly reflects the continued reliance of the new urban history on manuscript census data, which has only recently become available for 1910.

The now perceived weaknesses of an exclusively quantitative approach to urban history research have liberated urban historians to pursue many other diverse paths of the urban experience, to follow their instincts and their interests. The results have been fruitful and stimulating. Historians of the American city have begun to carve out a variety of new and exciting areas of urban research. Meanwhile, suggests Bruce M. Stave, the heavy emphasis on quantification has diminished considerably. Readers, Stave writes, "will be less overtly confronted by the numbers as historians increasingly recognize the problems of sometimes imprecise data and flawed methodology. Qualitative rather than quantitative analysis will be the historian's prime goal."[17]

Stave's epitaph for the new urban history has sparked surprisingly little comment, which suggests that his observation may be right on target.[18] But if the now old, quantitative urban history is dead, or dying, the larger field itself is brimming with new approaches, new interpretations, and new ideas. The remainder of this article will survey briefly a dozen or so of these new perspectives on American urban history.

Urban Politics and Government. Studies of urban politics traditionally focused on the urban political machines that emerged in the late nineteenth century and on the reformers and reform organizations that challenged the city bosses. The traditional view was highly moralistic; the bosses and machines were corrupt and venal, while the reformers upheld the democratic ideal. In the 1950s and 1960s sociologists and historians reversed these widely accepted stereotypes, suggesting instead that the bosses extended democratic politics down to the neighborhood level, provided needed services, supported urban growth and development, and centralized power and decision making at a time of rapid urbanization and social change. As one of these bosses, George B. Cox of Cincinnati, had argued in 1892, the boss was "not necessarily a public enemy."[19]

The defense of the machine reached its epitome in Leo Hershkowitz's study of Boss William Tweed of New York City. Often singled out as the most notorious of the bosses, Tweed became, in Hershkowitz's account, "a pioneer spokesman for an emerging New York" and "a progressive force in shaping the interests and destiny of a great city and its people."[20] Few historians carried the revisionist argument that far. More recent studies of the urban political machine and its origins have made fewer expansive claims for the city boss, seeking instead to locate the machine within the broader pattern of American political and social processes.[21]

Meanwhile, the historians of the 1960s and 1970s were revising the traditional picture of the urban reformer. Increasingly, urban reform was perceived as badly splintered, a congeries of separate little movements devoted to single issues like the saloon or playgrounds or civil service reform. The general thrust of recent research suggests that urban reform was a complex, constantly shifting, multidimensional movement. Reformers, it seems, came from all social and economic classes, and they supported a diversity of often conflicting reform legislation, programs, and causes. Some reformers, it now appears, took extremely elitist and undemocratic positions in their attack on the electoral base of the machine. At the same time, other reformers supported social causes dear to the heart of the bosses; indeed, some reformers were bosses and vice versa. As a result of this research, the traditional practice of portraying urban politics as a sharply defined struggle between bosses and reformers seems less useful now than it did a decade or so ago.[22]

The now acknowledged weaknesses of the boss-reformer interpretive model have forced urban historians to pose new questions and view the evidence in alternative ways. In the past decade, for instance, some historians have begun to challenge the functional view of the boss as a provider of positive government. More research is needed, Jon C. Teaford has written, to determine "to what degree the boss actually bossed." Teaford's important book, *The Unheralded Triumph: City Government in America* (1984), demonstrated the powerful and decisive role of urban professionals and experts in running the industrial city. More important than bosses or reformers, Teaford contended, the growing army of city bureaucrats and technicians may have been the real shapers of the city. Public policymaking depended on what was technically or financially feasible. Thus, the politicians came to rely on the experts, who by the twentieth century staffed the administrative departments in city government. They were municipal engineers, landscape architects, city planners, public health officials, accountants, attorneys, educators, even librarians. Neither the bosses nor the reformers, this new interpretation suggests, had as much power or influence as historians once believed.[23]

Political Power. Other historians have begun addressing the issue of urban political power, particularly its distribution and uses. Established political science models advocate either elitist or pluralist positions regarding the distribution of power: political power is either concentrated among the wealthy or widely dispersed among competing social groups. Recent historical research offers some alternatives to these political science models, while illuminating new dimensions of the American urban experience.

In his book, *Political Power in Birmingham, 1871–1921* (1977), for instance, Carl V. Harris focused on two interrelated aspects of political power, office holding and governmental decision making. He concluded that the elitist model did fit electoral patterns in Birmingham, where office holding was concentrated heavily among the richest 20 percent of the city's population. But these office-holding patterns did not always dictate public policy outcomes. Indeed, decision-making power in Birmingham was distributed in complex ways. Depending on the policy issue involved, the city's politics were complicated by shifting alliances among and within economic groups, and by religious, ethnic, and racial influences. Neither the power-elite thesis nor the pluralist interpretation matched perfectly the political reality in this growing industrial city of the new South. Nevertheless, by abandoning the boss-reformer framework and by posing new questions, Harris was able to bring a fresh perspective to urban political history.[24]

Similar conclusions were reached by David C. Hammack in his important study, *Power and Society: Greater New York at the Turn of the Century* (1982). Hammack examined both the pattern of mayoral politics and the conflicts surrounding three big public policy issues: the consolidation of greater New York City in 1898, the building of the city's first subway, and the centralization of the public school system. The city's increasing ethnic and economic heterogeneity, he argued, stimulated a shift from elitist politics "to a politics of competing elite and nonelite economic, social, and cultural interest groups mediated and managed by specialized professional politicians."[25]

Several forces coalesced in Hammack's New York to undermine the earlier dominance of power elites. First, the elites were divided among themselves, which was also the case in Harris's Birmingham. They often had different economic interests and competing political ambitions. Second, as the city's population grew through immigration and economic diversification, varied nonelite groups (ethnic communities, small business interests, labor unions) developed into active pressure groups. The community-based political parties that represented these interest groups siphoned off political power from the elites. Finally, as the political arena became a place where different interests were compromised and mediated, technical experts, professionals, and bureaucrats came to exercise a great degree of governmental power and authority. The chief interpretive thrust of these new studies is that political decision making reflected the economic, ethnic, and cultural complexity of the cities. The new city of the industrial era, it now appears, was shaped by the continual political interaction of competing elites, pluralistic interest groups, and urban technicians.

Suburbanization. Recent historians of the American city have demonstrated great interest in suburbs. Census statistics have revealed that more Americans now live in the suburban rings surrounding the big cities than in the central cities themselves. Thus, it is appropriate that the historical process that created this demographic reality has been brought under scholarly examination. Warner initiated this sort of study more than twenty years ago in *Streetcar Suburbs*, but few followed his lead. However, the subject has been revitalized in the past few years with the publication of a number of books and articles on the history of suburbanization.

The most important of these studies is Kenneth T. Jackson's *Crabgrass Frontier: The Suburbanization of the United States* (1985). His masterful and literate book provides a synthesis of two centuries of the suburbanization process in the United States. It begins with the preindustrial "walking city" of the eighteenth and early nineteenth century, a residential pattern gradually altered by new transit provisions and the romantic lure of suburbia. By the 1850s and after, revolutionary transit technology—first the horsecar, later the electric trolley—encouraged the deconcentration of population to the urban periphery. There was a political dimension to the process as well, as cities sought to recapture lost population through the annexation of the suburbs. Much of the municipal political history of the late nineteenth century reflected the conflict between the center and the periphery. For the twentieth century, Jackson focuses on the impact of the automobile and on the role of the federal government. Since the 1930s, especially, the suburbanization process has been shaped by federal policymaking; government highway construction, federal housing programs, and federal mortgage and tax policies have all propelled the suburban drift of population and economic activities. Jackson's study is the most sophisticated and thorough account of these subjects.[26]

Jackson's *Crabgrass Frontier* has been joined by a number of more specific studies of suburbs and the suburbanization process. Henry C. Binford's *The First Suburbs: Residential Communities on the Boston Periphery, 1815–1860* (1985) pushes suburbanization back well before the development of mass transit in midcentury. This study of Cambridge and Somerville sees the suburbanization process stemming from a variety of "fringe" economic activities, an emerging sense of middle-class domesticity, and the rise of new commuter patterns.[27] In *City and Suburb* (1979), Jon C. Teaford provides the first sustained historical analysis of the politics of metropolitan deconcentration, governmental fragmentation, annexation, and consolidation. With a wealth of detail on city-suburban political conflicts from 1850 to 1970, Teaford's book charts some new territory for urban historians.[28] Not to be overlooked are new studies of such planned suburban communities as Radburn in New Jersey and Forest Park in Ohio, and of such classic suburbs as Scarsdale, New York, and the North Shore near Chicago.[29] For the suburban patterns of the late twentieth century, two studies by urban geographer Peter O. Muller remain essential: *The Outer City* (1976) and *Contemporary Suburban America* (1981).[30] Michael H. Ebner's 1985 survey of suburban historiography provides an excellent introduction to the literature and the key interpretive issues.[31]

The New Regionalism. Increasingly, some urban historians have sought to link the American city to its hinterland, to the surrounding region of which it is a part. As historian David R. Goldfield has suggested, by the 1970s historians in the United States and elsewhere had begun to pursue urban research within a regional framework. The regionalist idea in the United States derived largely from the work of sociologist Howard W. Odom, who argued in the 1930s that "cultures evolve and can be understood only through the study of regional areas." As Goldfield put it, regionalist research was based on a convergence of geography and history, and it hoped to discover links between environment and culture. For urban historians, the regional approach promised to broaden the study of the city to the wider region to which it was linked geographically, economically, and culturally. By this method, it has been argued, the city and the character of its development might be more precisely examined and defined.[32]

Goldfield himself has provided the best example of how the regionalist approach can invigorate the writing of urban history. His book, *Cotton Fields and Skyscrapers: Southern City and Region, 1607–1890* (1982), analyzed southern urbanization within the context of southern history and culture.[33] Goldfield challenged earlier views that the pattern of southern urban development was similar to the national urban experience, a position that he himself had once taken.[34] As Goldfield put it, "The southern city is different because the South is different"; the southern city "is much closer to the plantation than it is to Chicago and New York." More specifically, he argued that three distinctive aspects of southern regional history and culture have shaped southern urbanization. These are, first, a rural life-style in which the cities maintained a symbiotic relationship with staple agriculture, cotton especially; second, the importance of race and the reality of a biracial society; and third, a colonial economy in which southern cities remained "in economic servitude to the North not only for manufactured products but for all of the financial, credit, legal, accounting, and factoring services that attend a national economy." The application of this regional model of explanation resulted in a stimulating reinterpretation of southern urban history.[35]

Goldfield has presented the most fully developed regional interpretation of U.S. urban history. A number of other recent studies, when taken together, also suggest the utility of such a regional research strategy. These include Francis X. Blouin's study of the Boston region between 1810 and 1850, Gary Lawson Browne's book on early nineteenth-century Baltimore, Burton W. Folsom's study of urban growth in the coal and iron regions of eastern Pennsylvania, Diane Lindstrom's analysis of economic change in the Philadelphia region between 1810 and 1850, and Goldfield's study of urban growth in antebellum Virginia.[36] Some other new or recent studies of urban development in various regions, while not specifically regionalist in the Goldfield tradition, nevertheless provide more grist for the interpretive mill. These include studies of the urban South by Lawrence H. Larsen and James C. Cobb, and books on the urban West by Larsen, Gunther Barth, and Gerald D. Nash.[37]

Sunbelt Cities. One of the most dramatic demographic and structural shifts in American history has occurred in the years since 1940 with the growth of the so-called sunbelt cities. Carl Abbott's *The New Urban America* (1981) presented the first full-scale historical analysis of sunbelt city growth. Abbott identified two distinct growth regions—a seven-state sunbelt Southeast, and a ten-state sunbelt West. Since 1950 these regions experienced population increases, urban and metropolitan growth, and expansion in government employment and per capita income. These growth patterns, Abbott suggested, began during World War II, when the federal government built military bases and training facilities in the South and Southwest. Defense industries such as shipbuilding and aircraft manufacture were concentrated in those regions, as well. Wartime migration and new federal contracts made boomtowns of Atlantic, Gulf, and Pacific coastal cities. By 1980 five of the nation's ten largest cities—Houston, Dallas, Phoenix, San Diego, and Los Angeles—were located in the Southwest.[38]

The post-World War II sunbelt boom was characterized by sustained economic growth, particularly in defense and high-technology industries, as well as in tourism, recreation, and retirement activities. In the automobile era, speedy population dispersal from the central city was commonplace, often following new highway construction and the decentralization of economic activities. Suburban growth accompanied the rise of the sunbelt cities, as the social ecology of the central cities was reproduced at the metropolitan periphery. Population growth and dispersal eventually led the sunbelt cities to active programs of annexation, often on a massive scale. Between 1950 and 1980, typically, Houston grew in area from 160 to 556 square miles, while Oklahoma City expanded from 51 to 603 square miles. Rapid growth created urban-management problems and occasionally led to governmental experimentation, such as in the implementation of metropolitan government in Miami-Dade

County in 1957 and city-county consolidations in Nashville in 1962 and Jacksonville in 1967. Relaxed state annexation laws, a tradition of single-party politics in the South, and the fear of a growing black vote in the central cities all hastened the annexation and consolidation process in the sunbelt in the 1950s and 1960s.

In an innovative section on sunbelt city politics, Abbott identified three successive stages in postwar political development. In the immediate postwar era, the urban boosters and chamber-of-commerce reformers who controlled city governments sought to manage physical and economic growth so as to benefit central city business interests. A new political pattern began to emerge by the 1950s, as vigorous suburban politicians and interest groups fought central city establishments on various issues. More recently, urban politics in the sunbelt has been characterized by neighborhood and ethnic conflict in which local communities within the urban region have become "focal points for political action." Metropolitan politics in the sunbelt, Abbott has argued, reflected urban spatial and territorial realities. Indeed, the crucial issues of local politics—growth policies, annexation, consolidation, school integration, urban renewal, public housing location, highway planning, environmental protection, taxes, and services—are at least partly spatial issues, and local political actors perceive them in terms of their spatial consequences. These are only some of the conclusions drawn in this pioneering study of the sunbelt cities.

If there are common patterns among sunbelt cities, however, the differences among them may be as great as those between sunbelt and frostbelt. This point certainly emerged in a collection of original essays edited by Richard M. Bernard and Bradley R. Rice, *Sunbelt Cities: Politics and Growth since World War II* (1983). Examining twelve sunbelt cities, ranging from Miami and Tampa in the East to Los Angeles and San Diego in the West, the Bernard-Rice volume demonstrated the incredible variety in the demographic, cultural, economic, and political patterns in the sunbelt. More focused is Bradford Luckingham's *The Urban Southwest* (1982), which examines the common patterns in the growth and development of Albuquerque, El Paso, Phoenix, and Tucson.[39]

Technology and the City. From the mid-nineteenth century, technological innovation has provided one of the chief stimulants to urban growth and development. New transit technology encouraged the outward movement of population, new or improved municipal services made urban life safer and more pleasant, new building technology permitted the rise of the skyscraper. A number of studies have elaborated on these aspects of urban history. For example, Charles W. Cheape's *Moving the Masses: Urban Public Transit in New York, Boston, and Philadelphia, 1880–1912* (1980) provides an excellent analysis of the financial, political, and technological context of the building of city transit systems, particularly subways. Other books examining aspects of improving technology and municipal service delivery include Joel A. Tarr's study of transportation patterns in Pittsburgh, Harold L. Platt's book on public utilities in Houston, Judith Walzer Leavitt's treatment of public health in Milwaukee, and Louis P. Cain's analysis of water supply and sanitation in Chicago.[40] Martin V. Melosi's *Pollution and Reform in American Cities,*

1870–1930 (1980) is a collaborative work that carves out some new research areas for urban historians. Covering various sorts of pollution (water, air, noise), the individual essays highlight the role of technological innovation and of the municipal engineer in developing new systems of sewage disposal, water purification, and environmental reform. Melosi's *Garbage in the Cities* (1981) analyzes changing patterns of solid waste disposal, a rather unappealing but nevertheless ubiquitous urban problem.[41]

Moving into the twentieth century, an especially useful book is Mark S. Foster's *From Streetcar to Superhighway* (1981), a study of city planners and urban transportation between 1900 and 1940. The chief innovation of these years was the automobile and the consequent decline of city streetcar systems. Foster attributes the decline of mass transit to the perceived flexibility and economy of the automobile, an interesting conclusion in light of an extensive recent literature advancing a conspiracy theory by which automobile, highway, and related interest groups set out to dismantle and destroy fixed-rail mass transit.[42] In a specific case study of Chicago, Paul Barrett refines Foster's interpretation, suggesting that a "misguided city policy" between 1900 and 1930 ended rapid transit development, weakened the transit companies, and essentially fostered the use of the automobile. The automobile also doomed rail transit in cities ranging from Atlanta to Los Angeles.[43] In *Interstate: Express Highway Politics, 1941–1956*, Mark H. Rose shifts from the municipal to the national level, where public policies affecting the automobile and the city were also being made. It should be no surprise that the 1956 legislation creating the interstate highway system, supported by massive federal subsidies, has had a tremendous impact on urban-suburban America. Rose details the postwar, interest-group politics behind the highway program.[44] The central achievement of these varied recent works on technology has been to demonstrate the important link between technological change and urban development.

Planning and Housing. Technology is related closely to the ways in which Americans planned and built their cities. Technological innovation established the parameters of what was possible and feasible in the built environment. Studies of planning history published in the 1960s and 1970s focused inordinately on the nineteenth-century roots of city planning. These works emphasized the landscape architecture tradition, in which Frederick Law Olmsted played such a major role, and the emergence of the "city beautiful" movement under the leadership of such Chicago figures as architect and planner Daniel Burnham and architect Louis Sullivan.[45] These traditions, and Olmsted especially, continue to attract scholarly interest.[46] However, planning history in recent years has moved solidly into the twentieth century and has concentrated on the practical and utilitarian side of planning: the efficient implementation of zoning policies, urban transit, highway building, public utilities, and central-city development and redevelopment. Moreover, current writing in planning history tends strongly toward placing planning decisions into a wider political and social context. This is particularly true of planning histories by Judd Kahn on San Francisco, Christopher Silver on Richmond, and Carl Abbott on Portland.[47]

Twentieth-century planning has been centrally related to the expansion of modern government. Governmental decision making in this area often stems from motives other than those originally conceived by planners—making cities more rational, more pleasant, and more livable. The recent planning histories emphasize the government role in urban planning, and they demonstrate the often negative consequences of governmental action such as highway construction that helped destroy central city areas, or urban renewal programs that leveled vibrant inner-city neighborhoods. A full-scale critique of the role and function of planners can be found in M. Christine Boyer's *Dreaming the Rational City: The Myth of American City Planning* (1983). Boyer contends that city planning served the interests of the dominant capitalist economy and sought to impose order and control on the urban masses. So much for the dream and the promise of the early city planners.[48]

One aspect of urban planning that generally received short shrift in the United States was housing. In European nations, from the late nineteenth century on, the provision of housing was linked integrally to all other facets of planning.[49] Not so in the United States, where housing reform was generally a matter for private action. The Progressive era did see some basic protective legislation, but the prevailing view was that the private building market was responsible for the provision of decent housing. A good account of housing reform can be found in Thomas L. Philpott's *The Slum and the Ghetto* (1978).[50] Gwendolyn Wright places housing history in the broad context of modern urban and suburban development in *Building the Dream: A Social History of Housing in America* (1981).[51] More specific studies by Arnold R. Hirsch and Dominic J. Capeci trace the agonizing question of housing for blacks in Chicago and Detroit since 1940. In both cities, racial conflict and violence accompanied black efforts to widen their housing opportunities. John F. Bauman's history of housing in Philadelphia, *Public Housing, Race, and Renewal* (1987), explores another important dimension of this subject.[52] The best of the housing histories go beyond the purely physical aspect of housing provision and focus on the political, social, and racial context within which housing decisions were made by governments and by individuals.

The Urban Working Class. Building on the insights of the British historian E. P. Thompson, students of the American working class have been revamping our understanding of workers and of class relations in the American city. Herbert Gutman's important study, *Work, Culture, and Society in Industrializing America* (1976), led the way. His research on the first generation of industrial workers in America demonstrated the surprising strength and persistence of the communal, preindustrial work pattern, even in the midst of the drive toward industrialization. The chief thrust of Gutman's work has been that workers had some control over their lives and over the workplace.[53]

Other historians have pushed the rise of working-class activism back into the preindustrial era. In *The Urban Crucible* (1979), colonial historian Gary B. Nash concluded that social and economic distinctions developed very early in New York, Philadelphia, and Boston. During the economic dislocations of the mid-eighteenth century, Nash contended, the urban working class developed an increasingly radical and participatory politics; as a sense of class consciousness emerged, the urban working class began to take charge of their lives in new and dramatic ways. Crowd action in the cities, for instance, became an instrument of collective power, the means by which cohesive colonial communities protected their perceived interests. The American Revolution, Nash asserted, was one result.[54] Sean Wilentz, in a detailed and important study of the New York City working class, has pushed the class analysis into the early nineteenth century. Adhering fiercely to an egalitarian ideology, the urban artisans emerged after the American Revolution as a powerful anticapitalist force with a strong sense of working-class consciousness. Charles G. Steffen makes a similar point about the artisans in Baltimore during the age of revolution.[55]

During the industrialization process, urban artisans became factory workers; skilled craftsmen suffered loss of status and economic position as the production process was mechanized and skill became less important. A number of studies have focused on the ways in which the urban working class resisted, protested, and adapted to the changes brought about by industrialization. In *Worker City, Company Town* (1978), Daniel J. Walkowitz traces the divergent patterns in Troy and Cohoes, New York. Alan Dawley and Paul G. Faler have analyzed the workingman's response to industrialization in Lynn, Massachusetts. Other recent studies have examined the process and its impact on the working class in Newark, Philadelphia, Pittsburgh, Cincinnati, Detroit, Albany, and Chicago. The general thrust of this work is that workers did not accept industrialization passively, that they resisted the new work disciplines of the industrial era, that preindustrial values and traditions persisted, and that workers exerted some control over their own lives.[56] As Daniel T. Rodgers suggested in *The Work Ethic in Industrial America, 1850–1920* (1978), "There is ample evidence that large numbers of industrial workers failed to internalize the faith of the factory masters." Closely allied to this position is David Montgomery's argument in *Workers' Control in America* (1979) that trade unions ultimately became the mechanism for maintaining craft-worker autonomy and for enforcing traditional work rules.[57]

Race and Ethnicity. Recent historians have altered dramatically the portrait of immigrants and ethnic groups in the American city. The traditional view had been summarized ably in Oscar Handlin's *The Uprooted* (1951). Handlin depicted the immigrants as a displaced peasantry wrenched from the communal past and thrust into the industrial city in a harsh, foreign land. In the urban ghettos of industrial America, the newcomers suffered the destruction of their traditional cultures, social breakdown and disorganization, and eventual assimilation.[58] Virtually every aspect of Handlin's "ghetto hypothesis" of immigrant adjustment has been rewritten by recent historians.

The historical scholarship of the past decade has provided new perspectives on the migration process, the creation of the ethnic village in the American city, and the development of immigrant institutional life. Historians have discovered the importance of "chain migration"—the family- and community-based process which brought most immigrants to America.[59] Once in the new land, the immigrant family structure remained a powerful determinant of life and culture. For Italians, French-Canadians, and others, the family bolstered ethnic culture and aided in the adaptation to industrial work. Old country cultural, religious, and folk patterns did not disappear but persisted as vital ingredients of the ethnic community.[60]

Rather than weakening under the strains of migration and urban life, historians have concluded, the ties of family, kinship, and community remained strong in the American industrial city. Ethnic churches, parochial schools, and a bewildering variety of cultural and fraternal groups kept ethnicity alive despite the powerful forces of assimilation.[61] As historian Dino Cinel suggested in a recent study of Italian immigrants in San Francisco, the newcomers "used their native culture both to preserve their traditions and to cope with the challenge of the new environment."[62]

Moreover, as historian Rudolph J. Vecoli has argued, the immigrants demonstrated "a powerful tendency to reconstitute community in accordance with Old World origins." Thus, Chicago's "Little Italies" were, in reality, dozens of old-country village groups reorganized and reconstituted in the new land. Similarly, in his study, *Ethnics and Enclaves: Boston's Italian North End* (1981), historian William DeMarco noted the importance of old-country village and regional loyalties and concluded that, "in terms of subcultural neighborhoods, the North End resembled the Italian countryside by 1920." Among the Poles in Philadelphia, Caroline Golab wrote in *Immigrant Destinations* (1977), settlement and work patterns "strongly reflected their feudal past and peasant culture."[63]

Such research has uncovered important dimensions of the immigrant experience. Portraying dynamic and vibrant ethnic communities in the industrial city, this new work effectively demolished the traditional ghetto hypothesis of Handlin and others. The most sophisticated summary of recent interpretations may be found in John Bodnar's *The Transplanted: A History of Immigrants in Urban America* (1985), which pulls together in a seamless account the many and varied strands of immigrant history research.[64]

Immigrants were not the only newcomers to the industrial city who sought to keep alive the communal traditions of the premodern past. Among black migrants from the rural South to the urban and industrial North, the old folkways and family patterns persisted into the twentieth century. Buffetted first by slavery and then by modernization, nineteenth-century urban blacks found it difficult to enjoy the full measure of freedom in the city, as Leonard P. Curry has suggested in *The Free Black in Urban America, 1800–1850* (1981). Nevertheless, the black family remained a strong and vital institution, as Herbert Gutman demonstrated in *The Black Family in Slavery and Freedom, 1750–1925* (1976). Similarly, more recent studies of blacks in Boston and Cleveland revealed that southern blacks in northern cities maintained stable, two-parent families supported by extended kin networks. In his innovative study, *Alley Life in Washington* (1980), historian James Borchert found a remarkable persistence of black folklife in the capital city. Blacks retained their old cultural patterns and "were able to maintain stability through their primary groups of family, kinship, neighborhood, community, and religion." These cultural patterns, Borchert maintained, helped black migrants in their "adjustment to a harsh and difficult urban experience."[65] These works, along with recent studies of blacks in Philadelphia, San Francisco, Milwaukee, Louisville, and

Pittsburgh, suggest the ways in which urban blacks coped with industrialization, fought segregation and discrimination, and developed a sense of power
and community.[66] As in the case of the white immigrants, the new historical
research depicts a group of urban Americans who rejected passivity before
powerful forces of change and who sought to shape their own lives despite
pressures of the city, the factory, and the reality of white racism.

Urban Culture. Some historians of the city have turned their attention to
aspects of urban culture, to the popular institutions and ideas that shaped
the way people thought and behaved. The best example of this genre of
writing can be found in Gunther Barth's *City People: The Rise of Modern City
Culture in Nineteenth-Century America* (1980). In this somewhat eclectic book,
Barth contends that out of diversity and heterogeneity American urbanites
created a modern city culture oriented around common institutions and forms.
These common cultural patterns, he argues, helped Americans of vastly different backgrounds "cope with the complex demands of a strange cityscape."
Barth concentrates on five new elements that contributed to this common
urban culture: the apartment house, the metropolitan newspaper, the department store, the ballpark, and the vaudeville house. These new institutions
"came into existence with the modern city." Moreover, Barth writes, they
"contributed more directly and extensively to the emergence of modern city
culture than did the factory and the political machine." This interpretation
is asserted rather than proven, but the argument provides a fascinating new
perspective on the rise of the industrial city.[67]

Other aspects of urban culture have been addressed, as well, by historians
of the city. In an influential earlier study, *The Intellectual versus the City* (1962),
Morton and Lucia White traced deep-seated patterns of antiurbanism among
the American intelligentsia from the colonial era to mid-twentieth century.
By contrast, Adrienne Siegel, in *The Image of the American City in Popular Literature, 1820–1870* (1981), demonstrated that widely read popular books,
although perhaps not great literature, presented a positive, upbeat, even
exciting picture of urban life. As Siegel put it, "Literary hacks offered a view
of the city that was often at odds with the somber images painted by writers
of belles-lettres." Urbanites were bombarded with an avalanche of popular
fiction books that "whetted the appetite of Americans for city life." In *From
Main Street to State Street* (1977), historian Park Dixon Goist deals with the
place of the city in some of the more sophisticated literary writing between
1890 and 1940.[68]

Research on the history of urban sports also has begun to fill in gaps in
our knowledge of urban culture and the uses of leisure time. Baseball, in
particular, was extremely popular in the city from the late nineteenth century,
but other sporting and recreational activities also caught on. As sports historian Stephen Hardy has suggested in *How Boston Played* (1982), "The athletic
germ that infected the country after the Civil War found its most fertile ground
in cities." Baseball, boxing, horse racing, and other sports also were linked
to city politics and to city gambling activities.[69] And some playground reformers thought of baseball as a means of socializing and controlling urban and
immigrant children. As Dominick Cavallo suggested in *Muscles and Morals*

(1981), with its clearly defined rules and roles, baseball seemed a perfect way of teaching "respect for law, order, and justice" and restoring "the social cohesion damaged by urban mobility and anonymity."[70] It is hardly likely that city kids thought of baseball in exactly this way.

Another urban leisure institution—the saloon—has been investigated by recent urban historians. Serving many functions (social, political, and economic), the saloon became a ubiquitous urban institution. The most detailed recent study is Perry R. Duis's *The Saloon: Public Drinking in Chicago and Boston, 1880–1920* (1983), which details the multifaceted roles of these city watering holes, while contrasting their place in two very different cities. Complementing the Duis analysis are two other new city-specific saloon studies: Thomas J. Noel on saloons in Denver and Roy Rosenzweig on saloons and leisure in Worcester.[71] The general thrust of these urban culture studies seems to be that working-class urban institutions had important social and other functions, and that such agencies demonstrate the complexity and diversity of urban culture rather than the cultural consensus suggested by Barth.

Most of the recent research on urban culture has focused on nonelite groups, especially the working class, but a few studies of urban elites have been published. Among these is Frederic Cople Jaher's monumental book, *The Urban Establishment* (1982), which concentrates on the rich, the wellborn, and the powerful in Boston, New York, Charleston, Chicago, and Los Angeles from the nineteenth to the twentieth century. The cities offered unparalleled opportunities for the acquisition of wealth, power, and knowledge. In contrast to the studies of working-class culture, Jaher's perspective offers an alternative analysis of the dynamics of economic, political, and social change in urbanizing America.[72] One additional perspective is provided by Thomas Bender in several essays on professional and intellectual elites in the American city.[73] Taken together, the work of Jaher and Bender provides a more complete picture of American urban culture.

Federal-City Relations/Urban Public Policy. As urban history has begun to focus on the twentieth century, the increasingly powerful role of the federal government in urban policymaking has come under study. Two books in the mid-1970s initiated research on this subject: Mark I. Gelfand's *A Nation of Cities: The Federal Government and Urban America, 1933–1965* (1975) and Philip Funigiello's *The Challenge to Urban Liberalism: Federal-City Relations during World War II* (1978). Both volumes demonstrated the hesitant effort of the federal government to grapple with urban issues during the economic disaster of the 1930s and the wartime emergency of the early 1940s. While government did embark on a range of new programs for relief, employment, and wartime planning—programs particularly welcomed in America's big cities—what is remarkable is the lack of any really national political commitment to the city. Indeed, governmental initiatives were usually undermined by the enduring strength of a localist tradition, the power of entrepreneurialism and privatism, and destructive competition among various interest groups for governmental favoritism.[74]

Several more recent books have developed some of these themes. Roger W. Lotchin's edited collection, *The Martial Metropolis: U.S. Cities in War and Peace*

(1984), explores the connection between federal military spending and urban development. In what is now referred to as the Lotchin thesis, the city and the sword are seen as inseparably linked in such cities as Norfolk, San Francisco, San Antonio, Los Angeles, Seattle, and Portland. John Mollenkopf's *The Contested City* (1983) is an ambitious overview of the development of urban public policy since the New Deal era. Mollenkopf argues that the Democratic party put together a national progrowth coalition that altered the urban environment and not incidentally kept the party in power throughout much of the period between the 1930s and 1980. Mollenkopf also demonstrates that the Democrats' urban liberalism often worsened conditions for inner-city residents, while stimulating conservative countermovements. The book does have certain weaknesses, but it still presents a powerful account of federal interventionism since the 1930s. However, a second work on the same subject rejects the interpretation that politics motivated public policymaking. In *Metropolitan America: Urban Life and Urban Policy in the United States, 1940–1980* (1986), Kenneth Fox contends that social science research, governmental data, and rational argument have had a greater impact in shaping urban public policy. He illustrates his argument with a detailed account of governmental involvement in the making of metropolitan America. Despite their varied interpretations, all of the authors cited here would agree to the basic proposition that federal decision making has determined the shape of urban America over the past fifty years.[75]

Comparative Urban History. In the past decade, American urban historians have become much more aware of the international dimensions of urban history research. Some efforts at comparative urban research have proven fruitful, particularly geographer Brian J. L. Berry's *Comparative Urbanization: Divergent Paths in the Twentieth Century* (1981). Berry placed American urban patterns in the perspective of the larger forces reshaping the city in postwar Europe and Japan, and more recently the Third World. British geographer and planner Peter Hall takes a different approach in *The World Cities* (1984), presenting separate chapters on the urban development of such cities as New York, London, Paris, Tokyo, Moscow, Hong Kong, and Mexico City. A still different sort of analysis is that offered by Charles Tilly in *Big Structures, Large Processes, Huge Comparisons* (1984), which examines in sweeping strokes such forces as urbanization, industrialization, and capitalism that shaped the urban world in the nineteenth and twentieth centuries.[76]

Few urban historians have taken the sweeping approaches of Berry, Hall, and Tilly. But an enormous secondary literature has emerged on the history of cities throughout the world, making it possible for American urbanists to draw their own parallels with the urban experience of Canada, Australia, Great Britain, Europe, India, Latin America, Africa, and the Middle East. Graeme Davison, Weston Bate, J. B. Hirst, Peter Spearritt, and C. T. Stannage, among others, have led a vigorous effort to explore the urban dimensions of Australian history.[77] Alan Artibise and Gilbert Stelter have published a number of studies documenting the growth of the Canadian city.[78] For many years H. J. Dyos provided the inspiration and energy for the study of British urban history, and his legacy is reflected in the *Urban History Yearbook*, which began publication in 1975.[79] In three new studies, Josef W. Konvitz, Jan DeVries, and Paul M. Hohenburg and Lynn Hollen Lees have provided an extensive, and in some cases massively detailed, overview of European urbanization.[80] Work on the urban history of other nations and regions of the world has mushroomed over the past decade, work that can provide broadening insights for the historians of the American city.[81]

The Search for Synthesis. The foregoing general topics all represent important new thrusts of urban history research in the United States. With sufficient space, attention might have been given as well to new studies on women and gender relations in the city, to work on the visual dimension of the city, to biographical studies of urban movers and shakers like Robert Moses, to work on the city in American thought, to studies of urban architecture, crime, violence, and a dozen or more other subjects.[82] This essay has concentrated on books and monographs, but the reader also should be aware of an enormous article literature on all of these subjects.[83] The field, in short, has been livened and invigorated with a monumental amount of new research.

It is also true, however, that the outpouring of scholarship has fragmented the field and created problems of comprehension and analysis. As historian Bernard Bailyn put it in a recent address: "It is a confusing time in historical study, and yet a creative time—in which all sorts of new departures are being made, new materials being assembled, and new viewpoints being aired. But it calls for an occasional reassessment." It is time for a new synthesis pulling together social, political, and cultural history, Bender has written, time to "make history whole again."[84]

Three recent books have attempted at least a partial synthesis for urban history, pulling together the new research in the field in an organized and interpretive format: Raymond A. Mohl's *The New City: Urban America in the Industrial Age, 1860–1920* (1985); Carl Abbott's *Urban America in the Modern Age, 1920 to the Present* (1987); and Jon C. Teaford's *The Twentieth-Century City: Problem, Promise, and Reality* (1986).[85] More synthesis is needed, obviously, and works of this sort will probably emerge over the next several years. Meanwhile, the recent scholarship detailed in this essay should provide a sufficiently marked pathway leading interested students, teachers, and researchers into the exciting field of American urban history.

NOTES

[1]Richard C. Wade, "Urbanization," in C. Vann Woodward, ed., *The Comparative Approach to American History* (New York, 1968), 203.

[2]Arthur M. Schlesinger, "The City in American History," *Mississippi Valley Historical Review* 27 (June 1940): 43–66. See also Arthur M. Schlesinger, *The Rise of the City, 1878–1898* (New York, 1933).

[3]Blake McKelvey, "American Urban History Today," *American Historical Review* 57 (July 1952): 919–29; Carl Bridenbaugh, *Cities in the Wilderness* (New York, 1938); Carl Bridenbaugh, *Cities in Revolt* (New York, 1955); Oscar Handlin, *Boston's Immigrants* (Cambridge, 1941); Richard C. Wade, *The Urban Frontier: The Rise of Western Cities, 1790–1830* (Cambridge, 1959). For a model urban biography from this period, see Bayrd Still, *Milwaukee: The History of a City* (Madison, 1948). For an outstanding example of the multivolume genre of urban biography, see Bessie L. Pierce, *A History of Chicago*, 3 vols. (Chicago, 1937–57).

[4]Olivier Zunz, "The Synthesis of Social Change: Reflections on American Social History," in Olivier Zunz, ed., *Reliving the Past: The Worlds of Social History* (Chapel Hill, 1985), 54. See also Irwin Unger, "The 'New Left' and American History: Some Recent Trends in United States Historiography," *American Historical Review* 72 (July 1967): 1237–63; Michael Kammen, "The Historian's Vocation and the State of the Discipline in the United States," in Michael Kammen, ed., *The Past before Us: Contemporary Historical Writing in the United States* (Ithaca, 1980), 19–46.

[5]W. O. Aydelotte, "Quantification in History," *American Historical Review* 71 (April 1966): 803–25; Jerome M. Clubb and Howard Allen, "Computers and Historical Studies," *Journal of American History* 54 (December 1967): 599–607; Edward Shorter, *The Historian and the Computer* (Englewood Cliffs, NJ, 1971); Allan G. Bogue, "Numerical and Formal Analysis in United States History," *Journal of Interdisciplinary History* 12 (Summer 1981): 137–75; Jerome M. Clubb, "Computer·Technology and the Source Materials of Social Science History," *Social Science History* 10 (Summer 1986): 97–114. On the monographic explosion since the 1960s, see Bernard Bailyn, "The Challenge of Modern Historiography," *American Historical Review* 87 (February 1982): 1–24.

[6]Sam Bass Warner, Jr., *Streetcar Suburbs: The Process of Growth in Boston, 1870–1900* (Cambridge, 1962). See also Sam Bass Warner, Jr., "If All the World Were Philadelphia: A Scaffolding for Urban History, 1774–1930," *American Historical Review* 74 (October 1968): 26–43; *The Private City: Philadelphia in Three Periods of Its Growth* (Philadelphia, 1968); *The Urban Wilderness: A History of the American City* (New York, 1972); *The Way We Really Live: Social Change in Boston since 1920* (Boston, 1977); and with Sylvia Fleisch, *Measurements for Social History* (Beverly Hills, CA, 1977).

[7]Eric E. Lampard's articles include "American Historians and the Study of Urbanization," *American Historical Review* 67 (October 1961): 49–61; "Urbanization and Social Change: On Broadening the Scope and Relevance of Urban History," in Oscar Handlin and John Burchard, eds., *The Historian and the City* (Cambridge, 1963), 225–47; "Historical Aspects of Urbanization," in Philip M. Hauser and Leo F. Schnore, eds., *The Study of Urbanization* (New York, 1965), 519–54; "Historical Contours of Contemporary Urban Society: A Comparative View," *Journal of Contemporary History* 4 (July 1969): 3–25; "The Dimensions of Urban History: A Footnote to the 'Urban Crisis,'" *Pacific Historical Review* 39 (August 1970): 261–78; "The Pursuit of Happiness in the City: Changing Opportunities and Options in America," *Transactions of the Royal Historical Society* 23 (1973): 175–220; "The Urbanizing World," in H. J. Dyos and Michael Wolff, eds., *The Victorian City*, 2 vols. (London, 1973), 1:3–57; "City Making and City Mending in the United States," in Woodrow Borah et al., *Urbanization in the Americas* (Ottawa, 1980), 105–18; and "The Nature of Urbanization," in William Sharpe and Leonard Wallock, eds., *Visions of the Modern City* (New York, 1983), 47–96. See also Bruce M. Stave, "A Conversation with Eric E. Lampard," *Journal of Urban History* 1 (August 1975): 440–72.

[8]Roy Lubove, "The Urbanization Process: An Approach to Historical Research," *Journal of the American Institute of Planners* 33 (January 1967): 33–39; Roy Lubove, *Twentieth-Century Pittsburgh: Government, Business and Environmental Change* (New York, 1969).

[9]Stephan Thernstrom, *Poverty and Progress: Social Mobility in a Nineteenth-Century City* (Cambridge, 1964); Stephan Thernstrom and Richard Sennett, eds., *Nineteenth-Century Cities: Essays in the New Urban History* (New Haven, 1969); Leo F. Schnore, ed., *The New Urban History: Quantitative Explorations by American Historians* (Princeton, 1975). See also the extensive discussion of *Poverty and Progress* in *Social Science History* 10 (Spring 1986): 1–44.

[10]For a small sampling of this mobility literature, see Richard J. Hopkins, "Occupational and Geographical Mobility in Atlanta, 1870–1896," *Journal of Southern History* 34 (May 1968): 200–13; Peter R. Knights, *The Plain People of Boston, 1830–1860: A Study in City Growth* (New York, 1971); Howard P. Chudacoff, *Mobile Americans: Residential and Social Mobility in Omaha, 1880–1920* (New York, 1972); Michael B. Katz, *The People of Hamilton, Canada West: Family and Class in a Mid-Nineteenth-Century City* (Cambridge, 1975); Dean R. Esslinger, *Immigrants and the City: Ethnicity and Mobility in a Nineteenth-Century Midwestern Community* (Port Washington, NY, 1975); Thomas Kessner, *The Golden Door: Italian and Jewish Mobility in New York City, 1880–1915* (New York, 1977).

[11]Stephan Thernstrom, "Reflections on the New Urban History," *Deadalus* 100 (Spring 1971): 359–75.

[12]Michael Frisch, "American Urban History as an Example of Recent Historiography," *History and Theory* 18 (1979): 350–77.

[13]Stephan Thernstrom, *The Other Bostonians: Poverty and Progress in the American Metropolis, 1880–1970* (Cambridge, 1973); Bruce M. Stave, "A Conversation with Stephan Thernstrom," *Journal of Urban History* 1 (February 1975): 189–215.

[14]John B. Sharpless and Sam Bass Warner, Jr., "Urban History," *American Behavioral Scientist* 21 (November–December 1977): 221–244. See also Bruce M. Stave, "A Conversation with Sam Bass Warner, Jr.," *Journal of Urban History* 1 (November 1974), 85–110; and Bruce M. Stave, "A Conversation with Sam Bass Warner, Jr.: Ten Years Later," ibid. 11 (November 1984): 83–113.

[15]Theodore Hershberg, "The New Urban History: Toward an Interdisciplinary History of the City," *Journal of Urban History* 5 (November 1979): 3–40; Theodore Hershberg, ed., *Philadelphia: Work, Space, Family and Group Experience in the Nineteenth Century* (New York, 1981), 3–35.

[16]For earlier historiographical surveys, see Charles N. Glaab, "The Historian and the American City:

A Bibliographic Survey," in Hauser and Schnore, eds., *The Study of Urbanization*, 53–80; Dwight W. Hoover, "The Diverging Paths of American Urban History," *American Quarterly* 20 (Summer 1968): 296–317; Dana F. White, "The Underdeveloped Discipline: Interdisciplinary Directions in American Urban History," *American Studies: An International Newsletter* 9 (Spring 1971): 3–16; Raymond A. Mohl, "The History of the American City," in William H. Cartwright and Richard L. Watson, Jr., *The Reinterpretation of American History and Culture* (Washington, DC, 1973), 165–205; Michael H. Ebner, "Urban History; Retrospect and Prospect," *Journal of American History* 68 (June 1981); 69–84; Bruce M. Stave, "Urban History: A Tale of Many Cities," *Magazine of History* 2 (Winter 1986): 32–37.

[17]Bruce M. Stave, "In Pursuit of Urban History: Conversations with Myself and Others—a View from the United States," in Derek Fraser and Anthony Sutcliffe, eds., *The Pursuit of Urban History* (London, 1983), 424.

[18]For one objection to Stave's conclusion, see Terrence J. McDonald, "The Pursuit of Urban History: To the Rear March," *Historical Methods* 18 (Summer 1985): 116.

[19]Zane L. Miller, *Boss Cox's Cincinnati: Urban Politics in the Progressive Era* (New York, 1968), 94. The reinterpretation of the urban political machine began with Robert K. Merton, *Social Theory and Social Structure* (New York, 1967). Other revisionist studies include Seymour J. Mandelbaum, *Boss Tweed's New York* (New York, 1965); and John M. Allswang, *Bosses, Machines, and Urban Voters: An American Symbiosis* (Port Washington, NY, 1977). For a comprehensive collection of readings, see Bruce M. Stave and Sondra Astor Stave, eds., *Urban Bosses, Machines, and Progressive Reformers* (Malabar, FL, 1984).

[20]Leo Hershkowitz, *Tweed's New York: Another Look* (Garden City, NY, 1977), 348.

[21]For recent studies of the machine, see Amy Bridges, *A City in the Republic: Antebellum New York and the Origins of Machine Politics* (Cambridge, England, 1984); Edward K. Spann, *The New Metropolis: New York City, 1840–1857* (New York, 1981); Roger Biles, *Big City Boss in Depression and War: Mayor Edward J. Kelly of Chicago* (DeKalb, IL, 1984); and Paul Kleppner, *Chicago Divided: The Making of a Black Mayor* (DeKalb, IL, 1985).

[22]John D. Buenker, *Urban Liberalism and Progressive Reform* (New York, 1973); Michael H. Ebner and Eugene M. Tobin, eds., *The Age of Urban Reform: New Perspectives on the Progressive Era* (Port Washington, NY, 1977).

[23]Jon C. Teaford, "Finis for Tweed and Steffens: Rewriting the History of Urban Rule," *Reviews in American History* 10 (December 1982): 136; Jon C. Teaford, *The Unheralded Triumph: City Government in America, 1870–1900* (Baltimore, 1984). For a focus on the fiscal constraints imposed on municipal government, see Terrence J. McDonald, *The Parameters of Urban Fiscal Policy: Socioeconomic Change and Political Culture in San Francisco, 1860–1906* (Berkeley, 1986).

[24]Carl V. Harris, *Political Power in Birmingham, 1871–1921* (Knoxville, 1977).

[25]David C. Hammack, *Power and Society: Greater New York at the Turn of the Century* (New York, 1982), 180. For a different approach to the question of political power, see William Issel and Robert W. Cherny, *San Francisco, 1865–1932: Politics, Power, and Urban Development* (Berkeley, 1986).

[26]Kenneth T. Jackson, *Crabgrass Frontier: The Suburbanization of the United States* (New York, 1985).

[27]Henry C. Binford, *The First Suburbs: Residential Communities on the Boston Periphery, 1815–1860* (Chicago, 1985). See also Matthew Edel, Elliott D. Sclar, and Daniel Luria, *Shaky Palaces: Homeownership and Social Mobility in Boston's Suburbanization* (New York, 1984).

[28]Jon C. Teaford, *City and Suburb: The Political Fragmentation of Metropolitan America, 1850–1970* (Baltimore, 1979).

[29]Daniel Schaffer, *Garden Cities for America: The Radburn Experience* (Philadelphia, 1982); Zane L. Miller, *Suburb: Neighborhood and Community in Forest Park, Ohio, 1935–1976* (Knoxville, 1981); Carol A. O'Connor, *A Sort of Utopia: Scarsdale, 1891–1981* (Albany, 1983); Michael H. Ebner, "'In the Suburbes of Toun': Chicago's North Shore to 1871," *Chicago History* 11 (Summer 1982): 66–77.

[30]Peter O. Muller, *The Outer City: Geographical Consequences of the Urbanization of the Suburbs* (Washington, DC, 1976); Peter O. Muller, *Contemporary Suburban America* (Englewood Cliffs, NJ, 1981).

[31]Michael H. Ebner, "Re-reading Suburban America: Urban Population Deconcentration, 1810–1980," *American Quarterly* 37 (1985), 368–81.

[32]On the concept of regionalism, see David R. Goldfield, "The New Regionalism," *Journal of Urban History* 10 (February 1984): 171–86. See also David R. Goldfield, "The Urban South: A Regional Framework," *American Historical Review* 86 (December 1981): 1009–34.

[33]David R. Goldfield, *Cotton Fields and Skyscrapers: Southern City and Region, 1607–1980* (Baton Rouge, 1982). See also Bradley R. Rice, "How Different is the Southern City?" *Journal of Urban History* 11 (November 1985): 115–21.

[34]See the essays in Blaine A. Brownell and David R. Goldfield, eds., *The City in Southern History: The Growth of Urban Civilization in the South* (Port Washington, NY, 1977); and Leonard P. Curry, "Urbanization and Urbanism in the Old South: A Comparative View," *Journal of Southern History* 40 (February 1974): 43–60.

[35]Goldfield, *Cotton Fields and Skyscrapers*, 3, 8.

[36]Francis X. Blouin, Jr., *The Boston Region, 1810–1850: A Study of Urbanization* (Ann Arbor, 1978); Gary Lawson Browne, *Baltimore in the Nation, 1789–1861* (Chapel Hill, 1980); Burton W. Folsom, Jr., *Urban*

Capitalists: Entrepreneurs and City Growth in Pennsylvania's Lackawanna and Lehigh Regions, 1800–1920 (Baltimore, 1981); Diane Lindstrom, *Economic Development in the Philadelphia Region, 1810–1850* (New York, 1978); David R. Goldfield, *Urban Growth in the Age of Sectionalism: Virginia, 1847–1861* (Baton Rouge, 1977); Cynthia J. Shelton, *The Mills of Manayunk: Industrialization and Social Conflict in the Philadelphia Region, 1787–1837* (Baltimore, 1986).

[37]Lawrence H. Larsen, *The Rise of the Urban South* (Lexington, 1985); James C. Cobb, *Industrialization and Southern Society, 1877–1984* (Lexington, 1984); Lawrence H. Larsen, *The Urban West at the End of the Frontier* (Lawrence, KS, 1978); Gunther Barth, *Instant Cities: Urbanization and the Rise of San Francisco and Denver* (New York, 1975); Gerald D. Nash, *The American West Transformed: The Impact of the Second World War* (Bloomington, IN, 1985). See also Bradford Luckingham "The Urban Dimension of Western History," in Michael Malone, ed., *The West in American Historiography* (Lincoln, 1983), 323–43.

[38]Carl Abbott, *The New Urban America Growth and Politics in Sunbelt Cities* (Chapel Hill, 1981).

[39]Richard M. Bernard and Bradley R. Rice, eds., *Sunbelt Cities: Politics and Growth since World War II* (Austin, 1983); Bradford Luckingham, *The Urban Southwest: A Profile History of Albuquerque, El Paso, Phoenix, and Tucson* (El Paso, 1982).

[40]Charles W. Cheape, *Moving the Masses: Urban Public Transit in New York, Boston, and Philadelphia, 1880–1912* (Cambridge, 1980); Joel A. Tarr, *Transportation Innovation and Changing Spatial Patterns in Pittsburgh, 1850–1934* (Chicago, 1978); Harold L. Platt, *City Building in the New South: The Growth of Public Services in Houston, Texas, 1830–1910* (Philadelphia, 1983); Judith Walzer Leavitt, *The Healthiest City: Milwaukee and the Politics of Health Reform* (Princeton, 1982); Louis P. Cain, *Sanitation Strategy for a Lakefront Metropolis: The Case of Chicago* (DeKalb, IL, 1978). See also Ann Durkin Keating et al., *Infrastructure and Urban Growth in the Nineteenth Century* (Chicago, 1985).

[41]Martin V. Melosi, ed., *Pollution and Reform in American Cities, 1870–1930* (Austin, 1980); Martin V. Melosi, *Garbage in the Cities: Refuse, Reform, and the Environment, 1880–1980* (College Station, TX, 1981). See also Melosi, *Coping with Abundance: Energy and Environment in Industrial America* (New York, 1985).

[42]Mark S. Foster, *From Streetcar to Superhighway: American City Planners and Urban Transportation, 1900–1940* (Philadelphia, 1981). For the conspiracy theory, see Bradford C. Snell, U.S. Subcommittee on Antitrust and Monopoly of the Committee on the Judiciary, *American Ground Transport* (Washington, DC, 1974); Delbert A. Taebel and James V. Cornehls, *The Political Economy of Urban Transportation* (Port Washington, NY, 1977); and David J. St. Clair, *The Motorization of American Cities* (New York, 1986).

[43]Paul Barrett, *The Automobile and Urban Transit: The Formation of Public Policy in Chicago, 1900–1930* (Philadelphia, 1983); Howard L. Preston, *Automobile Age Atlanta: The Making of a Southern Metropolis, 1900–1935* (Athens, GA, 1979).

[44]Mark H. Rose, *Interstate: Express Highway Politics, 1941–1956* (Lawrence, KS, 1979).

[45]Albert Fein, *Frederick Law Olmsted and the American Environmental Tradition* (New York, 1972); Laura Wood Roper, *FLO: A Biography of Frederick Law Olmsted* (Baltimore, 1973); Elizabeth Stevenson, *Park Maker: A Life of Frederick Law Olmsted* (New York, 1977); Thomas S. Hines, *Burnham of Chicago: Architect and Planner* (New York, 1974); Robert Twombly, *Louis Sullivan: His Life and Work* (Chicago, 1986).

[46]Cynthia Zaitzevsky, *Frederick Law Olmsted and the Boston Park System* (Cambridge, 1982); Charles E. Beveridge and David Schuyler, eds., *Creating Central Park, 1857–1861*, vol. 3 of *The Papers of Frederick Law Olmsted* (Baltimore, 1983); Galen Cranz, *The Politics of Park Design: A History of Urban Parks in America* (Cambridge, 1982); Giorgio Ciucci et al., *The American City* (Cambridge, 1979); David Schuyler, *The New Urban Landscape: The Redefinition of City Form in Nineteenth-Century America* (Baltimore, 1986); Irving D. Fisher, *Frederick Law Olmsted and the City Planning Movement in the United States* (Ann Arbor, 1986).

[47]Judd Kahn, *Imperial San Francisco: Politics and Planning in an American City* (Lincoln, 1979); Christopher Silver, *Twentieth-Century Richmond: Planning, Politics, and Race* (Knoxville, 1984); Carl Abbott, *Portland: Planning, Politics, and Growth in a Twentieth-Century City* (Lincoln, 1983).

[48]M. Christine Boyer, *Dreaming the Rational City: The Myth of American City Planning* (Cambridge, 1983). For a similarly critical analysis of planning history, see Richard E. Fogelsong, *Planning the Capitalist City: The Colonial Era to the 1920s* (Princeton, 1986). See also Christine Meisner Rosen, *The Limits of Power: Great Fires and the Process of City Growth in America* (Cambridge, England, 1986).

[49]Anthony Sutcliffe, *Towards the Planned City: Germany, Britain, the United States, and France, 1780–1914* (Oxford, 1981), 88–125; Peter Marcuse, "Housing in Early City Planning," *Journal of Urban History* 6 (February 1980): 153–76.

[50]Thomas L. Philpott, *The Slum and the Ghetto: Neighborhood Deterioration and Middle-Class Reform, Chicago, 1880–1930* (New York, 1978). For an earlier study in this tradition, see Roy Lubove, *The Progressives and the Slums: Tenement House Reform in New York City, 1890–1917* (Pittsburgh, 1962).

[51]Gwendolyn Wright, *Building the Dream: A Social History of Housing in America* (New York, 1981).

[52]Arnold R. Hirsch, *Making the Second Ghetto: Race and Housing in Chicago, 1940–1960* (Cambridge, England, 1983); Dominic J. Capeci, Jr., *Race Relations in Wartime Detroit: The Sojourner Truth Housing Controversy, 1937–1942* (Philadelphia, 1984); John F. Bauman, *Public Housing, Race, and Renewal: Urban Planning in Philadelphia, 1920–1974* (Philadelphia, 1987).

[53]E. P. Thompson, *The Making of the English Working Class* (New York, 1963); Herbert G. Gutman, *Work, Culture, and Society in Industrializing America* (New York, 1976).

[54]Gary B. Nash, *The Urban Crucible: Social Change, Political Consciousness, and the Origins of the American Revolution* (Cambridge, 1979). See also Dirk Hoerder, *Crowd Action in Revolutionary Massachusetts, 1765–1780* (New York, 1977); and Gary B. Nash, "The Social Evolution of Preindustrial American Cities, 1700–1820: Reflections and New Directions," *Journal of Urban History* 13 (February 1987): 115–45.

[55]Sean Wilentz, *Chants Democratic: New York City and the Rise of the American Working Class, 1788–1850* (New York, 1984); Charles G. Steffen, *The Mechanics of Baltimore: Workers and Politics in the Age of Revolution, 1763–1812* (Urbana, 1984). See also Howard B. Rock, *Artisans of the New Republic: The Tradesmen of New York City in the Age of Jefferson* (New York, 1979).

[56]Daniel J. Walkowitz, *Worker City, Company Town: Iron and Cotton-Worker Protest in Troy and Cohoes, New York, 1855–84* (Urbana, 1978); Alan Dawley, *Class and Community: The Industrial Revolution in Lynn* (Cambridge, 1976); Paul G. Faler, *Mechanics and Manufacturers in the Early Industrial Revolution: Lynn, Massachusetts, 1780–1860* (Albany, 1981); Susan E. Hirsch, *Roots of the American Working Class: The Industrialization of Crafts in Newark, 1800–1860* (Philadelphia, 1978); Bruce Laurie, *Working People of Philadelphia, 1800–1850* (Philadelphia, 1980); Frances G. Couvares, *The Remaking of Pittsburgh: Class and Culture in an Industrializing City, 1877–1919* (Albany, 1984); Stephen J. Ross, *Workers on the Edge: Work, Leisure, and Politics in Industrializing Cincinnati, 1788–1890* (New York, 1985); Richard Oestreicher, *Solidarity and Fragmentation: Working People and Class Consciousness in Detroit, 1875–1900* (Urbana, 1986); Brian Greenberg, *Worker and Community: Response to Industrialization in a Nineteenth-Century American City, Albany, New York, 1850–1884* (Albany, 1985); Louise C. Wade, *Chicago's Pride: The Stockyards, Packingtown, and Environs in the Nineteenth Century* (Urbana, 1986); James R. Barrett, *Work and Community in the Jungle: Chicago's Packinghouse Workers, 1894–1922* (Urbana, 1987).

[57]Daniel T. Rodgers, *The Work Ethic in Industrial America, 1850–1920* (Chicago, 1978), 155; David Montgomery, *Workers' Control in America* (Cambridge, England, 1979).

[58]Oscar Handlin, *The Uprooted: The Epic Story of the Great Migrations that Made the American People* (Boston, 1951).

[59]On chain migration, see Josef J. Barton, *Peasants and Strangers: Italians, Rumanians, and Slovaks in an American City, 1890–1950* (Cambridge, 1975); John Bodnar, *Immigration and Industrialization: Ethnicity in an American Mill Town, 1870–1940* (Pittsburgh, 1977); John W. Briggs, *An Italian Passage: Immigrants to Three American Cities, 1890–1930* (New Haven, 1978); Dino Cinel, *From Italy to San Francisco: The Immigrant Experience* (Stanford, 1982).

[60]Virginia Yans-McLaughlin, *Family and Community: Italian Immigrants in Buffalo, 1880–1930* (Ithaca, 1977); Tamara K. Hareven, *Family Time and Industrial Time: The Relationship between the Family and Work in a New England Industrial Community* (Cambridge, England, 1982); John Bodnar et al., *Lives of Their Own: Blacks, Italians, and Poles in Pittsburgh, 1900–1960* (Urbana, 1982); Olivier Zunz, *The Changing Face of Inequality: Urbanization, Industrial Development, and Immigrants in Detroit, 1880–1920* (Chicago, 1982).

[61]On the immigrant church, see Jay Dolan, *The Immigrant Church: New York's Irish and German Catholics, 1815–1865* (Baltimore, 1975); Victor Greene, *For God and Country: The Rise of Polish and Lithuanian Ethnic Consciousness in America* (Madison, 1975); and Randall M. Miller and Thomas D. Marzik, eds., *Immigrants and Religion in Urban America* (Philadelphia, 1977). On schooling, see James W. Sanders, *The Education of an Urban Minority: Catholics in Chicago, 1833–1965* (New York, 1977); Ronald D. Cohen and Raymond A. Mohl, *The Paradox of Progressive Education: The Gary Plan and Urban Schooling* (Port Washington, NY, 1979), 84–109. On immigrant associational life, see Raymond A. Mohl and Neil Betten, *Steel City: Urban and Ethnic Patterns in Gary, Indiana, 1906–1950* (New York, 1986); and Scott Cummings, eds., *Self-Help in Urban America: Patterns of Minority Economic Development* (Port Washington, NY, 1979).

[62]Cinel, *From Italy to San Francisco*, 13.

[63]Rudolph J. Vecoli, "*Contadini* in Chicago: A Critique of *The Uprooted*," *Journal of American History* 51 (December 1964): 404–16; Rudolph J. Vecoli, "The Formation of Chicago's 'Little Italies,'" *Journal of American Ethnic History* 2 (Spring 1983): 5–20; William DeMarco, *Ethnics and Enclaves: Boston's Italian North End* (Ann Arbor, 1981); Caroline Golab, *Immigrant Destinations* (Philadelphia, 1977).

[64]John Bodnar, *The Transplanted: A History of Immigrants in Urban America* (Bloomington, IN, 1985). Books pursuing the interpretive lines laid out by Bodnar include Gary R. Mormino, *Immigrants on the Hill: Italian-Americans in St. Louis, 1882–1982* (Urbana, 1986); Gary R. Mormino and George E. Pozzetta, *The Immigrant World of Ybor City: Italians and Their Latin Neighbors in Tampa, 1885–1985* (Urbana, 1987); Robert Anthony Orsi, *The Madonna of 115th Street: Faith and Community in Italian Harlem, 1880–1950* (New Haven, 1985); Ewa Morawska, *For Bread with Butter: Life-Worlds of East Central Europeans in Johnstown, Pennsylvania, 1890–1940* (Cambridge, England, 1985); Judith E. Smith, *Family Connections: A History of Italian and Jewish Immigrant Lives in Providence, Rhode Island, 1900–1940* (Albany, 1985); and Robert A. Rockaway, *The Jews of Detroit: From the Beginning, 1762–1914* (Detroit, 1986).

[65]Leonard P. Curry, *The Free Black in Urban America, 1800–1850: The Shadow of a Dream* (Chicago, 1981); Herbert G. Gutman, *The Black Family in Slavery and Freedom, 1750–1925* (New York, 1976); Kenneth L. Kusmer, *A Ghetto Takes Shape: Black Cleveland, 1870–1930* (Urbana, 1976); Elizabeth Pleck, *Black Migration and Poverty: Boston, 1865–1900* (New York, 1979); James Borchert, *Alley Life in Washington: Family, Community, Religion, and Folklife in the City, 1850–1970* (Urbana, 1980).

[66]Vincent P. Franklin, *The Education of Black Philadelphia: The Social and Educational History of a Minority Community, 1900–1950* (Philadelphia, 1979); Douglas Henry Daniels, *Pioneer Urbanites: A Social and Cultural*

History of Black San Francisco (Philadelphia, 1980); Joe William Trotter, Jr., *Black Milwaukee: The Making of an Industrial Proletariat, 1915–45* (Urbana, 1985); George C. Wright, *Life Behind a Veil: Blacks in Louisville, Kentucky, 1865–1930* (Baton Rouge, 1985); Dennis C. Dickerson, *Out of the Crucible: Black Steelworkers in Western Pennsylvania, 1875–1980* (Albany, 1986); Peter Gottlieb, *Making Their Own Way: Southern Blacks' Migration to Pittsburgh, 1916–30* (Urbana, 1987).

[67]Gunther Barth, *City People: The Rise of Modern City Culture in Nineteenth-Century America* (New York, 1980), 5, 230.

[68]Morton and Lucia White, *The Intellectual versus the City* (Cambridge, 1962); Adrienne Siegel, *The Image of the American City in Popular Literature, 1820–1870* (Port Washington, NY, 1981), 5; Park Dixon Goist, *From Main Street to State Street: Town, City, and Community in America* (Port Washington, NY, 1977). See also Janis Stout, *Sodoms in Eden: The City in American Fiction before 1860* (Westport, 1976).

[69]Stephen Hardy, *How Boston Played: Sport, Recreation, and Community, 1865–1915* (Boston, 1982), 3. See also Dale Somers, *The Rise of Sports in New Orleans, 1850–1900* (Baton Rouge, 1972); Steven A. Riess, *Touching Base: Professional Baseball and American Culture in the Progressive Era* (Westport, 1980); Melvin A. Adelman, *A Sporting Time: New York City and the Rise of Modern Athletics, 1820–1870* (Urbana, 1986); Rob Ruck, *Sandlot Seasons: Sport in Black Pittsburgh* (Urbana, 1987); and Elliott J. Gorn, *The Manly Art: Bare-Knuckle Prize Fighting in America* (Ithaca, 1986).

[70]Dominick Cavallo, *Muscles and Morals: Organized Playgrounds and Urban Reform, 1880–1920* (Philadelphia, 1981).

[71]Perry R. Duis, *The Saloon: Public Drinking in Chicago and Boston, 1880–1920* (Urbana, 1983); Thomas J. Noel, *The City and the Saloon: Denver, 1858–1916* (Lincoln, 1982); Roy Rosenzweig, *Eight Hours for What We Will: Workers and Leisure in an Industrial City, 1870–1920* (Cambridge, England, 1983). On women's use of leisure in the city, see Kathy Peiss, *Cheap Amusements: Working Women and Leisure in Turn-of-the-Century New York* (Philadelphia, 1986). On popular uses of the streets, see Susan G. Davis, *Parades and Power: Street Theatre in Nineteenth-Century Philadelphia* (Philadelphia, 1986).

[72]Frederic Cople Jaher, *The Urban Establishment: Upper Strata in Boston, New York, Charleston, Chicago, and Los Angeles* (Urbana, 1982). See also Don H. Doyle, "History from the Top Down," *Journal of Urban History* 10 (November 1983): 103–14. For variations on the theme of class and culture, see John S. Gilkeson, Jr., *Middle-Class Providence, 1820–1940* (Princeton, 1986); and William H. Pease and Jane H. Pease, *The Web of Progress: Private Values and Public Styles in Boston and Charleston, 1828–1843* (New York, 1985).

[73]Thomas Bender, "The Cultures of Intellectual Life: The City and the Professions," in John Higham and Paul K. Conkin, eds., *New Directions in American Intellectual History* (Baltimore, 1979), 181–95; Thomas Bender, "The Erosion of Public Culture: Cities, Discourses, and Professional Disciplines," in Thomas L. Haskell, ed., *The Authority of Experts: Studies in History and Theory* (Bloomington, IN, 1984), 84–106.

[74]Mark I. Gelfand, *A Nation of Cities: The Federal Government and Urban America, 1933–1965* (New York, 1975); Philip Funigiello, *The Challenge to Urban Liberalism: Federal-City Relations during World War II* (Knoxville, 1978).

[75]Roger W. Lotchin, *The Martial Metropolis: U.S. Cities in War and Peace* (New York, 1984); John Mollenkopf, *The Contested City* (Princeton, 1983); Kenneth Fox, *Metropolitan America: Urban Life and Urban Policy in the United States, 1940–1980* (Jackson, MS, 1986).

[76]Brian J. L. Berry, *Comparative Urbanization: Divergent Paths in the Twentieth Century* (New York, 1981); Peter Hall, *The World Cities*, 3d ed. (New York, 1984); Charles Tilly, *Big Structures, Large Processes, Huge Comparisons* (New York, 1984).

[77]Graeme Davison, *The Rise and Fall of Marvellous Melbourne* (Melbourne, 1978); Weston Bate, *Lucky City: The First Generation at Ballarat, 1851–1901* (Melbourne, 1978); J. B. Hirst, *Adelaide and the Country, 1870–1917* (Melbourne, 1973); Peter Spearritt, *Sydney since the Twenties* (Sydney, 1978); C. T. Stannage, *The People of Perth* (Perth, 1979); R. J. Solomon, *Urbanisation: The Evolution of an Australian Capital* (Sydney, 1976). See also Graeme Davison, "Australian Urban History: A Progress Report," *Urban History Yearbook, 1979* (Leicester, 1979), 100–9; C. T. Stannage, "Australian Urban History," in G. Osborne and W. F. Mandle, eds., *New History: Studying Australia Today* (Sydney, 1982), 164–74.

[78]Gilbert A. Stelter and Alan F. J. Artibise, eds., *The Canadian City: Essays in Urban History* (Toronto, 1977); Alan F. J. Artibise and Gilbert A. Stelter, *Canada's Urban Past: A Bibliography to 1980 and Guide to Canadian Urban Studies* (Vancouver, 1981); Gilbert A. Stelter and Alan F. J. Artibise, eds., *Power and Place: Canadian Urban Development in the North American Context* (Vancouver, 1986).

[79]H. J. Dyos, ed., *The Study of Urban History* (London, 1968); David Cannadine and David Reeder, eds., *Exploring the Urban Past: Essays in Urban History by H. J. Dyos* (Cambridge, England, 1982); Fraser and Sutcliffe, *The Pursuit of Urban History*.

[80]Josef W. Konvitz, *The Urban Millennium: The City-Building Process from the Early Middle Ages to the Present* (Carbondale, IL, 1985); Jan DeVries, *European Urbanization, 1500–1800* (Cambridge, 1985); Paul M. Hohenburg and Lynn Hollen Lees, *The Making of Urban Europe, 1000–1950* (Cambridge, 1985).

[81]For examples of this work, see Michael F. Hamm, "The Modern Russian City: An Historiographical Analysis," *Journal of Urban History* 4 (November 1977): 39–76; Gary D. Allinson, "Japanese Cities in the Industrial Era," ibid. 4 (August 1978): 443–76; Howard Spodek, "Studying the History of Urbanization

in India," ibid. 6 (May 1980): 251–95; Susan Migden Socolow and Lyman L. Johnson, "Urbanization in Colonial Latin America," ibid. 8 (November 1981): 27–59.

[82]For a sampling of this work, see Christine Stansell, *City of Women: Sex and Class in New York, 1789–1860* (New York, 1986); Marjorie Murphy, "Gender Relations on an Urban Terrain: Locating Women in the City," *Journal of Urban History* 13 (February 1987): 197–206; Peter Bacon Hales, *Silver Cities: The Photography of American Urbanization, 1839–1915* (Philadelphia, 1984); Peter Conrad, *The Art of the City: Views and Versions of New York* (New York, 1984); Robert A. M. Stern et al., *New York 1930: Architecture and Urbanism between the Two World Wars* (New York, 1987); Robert A. Caro, *The Power Broker: Robert Moses and the Fall of New York* (New York, 1974); Sam Bass Warner, Jr., *The Province of Reason* (Cambridge, 1984); Andrew Lees, *Cities Perceived: Urban Society in European and American Thought, 1820–1940* (New York, 1985); Paul Goldberger, *The Skyscraper* (New York, 1981).

[83]For guides to the scholarly journal literature, see John D. Buenker, ed., *Urban History: A Guide to Information Sources* (Detroit, 1981); Neil Shumsky and Timothy Crimmins, eds., *Urban America: A Historical Bibliography* (Santa Barbara, 1983); and the key journals in the field: *Journal of Urban History, Urban History Yearbook, Urbanism Past and Present,* and *Urban History Review.*

[84]Bernard Bailyn, *History and the Creative Imagination* (St. Louis, 1985), 3; Thomas Bender, "Making History Whole Again," *New York Times Book Review* (October 6, 1985), 1, 42–43; Thomas Bender, "Wholes and Parts: The Need for Synthesis in American History," *Journal of American History* 73 (June 1986): 120–36. See also Eric H. Monkkonen, "The Dangers of Synthesis," *American Historical Review* 91 (December 1986): 1146–57.

[85]Raymond A. Mohl, *The New City: Urban America in the Industrial Age, 1860–1920* (Arlington Heights, IL, 1985); Carl Abbott, *Urban America in the Modern Age, 1920 to the Present* (Arlington Heights, IL, 1987); Jon C. Teaford, *The Twentieth-Century American City: Problem, Promise, and Reality* (Baltimore, 1986). Older and still useful works of synthesis include Blake McKelvey, *The Urbanization of America, 1860–1915* (New Brunswick, NJ, 1963); Blake McKelvey, *The Emergence of Metropolitan America, 1915–1966* (New Brunswick, NJ, 1968); and Maury Klein and Harvey A. Kantor, *Prisoners of Progress: American Industrial Cities, 1850–1920* (New York, 1976).

Index